I0335253

ISLAMIC BELIEFS:

RECLAIMING THE NARRATIVE

بِسْمِ ٱللَّهِ ٱلرَّحْمَٰنِ ٱلرَّحِيمِ

In the Name of Allah

the Most Beneficient

the Most Merciful

Islamic Beliefs

Reclaiming the Narrative

Ayatollah Sayyid Ali Khamenei

Translated by
Alexander Khaleeli

Edited by
Hamid Tehrani

Second Edition in 2023
First Published in 2021
by
Ahlulbayt Islamic Mission (AIM)

ISBN: 978-0-9957589-1-9

Typesetting and Editorial Services by
University Press of London (UPL)

Ayatollah Sayyid Ali Khamenei, 1974.

Contents

Preface 1
Author's Introduction 6

Section 1: Faith (*Īmān*) 11
This is *Taqwā* 12
Virtues of the Believers 24
Faith Based on Understanding 41
Faith Through Action 55
Faith and Selective Duty 67
Divine Promises, Part One 85
Divine Promises, Part Two 101

Section Two: Divine Unity (*Tawḥīd*) 121
Tawḥīd: An Islamic Worldview 122
Outcomes of Understanding *Tawḥīd* 139
Worship Belongs Only to God 157
Service Belongs Only for God 172
Tawḥīd and the Abolition of Social Classes 191
The Psychological Effects of Belief in *Tawḥīd* 210

Section Three: Prophethood (*Nubuwwah*) 229
The Philosophy of Prophethood 230
The Mission of the Prophets 246
The Prophetic Resurrection of Society 265
The Goals of Prophethood 286
The First Note of the Prophetic Call 304
Opposition to the Prophetic Mission 324
The Outcome of Prophethood, Part One 341
The Outcome of Prophethood, Part Two 364
The Responsibility of Belief in Prophethood 382

Section Four: Authority (*Wilāyah*) 399
Introduction to *Wilāyah* 400
Relations of the Ummah 420
The Paradise of *Wilāyah* 435
The *Walī*: The Central Authority 450
Wilāyah to the *Ṭāghūt* 466
Migrating to the *Wilāyah* of God 482

Preface

Islam is a revolutionary way of life which has liberated humanity from the depths of deprivation and destruction and brought the solution for attaining a goodly life (*ḥayāt ṭayyibah*) as God had intended it to be.

The main sources for our guidance have remained the same throughout the centuries, as told to us by the Final Prophet of God, Muhammad (peace and blessings be upon him and his family), who said:

إنّي تارِكٌ فيكم الثَّقلين ما إن تَمَسَّكم بهما لن تضلّوا
بعدي: كتابَ الله وعترتي أهلَ بيتي

"I leave you two weighty things, if you [do] hold tight to both you will never go astray after me: the Book of Allah and my progeny, the Ahlulbayt."

These are the words that have echoed throughout the centuries and have served as the blueprint for our salvation.

Many centuries have passed since the advent of Islam and with the passing of time came many challenges to our understanding of God's desire and plan for us. The task of finding the goodly life and attaining our salvation became ever so difficult but we have always had a blueprint, a guide, the 'two weighty things': the Qur'an and the Ahlulbayt.

This is not something known only to us as Muslims, but also to the adversaries of Islam who for centuries have made every effort to undermine the faith and disconnect people from these divine teachings.

Since the occultation of Imam Mahdi (atf), the 12th infallible Imam of the Ahlulbayt (as), the affairs of the Muslims were challenged in the most dire circumstances. With no direct communication to the hidden Imam, and as the successive illegitimate regimes continued to brutally oppress the faithful, people began to further descend into darkness and the true meanings of the divine teachings were no longer clear in the collective conscience of the faithful. The trajectory of the Islamic faith was looking bleak and the faithful were faced with the serious challenge of turning around their state of affairs.

These were the circumstances that the scholars of Islam had to overcome. Through strenuous efforts analysing the holy scriptures and their contexts, the scholars were looking for answers to the deepest issues of faith and how that can help us reconnect with our purpose.

It is this huge challenge that a young Sayyid Ali Khamenei found himself confronted with in the politically charged environment of Iran prior to the victory of the Islamic Revolution.

Setting the Scene

The year was 1974 and Iran in this period was a secular country governed by a tyrannical monarch who boasted centuries of monarchical authority while enjoying the backing of major global powers.

It was Ramadan in the holy city of Mashhad in northeastern Iran and with the call for afternoon prayers sounding in the background, the streets leading to the masjid would be buzzing with men and women of different ages, who in spite of the summer heat and the toll it takes on anyone fasting long hours, would come in droves to a tiny structurally incomplete masjid to gather in anticipation of the new ideas being delivered from the pulpit.

A relatively unknown young cleric, donning a black turban and a matching colour cloak, stood behind the pulpit to deliver his talk. The young cleric known as Sayyid Ali Aqa was the resident Imam for this small masjid and during the holy month of Ramadan, he would deliver his daily lectures while fasting. With his piercing eyes and an eloquent tongue, he would capture the imagination of the audience with ideas that would change the world in their minds, but these were ideas that had the potential to change a lot more than that. Little did the world know at the time that this young Sayyid Ali would be destined for greatness.

These were no ordinary gatherings and those were no ordinary times. The people of Iran were suffocating under the tyranny of the Pahlavi monarchy and religious discourses were being stifled and silenced. The regime of the Shah feared the threat posed by anything 'Islamic' and was cracking down on anyone who propagated Islamic ideas. In such times, public gatherings that were held to discuss Islam, beyond traditionally held rituals or recitations, were an act of defiance. Yes, these were no ordinary times but as the world was to find out, Sayyid Ali was also no ordinary person.

At the same time, revolutionary ideas were coming to the surface and Imam Khomeini, the exiled leader of the revolution, was delivering his famous talks on Islamic Government from neighbouring Iraq.

A culmination of sacrifices and efforts from the depths of history were finally showing signs of fruition under a wise and divine leadership. A storm of huge magnitude was brewing, and the waves of the revolution were arriving to change the course of history.

About the book

The contributions of Ayatollah Khamenei to Islamic revival are many but in this book we seek to show his theological and ideological viewpoints through his own words prior to the victory of the 1979 Islamic Revolution.

It is Ayatollah Khamenei's view that over the centuries, we have seen the narrative of Islam defined and even dictated by everything except from the Holy Qur'an and the real leaders of the divine movement. Therefore, he delivered these lectures with a focus on revisiting the sacred scripture to better understand the true purpose of faith, consequently changing the way we see life and the world around us.

It was from a small masjid in Mashhad that Ayatollah Khamenei delivered these lectures that inspired a generation. We believe these words will continue to enlighten future generations in their understanding of faith and religion, and ultimately their understanding life and the world.

It is important to mention that this book contains the lectures delivered by Ayatollah Khamenei, at the age of 35, in the exceptional circumstances prior to the Islamic revolution and although it is in that context that this book should be read, the ideas and meanings presented are treasures that are relevant for the development of the Ummah in every era.

Acknowledgements

It is noteworthy to mention that the collection and preservation of the contents of this book took mammoth efforts from those involved who unearthed the recordings and notes to make them available for us today. As you can imagine much has happened since these lectures were delivered and if it had not been for the remarkable efforts of some individuals, these works would have been lost forever. Special gratitude is due to the Sahba organisation who turned these recordings and notes into a Farsi publication entitled *Tarḥ-e Kullī-ye Andīsheh-ye Islāmī dar Qur'ān* in 2014.

It was thereafter that we at the Ahlulbayt Islamic Mission (AIM) started working on this important text to make it available in the English language as well. It has been a great honour for us to have worked on this project from 2017 until its first publication in 2021. We can vouch for the sheer hard work and effort that has gone into bringing this book to you not only by ourselves but by those who worked on this text in the Farsi language as well.

We would like to take this opportunity to thank the many people who helped in making this publication a reality and whilst we are only naming a few, there are many who are unsung heroes who assisted with their time, efforts and donations. They remain the selfless and anonymous helpers whose reward is with God.

Having said that, there are those who have made significant contributions to this publication whom we would like to thank and acknowledge, they include Alexander Khaleeli for his thorough translation of the text, Hamid Tehrani for his meticulous editing, and Sayyid Mohsin Jafri for his general role in facilitating this publication. We would also like to thank the Islamic Humanitarian Services in Canada for their support in making this publication a reality.

Finally, we thank the Almighty God who blessed us with this opportunity to serve and ask that He accepts this little that we offer in His way.

Sayyid Samir Al-Haidari
Ahlulbayt Islamic Mission (AIM)
25th January 2021

Author's Introduction

One of the most pressing issues facing religious thought today is to understand Islam as a creed that is fundamentally concerned with the social life of the human being and one which provides principles for the creation of a harmonious and cohesive society.

So far, the majority of the Islamic discussions and research have largely overlooked these two extremely important facets of the religion. This is why, in comparing Islam to other contemporary ideologies and schools of thought, researchers and thinkers have not been able to arrive at a definitive conclusion about this religion. In other words, they have been unable to offer a coherent and unified account of Islamic doctrine and to explain its relationship to other philosophies and schools of thought.

In addition to this, because the debates of Islamic scholars have remained largely abstract and walled-off from other intellectual, personal and especially social influences, the conclusions these debates produced have been equally abstract and have had little to offer in the way of actual concrete guidance about the social lives of human beings, particularly about how a society should be configured with regard to the rights and responsibilities of its members. In fact, these theories of religious scholars do not even offer a general theory for human social life.

Furthermore, in most cases, the Qur'an, Islam's foundational text, has played no role in guiding or directing human affairs. Instead, the floor has been given over to pseudo-intellectual pedantry and narrations of questionable authenticity. As a result, theological discussions have taken place isolated from the Qur'an and, indeed, without regard for it. Perhaps this is down to a lack of attachment to the Qur'an, a sense of not needing it, or perhaps, pessimism about our ability to draw firm conclusions from its text, each of which is the result of its own particular array of factors. In any case, the overall result of this trend is that people recite the words of the Qur'an without pondering on their meaning, so that they have no worldly reward or benefit, and their only purpose is otherworldly reward and recompense. In short, the Book of God has become the stock-in-trade of the masses and those who would mislead them.

It is with this in mind that we can identify, in a general sense, three major qualities that are necessary but lacking in discussions of Islamic thought, of which all contemporary thinkers must be aware and for which they bear responsibility:

First, we must look to bring the ideas and system of Islam out of the realm of pure mental abstraction–like all schools of social thought–by looking at practical responsibilities, especially in the realm of social affairs, and reorienting theoretical discussions to see what their implications are for human life, what their goals are, and what methods they prescribe for reaching these goals.

Second, we must study the different issues within Islamic thought as connected to one another and parts of a single and cohesive whole, seeing each as one component of a greater structure that is linked to all other components rather than viewing each issue atomically and separate from others. By understanding the principles of the religion in this way, we are able to derive a comprehensive blueprint of the religion as a complete ideology–one which is without ambiguity and whose different aspects relate to various aspects of living human existence.

Third, when we set out to extract and understand the fundamental principles of Islam, this must be on the basis of the fundamental sources and texts of the religion, not according to personal tastes and opinions or the accretions of speculative thought, so that the output will be something genuinely 'Islamic' and nothing other than that. In this regard, the Qur'an is the most complete and dependable source upon which we can rely, which falsehood cannot approach from any direction[1] and which was sent down as a clarification for all things[2] but only when we ponder deeply upon it as it itself commands us.[3]

This treatise represents a humble effort on the part of the author to achieve the aforementioned goals by presenting a sketch of Islamic thought in a series of lectures.

These lectures strive to discuss the fundamental precepts of Islam from their aspects which are most relevant to human existence through an exposition of the Qur'anic verses of peerless eloquence. In the course of clarifying and explaining these verses so that the audience will grasp these aforementioned principles, the author will make use of authentic traditions narrated from the Prophet (s) and the Infallible Imams (a) to further illuminate their meanings. So that, through making these verses of the Qur'an the locus of our contemplation and comprehension, the most foundational precepts of Islam will attain clarity, both as an element of Islamic thought and ideology and, from a practical point of view, as a source of rights and obligations.

Sayyid Ali Khamenei
Friday 25th October 1974

---

1 See Q41:42: 'falsehood cannot approach it, at present or in future'.

2 See Q16:89: 'We have sent down the Book to you as a clarification of all things'.

3 See Q38:29: '[This is] a blessed Book that We have sent down to you, so that they may contemplate its signs, and that those who possess intellect may take admonition!'

Section One

Faith
(Īmān)

This is Taqwā

Thursday 2nd Ramadan 1394
19th September 1974

وَأَطِيعُوا اللَّهَ وَالرَّسُولَ لَعَلَّكُمْ تُرْحَمُونَ (١٣٢) وَسَارِعُوا
إِلَى مَغْفِرَةٍ مِنْ رَبِّكُمْ وَجَنَّةٍ عَرْضُهَا السَّمَاوَاتُ وَالْأَرْضُ
أُعِدَّتْ لِلْمُتَّقِينَ (١٣٣) الَّذِينَ يُنْفِقُونَ فِي السَّرَّاءِ وَالضَّرَّاءِ
وَالْكَاظِمِينَ الْغَيْظَ وَالْعَافِينَ عَنِ النَّاسِ وَاللَّهُ يُحِبُّ
الْمُحْسِنِينَ (١٣٤)

'And obey God and the Messenger so that you may be granted mercy. And hasten towards your Lord's forgiveness and a Paradise as vast as the heavens and the earth, prepared for the Godwary: Those who spend in ease and adversity, and suppress their anger, and excuse the people, and Allah loves the virtuous.'
- Sūrat Āl-i ʿImrān (3):132–134

To keep their hearts free from sin, some Christians adopted a monastic way of life; they sought refuge in the solitude of caves and mountains. The Qur'an says 'But as for monasticism, they innovated it–We had not prescribed it for them'[1]. However, the Islamic scholar cannot live the life of a monk; he cannot withdraw from society; he cannot retreat to the mountains. The Islamic scholar is the one who rushes in to save

1 Q57:27.

others. A thinking Muslim is like this. Any Muslim person, insofar as being a Muslim and bearing moral responsibility go hand in hand, is like this: They rush to rescue one who is drowning, to save one who is in danger, to care for one who is sick–they do not run away! A Muslim makes himself Godwary (*muttaqī*) by equipping himself with piety (*taqwā*, literally 'protection'), meaning the necessary arms and armour to protect himself from sinning, before entering the place of sin in order to take the sinners out. This is the essence of *taqwā*!

If this is *taqwā*, does this mean that *taqwā* is a necessary requirement and means of attaining success or not? As you can see, the answer is straightforward: It is a means of attaining success. If someone wants to treat an outbreak of disease in a particular area and he is constantly worrying that he will be infected just by being there, how can he possibly hope to save others from it? Before he can go to the affected area and rescue others, he must first be sure about himself. It is then that he will succeed. It is then that he can easily undertake his mission. As God says: 'And be wary of God so that you might be successful.'[2]

'And beware of the Fire that has been prepared for the faithless, and obey God and the Apostle so that you may be granted [His] mercy.'[3] Now, there is no difference between obeying God and obeying the Prophet, so why would God say to obey God *and* to obey the Prophet? If the two are one and the same, then isn't it unnecessary to mention them separately? No, because if God only says: 'Obey God' without mentioning the Prophet or telling people to obey him, people can have a counter argument against the Prophet. They might say: 'We are obeying God!' People can make all sorts of claims easily, including outward claims of religiosity, piety and faith. The same sort of people

2 Q3:130.

3 Q3:131–132.

who make these claims are the ones who will say they are obeying God and are His devoted servants!

During the lifetime of the Prophet, he was not the only one calling people to worship and obey God. Those who were on the other side–the ones who were fighting him–claimed exactly the same thing. The leaders of the Jews and the Christians, their priests and their rabbis, also said this: 'The Jews and the Christians say, "We are God's children and His beloved ones."'[4] So they say they are a step above the Prophet, because the Prophet claimed to be God's servant while they claim to be God's children. They thought that only they could decide what constituted obedience to God. Or, to put it another way, they didn't think at all. They pretended that some acts of disobedience to God were in fact obedience to him. Isn't that right? There were those of them that when they were alone with themselves, they realised what a dark record of deeds they had; they saw that they were saying nothing but lies, and yet they continued to pretend in front of people that they were good and devoted servants of God who worshipped and obeyed Him. So we must distinguish between these hypocrites and those who truly worshipped God–we have to find a way to identify one from the other. This is why when God sets out to explain obedience and why it is necessary to the faithful, He doesn't just say to obey Him, instead He says: 'Obey God and obey the Apostle!' If God did not say 'the Apostle' then the enemies of the Prophet could have said that they were obeying God in their own way too. Therefore, there must be a definition of what obedience to God means. Those who claim they are servants of God while they disregard the precepts of the divine law and do not act upon it in their daily lives, are not fulfilling the conditions of being God's servants, so how can they claim that 'we are God's servants'? That is why God says: 'and obey God and the Apostle so that you may be granted [His] mercy!'

---

4 Q5:18.

Now let us turn to the latter part of this verse–what is God's mercy (*raḥmah*)? Let us compare what the Qur'an says about this and our own naive understanding of mercy. We think that if we commit a sin, or disobey God, or fail to perform our religious duties, if we do not avoid the places where God does not want us to go, we have only one hope–and what is that? God's mercy! We think that God will treat us mercifully, that He will be kind to us even though we have sinned. This is what we claim, and this is what most people in society imagine when we speak of God's mercy. What do we think God's mercy is for? We think it is for the duties we neglected, for the commands we disobeyed, for the sinful places we frequented, for all the times we forgot about our moral responsibility towards God. In other words, we think that there is nothing for us to do, God must be merciful to us. We think that mercy–God's divine mercy–exists to replace the things that we don't do. However, the verse of the Qur'an we are discussing here says exactly the opposite of this! It says that you must take action, you must obey, so that *perhaps* you will receive God's mercy. God's mercy is there for the times when a nation takes up their moral responsibilities. God shows mercy to people when they obey Him and when they do their duties. Seven hundred million Muslims are sitting just waiting for God's mercy to come to them and allowing people to violate their dignity, trample upon their faith, and take everything they have! Are you sitting hoping for God's mercy in these circumstances? In that case, you may as well get comfortable!

God says: 'And obey God and the Apostle so that you may be granted [His] mercy.' What does it mean to obey God? In what are we supposed to obey Him? To convey all of the divine duties and proofs to the enemy; to do our duty, whatever that may be. God says in the Qur'an that the truly faithful are those who, when any dispute occurs between them, they refer it to God's Messenger and when the Messenger judges between them, 'They do not find in their hearts any dissent to your verdict and submit to it in full submission.'[5] This is the mark of a true believer. If there were a people or a nation, if there were a society, that obeyed God in this manner, that is when His limitless mercy and kindness would surround them! That is when these people would attain dignity! That is when these people would grow to be fully-fledged human beings! That is when they would be freed from the chains and fetters that bind them! That is when they would receive God's mercy. So 'and obey God and the Apostle so that you may be granted [His] mercy.'

'And hasten towards your Lord's forgiveness and a Paradise as vast as the heavens and the earth, prepared for the Godwary.'[6] Here we see that God not only gives one example of *taqwā*, but also describes a consequence of it. Then he mentions further examples of what constitutes *taqwā* below.

In this world, many are willing to race each other to gain ownership of a plot of land, which is only a bit of water and dirt and they are ready to overtake others for this. They are ready to give all of their strength and energy so that, as well as obtaining the land, they are able to make a living from it? Perhaps to run a shop, to gain the ear of a powerful person or to manage a company somewhere in the world? To gain whatever material advantages they can? For these things, you are ready! To race! To leave others behind! Even if it means trampling on all virtues and dignities in the process. O human! Religion will never tell you not to rush, it will never tell you to stay at home and rest, it will never ever tell you not to use your energy–anyone who tells you this in the name of religion is either ignorant or a liar. True religion never tells you to leave your energies idle. True religion tells you to do your utmost, to do your best, but to what end? True religion tells you to use your energy

5 Q4:59–65.

6 Q3:133.

for something worthy of you, not for a bit of water and dirt, not for some paltry price, not for some worldly existence which, no matter how grand it is, will always be small for you. O human! Strive for something that is worthy of your magnificence and equal to your stature! The human being is the greatest being in the cosmos, the most magnificent wonder of existence, second only to God, and yet it inhabits this tiny and limited form. O human! Strive! Make haste! But towards what? 'Towards your Lord's forgiveness and a Paradise as vast as the heavens and the earth!' Strive for a Paradise that is so great that it makes the heavens seem small and the earth seem insignificant. What does this mean? Pay close attention to the Qur'an's words so that you may understand. The Qur'an says: If you want to aim for something, the heavens and the earth are not worthy of you, they are small for you, so aim for something greater than these. O human! God's forgiveness is important for you. God's forgiveness is higher than everything else, and after forgiveness there is something whose value and magnificence is greater than the heavens and the earth combined!

Now, what does forgiveness mean? We think it is when we say to someone: 'I apologise. I was rude to you. Please forgive me.' And that person, whether with kindness and magnanimity or in any other form says: 'That's ok. Don't worry about it.' We think it means when we do something wrong by accident and we go to the person we wronged and ask for forgiveness: 'I am sorry. Please forgive me.' And he says: 'That's ok, I forgive you.' We think it means when we go to a government office because you've been overcharged on your taxes, and you ask them kindly to help you solve your problem, perhaps you take someone with you, or a letter, or ask someone to call on your behalf, and they say: 'OK. We will refund you such-and-such an amount.' This is how we imagine God's forgiveness: Someone does something wrong, they caused corruption in the earth and were worthy of God's punishment. Then, on the Day of Judgement, because of a tear they shed, or a plea they made, God will say: 'That's ok, I forgive you.' Is that what we mean by God's forgiveness? Does this sound like something we are supposed to *hasten* towards? No, of course not!

Outside of these lectures, we have spoken a lot about the meaning of God's forgiveness (*ghufrān*). Those of you dear brothers who were in our discussions, try to recall what we said. Bring it out from the recesses of your minds! The Arabic word we use for 'forgiveness', *ghufrān*, means to heal a wound or fill a gap. Imagine you are given a deep wound on your arm or leg and your flesh is cut open, what would you do? You'd have the wound treated. They would clean it, sew it up, give you ointment to put on it, medicine and vitamins to take to help it heal and, eventually, your flesh would heal, and the wound would disappear. In other words, you would do everything in your power to close the wound. This is how we close a physical wound. Now let us draw a comparison between this and how to close a spiritual wound, so that we can understand the meaning of *ghufrān*.

Imagine your soul as a body, and every sin you commit is like a wound that you inflict on your body. Why do we say this? Why is a sin like a wound to one's soul? Because the soul must grow and develop, and a sin is anything that prevents the soul from doing so. So, as a wound, every sin creates a gap in the substance your soul. So every sin you commit diminishes you soul. If, God forbid, you steal the property of others, you drink wine, you take usury, you fornicate, you lie, you fabricate...each of these acts opens a fissure in your soul, it tears the substance of your soul, it leaves your soul wounded and depleted, and far from the ideal which it is destined to reach. Now, you must find forgiveness for this sin.

So what does forgiveness mean in this context? Forgiveness means to close the gap, to mend the tear and to heal the wound–this is *ghufrān*. How can this be achieved? How can this tear in the soul caused by sin be mended? By making up for it. When someone drags their soul down from the heights of human ideals and causes it to sink to a lower level, they must do something to make up for this in order for their soul to rise again.

Take another example. You get into a car and set off on a journey. Now, if the car breaks down on the way, what will happen to you? You'll be delayed. So how can you make up for this delay once you get it working again? By going a little faster, by denying yourself a little comfort, you can still arrive on time. If you just sit there and say: 'Oh no, what a mistake I made! Why didn't I set off sooner? O God, please forgive me.' This won't be of any use to you. Yes, you made a mistake, but now you should make up for it. Go a little faster so that you reach your destination on time!

God doesn't say that when you commit a sin there is nothing you can do to efface it. He is not vindictive! 'Surely, I am the all-forgiver!'[7] Those sins you commited, those mistakes you made, all of these can be forgiven if you are willing to make up for them. God does not say: Because you made one mistake, no matter how hard you try, no matter what you do, you cannot be forgiven. No! 'Surely, I am the all-forgiver!' I will forgive, I will heal you and make you whole again. But for what kind of person? 'For him who repents, becomes faithful and acts righteously, and then follows guidance.'[8] God says He will forgive the one who repents. And what is repentance (*tawbah*)? It means to come back. Your path to perfection was here, but you went that way instead. But you can be forgiven. When? When you come back to the path of perfection and follow the right way again. 'For him who repents'–for him who comes back, who strengthens his faith, and who acts righteously. One who *acts*! We should never forget the importance of right action and just rely on uttering nice words and thinking nice thoughts!

---

7 Q20:82.

8 Ibid.

Therefore, forgiveness means to heal the wounds of the human soul; by mending these tears, the human being attains perfection. This means that forgiveness is something that we should strive for, something we should compete to obtain, and something we should hasten towards. Divine forgiveness is very important. Divine forgiveness is not something that God bestows arbitrarily, according to whim or caprice; he does not make someone the object of His kindness unless that person has striven to become worthy of that kindness. 'And hasten towards your Lord's forgiveness and a Paradise as vast as the heavens and the earth, prepared for the Godwary.'

Sometimes we might say someone belongs in Paradise or that they will definitely go to Paradise, and we sincerely hope that we are people destined for Paradise. In all of our supplications, we ask God to grant us Paradise. And sometimes we are not content with merely asking for Paradise; we count out the blessings we want from it one by one; we ask God for the *ḥūr al-ʿayn*, for its food, the meat of its birds[9] and the like thereof. However, it is none other than God Himself who says that this Paradise is for those people who have *taqwā*. This feast has been prepared especially for them and only they will enter this place and sit at this table. So, if we want to enjoy this feat, we too must be people of *taqwā*.

Who are the people of *taqwā*? 'Prepared for the Godwary.' Pay close attention to the words of these verses: 'Prepared for the *muttaqīn*' means those who have *taqwā*. Who are those who have *taqwā*? 'Those who spend in ease and adversity'–those with *taqwā* are those who spend (*infāq*). To spend is a condition of having *taqwā*. And what does spending in the sense of *infāq* mean? This is something we have discussed in earlier lessons, but there is no problem in repeating it here so that these words become engraved upon your hearts. *Infāq* is more than spending in the ordinary sense of the word. To spend

9 See Q56:21: 'and such flesh of fowls as they desire'.

ordinarily means that a person spends some money for some reason. *Infāq* is also spending, but it is not just any kind of spending. *Infāq* means spending in such a way as to fill a gap, for a worthy cause. Where are those who spend millions, sometimes even for what appears to be a good cause, only for the Qur'an to say that they are the most ill-fated of people, because what they are doing is not called *infāq* in the Qur'anic sense of the term: Say, 'Shall we inform you about the biggest losers in regard to works? Those whose endeavour goes awry in the life of the world, while they suppose they are doing good.' They spend a fortune feeding some hungry people, and yet this is nothing but appearance and deception, it is not *infāq*. Why? Because it does not fill a gap.

When you give five *riyāls*[10] to someone who has five hundred riyals in his pocket and could add another hundred to this, this is not *infāq*. On the other hand, if you give this to someone who needs five riyals to buy a single loaf of bread to fill his stomach, *this* is *infāq*. However, I do not say this so that after the class everyone here will go and give five riyals to the first hungry person they find to fill their stomach. This is because filling an empty stomach is not necessarily *infāq* either, in some conditions this is the case. For example, when poverty and hunger are like countless weeds covering the ground, filling one stomach is like pulling out one weed. But what difference does one weed make? Ok, so you can see one weed has been uprooted, but how essential is this? How important is this? Therefore, *infāq* means to fill a gap. To satisfy a need. If some people today needed something like air and water, and you helped them by giving them something else, this also would not be *infāq*. Equally, if you gave them ill-gotten wealth, this would also not be *infāq*. Therefore, *infāq* is not something everyone does. *Infāq* is what clever people do. Clever people identify people's needs and are prepared to do what is necessary to fill the

10 [Currency in Iran.]

gap that gives rise to these. Spending in this sense is very important, one of the marks of *taqwā* is to spend in the good times and the bad.

'And suppress their anger' (*kāẓimīn al-ghayẓ*). They do not forget, they restrain their anger and displeasure. As it is only when a person holds their anger in check that they can, with reason and understanding, do what is correct.

'And excuse people' (*wa al-ʿāfīn ʿan al-nās*)–they forgive others for their faults and their mistakes. They overlook people's misdeeds. Of course, this is where people perform these by accident rather than by intent. The same is true of God, He overlooks mistakes. When someone does something evil by intent, this should not be overlooked. However, we should forgive the mistakes that all people make and excuse their flaws. 'And excuse people. And God loves the virtuous.'

What are the other marks of *taqwā*? 'And those who, when they commit an indecent act or wrong themselves, [immediately] remember God, and plead for forgiveness for their sins.'[11] They do not remain beneath the veil of heedlessness for long. There is a very strange verse in the Qur'an about the people of *taqwā* and the act of remembering God (*tadhakkur*). It reads: 'When those who are Godwary are touched by a group from Satan, they remember [God] and, behold, they perceive.'[12] Here, the Arabic word *shayṭān* is used in its broadest possible sense, meaning a group of devils or people with devil-like qualities. When one who has *taqwā* is afflicted by such a group and they surround him to try and lead him astray, separate him from the right path and make him forget God, 'they remember God' immediately. And the remembrance of God is an escape from the clutches of Satan. The remembrance of God is a rope we hold in our hands, which can save us from the traps laid for us by our

11 Q3:135.

12 Q7:201.

ever-watchful foes. Therefore, the remembrance of God is something truly precious to which we should hold fast.

'They remember God'–just as they do something wrong or wrong themselves, they remember God 'and plead for forgiveness for their sins.' In other words, they hasten to find a way to efface this sin and to heal the wound it has created in their soul. However, this is also not possible without God's help, as the verse continues: 'and who forgives sins except God?'[13] The effort is from you, the movement is from you, but the blessings are from God. We try our utmost, and God accepts our efforts. This means that it is our responsibility to take action, we cannot neglect this and simply expect God to do the work for us.

'And who do not persist in what they have committed while they know.' They do not keep committing sins while they know them to be such. 'Their reward is forgiveness from their Lord.'[14] These ones, who strive their utmost, who plead forgiveness for their sins, who do not persist in sinning and error, *these* are the people who will receive God's forgiveness 'and gardens with streams running in them, to remain in them [forever], How excellent is the reward of the workers!'[15] See how once again God emphasises the importance of working and making effort!

13 Q3:135.

14 Q3:136.

15 Ibid.

Virtues of the Believers

Friday 3rd Ramadan 1394
20th September 1974

إِنَّمَا الْمُؤْمِنُونَ الَّذِينَ إِذَا ذُكِرَ اللَّهُ وَجِلَتْ قُلُوبُهُمْ وَإِذَا تُلِيَتْ عَلَيْهِمْ آيَاتُهُ زَادَتْهُمْ إِيمَانًا وَعَلَى رَبِّهِمْ يَتَوَكَّلُونَ (٢) الَّذِينَ يُقِيمُونَ الصَّلَاةَ وَمِمَّا رَزَقْنَاهُمْ يُنْفِقُونَ (٣) أُولَئِكَ هُمُ الْمُؤْمِنُونَ حَقًّا لَهُمْ دَرَجَاتٌ عِنْدَ رَبِّهِمْ وَمَغْفِرَةٌ وَرِزْقٌ كَرِيمٌ (٤)

'The faithful are only those whose hearts tremble [with awe] when God is mentioned, and when His signs are recited to them, they increase their faith, and who put their trust in their Lord. Who maintain the prayer and spend out of what We have provided them. It is they who are truly the faithful. They shall have ranks near their Lord, forgiveness and a noble provision.'
- Sūrat al-Anfāl (8):2–4

'They ask you [O Prophet] concerning the *anfāl*.' Who are they for? Who has the right to distribute them? We can translate the word *anfāl* as follows: *Anfāl* means the wealth that belongs to all of the Muslims collectively. One example of this are the spoils that the Muslims win through warfare, so this is not every source of income but only some kinds of it. Another example of *anfāl* is mineral wealth (*maʿādin*) that is extracted from beneath the ground. Yet another example is the forests, the deserts or the great pastures in valleys or on mountains. In short, *anfāl* denotes any kind of wealth that does not belong to a single person or to a single group of people but rather is public property, belonging to the nation as a collective. However, one of the aforementioned examples are those spoils won by soldiers in warfare. The first time this question seems to have been raised was after the Battle of Badr when the Muslims were discussing how they should divide the spoils they had won. They disagreed with one another, so they referred the matter to the Prophet and asked him what they should do. Their answer came in the form of the aforementioned verse of the Qur'an. 'Say: The *anfāl* belong to God and the Apostle.' What does it mean when the Qur'an says they belong to God? It means that they do not belong to any one particular group of people. Anything that belongs to God, anything that is said to be God's property, actually means something that should be used for Godly aims. Clearly, when we say that something belongs to God, we do not mean that it should be spent for God's benefit, because God does not benefit from wealth. God does not have any needs. God does not have any wants. So there is no need to spend His wealth to fulfil these. On the contrary, when we speak of God's property, we mean the property of all of his servants. Therefore, this wealth should be used for those causes alone which God has specified. This is the meaning of saying something belongs to God.

'And the Apostle'–what does this mean? That it is the property of the Messenger. Yes, but what does *that* mean? Is the Prophet the polar opposite of God? Of course not. But when we say something belongs to God, someone might come along and give himself the right to do with it as he pleases because it belongs to no one in particular. He can say: 'This belongs to God, and we are all God's servants!' So using this pleasant-sounding and attractive slogan, this person can use something that belongs to everyone for his own personal benefit.

Therefore, while God's wealth is supposed to be used for the benefit of all the Muslims and all of God's true servants, using it for the public good does not mean it can be used haphazardly, as anyone pleases. On the contrary, there should be some management of this wealth, there should be someone in charge of it as God's representative, who will look after people's interests. Who can serve this purpose? The Prophet, of course! So the Prophet here is not mentioned as a divine messenger, but as a divine *ruler*. And, in times when there is no Infallible Imam to rule over people, it is the responsibility of whoever is ruling over people to take charge of these *anfāl* and associated sources of wealth.

In any case, these sources of wealth such as mines, forests, pastures and glades are considered public property, the spoils the Muslims take from the enemy belong to everyone. The treasures of the kings are for everyone. These are the sort of things that are mentioned as belonging to the category of *anfāl*. However, even though they are for everyone, someone has to manage them on behalf of God and that someone is the Islamic ruler. Who is that? When the Prophet was alive, he was the Islamic ruler. After him, it was the Infallible Imam, who was known as the divinely appointed just leader. The one in whose hands the reins of power should rightfully be, it is he who is responsible for the *anfāl* and how they are used. However, this is not the part of the verse on which we wish to focus most of our attention.

After God specifies the method by which the *anfāl* are to be distributed (i.e. in accordance with the Prophet's directives), He says: 'So be wary of God and settle your differences, and obey God and His Apostle, should you be faithful.' If you are truly faithful, do these three things: First, be wary of God. Then, settle your differences with one another and put aside your disagreements. For the sake of the truth, those who do not speak the truth will give up their claims, and disagreements between you will disappear. Also, do not become caught up in trivial disputes, do not look for excuses to fight one another. The sort of people who fight their friends as well as their enemies are the sort who look for the slightest excuse to fight, argue and bring about disagreements. God and His Messenger advise people that, instead of looking for reasons to fight amongst yourselves do not ignore the real reasons why you should fight your enemies. If you want to fight, fight your enemy. Why should you fight your brother? Why should you fight your friend? Set aside your disagreements and put things right amongst yourselves. These are the first two pieces of advice: Be wary of God and settle your differences. The third is something universal that applies to whatever it is you are doing, and it means to do whatever is good and avoid whatever is bad: 'Obey God and His Apostle' by following their commands. 'Should you be faithful' then you will do all of this.

The issue of faith, this pledge of the heart, this bond of thought, belief and mind to a single issue, to a single person, to a single pole, to a single core, this thing we call faith cannot come about simply by these means, simply by a person feeling an attachment in their heart. No, the time when faith truly inheres in a person, when it becomes actualised, is when that person acts on it. Then, and only then, can a person claim that they are truly faithful, when they fulfil the requirements of faith and they act in accordance with faith. Then they can say they are truly faithful, that they truly believe, because it is only then that their life and the very fabric of their being differs from someone who denies God and rejects the truth. Today, what is the difference in behaviour between someone who denies God and someone who claims to believe in Him? They both do wrong. They are both absorbed by materialistic concerns until their last breath. They are both willing to trade all virtue and all goodness for two more morrows, for two more morsels, for two more breaths. The only difference is that one honestly says: 'I don't believe in God.' The other claims that he believes in God. What kind of faith is this? The Qur'an is clear about what faith means. This is not some philosophical argument about which there can be doubt–if you truly believe, do these things. And one of these things is that you obey God and obey the Apostle, that you do as they command.

What is God's command? It is self-evident that every person has certain duties and responsibilities whether this is with regards to their own property, life and soul, or whether it is with regard to their relationship with other human beings, their relationship with God, their relationship with animals or even their relationship with plants. If you obey God in all of these different fields of your life, then you can say you are a true believer. Otherwise, faith merely in the sense of feeling an attachment to some principle or cause but without this attachment being reflected in one's words or deeds, in one's limbs or behaviour, is of no use. In fact, this is not something that Islam would even recognise as faith (*īmān*)! This is the logic of the Qur'an. 'Be wary of God and settle your differences, and obey God and His Apostle, should you be faithful.'

Now, because the word 'faithful' (*muʾmin*) appears at the end of this verse, the next verse continues by describing the conditions one must meet to be faithful: 'The faithful are only those whose hearts tremble [with awe] when God is mentioned, and when His signs are recited to them, they increase their faith, and who put their trust in their Lord, Who maintain the prayer and spend out of what We have provided them. It is they who are truly the faithful. They shall have ranks near their Lord, forgiveness and a noble provision.'[16] Here, the Qur'an lays out five qualities that one who is truly faithful will possess. It is possible that not all of these will be on show to others. However, anyone who is trying to cultivate these five qualities in themselves is on the path of faith: they are pursuing faith and worthy of the title 'faithful'. A true believer will have these five qualities.

16 Q8:2–4.

First, 'the faithful are only those' (*innamā al-mūʾminūn alladhīna*)–this shows that only the people with these qualities count as faithful–'whose hearts tremble when God is mentioned.' What does it mean for their hearts to tremble? In what sense are they afraid of God? Are they like a criminal who is afraid of a judge? Or is fear here something more subtle than this? Someone might say: 'I haven't done anything wrong and I'm not afraid of God.' Of course, the only person who is afraid of a judge is someone who has committed a crime for which they deserve to be punished. But if someone is innocent, they will not be afraid. Then again, what person can be sure that they have no sins?

However, there is another kind of fear–one that does not spring from guilt but from knowledge. When a person comes face-to-face with something great and magnificent, they feel awe and wonder. This is part of what it is to be human; our bodies and souls react in this way. Whenever a person is in the presence of something great, they feel a sense of awe. This awe is not the same as common fear, as the person might not have anything to fear in the sense of anything being done to him. On the contrary, awe comes from a realisation of something else's greatness and a corresponding sense of one's own insignificance. This kind of fear is what we should feel towards God, and it is this kind of fear that is of benefit to us. Someone who feels small and insignificant before their Lord and sees that God has power and control over all things will only follow the path which God has traced out for him without swerving onto any other path. This is the best guarantee that a Muslim individual or society will take action and strive for the sake of God.

When you see that Imam ʿAlī would awaken in the middle of the night, especially in the nights of the month of Ramadan and shed tears; when you see that Imam Zayn al-ʿĀbidīn would sometimes cry out; when you see that God's Messenger, despite his greatness, would not sleep in the last ten nights of Ramadan, meaning he did not see those nights as a time for sleep but for worship, for prayer, for submitting to one's Lord–do you think these actions are things the Prophet and Imams only did for our benefit? How foolish it is to say that Imam ʿAlī only uttered the *duʿā* of Abū Ḥamzah Thumālī in order to teach people something rather than uttering these words from his own heart. How unaware someone must be of the spirit of supplication to imagine that Imam ʿAlī only shed tears in order to teach us! Do you seriously mean to say that he made a show of weeping for us to learn? This is wrong. He truly shed tears–why did he shed tears? Because he knew God better than we did. The Commander of the Faithful [Imam ʿAlī] saw the greatness of God's being–a greatness which the short-sighted vision of you and I cannot see. 'You are too great to be seen in a tiny mirror!'[17] This tiny mirror of our soul cannot fully reflect that magnificent greatness of God–but what about the soul of the Commander of the Faithful? His soul can. He understands God's greatness. He comprehends. That is why he would spend time alone and weep out of fear of God!

When God is mentioned, that is when the believer's heart is gripped by a state of awe, a feeling of humility, a sensation of fear that stems from their own awareness of their insignificance before God's grandeur. Their hearts tremble with awe when God is mentioned. That occurs when God ceases to be an imaginary thing to them, and when the name of God ceases to be something we utter habitually. In a gathering, someone who sits says 'O God!' as an expression of respect to others around him. Someone yawns and says 'There is no God but God' out of tiredness. If this is how we mention God, it shows our lack of concern for Him, our lack of comprehension of Him, and our utter indifference to His greatness. However, this is not how someone who is aware of God's magnificence or comprehends His grandeur behaves. 'The faithful are only those whose hearts tremble

17 A line from the Persian poet, Shahrīyār.

[with awe] when God is mentioned.' This sensation fills their hearts! So this is the first quality of a believer.

'And when His signs are recited to them, they increase their faith.' The second mark of a true believer is that when God's signs are recited, whether they recite them to themselves or someone else recites them to them, their faith increases. In other words, this faith is like a seed that has been planted in their hearts, with roots in their souls. Slowly, this seed grows, like a plant reaching upwards, like a great tree with a trunk and branches, with roots so firm that it could never be uprooted. Faith that sits still like stagnant water in the heart of a believer is meaningless. Someone might learn a formula as a child and, as a result of the doubts they feel as they grow up, it cannot penetrate the hardness of their heart. So it shrinks, withers and fades. A sort of half-faith or half-truth remains in their hearts. But this grows dimmer and dimmer with the passage of time. Such faith can be easily taken from a person. It is a surface faith. But a true believer is not like this. A true believer is someone who, if a single word of the truth and knowledge of God or religion enters his heart, he will ponder on it, examine it, and think about it and anything that comes to the aid of that word will cause their faith to grow. This faith cannot be erased. And the person who has it is a true believer.

From this verse and from this sentence we can deduce that when a faithful human being recites the Qur'an, their faith should increase. This sentence is proof of something. Pay close attention to God's words here and you will see what. There are those who say: 'Do not translate the Qur'an!' 'Do not explain the Qur'an!' 'Do not comment on the Qur'an!' 'Our intellects cannot understand it!' To those people we say: If we cannot understand the Qur'an then how will the Qur'an increase our faith in God? It is clear that the Qur'an is not a book of codes. The Qur'an is a book that is supposed to be read in order to be understood, and understood in order that it increases and strengthens one's faith! 'And when His signs are recited to them, they increase their faith.' This is the second condition of being a true believer.

Next, the verse says: 'and who put their trust in their Lord.' This is the third mark of the true believer–that he places his trust in God and relies on Him. What does trust in God (*tawakkul*) mean? Does it mean to fold your arms and say: 'God will take care of it'? No, this is not placing one's trust in God. Someone who folds their arms instead of undertaking their duties, obligations and responsibilities, instead of using their own abilities, and instead expects God to work a miracle on their behalf–such a person should know that the Qur'an utterly rejects this attitude. God delivers a harsh rebuke to the Israelites who told Moses: 'Go ahead, you and your Lord, and fight! We will be sitting right here.'[18] In other words: You go and fight our enemies and let us know when you've won–then we'll come! The Qur'an rejects this utterly. This approach is that of the Israelites whom God cursed and denied the joys of faith. This is not worthy of someone who claims to submit to God! This is not the meaning of trusting in God. This idea that has gained currency amongst people–I'm saying this so everyone will hear and understand–this idea people have, in which they say: 'God needs to fix this. No one can do anything about this.' This is an error. If no one could do anything. If no one had it in them to fight corruption and make the world better, then God would not have sent prophets. He would not have summoned people to follow the prophets. He would not have given the prophets weighty messages to deliver to this world. But we see that God *has* sent people to fight corruption and make the world better, and we see that they *are* human beings. Therefore, you should know that it is up to *human beings* to fight *human corruption*.

So then what *does* it mean to place one's trust in God? *Tawakkul* means that in every situation you rely on God and place your hopes

18 Q5:24.

in Him. Notice that the definition I am giving here–to rely on God and place your hopes in Him in every situation–makes trusting in God a basis for action rather than an obstacle to it, and a source of motivation rather than a source for indifference.

Have you seen how when some people face difficulties in life, when they go through hardship, and they exhaust every visible means at their disposal to rectify their situation without success–what do they do? Have you seen or heard this? They will do one of a few things, either they will surrender, when nothing they do seems to work, or they will resign themselves to fate; or they will take the path of least resistance–they won't give up but in practice they will do whatever is easiest. They won't make any effort to change their circumstances and go wherever life takes them. But even if this person has not visibly surrendered like in the first case, inwardly their mentality is the same. So this is one response people have when they face hardships. Others end their own lives. For example, someone gains power in a country, and little-by-little, other powers wear him down. Every day, somewhere in his dominion, there is some clamour against him. Then when he has no choices left, when he is utterly humiliated, tired and dejected, he takes his own life. He ends it.

These are the routes open to someone when they don't have God and find themselves in a blind alley. When they reach a dead end and they see that they have nowhere left to turn, no escape, these people will take one of three options. They will either surrender to fate, take the path of least resistance, or they will kill themselves. However, for someone who believes in God and finds themselves at a dead end, these options are not available to them. Their dignity won't let them follow these paths. But there is one door that is always open to them. And what door is that? Placing their trust in God. They will say: 'This is a dead end. But the God I know makes doors out of dead ends.' What is a dead end? For God, there are no dead ends for us. In God's hands, every dead end is a door. There is always a way.

Is there a dead end worse than the Battle of *Uḥud*? The few soldiers of Islam, preoccupied with the pursuit of spoils on the battlefield, forgot to guard the flanks. Because of the heedlessness of a few soldiers, the Quraysh were able to outflank the Muslims, who had laid down their swords and dismounted their horses to collect spoils. Suddenly, they see themselves surrounded by the enemy on all sides, attacking them. Now, it's clear what an unarmed, unprepared soldier will do in this situation, isn't it? He runs. He runs for his life! Satan calls out through the voice of a wicked person that the Prophet has been slain. It's obvious–Satan is always doing this. Satan's plans are clear, and his helpers are clear: He is always putting doubts into people's minds. He is always sapping their morale. Telling them they failed. That the Prophet has died! In this crisis, in this dead end, what does a faithful person who relies on God do? Is there a dead end greater than this? There is no way out. Your own soldiers have thrown down their weapons and fled. The enemy have surrounded you on all sides. No one is coming to your aid. But there is still a way out. To put your trust in God. To have hope. What dead end? Even if the Prophet of God has been slain. The God of the Prophet will never be slain! We still have our moral duties! In such a situation, how will a person who places their trust in God behave? Like the Commander of the Faithful, ʿAlī ibn Abī Ṭālib! Like Abū Dajjānah![19] Like those few who stood their ground. Those who had no trust in God, who were they? Those who fled for their lives back to Madinah without ever looking back, who ran until they were safely inside the city. Now you can see the meaning of *tawakkul*!

19 A companion of the Prophet who was slain after the death of the Prophet at the Battle of *Yamāmah*. He was also at the Battle of *Uḥud*, where his bravery and selflessness were such that the verse Q61:4 'Indeed God loves those who fight in His way in ranks' was revealed about him. There are even traditions which foretell he will be brought back to life to fight alongside Imam al-Mahdī (aj).

Those who fold their arms in the name of *tawakkul*, who sit back and do nothing in the hope of some unknown future, choose to forsake their own faith and their own power as human beings. Those who think *tawakkul* means to strike out human free will and human ability either do not understand *tawakkul* or they understand it perfectly but want to change its meaning in the minds of others so they will no longer place their trust in God. But when God says the faithful are those 'who put their trust in their Lord', He means that the human being has two powerful wings to carry them through life: One is steadfastness (*ṣabr*) and the other is relying on God (*tawakkul*). Any nation which has these two wings will fly beyond the reach of their enemies. The wing of steadfastness and the wing of reliance! 'And who put their trust in their Lord'–this is the third quality of the faithful!

Fourth, 'who maintain the prayer.' Now, pay attention to the expression God uses here. Consider the difference between 'those who pray' (*alladhīna yuṣallūn*) and 'those who maintain the prayer' (*alladhīna yuqīmūn al-ṣalāt*). If God was only referring to those who say their prayers, there would be no need to say 'those who *maintain* the prayer' because the use of the word 'maintain' would be superfluous. God could have just said 'those who pray' and be finished with it. Clearly, those who *maintain* the prayer are not the same as those who pray, there is something else there too; there is some higher reality. What do you think this could be? What does it mean to '*maintain*' prayer?

There are several possibilities, any one of which could be correct. One is that maintaining the prayer means performing prayer perfectly or completely, as this is one of the meanings for the verb *iqāmah* ('to maintain') in Arabic. In other words, it means to do something completely or fully, as in: 'So set your countenance (*fa aqim wajhaka*) on the religion as a people of pure faith.'[20] In other words, turn your

20 Q30:30.

countenance in its entirety, your being in its entirety, towards the religion, completely and utterly. This is one meaning. And it makes sense in this context. If someone maintains the prayer in this way, this means to perform it fully and completely, on the correct basis, paying attention to the teachings and inspirations of prayer. If someone offers prayer in this matter, then success and salvation are really expected for them.

When someone prays properly, all problems become easy for them. Have you not heard of those people of great faith who, whenever they face any difficulty or hardship, offer two *rakʿats* of prayer? Have you heard that when the Prophet faced trials and tribulations, he would turn to his companion, Bilāl and say: 'Grant us relief, O Bilāl!' or 'Cool us, O Bilāl!' By this he meant that Bilāl should recite the call to prayer. If someone truly *maintains* their prayers, with attentiveness, with humility, with awe of God, with presence of mind, and with an understanding of the significance of what they are saying and doing, intending to get something out of their prayer...if someone who prays, prays like this and maintains their prayer in this sense, then he will definitely receive those things which have been promised to the faithful.

This was one possibility. Another possibility is that 'those who maintain the prayer' means that they pray in a community–that they make a community that prays. Some people feel happy when they pray alone. Instead of seventeen *rakʿats* a day, they offer fifty-one *rakʿats* a day, not to mention other supererogatory prayers! Someone tells them: 'People are leaving the religion in droves!' This does not concern them. As Saʿdī says: 'They pull their own rug back from the wave.' They say: 'It's hard enough to save ourselves, let alone anyone else!' Some people think this way. But the kind of action that is a mark of faith is not this! Anyone who prays well but prays by themselves, without any concern for the prayers of others, this is not correct. It is not, as we said above, complete!

What is the mark of true faith? *Maintaining* the prayer. Maintaining it by praying in a community, by making everyone worshippers, although not necessarily in the sense that everyone worships together. (I want you to think beyond the words. I want you to think more broadly. Words are too small to express this!) This doesn't mean that we make the person who doesn't pray say his prayers, it means making a community which prays, a community which is always mindful of God and is always following the path of God. A community which says: 'You alone we worship and your aid alone we seek!'[21] A community that only worships and serves God, and a community that relies on no one except God. A prayerful community means one which in its daily life distances itself from the leaders of corruption, those upon whom is God's wrath (*maghḍūbi ʿalayhim*), and those who follow corruption–those who are astray (*ḍāllīn*).[22] This is what prayer means!

If someone tries to make other people prayerful in this sense, this is a mission done in the service of the Truth, for the sake of removing corruption, for the sake of removing 'us' and 'them', for the sake of the unity of a society and the unity of all human beings! This is what it means to *maintain* the prayer. In other words, you do something so that everyone, five times every day, will repeat the words: 'You alone we worship and your aid alone we seek.' God! We only serve you. We only bend to you. And to no one else! Five times every day, they will disassociate from 'those who have incurred Your wrath' (*maghḍūbi ʿalayhim*) and those who are 'astray' (*ḍāllīn*) from the leaders of corruption and the followers of corruption. Another of the meanings of 'to *maintain* the prayer' could be to create a society like this.

Then the Qur'an says: 'and spend out of what We have provided them.' What is the next mark of the faithful? That they give to others

---

21 Q1:5.

22 Q1:7.

out of the provision we have given them. What does spending (*infāq*) mean? (You will recall I discussed this in the previous lecture.) *Infāq* means to fill a gap or to meet a need. Therefore, it only refers to those kinds of spending which fill gaps or meet needs. They say the meaning of *infāq* is this. Just as if the wall of this mosque is already painted, but you come and spend money having it painted again–this is not *infāq*. Why? Because there was no need to do this–it was already painted. Or even if it was not painted, there was no need to do so. If you come and paint the earth around the Imam Ḥasan Mosque and said: 'We spent our wealth on the Imam Ḥasan Mosque. We took several crates of paint to the mosque and used them there.' What have you actually done? You've painted some clods of earth and some dust. Yes, you've spent some money, but this is not what God means by *infāq*! *Infāq* means to spend for the sake of closing gaps that need to be filled in the fabric of society and fulfilling actual needs, not just spending for the sake of spending.

What does 'and spend out of what We have provided them' mean? It means the true believers are those who give out of whatever God has given them. This doesn't just mean money. Does God say: 'and spend out of the money we have provided them?' No. God draws no distinction between the wealth He has given them, the life He has given them, the children He has given them, the dignity He has given them, the physical strength He has given them, the power of speech which He has given them and the mind and ideas He has given them. So 'what We have provided them' includes all of the abilities and resources that God has placed at their disposal. And what do the truly faithful do with the things God has provided them? They spend out of them–they do *infāq*. In other words, they spend it where it is needed, not haphazardly. This is one of the marks of the true believer.

O my brother believer, live up to your name! O my brother! If someone calls you a believer you are happy, but if someone raises the slightest doubt about your faith, you are upset. You might tell me: 'What's the point in you telling us we don't really have faith and we don't really believe in your speeches?' O my so-called believing brother, do you do *infāq*? Remember, this isn't just about whether you spend money–you spend a lot of money. You spend so much money during the Month of Ramadan, you cook delicious food, you lay out an impressive spread, you invite your friends and family. You spend a lot! But do you also do *infāq*?

Dear speaker! How much you speak, how much you breathe, how much you use your lungs, your chest, your existence, your body and your limbs! How much you deploy your powers of explanation! But do you do *infāq* from this power? It is not artful to speak a lot. Rather, saying that which needs to be said–that is artful. The first is not *infāq*. Only the second is. O you who spends his dignity and prestige–you write a letter to someone; you have a meeting with someone to achieve something; you see someone to make sure they do what you wanted; someone tells someone else to do something, someone worthy of respect uses someone to get somewhere. You spend your dignity and prestige; but do you do *infāq* with it? O you who spends his wealth in various ways, whether in the name of religion or the name of something else–yes, sometimes a person spends his money in the name of religion without this being *infāq*; do not be surprised about this, as it does happen. And how bitter it is when it does! You give so much money in the name of religion, you spend so much, but this still isn't *infāq* because you aren't filling a gap, because you are not curing an ailment, because you are not meeting a need that is present in society! No, the real capital of the believer, the thing that is the mark of a true believer, is nothing other than *infāq*–'and spend (*yunfiqūn*) out of what We have provided them.' So if you really want to give your time, or your dignity, or your money for something, you had better think long and hard. Is this really *infāq* or are you just spending haphazardly?

'It is they who are the truly faithful. They shall have ranks near their Lord, forgiveness'.[23] This is the same forgiveness (*maghfirah*) whose meaning we explained in yesterday's lecture and I hope that you can recall what we discussed. If God wishes to grant forgiveness to someone, this means healing the wound he inflicted on his own soul through sinning. So these true believers are those whose spiritual wounds God will heal; 'forgiveness and a noble provision.' They shall have a provision without any abasement or humiliation, without any difficulty or grief. This is the kind of provision God will grant them.

Whenever a faithful *society* comes into being...I am not talking about an *individual*, so do not say 'Thank God, we have a morsel of bread to eat, so we are ok. We have no grief. We don't lord it over anyone.' Because when you really examine such a person's behaviour, you see it is all misfortune and mistreatment of others. They do degrading work and they don't even see that what they do is degrading, or that this morsel of bread they have is a morsel of humiliation...I am talking about a society; when a society's morsel of bread is clean, when it is noble, when it is earnt with dignity, this is when its provision is noble and distinguished, and this happens when a society is truly faithful and displays the qualities I am describing. If this was the case, all of the slogans that political parties in the world today are loudly proclaiming from every quarter to every people–whether truly or falsely–in order to win votes...all of these slogans and promises could be achieved in a truly faithful society. Peace, freedom, prosperity and ease...achieved without war, without bloodshed, through fraternity, through friendship...a high level of culture, a high level of prosperity, a high level of living... all of these slogans and mottos–some of which are meaningful, others of which are meaningless–all of them would be actually achieved in a faithful society ('and a noble provision').

23 Q8:4

Faith Based on Understanding

Saturday 4th Ramadan 1394
21st September 1974

إِنَّ فِي خَلْقِ السَّمَاوَاتِ وَالْأَرْضِ وَاخْتِلَافِ اللَّيْلِ وَالنَّهَارِ لَآيَاتٍ لِأُولِي الْأَلْبَابِ (١٩٠) الَّذِينَ يَذْكُرُونَ اللَّهَ قِيَامًا وَقُعُودًا وَعَلَى جُنُوبِهِمْ وَيَتَفَكَّرُونَ فِي خَلْقِ السَّمَاوَاتِ وَالْأَرْضِ رَبَّنَا مَا خَلَقْتَ هَذَا بَاطِلًا سُبْحَانَكَ فَقِنَا عَذَابَ النَّارِ (١٩١)

'Indeed in the creation of the heavens and the earth and the alternation of night and day, there are signs for those who possess intellects. Those who remember God standing, sitting, and lying on their sides, and reflect on the creation of the heavens and the earth [and say], "Our Lord, You have not created this in vain! Immaculate are You! Save us from the punishment of the Fire."'
- Sūrat Āl-i ʿImrān (3):190–191

Today, we will look at a few more verses on the topic of faith. There are a few points we must consider. Firstly, faith is one of the foremost qualities of God's prophets and the true believers who follow them; they have faith in their own message. This is the difference between divine leaders and the political leaders of the world today. A divine leader, as someone who follows this path, by whatever he says, by every step he takes, by the path that he follows, with all of his being is a sincere believer. On the other hand, the world's political leaders might sometimes say nice things and give moving speeches, but this does not necessarily mean that they necessarily believe in what they say to even the slightest degree.

There is a story about the leaders of one of the communist nations of the Eastern Bloc, who professed atheism and utterly rejected any culture or philosophy that was not based on materialism. This story takes place shortly after Indian independence. In order to win the hearts of the massed millions of Indians who have just won their independence, these leaders visit India. There, the people of India were amazed to see that the leaders of this communist nation had *tilaka* marks on their foreheads. Tilak[24] was one of the leaders of the Indian Independence movement, as well as a Hindu religious scholar. He was one of the greatest leaders of the Hindu religion and both a leader and a pioneer of the independence movement for a period of time.

It is worth me taking some time to mention this to you, even though it is not directly relevant to our present discussion, because it is good to know about such things. From beginning to end, the Indian independence struggle lasted ninety years and, from beginning to end, its most important leaders were all men of religion; whether Muslim or Hindu. Some of the most important Muslim leaders were Mawlānā Shāh Maḥmūd Dihlawī, Mawlānā Maḥmūd al-Ḥasan, Mawlānā Abū al-Kalām Āzād, Mawlānā Muḥammad ʿAlī, and Mawlānā Shawkat ʿAlī. The term 'Mawlānā' amongst Indian Muslims at this time is roughly equivalent to our term 'Ayatollah'. Therefore, these Muslim scholars were amongst the major leaders of the Indian Independence movement. There were also Hindu figures, such as Mahatma Ghandi, and figures belong to the Jain faith who were also part of it.

24 Bal Gangadhar Tilak (1856–1920).

Coming back to Tilak, he was a Hindu monk–although perhaps 'monk' is not the proper term–but, in any case, he was a Hindu religious leader and an amazing figure. He really was quite a remarkable person, although he died while the struggle was ongoing and did not live to see a free India. However, thirty years, forty years after his death, his followers saw his vision for a free India realised and wore the *tilak* mark to memorialise him. This mark is a religious symbol with spiritual and metaphysical significance. And Tilak himself was, for the Hindus, a religious leader.

In any case, when these communist leaders–who espoused atheism and materialism–went to India, in order to win people over to their cause, they put the *tilak* mark on their heads. In other words, they wanted to say: 'Yes, us too. We believe the same as you.' This, even though their own words and beliefs contradicted this statement!

Those political leaders who are removed from spiritual, religious or divine responsibilities are like this. But, the prophets of God believed in whatever they spoke with the totality of their being. Whatever they called people towards; they were rushing towards it already. It means nothing if I lay down at the bottom of a mountain, dying of thirst, and tell you: 'There is cool fresh water to be had on top of this mountain. Quick! Go and get it! Hurry! I'll be waiting here.' You would all be right to tell me: 'If what you're saying is true, if you really knew there was a spring atop this mountain, when you yourself are dying of thirst, you would have gone yourself! You must be lying for you yourself do not believe what you have said!' Therefore, divine leaders must, before anyone else, like trailblazers with the banner in their hands set out on the path, stand tall and lead the way for others to follow. Abraham says: 'I am the first to submit'[25]–before anyone or anything else, he says he is the first to humble himself before his Lord. This is the quality of divine leaders. Divine leaders must be

25 Q6:163.

like this and they are like this. The Prophet was present for all the most important and most dangerous events at the advent of Islam. True, ʿAbd Allāh ibn Masʿūd was beaten, Khabbāb was tortured, and ʿAmmār was tortured too, but the persecution the Prophet suffered was no less than any of these. In fact, if you compare the situation of these devoted companions to the Prophet himself, you will see the Prophet's task was even more difficult and trying–because, as their leader, he was always at the forefront.

Faith is one of the most important qualities we find in God's messengers. Here, 'faith' means to believe in what you say with all of your being. The mark of their faith is that they themselves, before anyone else, set out on the path. That is why the Qur'an tells us: 'The Messenger has faith in what has been sent down to him from his Lord, and all the faithful.'[26] The faithful, those who have been converted by him, those outstanding people who have joined him, and are now the loudspeakers for his message, are like him also: 'each has faith in God'–each and every one of them believe in God, they accept God with all of their being–'His angels, His scriptures'–the holy books which are from the first to the last in harmony with one another–'and His messengers'–and all of His prophets. The Prophet and his followers believe in all of the prophets, because all follow the same path:

'In this path, the prophets are like camel drivers,
Guiding the caravan along the way'[27]

The prophets are all drivers of a single caravan, guiding the caravan on a single path, leading it to a single destination, with people from all places, all going together towards a single terminus. The faithful say: 'We make no distinction between any of His apostles.'[28] We respect

26 Q2:285.

27 A verse from Shaykh Maḥmūd Shabistarī.

28 Q2:285.

Jesus, Moses, Abraham and Idrīs, just as much as Jacob and George[29], just as much as Noah. We respect all of the prophets from the first to the last. All of them were acting by God's command. All of them were directed by Him to the same destination. All of them gave glad tidings of the same felicity and the same Paradise. All of them followed the same line. 'We make no distinction between any of His apostles.' (As for why we believe in the prophethood of this line of prophets, we will–with God's leave–discuss this in turn on another occasion.)

'And they say'.[30] Pay attention to these two or three sentences, as they illustrate something that we will return to later. So, the prophets have faith. Our Prophet has it. The believers and those that follow him also all have faith. 'And they say: "We hear and obey."' In other words, they hear, they *understand*, and they obey. Hearing here does not simply signify sounds reaching their ears. Hearing is more than this. Because the act of hearing involves more than just one's ear. You might tell someone to 'lend an ear' when you are speaking to them but at the end, what do you ask them? You ask: 'Did you *hear* what I said?' Now, obviously, when you are talking to someone there is no more than half a metre separating you. Your normal speaking voice can carry for ten metres or more. So of course, he *heard* what you said but what you really mean is did he *understand* it? Of course, it went into his hear but what you want to know is did it go into his *mind*? So when those with faith say, 'we hear' this means: 'We understand, with the totality of our being, what God sent down to us and what He specified for us.' 'And obey'–what does this mean, then? It does not mean blind obedience. It means that they obey based on knowledge and understanding of what they have heard! 'Our Lord, forgive us'–pardon us, our Lord, we want only your reward and your forgiveness,

29 Possibly a reference to Saint George, who is also sometimes revered as one of the prophets after Jesus in the Islamic tradition.

30 Q2:285.

and nothing else–'and toward You is the return'–we are going back to You. (There are many important things to be said about returning to God that we will, God willing, explain in this series of lectures when we come to the topic of the Resurrection in the Qur'an, if God grants us the opportunity until then!)[31]

So what have we understood from these verses so far? First that faith and belief are two qualities possessed by those who answered the call to submit to God. Those people who have no faith, who have no belief, who just followed everyone else to be on the safe side, they are not within the domain of Islamic thought–there is no shame in saying so–because faith is necessary. Faith means belief, to accept what is clearly and unimpeachably true, it means attaching oneself to a cause. If this cause is not the thought of the religion and the Qur'an, and your heart will not be subdued–meaning if there is no faith in this heart–then this heart is a dead heart. It does not live in the light of Islam. It can never be called a submitting heart...a *Muslim* heart. Therefore, faith is necessary. This is first.

Second, is that faith is of two varieties. There is the faith of those who blindly follow because they have a tribal mentality; their fathers and grandfathers believed, so they believe too. Because our holy scripture says this, because our religion says this, we say the same. And even if you bring them evidence to the contrary, they will never listen to you. This is one kind of faith or belief. But even this has two kinds. There are those who blindly follow (*taqlīd*), like most people today. Such that if you ask them: 'How do you know that the Prophet of Islam was true?' They have no idea what to say. They don't know anything! Their forefathers said so. Their schoolteachers say so. The people they see in the streets and market say so. So, if all of these tell them that the Prophet was true, they will say so as well. Now they believe...they really do believe that the Prophet was true, but this

31 Unfortunately, this series of lectures did not reach the topic of Resurrection.

is just something they heard from someone who they trusted and blindly accepted without checking for themselves.

Similar to the belief of those who blindly follow is the belief of those who follow tribally (*taʿaṣṣub*). Some of these people are ready–may God protect us–to insult other prophets to please our Prophet! They think that these prophets are fighting with one another in the heavens! They say things like: 'Moses! Who on earth was Moses? Our Prophet is the best!' Sadly, this is not something you find only amongst the uneducated. Sometimes you see people speaking like this whom you expected better from, people who should know better, people who should understand, and you see them making these sorts of mistakes, you hear them saying these sorts of things! This is what we call tribalism. 'Because Islam says this, this is right and whatever any other religion says is nonsense!' 'Because we Muslims do this, this is right, and because other people do this, this is wrong!' I suppose this is a kind of faith, but it is not one that rests on evidence, but on tribal identity. And you know that tribalism means taking a side without any basis, taking sides based on your feelings rather than based on reason. This is what we call tribalism.

So, these are blind faith and tribal belief. But, my friends, I must tell you that the kind of faith Islam values is not either of these. Blind faith and tribal belief have no value. You want proof of this? I will show you that when you believe blindly or tribally, you can lose such belief just as easily as you acquired it. Just as a child, without any effort, or a student, without any difficulty, can acquire simple faith from their parents or teachers, those who steal faith can just as easily come along and take it. And, all of a sudden, you see a generation growing up without any faith, a generation whose belief has been pillaged, gone; everyone's faith is left hollowed out and empty. In the fires of materialism, faith melts into the earth like snow in the summer heat. Who am I talking about? Normally, we talk about the younger generation like this. But I want you to know that when I talk about the generation that is losing its faith, I am not talking about the younger generation. Because, what we are witnessing today is the blossoming of faith in the younger generation, as it is the younger generation who are looking for a faith that is not based on blind following or tribal identity, but rather is based on understanding. No, I am talking about the generation before the youth of today. The older generation of our society. These who believe in some things blindly: Yes, they come to the *majlis* in the mosque to hear the sermons and storytelling; yes, they come to the congregational prayers at the mosque; but, because none of this is based on reason or logic, they can also be easily convinced to burn down the very same mosque, to trample Imam Ḥusayn, and to give up all their religiosity for those things they think have real value. They do this, and you can see them do this! Today, one of the real crises that we are facing is in the generation before the youth. Those who lack the awareness and understanding of the Muslim youth today and who sadly also lack the deep, unshakable faith of two generations past. They lack the thoughtfulness and understanding by virtue of which they could nurture a strong and abiding faith in themselves, and are instead held by the bonds of money, position, status, desire, prosperity and comfort. Nor do they have a strong ark or impregnable fortress, like one or two centuries ago, in which, at the very least, they could shelter their faith; even if this was only acquired blindly.

A hundred years ago, these snares for one's thoughts, faith and beliefs did not exist. In those days, the hands of the enemy, those treacherous fingers, had not penetrated so deeply into the fabric of our society. There were still plots which had yet to come to fruition. They still had to deprive people of their fundamental religious faith if they wanted to heap misery on them. But these plots have since succeeded. The generation before the youth, the generation who are no longer young but are rather the youth of yesteryear, they are trying to build their faith and belief in the face of a flood, without even having a firm foundation on which to build. How lucky are those who chose their faith based on understanding, comprehension, awareness and knowledge. A flood will sometimes carry off great trees, while leaving those tender saplings unscathed, because their roots go twice as deep into the ground. Those things that have a foundation do not shake so easily. They do not fall so easily.

In any case, this is a reality that is present in Islam. My brothers! The faith that has value is faith based on understanding. The faith that is joined with comprehension and awareness. Faith based on insight. With open eyes. Without fear of criticism. The faith of some Muslims is such that, in order to keep it safe, they should never open a newspaper. They should never read a book. They should never open their eyes. They should never speak to anyone. They should never leave their home. They should never go outside. Such faith cannot last. The faith that is needed is a faith chosen based on awareness. This is a faith that will endure even in the most difficult and dire of circumstances 'barring someone who is compelled while his heart is at rest in faith'[32]–which was revealed about the Prophet's Companion, ʿAmmār Yāsir. The Qur'an says that if you are being tortured and, in order that the enemy leave you alone, you tell them what they want to hear, your faith is not a faith that can be diverted from its proper direction by persecution. The faith of Khabbāb ibn Aratt, when they pointed red-hot irons at his throat, is no joke! When they brought these hot irons close to his body and touched them against his skin, his faith was so deep and so strong that even these burning irons could not make him surrender it.

This faith that is based on understanding, based on comprehension, based on thought, based on correct calculations–when we have this faith, it is not necessary to put this faith under a cover or lock it away to keep it safe from the trials and travails of this world, because

32 Q16:106.

nothing can harm it in the first place. It is only these unthinking kinds of faith that some people have with which we need to concern ourselves: Unless this happens, or unless that happens, or unless something else happens. If we want faith to stand firm, if we want faith not to vanish and if we want faith to be based on understanding, then we must give knowledge to those people who we want to be believers! We should not feel threatened by them learning. We should not deprive them of the enjoyment of gaining knowledge. Instead, we must make sure that the right knowledge is available for their hearts and minds so that, on the basis of this knowledge, they can nurture a true and strong belief, so that they will have a concrete foundation for their faith, so that their faith won't vanish when someone takes a shot at it. Islam says that faith must come from understanding. It is precisely this kind of faith that these verses at the end of *Sūrat Āl-i ʿImrān* are describing:

'Indeed in the creation of the heavens and the earth and the alternation of night and day, there are signs'.[33] For whom? For those who do not observe? For those who do not think? Of course not, 'for those who possess intellects'–for those who have the power of thought and understanding. Now, this would be all people, if everyone used the mind that God had given them! Otherwise, from the moment they were born, those with intellects would enjoy a special peace of mind, and we would say: 'We are not of them and we can never be of them. Those with intellects and these or those.' No, when God says 'possessors of intellects', this means all people...all of the three billion people in the world today possess intellects, so long as they use this gift that God has given them. Just as if you buy a car and keep it in the garage without ever getting in and driving it. Then, sometime later, you turn the key in the ignition and see that it doesn't start. You inspect the car: Maybe it is corroded or maybe the battery has

33 Q3:190.

gone flat. But this isn't the fault of the car. It's your fault for not using it and taking care of it. So 'those with intellects' are those who actually make use of the minds that God has given them in order to become wise.

So, who are 'those who possess intellects' (*ulu al-albāb*)? Now, pay attention to how the Qur'an addresses this question, because it uses a very subtle approach. When it wants to say who 'those who possess intellects' are and who the wise ones are, if these were ordinary people it was describing, it would say 'those who possess intellects are those who get ahead in whatever they do, who are never duped, in business, in politics, in competitions, in confrontations, in professions...whatever they do, they do well.' But the Qur'an doesn't accept any of these ploys, because the real value the human being has is not through any of the above, but through his connection with God. Therefore, the Qur'an describes 'those who possess intellects' in terms of their relationship with God. And, according to the Qur'an, those who possess intellects are the ones who are concerned with this highest of values, more than anyone or anything else. 'Those who remember God'[34]–this is the mark of someone who has an intellect: they remember God–'standing, sitting, and laying on their sides.' In other words, in every circumstance, they remember. However, remembering God here does not refer to the mystical trance-like state of the dervish that some people crave–always remembering God, always chanting–'*hū*!'[35]–but that is not what we mean. We mean *actively* remembering God. But what is it to actively remember God, such that this remembrance is counted as an act? How can one achieve this?

'And reflect on the creation of the heavens and the earth.' Do you see? Those who have intellects–those who are truly wise–are those

34 Q3:191.

35 *Hū* ('He'), is the pronoun used for Allah which Sufis use in their chanting.

who ponder and think: 'And reflect on the creation of the heavens and the earth.' And, as they ponder on this, they say, whether inwardly in their hearts or outwardly with their tongues: 'Our Lord! You have not created this in vain! Immaculate are you!' You have not created this without a purpose. You are too immaculate to have made this without a purpose. In other words, this is the most fundamental principle of their belief system or worldview.

Each and every worldview starts from a simple fact: We are here for some purpose. If you believe in God, you say you were created for a purpose. And if you do not believe in God, you say you have a purpose here. Do you see? The most fundamental idea of a philosophy that is meant to inspire a way of life, whether for an individual or a society, is this: 'Our Lord! You have not created this in vain.' He is a theist. He believes in God. So he says: 'Our Lord, you did not create the heavens and the earth and all they contain for no reason. You are too immaculate and wise to do such a thing! Therefore, I have a moral responsibility. I must follow a path. I am but a speck amongst the wonders of the cosmos. But I am here for a reason. In this grand edifice, you have made a place for me and given me a purpose to fulfil. But I might disrupt the harmony of this system.' 'Immaculate are you! So save us from the punishment of the Fire!' While the Fire of the Resurrection is real, it is also a symbol of the Fire of God's wrath, anger and retribution, and of the cosmos.

You must pay attention this because this is all a prelude, a prelude so that we can apprehend the meaning of faith based on understanding from these verses. Dear friends, you must have grasped by now how understanding arises from these signs but pay attention to what comes next: 'Our Lord! Whoever that You make enter the Fire will surely have been disgraced by You, and the wrongdoers will have no helpers.' The wrongdoers that you consign to the Fire will have no help, whether from the material realm or from the unseen realm, in any way, shape or form. In other words, those who follow the path of wrongdoing and injustice, the path of faithlessness and hypocrisy, and the path of falsehood, are condemned to fade away to nothingness–no part of this world will preserve them or protect them.

Now, 'Our Lord!' they call out–these possessors of intellect, these wise people, these who ponder on the heavens and the earth, these who understand that there is nothing in this world without a purpose and that this world would not have been created without a purpose–they continue: 'Our Lord! We have indeed heard', we have heard with our ears and *understood* with our hearts, 'a summoner calling to faith, declaring, "Have faith in your Lord!" So we believed.' How exactly did they believe? Someone came along and told them to believe, so they believed? Of course not! These are the possessors of intellects. These are the thinkers. This caller could be a manifest caller, like a prophet, but there is also an inner prophet in the form of their intellect, thought, and insight which calls them to believe in God. So, a caller told them to have faith and they, *based on their full understanding, comprehension, awareness and insight*, answered the call. This is the second point.

There is a third point that I want to deal with briefly here. That is that, since it is faith based on understanding that Islam wants, since God Almighty does not accept faith without understanding and places no value or importance on this, that is why we see the Qur'an in several places criticising blind or tribal belief. Sadly, it is this sort of belief that people adopt by leaving their brains behind. But it is this belief that the Qur'an harshly criticises.

'And when they are told, "Come to what God has sent down and to the Apostle"'[36]–this is addressed to the faithless and I would translate its meaning as saying: 'Come to what God has sent down and to the Prophet, come and see and understand.' So, the faithless are told to come and understand, to come and listen, to see what

36 Q5:104.

the Prophet says. And what is their response? Instead of coming, instead of thinking, instead of trying to understand and choosing their own way, 'They say: "Sufficient for us is what we have found our fathers following."' In other words, we will follow the same path as our fathers and we will not follow anything new. One scholar says that when the Qur'an speaks about disbelievers (*kuffār*), they are always the reactionaries of every era. Whenever a prophet or a wise person says something new, opens a new path, or summons people to something new, the disbelievers are opposed to it; they are tribal, blind following, ossified and reactionary in their outlook. They will never accept a new approach. They always say the same thing: We will take the same way as those before us travelled. This is not the way we saw our mothers and fathers doing it, we want to see the world as they saw it and follow in their footsteps. But what does the Qur'an say in response? 'What, even if their fathers did not know anything and were not guided?!' The Qur'an asks: Will you still follow your forefathers even if they didn't understand anything? If they didn't find a path? If they couldn't work out what was right and wrong? Do you see how the Qur'an rebukes people for blindly following their forefathers?

Faith through Action

Sunday 5th Ramadan 1394
22nd September 1974

وَجَاهِدُوا فِي اللَّهِ حَقَّ جِهَادِهِ هُوَ اجْتَبَاكُمْ وَمَا جَعَلَ
عَلَيْكُمْ فِي الدِّينِ مِنْ حَرَجٍ مِلَّةَ أَبِيكُمْ إِبْرَاهِيمَ هُوَ سَمَّاكُمُ
الْمُسْلِمِينَ مِنْ قَبْلُ وَفِي هَٰذَا لِيَكُونَ الرَّسُولُ شَهِيدًا عَلَيْكُمْ
وَتَكُونُوا شُهَدَاءَ عَلَى النَّاسِ فَأَقِيمُوا الصَّلَاةَ وَآتُوا الزَّكَاةَ
وَاعْتَصِمُوا بِاللَّهِ هُوَ مَوْلَاكُمْ فَنِعْمَ الْمَوْلَىٰ وَنِعْمَ النَّصِيرُ (٧٨)

'And strive for the sake of God, a striving which is worthy of Him. He has chosen you and has not placed for you any obstacle in the religion, the faith of your father, Abraham. He named you 'muslims' before and now, so that the Apostle may be a witness to you, and that you may be witnesses to mankind. So maintain the prayer, give the zakat, and hold fast to God. He is your master, and an excellent master and an excellent helper is He.'

- Sūrat al-Ḥajj (22):78

The issue we will address today is this: Faith (*īmān*) in the Qur'an's lexicon is not purely a matter of the heart. It is true that faith means belief, and belief is something related to the heart, but the Qur'an does not recognise every kind of faith or belief as valid. 'Pure' faith, faith 'of the heart', is something dried-out and hollow; it is a belief whose rays cannot be seen in the body and limbs of the believer, and Islam does not consider such belief to be valuable. If this is what is meant by belief, then Satan would be the first believer in God. Before Satan became the tempter of mankind who brought about Adam's fall, he had worshipped God for aeons and his heart was filled with the knowledge of God. However, in that moment where faith truly counts–meaning when it came to making a choice and deciding one's final fate–this belief did not matter because it was only in his heart. What I am saying is that a faith that only remains in the heart will wither and die. You might think it won't, that it will survive. We make this erroneous assumption that faith will somehow survive in the depths of one's heart. But the faith that remains in the heart without ever reaching your hands, your feet, your eyes, your ears, your brain, your limbs, your life, your potential, or your energy–according to the Qur'an, this faith has no value. I've tried to sum this up in the title I gave to this lecture: 'Life-giving Faith'. A faith which works like an overflowing spring, a faith that is accompanied by duty, a faith that is a weight on the shoulders of the believer, a faith that is accompanied by action.

When we read the Qur'an, we notice the phrase 'those who have faith and do righteous deeds'[37] repeatedly associates faith with good works. Faith alone, faith without duty, faith without any sense of responsibility, is of no use in this world and of no use in the Hereafter. This is the Qur'an's logic. (Our reading tomorrow will be on roughly the same topic and the verses we will ponder on tomorrow, God-willing, will illuminate this further, so that there will be no doubt). Those who think that faith is something that resides only in the human heart believe that even if a person pays no attention to the duties this faith imposes on him or the demands it makes of him, they are still a believer. They imagine that one can be a believer through

37 See, for example, Qur'anic verses: 2:25, 2:83, 3:57, 4:57, 4:122, 4:173, 5:9....

belief alone, without action, without effort, without struggle, they make the promises God has given to the faithful promises to almost everyone. They suppose that Paradise is granted because of something in the heart without any action to back it up, and that dominion over the earth is granted because of something in the heart rather than action. In short, they imagine that if we put action to one side, something of faith still remains. But the people who believe this must read these verses and the tens of others which are found throughout the Qur'an which make it clear that the faith that Islam values, is a faith accompanied by action, by responsibility and by duty.

If you feel no sense of moral responsibility, then you should doubt whether you are in fact, a believer. A society which does not act on the duties of faith cannot call itself a believing society. Those who hear the Qur'an's words: 'Do not weaken or grieve: you shall have the upper hand, should you be faithful'–those who hear this amazing reassurance from the Qur'an only to see that, when they look at reality, those who believe in the Qur'an are no better than anyone else (in fact, they see that they are dependent on everyone else!), they are going to wonder what happened to the Qur'an's promise? And if they do not find any time when this promise was fulfilled, they are going to await the appearance of the Twelfth Imam (aj). They will convince themselves that, yes, this promise is true–it will come to pass when the Mahdi (aj) appears and everywhere that faith takes root. However, the faith the Qur'an is speaking about is a faith that is never separated from duty because, according to the Qur'an, faith is more than something in one's heart.

If assenting to or accepting some beliefs was enough to have this thing we call faith, then I tell you that the first believer in the Prophet was Abū Lahab or Walīd ibn Mughīrah! They were men of intelligence; they knew full well that the Prophet was not lying. They knew he was telling the truth. Do you want proof of this fact? The proof is that they would sit together and plot how to defame the Prophet. They said: 'Let's go and listen, see what he says, then point out its flaws!' Then, once they had gone and listened, they sat together the next night and said: 'No, this is not the words of a human being. These are the words of God!' So they accepted this fact, they accepted that these words were not emanating from the Prophet but from God. However, even fourteen centuries after this fact, we still don't accept Abū Lahab as a believer. He was not a believer because his belief did not lead him to feel any sense of duty. So what do you say?

If it was enough to know what was true on a theoretical level and to have belief in one's heart, then ʿAmr ibn ʿĀṣ should be the first Shiʿa in the world. The same ʿAmr ibn ʿĀṣ, who either witnessed the events of Ghadīr with his own eyes or heard about it from those who had.You and I can only read about that event in books some thirteen centuries later. The same ʿAmr ibn ʿĀṣ even composed verses of poetry in praise of ʿAlī. ʿAmr ibn ʿĀṣ who, on his deathbed, at that sensitive moment of a person's life, expressed regret and showed remorse, who said that he had sold his religion for the worldly promises of Muʿāwiyah and fought ʿAlī, even though he knew ʿAlī was right. So, from where I'm sitting, ʿAmr's faith was deeper and more insightful than the Shiʿa of the fourteenth century who find out about the Imamate of the Commander of the Faithful (a) and believe in it. Is ʿAmr one of the Shiʿa? You say he's not. Why isn't he then? Because you and I both know that when you believe in the Imamate of the Commander of the Faithful (a), there are certain duties that become incumbent upon you. Your first duty is to *not* pledge allegiance to Muʿāwiyah ibn Abū Sufyān! But ʿAmr joined forces with Muʿāwiyah and fought Imam ʿAlī. In other words, because he did not observe the moral duties and responsibilities that this belief directs towards a person–that is why he isn't a Shiʿa.

This principle is correct and because it is correct, I want to apply it to us. On the same basis, let us ask: Am I sure I am a Shiʿa? Are you sure you are Shiʿa? Do we do our duties as Shiʿas? Do we uphold our moral responsibilities? The Qur'an speaks clearly and unambiguously about this. It explicitly negates faith from anyone who categorically neglects the moral duties that faith engenders. Therefore, the faith that Islam values and recognises–this is one of the fundamental principles of Islam and Shi'ism–is the faith that gives rise to moral duties and sustains these. It is the faith that is always accompanied by moral responsibility and if it is not, then it is not expected to have its desired effect. So do not expect any assistance in this world. Do not expect any security in this world.

'Those who have faith and do not taint their faith with wrongdoing for such there shall be safety, and they are the guided.'[38] A faith that is accompanied by wrongdoing does not bring forth safety. A faith that is not accompanied by moral duty, will not grant aid to the believer; it will not guarantee his success; it will not invoke God's help and the help of the very atoms of the cosmos; it will not grant him salvation or felicity in this world and–in a word–it will not grant him Paradise in the Hereafter.

The vain thoughts that spring from seeking a life of ease try to convince us that the opposite is true. One of the traits of the human being is that he is always looking for an easier way to do things, this state of desiring ease is something innate to humans. If you give a person a choice between two actions, all things being equal, they will choose whichever is easier, whichever requires less effort, whichever needs less investment. This is a human trait and people usually live in this manner. This is what is known as taking the path of least resistance. The easiest route. So, from this point of view, religious faith looks like it means giving up this paradise of ease! However, if we genuinely want to find ease, we should sit down and make sure we have the formula right for this. The formulas that tell us that a lazy person who never does anything for anyone can go to Paradise–what

38 Q6:82.

will it take for us to see that this cannot be right? Are we going to wait until we don't go to Paradise to notice that the formula is wrong? So I am saying let's look again at this formula right now, to see whether this is really going to give us the result we are after!

As well as the Qur'an, which is our infallible guide to truth, there are also countless narrations from the Imams which state that their intercession cannot be attained except through striving and effort. Now, we think we can sit here despondent about our past, present and future, accept humiliation, and do nothing to change our condition, and hope for intercession, even after the Imams themselves have said that their intercession is not for those who do not strive? Do you see how these narrations contradict what we imagine to be the case in our minds?

One night, Imam Zayn al-ʿĀbidīn (a) is worshipping in the mosque. He is weeping. This is someone who, according to a correct understanding of his life, was constantly striving so that truth would reign supreme. But at night, he was also constantly striving to serve God and humble himself before Him. He would cry, shed tears, and call out to his Lord. Some of his supplications are truly amazing–although now is not the time to delve into these. Then, along comes a simple and naive man, who says to the Imam: 'O son of God's Messenger! Why do you weep? When you have such a father, such a mother, and such a grandfather, all of whom were chosen by God? Leave weeping to us! You are the son of God's Messenger, the son of ʿAlī, the son of Ḥusayn, the son of Fāṭimat al-Zahrāʾ! What do you have to cry for?' Now, Imam Zayn al-ʿĀbidīn (a) wants to defend the following thesis, that humbling oneself before God, weeping to God, worshipping and supplicating to God is to polish the soul, to make oneself more determined, to make oneself more reliant on God, and not to slacken. He wants to defend this thesis, but this Shiʿa layperson also has an erroneous understanding that he wants to correct. What would you say? Look at the Imam's words: 'Let us not speak of my father, my mother and my grandfather...Paradise is for the obedient.' This is the thesis of Shiʿa Islam with regard to faith and actions.

Why am I placing so much emphasis on this issue? Because for many years–centuries even–the idea has been put into the minds of Muslims that it is not necessary to do anything in order to be a Muslim. They have been told that all you need to be a believer is a pure heart–you don't need to do anything else. And we have helped our enemies foster this idea in our minds through our own indolence and laziness. We think that we are going to Paradise and it will be given to us for the slightest thing. This false notion has been so successful in spreading because people are ignorant, and they want to believe this is true. They had no other motive in spreading this idea save that they were ignorant.

In fact, it was only a short time after the Prophet that this idea came into existence and began to spread. Muʿāwiyah ibn Abū Sufyān is a very interesting character. Do you know of anyone more impious than Muʿāwiyah? Do you know of anyone more wicked than Muʿāwiyah? Who is more villainous than he in history? In the early centuries of Islam? One day, people saw that Muʿāwiyah was advising his followers that when he dies there were two packages that should be buried with him in his grave. They asked: 'What are these things?' He tells them that one of the packages contains a piece of the Prophet's clothes. As for the other: Well, one day, the Prophet was trimming his hair or nails, and some clippings fell on the ground, which Muʿāwiyah He said to his followers: 'Put these in my grave so that God forgives me'. Do you see! Even Muʿāwiyah hoped for the Prophet's intercession and tried to obtain it. But how did he do this? By taking some hairs or nail clippings from the Prophet. Bravo! He was willing to strive to the extent that it was easy, to the extent that it has no cost to him. He will listen to the Qur'an, he will respect the Qur'an, but only to the extent that it is useful for him.

In any case, it is over the course of many long years that the enemies have been working on the minds of the Muslims so that they say that Islam is not action, faith requires no work, as long as there is love and faith and belief in your heart, there is nothing else you need to do. You don't need to move, to strive, to have an effect. It is years that they have been trying to convince of this. But what does the Qur'an say? It says loud and clear that 'they do not have faith.'[39] Those people who do not do what these verses describe (which we will continue to discuss tomorrow as well) are not believers. The faithful are those people who are with you, those people who are surrounded by God's grace, brotherhood, and submission, who are striving in the way of God in a way that befits their beliefs. They strive. They take action. This is the logic of the Qur'an.

'O you who have faith! Bow down and prostrate yourselves, and worship your Lord, and do good, so that you may be felicitous.'[40] If you do these actions, you will be successful, happy and saved. But if you had faith without bowing, prostrating, worshipping God or doing good, then will you be successful and happy? You can clearly see what the answer is!

'And strive for the sake of God, a striving that is worthy of Him. He has chosen you'.[41] It is He who has chosen you, O community of Islam! What does it mean when the Qur'an says He has chosen you? Does it mean you have been set aside like precious pearls? That you're cut from different cloth? They sin. They err. They disobey our commands. And Paradise has their name on it? This is what the Jews claimed at the time of the Prophet. They made the same mistake. Every Muslim has this same mistaken idea in their head. The Qur'an responds to the Jews, who believed themselves to be God's chosen and beloved or, in

39 Q24:47.

40 Q22:77.

41 Q22:78.

fact, the sons of God, by delivering a very sharp rebuke. It says that the chosen and beloved of God are those who obey His commands. 'Yes, O Children of Israel, We chose you.' God chose the nation of Islam but, before Islam, he chose the Israelites, but both acts of choosing are one and the same. In other words, God chose the people best prepared for His most important mission.

If you look amongst yourselves, you will see that one of you looks more determined in appearance, stronger in physique, and more healthy-looking in complexion. His hand is stronger. His arms are more powerful. His chest is broader. You'd ask that guy to help you carry a heavy load! You'd choose him for this task! And he'd probably rush to help too! So, if he was chosen...if he could undertake this task... meaning if he *wanted* to do it, because he definitely *could* do it...if he decided that he would carry this load, then he would stand out from his peers. You would say: 'Poor guy! No one else could do it, so we didn't ask them. Instead, we asked you.' When God chose the nation of Islam or the Israelites, it was in this sense. At their own time, the Israelites and the Muslims were the most able people to bear the responsibility of the divine mission, of leading and guiding mankind. That is why God entrusted them with this mission. Did they bear it faithfully or not? If they did, they would have carried this trust to its destination, and they would have been the best and most worthy of the Muslims. But if they didn't, then what? If they didn't, then they are in the same situation as the Israelites who did not fulfil the trust that God placed in them: 'So they were struck with abasement and poverty, and they earned God's wrath.'[42] This is in this world. And their 'refuge is Hell.' This is in the Hereafter.

'He chose you' to bear this responsibility 'and has not placed for you any obstacle in the religion'[43]–He has not created any difficulty or

---

42 Q2:61.

43 Q22:78.

hardship in the religion for you. This responsibility is not excessively burdensome. Being chosen is not a punishment. You are capable of bearing this duty. 'The Faith of your father, Abraham'–this is the same faith as that of Abraham. 'He named you *muslims* before and now.' This refers to Abraham's supplication in *Sūrat al-Baqarah*, 'and from our progeny a nation submissive to You.'[44] So God is saying that He gave them this name before and also now–why? For what reason? In order that you do what? 'So that the Apostle may be a witness to you, and that you may be witnesses to mankind'–so that the Prophet will be responsible for you, and you will be responsible for mankind. So that the Prophet watches over you and witnesses what you do, and so that you will watch over mankind and witness what they do. You are the leaders of humanity. You are the guides of the human race. You are responsible for leading this caravan. The leaders of caravans do not sleep!

'So that the Apostle may be a witness to you, and that you may be witnesses to mankind.' Now that this is the case, that your responsibility is heavy indeed, that you have been entrusted with a hard task by your Lord...'So, maintain the prayer.' Do you see? There is a moral duty here. Do you think this is just hollowed and withered belief? 'So, maintain the prayer, give the *zakat*'[45]–recall, we discussed the meaning of maintaining the prayer previously–'and hold fast to God.' Cleave to God and the religion of God. Seek refuge with God. Rely on God and no one else, and no other power! When all the ways are closed to you, do not despair of God's help, of God's kindness, of God's grace! 'He is your master.' God is your Lord, your protector, your helper. (The meaning of master–*mawlā*–and mastery–*wilāyah*–and other such terms requires a lengthy discussion. What does it mean

44 Q2:128.

45 Q22:78.

when God says He is the guardian (*walī*) of those who believe,[46] when He says He is their master? ʿAlī is the Master of the Faithful, the faithful should have the *wilāyah* of ʿAlī, what does that mean? This word, *wilāyah*, is a very profound and meaningful term. One day, we will–God willing–discuss the meaning of this term and the way it is used in the Qur'an). 'An excellent master and an excellent helper!'

There are a handful of other verses at the end of *Sūrat al-Anfāl* which restate the duties associated with faith mentioned here, such as prayer, zakat, holding fast to God. It also mentions some duties associated with faith from another perspective. Let us turn to these now:

'Indeed, those who have believed and migrated and struggled with their possessions and their persons'–and against their possessions and their persons–'and those who gave them shelter'–when they were refugees without a home–'and helped, they are guardians of one another'–they are bound together and on the same side. They are of a single substance. They are the bricks and mortar of a single structure. 'The likeness of the faithful is like an edifice; they support one another.' Have you seen how these bricks go together in these ornate ceilings? Each brick is a single believer. Each believer is a single brick. They fit together and support one another. Together they form a structure that takes great effort to demolish. Tens of bricks side-by-side. This one brick helps to protect the whole, and the whole all help to protect this one brick. 'They are guardians of one another.' Held together by strong bonds. United.

'And those who have believed'[47]–pay attention here. What about those who have believed, who have faith in their hearts 'but did not migrate'? They believed but they didn't act on the moral duties that arise from their faith. What about them? 'You have no guardianship

46 Q2:257.

47 Q8:72.

(*wilāyah*) in relation to them until they migrate.' These are not bound to you. They are not a part of you. There is no relationship or guardianship between the two of you. Until when? 'Until they migrate.' Until they follow through on the moral duties to which faith is attached. Hollowed-out faith is no use in this world, dear brother. It does not produce any effects in the Islamic society. As for the Hereafter, this is a separate discussion. 'You have no guardianship in relation to them until they migrate.'

There is another verse which is very relevant to what we are discussing here, and it comes just a few verses after those we have been discussing above. God says: 'Those who have believed, migrated, and struggled in the way of God, and those who gave them shelter and help, it is they who are the truly faithful.'[48] So, if those who emigrate, struggle, give shelter and help are the truly faithful, what are everyone else? They are false believers.

48 Q8:74.

Faith and Selective Duty

Monday 6th Ramadan 1394
23rd September 1974

إِنَّمَا كَانَ قَوْلَ الْمُؤْمِنِينَ إِذَا دُعُوا إِلَى اللَّهِ وَرَسُولِهِ لِيَحْكُمَ بَيْنَهُمْ أَنْ يَقُولُوا سَمِعْنَا وَأَطَعْنَا وَأُولَئِكَ هُمُ الْمُفْلِحُونَ (٥١) وَمَنْ يُطِعِ اللَّهَ وَرَسُولَهُ وَيَخْشَ اللَّهَ وَيَتَّقْهِ فَأُولَئِكَ هُمُ الْفَائِزُونَ (٥٢)

'All the response of the faithful, when they are summoned to God and His Apostle that He may judge between them, is to say, "We hear and obey." It is they who are the felicitous. Whoever obeys God and His Apostle, and fears God and is wary of Him it is they who will be the triumphant.'
- Sūrat al-Nūr (24):51–52

This is another very important issue in the discussion of faith. Namely, the moral duties of the believer do not only apply sometimes or whenever he feels like it. It is not the case that if someone calls himself a believer, even though he violates his moral code whenever it is convenient or beneficial for him, then he is a believer. Just because someone calls themselves a believer and makes a show of piety that he is such. That he has combined faith and action as he claims. It is only when faith and piety are of more benefit to him than transgression and sin that he returns to the names of Islam, faith, and morality.

Here, we are going to discuss this quality that the Qur'an discusses in various contexts and which we ascribe to people who are self-serving. We said that self-serving people are like this. But all people in this world are self-serving–after all, who goes out in search of loss? When we call someone self-serving, however, what we mean are those who are ready to sacrifice worldly benefits for their own personal interest; they transgress in serving themselves.

Their behaviour is like this: They believe and act piously to the extent that they desire and to the extent that is beneficial to them. They call themselves believers and make a show of morality and piety in the pursuit of personal benefit. From the point of view of Islam, these kinds of individuals are not believers. The Qur'an explicitly states that these people have no faith. Therefore, when we are discussing faith, which is one of the most fundamental topics in understanding Islamic thought, we draw the conclusion that if faith is not accompanied by a sense of duty and moral responsibility, if someone who claims to be a believer does not follow through by fulfilling these moral duties–or 'doing righteous deeds'–in the Qur'anic parlance, this is not genuine faith and such hollow and empty faith will have no effect. In addition to this, we must also see that the kind of moral duty we are discussing is permanent and unceasing.

Someone who is a believer and wishes to remain so in order to enjoy the fruits of his faith, must bear a sense of duty towards all of God's laws and must feel morally responsible at all times and places. Someone who believes that believing in God and believing in the Prophet give rise to moral duties will see that these moral duties are permanent and unceasing. One must always strive to be a servant of God. Each of us must do his utmost to serve God. Believing in the Prophet and announcing that you affirm him as God's messenger means that you now have a duty to follow the Prophet and adopt his path. If I affirm his prophethood like this and accept this moral duty, it means nothing if when something small happens and there is an opportunity to go against the way of the Prophet, I grit my teeth and clench my fists and stay strong, and make a show of being a good Muslim, but as soon as something serious happens, something more painful, I turn around and forget my moral conviction–as the Arabic proverb reads: 'A lion amongst friends and an ostrich amongst enemies'. So, on little issues, you are a lion but when it comes to serious ones, you are an ostrich. All your courage is gone! This proverb means that when it comes to your own, you are a lion, but when you are facing enemies with swords, you become an ostrich. How does an ostrich fight? Does it have claws and teeth?

Moral duties are not just for religious seasons. They are not for sometimes. They do not apply one day but not another. They do not apply to one person but not another. Duties are perpetual, universal and eternal. The Qur'an rebukes the Israelites for saying on one occasion 'our brethren must be protected' but on another, when it suited their personal interests, making war on these same brothers, killing them, taking them prisoner, enslaving them, selling them and looting their property. The Qur'an says: 'What! Do you believe in part of the Book and defy another part?'[49] Do you believe in part of the religion? Are you faithful and moral when it is easy and convenient, and then at other times you are faithless? Is this even possible? Can you really separate one command from another and one duty from another, even when these are both from the same source and the same Lord?

There is a well-known tradition from Imam al-Bāqir (a) which appears at the beginning of the chapter on 'Enjoining the Good and Forbidding the Evil' (*al-amr bi al-maʿrūf wa al-nahī ʿan al-munkar*) in *al-Kāfi*, one of our most important works of *ḥadīth*. There is also

49 Q2:85.

al-Wāfī by Fayḍ Kāshānī[50], which combines traditions from our major collections of *ḥadīth* and I believe the aforementioned tradition also appears at the beginning of its chapter on this topic. This tradition says that, as we have mentioned, there are people who pray and fast so long as it's easy and doesn't cost them anything, but who avoid the duty of enjoining good and forbidding evil because it is difficult and liable to cause them hardship or bring them harm. The Imam does not say these people are not believers or that they do not have faith. He does not say they are sinners or hypocrites. However, the Qur'an is clear about this: Those who are after their own interests do not really want the religion in its totality. They are not believers.

These are the people who, when they are in the right on an issue, go to the Prophet to seek his judgement, but when they are in the wrong and they know that the Prophet will rule against them in his judgement, they do not go to him. The Qur'an asks: Are they afraid? Are they in doubt? Have they some misgivings about the truth of this religion? 'Or do they have doubts or fear that God and His Apostle will be unjust to them?'[51] This is close to disbelief. Do they fear that God and His Messenger would mistreat them? In all issues, in all disputes, in all the ups and downs of daily life, a believing person is moral. They are not only moral when it suits them to be.

As everyone knows, when Muʿāwiyah ibn Abū Sufyān needed to, he brought pages of the Qur'an and had them raised on spears. When it suited him, he would talk about the Qur'an, prayer and the religion. When he wanted to win over someone who was on ʿAlī's side, he would even mention the virtues of the Commander of the Faithful. He would even shed crocodile tears as he recited these. You have heard this story countless times: Muʿāwiyah was sitting. ʿAbd Allāh

50 The Safavid-era traditionist, jurist and philosopher (lived 1007-1091 AH/1599–1680 CE).

51 Q24:50.

ibn ʿAbbās was sitting. Others were sitting also. He asks someone: 'O so-and-so, what do you know of ʿAlī's merits?' They would ask: 'Do you promise me safety?' He says: 'Yes, you are safe.' Then he began to praise ʿAlī and, as he did, Muʿawiyah would begin to shed tears. When he needed to, he would speak of his love for ʿAlī. When he needed to, he would portray himself as a devoted servant of God. When he was forced to in order to govern the masses of Muslims, he would respect their feelings, he would not want to offend their sentiments. He would speak of things that people cherish, i.e. the Qur'an and Islam.

These are all in circumstances when the religion was of benefit to him, when he could use it for personal gain and ambition. But when it was not profitable for him to observe the teachings of the religion, it was as though he had never heard of it! When we speak of justice, of observing fairness in society, of protecting the oppressed and dispossessed, of treating both friends and strangers equally–these are all religious teachings, these are all teachings of Islam–of raising the level of people's thinking, which was the goal of divine prophethood... when religion meant observing these things, Muʿāwiyah didn't know anything about the religion. He felt no sense of duty towards the moral content of the faith. I'm using Muʿāwiyah here as an example so that you and I can look at ourselves in this regard. So we can use him as a benchmark. Let us take someone as an example who everyone agrees was wicked.

What I want to say is that if we accept to follow one part of the religion while refusing to follow another but all the while still call ourselves believers...if this is how we see things...then we should recognise Muʿāwiyah as the foremost of the believers, because this is exactly how Muʿāwiyah was. He made a big show of piety when it came to one part of the religion. I have said, time and again, that Muʿāwiyah not only prayed, but he prayed in congregation, at the beginning of the time, that he led the congregations. The merit of the leader of a congregational prayer is higher than that of those who follow him. The reward God keeps in store for the one who leads the prayers is greater than the reward He keeps in store for those who follow in the congregation, according to the traditions we have. And Muʿāwiyah would lead prayers!

So, this is a very pleasant sort of religion. It is enjoyable. It is good. It is harmless. It wins people's sympathy. It wins their affection. It gets their attention. This is all very good. But what about the religion that says its Prophet was sent to educate and raise up mankind? 'God certainly favoured the faithful when He raised up among them an apostle from among themselves to recite to them His signs and to purify them, and to teach them the Book and wisdom.'[52] The Prophet was sent to mankind to teach them, to raise them up, to increase their insight and wisdom. Whatever opposes the human intellect, religion opposes it. Whatever stands against people's vision, thinking and comprehension, religion stands against it. Anything which, in any way, shape or form, impairs the human ability to comprehend, to see, to think...religion will not leave it standing.

This is the true religion. The religion which they call 'the opiate of the masses'[53] is something else entirely. We find no trace of that religion in the Qur'an. We find no trace of that religion in the practice of our Prophet or of our Imams. Islam fights against ignorance. Islam fights against that kind of religion. The Commander of the Faithful, our Imam, says that God sent the prophets to unearth the buried treasures of the human intellects.[54] So whatever buries the wisdom latent in each human being, whatever tries to extinguish the light of thought in the human mind, whatever tries to smother these in prejudice and falsehood, or anything else that tries to keep them

---

52 Q3:164.

53 A reference to Karl Marx.

54 See *Nahj al-Balāghah*, sermon no. 1.

hidden...anything which does this is the polar opposite of the *raison d'être* of prophethood. It does not matter what it is or at what time it is.

Prophethood works with human thought and intelligence. The more refined this intelligence, the more receptive it is to prophethood. Prophethood strives to raise the level of people's thinking. Anyone, anything, any force, any cause, whether within the human being himself or beyond the human being, which tries to hold the human intellect back from growth and development, that tries to prevent it from reaching its potential, that tries to restrain people from understanding things through the light of their own thought and insight, to prevent them from finding the right path, anything that obstructs them in this way, that opposes the intellect in this way, is utterly opposed to the religion of Islam as well. This is how Muʿāwiyah was. He wanted to stifle people's ability to think. Muʿāwiyah fundamentally did not understand what Islam was. When Islam told him to make sure no one was hungry, to break down class divisions within society, to do away with discrimination, to not appoint heartless tyrants to rule over people, not to select the most criminal of people to be your advisors and friends, not to drive people towards Hell and towards divine punishment...when religion told him not to oppress people, to let them think for themselves, Muʿāwiyah was far from this religion.

Muʿāwiyah told ibn ʿAbbās: 'Ibn ʿAbbās, do not recite the Qur'an!' He replied: 'How can I not recite the Qur'an?' Muʿāwiyah said: 'OK. Recite it. But do not explain it!' He exclaimed: 'How can I recite it without explaining it, Muʿāwiyah? What are you talking about?' Muʿāwiyah saw that this wouldn't work, so he tried again: 'Ok, explain it. But the explanation you have from your own family, the explanation you have received from ʿAlī, don't tell that to people.'[55] He didn't want people to understand the Qur'an. He didn't want people to

55 See *Kitāb Sulaym ibn Qays al-Hilālī*, tradition no. 26.

understand anything whatsoever. The less people knew, the better it was for Muʿāwiyah!

Therefore, when we assess Muʿāwiyah's actions, more than the wrongdoing, more than the killing, look closer! More than burying people alive, more than imprisoning people, more than executing the likes of Ḥujr ibn ʿAdī and Rushayd al-Hajarī, more than his brutal treatment of the likes of Maytham al-Tammār, which everyone knows about, which anyone can see...look closer! There is a crime that Muʿāwiyah committed that only someone with insight will understand. Muʿāwiyah's crime is towards this new religion, this Islamic society that was only some twenty years old, this trust that had fallen into his hands, not more than twenty years old...he set it back two hundred years. In what way did he set it back? Did he make them poor? No. If only his crime was making them poor! Did he lose their territories? No. Did he divide up their lands? No. Did some of them die pointlessly? If only! No, the way in which he set them back was in their thinking. In their morals. This is a crime for which he can never be forgiven. This is a sin whose consequences could not be fixed even with two decades of good governance. Some two to three decades after Muʿāwiyah's reign there came ʿUmar ibn ʿAbd al-ʿAzīz, who is known as the one just ruler of the Umayyad clan. But he couldn't do anything. He could not make up for Muʿāwiyah's crimes. He could not set right Muʿāwiyah's wrongs. He barely lasted two years in government before they poisoned him and killed him. Muʿāwiyah made it so that there was only corruption and nothing else would be accepted.

People who are ignorant and uninformed, who do not pay close attention or ponder on issues, listened to what Muʿāwiyah's propagandists were saying and they believed them. There are so many accounts of the ignorance of the people of Syria under the rule of the Umayyad clan. Some of these can be quite amusing and I've mentioned them on numerous occasions in discussions, lectures and lessons on *tafsīr*. It seems fitting to mention one here for a touch of humour:

Look what can happen to a community. During the time of the Umayyad Caliph, ʿAbd al-Malik ibn Marwān,[56] Makkah was recaptured by the ruthless and powerful Umayyad general, Ḥajjaj ibn Yūsuf. He was someone strongly opposed to anything remotely Shīʿī. However, in those days, Makkah had not been in the hands of the Shiʿa. It had been under the rule of ʿAbd Allāh ibn al-Zubayr. Now Ibn al-Zubayr was a little better than Ḥajjāj in his conduct and he did not last long. Ḥajjāj put an end to him, taking back control of Makkah for the Umayyad clan. He also took control of Mount Abū Qubays. Mount Abū Qubays, of course, is one of the mountains that surround Makkah and is just on the city's outskirts. He sent a letter to Damascus, to the Caliph, ʿAbd al-Malik, which said: 'Praise God, we have conquered Abū Qubays'–meaning Mount Abū Qubays. The Caliph gave the order that this letter should be proclaimed from the pulpits of Damascus. So, everyone gathered in the mosque on a Friday. The preacher took the letter and said: 'Praise God, the Caliph's general, Ḥajjāj, has conquered Abū Qubays.' All of a sudden, everyone was clamouring loudly. They said: 'No, we don't accept this. We don't believe you. He must send this heretic called Abū Qubays in chains to Damascus. Then we'll believe you!' They thought Abū Qubays was the name of a Shiʿa leader in Makkah–they didn't realise it was the name of the mountain! This shows you how uninformed these people were. And there are many other stories like this.

56 He ruled from 65 to 86 AH/ 685 to 705 CE.

Who did this? Who is responsible for keeping the people ignorant? Perhaps we should blame the judge, Shurayḥ ibn al-Ḥārith?[57] Perhaps it is the fault of Muḥammad ibn Shihāb al-Zuhrī?[58] Or maybe responsibility lies with Qāḍī Abū Yūsuf?[59] So, which is it? Is it Shurayḥ's fault? Al-Zuhrī's? Abū Yūsuf's? Or is someone else to blame? Yes, what they did was wrong, as we can see from Imam Zayn al-ʿĀbidīn's letter to al-Zuhrī, but who made these people? Who paid for them? The axis around which gathered the scholars who went against the religion and against the Qur'an–who was that? Was it anyone other than Muʿāwiyah? Therefore, the ultimate responsibility for these crimes must rest with Muʿāwiyah, with ʿAbd al-Malik ibn Marwān, with all the tyrants of the Umayyad and 'Abbasid clans and others. And these tyrants would speak of the Qur'an and the religion even while they were carrying out these crimes!

What is our responsibility here? Have you thought about that? When we are faced with someone like Muʿāwiyah, someone like Shurayḥ, someone like Mughīrah, someone like Zayd ibn ʿAmr? It doesn't matter on which level you are. When it comes to a person such as this, how should we judge them? In some places they accept religion, faith, and morality, while at others there is no trace of any religion, faith or morality in their lives! What should we say of such a person? Do we consider them a believer? The Qur'an clearly says that such a person is not a believer. Therefore, the kind of faith that

---

57 A corrupt judge from Kufah who sided with ʿUbayd Allāh ibn Ziyād. It was he who lied to the tribe of Hānī ibn ʿUrwah and told them that he was in good health. He also permitted the killing of Imam Ḥusayn. And, when Ḥajjāj became the governor of Kufah, he was considered one of his closest allies.

58 A jurist and scholar of traditions who was associated with the Umayyad government in Damascus.

59 A student of Abū Hanīfah, who was the chief judge of Baghdad under the early 'Abbasids.

is recognised in the framework of Islamic thought cannot be the faith of these kind of people–of which there are many like them in today's world! On the contrary, the kind of faith that Islam values is the faith that is preserved in every place, with every person, at every time, in every way, through a sense of moral duty and through doing what is right–'Surely those who believe *and* do righteous deeds'.

Therefore, the kinds of promises given for faith and given to the faithful are referring to this kind of faith–the kind that is backed up by right action. If we are told the believers will be victorious, it means those kinds of believers will be surely victorious! If we are told that the hand of God is with the believers, it means it is with those believers. If we are told that nature itself will help the faithful, it is those kinds of believers, not 'believers' like me and you! Therefore, the least we can take away from this discussion is that if we think we have faith, but our faith does not have the effects or the consequences faith is supposed to have, the promises that God makes to the faithful in the Qur'an, we should not be surprised, because now we know that the kind of faith to which these promises are given is not the faith we have.

Now, let us look at the following verses: 'Certainly We have sent down manifest signs'.[60] These verses of the Qur'an are clear. Those people who do not allow themselves to understand the Qur'an deny themselves this clarity–'and God guides whomever He wishes to a straight path.'

What does it mean to say God 'wishes' here? Does it mean he wishes for this person to be guided, but does not wish for that person to be guided? He singles some people out and decides that these will be guided and ignores some others? This is not the case! When we speak about God willing something (*irādah*) or wishing something (*mashīyyah*), in normal circumstances this takes the form of the

60 Q24:46.

system of cause and effect that governs the cosmos. If you chose this; if you listened to guidance and were guided, then this means God wanted to guide you. Equally, if you are lazy, if you can't be bothered, if you close the way to yourself, God willed for you not to understand. When we say God willed something or did not will something, we only mean that the causes necessary for a thing to transpire were either present or they were not. If the causes and means were there for you to do something you wanted to do, then God wanted you to do it, if you did not want to do it, then clearly God didn't want it. This does not mean that God didn't will it and His not willing it caused *you* not to will it, no. You are free to choose. When God doesn't will something, it simply means that the necessary cause for it isn't there.

Now, why don't we just say, 'the necessary cause was lacking' instead of 'God did not will it'? Because God is the cause behind all causes and the one who makes them causes. If I put my hand into a fire and my hand gets burnt, God willed that my hand be burnt. If I don't put my hand into a fire, God willed that it not be burnt! What does it mean when I say, 'God willed that my hand be burnt'? It means that the natural causes for my hand to be burnt were fulfilled. What are these? There is a fire. There is no barrier. I made a decision. I put my hand into the flame. And when we say, 'God willed that my hand not be burnt', this means the natural causes for my hand to be burnt were not fulfilled. Either my hand didn't go near the fire, or there was some barrier preventing it from being burnt, or maybe the fire wasn't very hot, and so on. Now, why do we attribute to God that which depends upon a cause to transpire? Because God is the creator of the causes! Therefore, when the Qur'an says 'whomever He wishes', it is in this sense. We have discussed this more fully elsewhere, so I will content myself with this brief explanation here.

'They say, "We have faith in God and His Apostle, and we obey."'[61] This is what they claim. It is easy to make this claim! But 'after that a part of them refuse to comply'–after making this claim, a group of them turn back. This is not talking about the disbelievers. This is not talking about the apostates, who leave the bounds of Islam altogether. No, this is talking about the so-called believers in Muslim society. What does the Qur'an say about them? 'And they are not believers.' The issue becomes even clearer when the Qur'an says: 'When they are summoned to God and His Apostle that He may judge between them, behold, a part of them turn aside.'[62] They are not ready to go and hear the judgement of God's Messenger. The apparent meaning of the verse is about judgement or arbitration. When we see the verb '*ḥukūmah*' used in the Qur'an, it is usually–thought not always–about judgement. However, while the immediate context of the verse concerns judgement, its meaning is broader than this. This is not just about those who turn away from the Prophet's judgement, it also includes those who do not obey the Prophet's commands in situations other than judgement. 'When they are summoned to God and His Apostle that He may judge between them, behold, a part of them turn aside. *But if justice be on their side, they come compliantly to him.*'[63] If they are in the right, they come to the Prophet and obey him. Whenever it benefits them to hear his judgement, they submit to the religion. However, when it seems like his judgement will go against them, they don't accept it.

Now the Qur'an asks them: Why is it that when religion doesn't benefit you, you reject it? There are three possibilities: 'Is there a sickness in their hearts?'[64] Do they suffer from the sickness of

61 Q24:47.

62 Q24:48.

63 Q24:49.

64 Q24:50.

hypocrisy? Of avarice and greed? Of ignorance and delusion? Is this why they won't accept the judgement of the Messenger? Or is it something worse? 'Or do they have doubts...?' Do they fundamentally doubt the religion? If you don't doubt the religion, if you don't have any misgivings about the religion, if you aren't hesitant about the religion, why is it that when it doesn't benefit you, or if it causes you some difficulty, you reject it by rejecting the judgement of God's Messenger? Or is it something more severe still–'or fear that God and His Apostle will be unjust to them?' This is worse than doubt, because it is utter disbelief. Could a person be so ignorant and ill-informed that they think it possible that God and His Messenger might oppress people? Someone who has this fear thinks that God or the Prophet might wrong him! Clearly such a person has no clue about God or His Messenger! 'Rather it is they who are the wrongdoers', God does not wrong anyone. In truth, it is they who wrong themselves and wrong others. If there is a degree worse than this, they wrong themselves, the truth, and other people. If there is still a further degree worse than this, they wrong humanity as a whole. These are the real wrongdoers!

'All the response of the faithful'.[65] What about the believers? How do they respond? The believers are not like those mentioned above. Look at how the Qur'an speaks. The Qur'an has a special language, a special style of dialogue. According to the terminology of the Qur'an, the believer is someone who behaves like this: 'All the response of the faithful, when they are summoned to God and His Apostle that He may judge between them, is to say, "We hear and obey."' As I've mentioned already, the phrase 'to hear' means 'to understand'; not merely to receive something with the ear, but to have grasped. The term 'hearing' (*samᶜ*)–as in, 'or gives ear, being attentive'[66]–appears frequently in the Qur'an in the sense of 'understanding' rather than

65 Q24:51.

66 Q50:37.

passively listening with one's ears. So the faithful say: 'We understand.' In other words, they consciously and knowingly become believers. As we have said in a previous lecture, faith must be founded on the basis of understanding!

'We hear and obey'–so as well as consciously believing, we also willingly obey. 'It is they who are the successful ones (*mufliḥūn*).'[67] It is they who will reach their destination. *Falāh* means success, victory and reaching one's goal or destination. Some lexicons also give it the meaning of felicity or salvation. However, when the word *falāḥ* is used for the faithful, it is in its usual linguistic sense of 'success.' 'It is they who are the successful ones.' They will reach their goal. And 'Whoever obeys God and His Apostle, and fears God and is wary of Him–it is they who will be the triumphant ones (*fāʾizūn*).'[68] Triumph (*fawz*) is similar in meaning to success (*falāḥ*).

The next two verses of *Sūrat al-Nūr* are not directly related to our discussion, so I would like to move onto the following verse: 'God has promised those of you who have faith'.[69], this is God's promise for the faithful and those who fulfil their moral duties. Pay close attention. God makes his promise clear in this verse: We have promised the faithful that they shall have dominion over the earth–your ideas, beliefs and thought will cover the world–and the fear and anxiety you feel in your hearts will be replaced by security and peace. If you have been persecuted and oppressed throughout history and then you attain a state of safety, respite and security, you will want to worship God and put aside any partners to God. This is God's promise in this verse. Although God gave this promise to the Muslims, it is specifically addressed to the believers who fulfil their moral duties.

67 Q24:51.

68 Q24:52.

69 Q24:55.

Some become very doubtful, their vision becomes very narrow, they say that this is only for the time of the Mahdi (aj). I don't doubt that this verse will be fully realised at the time of the Twelfth Imam–there is no doubt about this! However, where is it written that this verse *only* applies to that time? Tell me, where? Which narration says that this verse is *only* about that time? Why do we limit this verse? Did God not fulfil this promise to the faithful at the very advent of Islam? It was this very verse that God fulfilled! They came to Madinah and formed a government. Whereas before they dare not openly say 'there is no god but God' out of fear of the Quraysh, now Bilāl went up and loudly recited the call to prayer. Those, who before had been forced to worship three hundred idols, to worship people, to worship their own selves and desires, night and day without respite...these were all set up as rivals to God. They came to a land where they found safety and security, in which they could create an Islamic society without fear of persecution. In which there were no rivals to God, whether great or small, living or dead, from themselves or from others. So this verse was already fulfilled in Madinah and it can be fulfilled a thousand times more! What is the condition for this? It's condition is that the first sentences of the verse must be fulfilled in order that God's promise be fulfilled: 'God has promised *those of you who have faith and do righteous deeds*'–in other words, those who act upon the moral duties that emanate from their faith. God has promised these 'that He will surely make them successors in the earth.'

Some translators of the Qur'an erroneously render 'in the earth' (*fī al-arḍ*) as 'in this land.' This is not correct. 'This land' would mean the Arabian Peninsula–was it so unlikely that they would gain dominance over Arabia? They conquered an area forty or fifty times the size of Arabia! 'In the earth' means *all* of the earth. This is not to say that the translator had any ill intention in translating it this way, but it makes a big difference to the meaning! If we say it means 'this land' then the promise God is giving to the faithful who do righteous deeds is that they will only conquer Hejaz and the Arabian Peninsula, not Rome, not Persia, and not Spain!

In any case 'He will surely make them successors in the earth, just as He made those who were before them successors.' Sometimes we imagine that, from the beginning of the time and wherever they were, the faithful were always oppressed. This is how many Muslims see the world today: They think having faith means to take a beating! To be a Muslim, to be a believer, to be striving in the way of God, means suffering, means persecution, means oppression. The Qur'an wants to say the opposite is true–that from the moment religion came into being it was always moving forwards, it was always advancing, it was never going backwards. According to our beliefs, religion has never taken a single step backwards. Even the things that some people think are signs of 'backwardness' are actually steps towards progress.

In any case, the earth is yours to govern just as it was that of those before you–the faithful of previous generations. 'And He will surely establish for them their religion which He has approved for them'–the religion which is right for them and which He has made for them, meaning the religion of Islam which encompasses both this world and the Hereafter, the present and the future, the body and the soul and, in short, all aspects of human existence–it meets all human needs. 'And that He will surely change their state to security after their fear'–to what end? What are they supposed to do under the auspices of this security? Are they supposed to sit in its shade and sip their afternoon tea in the garden? Is this what security is for? So they can live carefree lives of ease and indolence? No. This security is there so that they can journey towards the human being's ultimate abode, towards perfection. So that they can serve God, obey Him, submit themselves to Him and, in doing so, grow and develop as human beings. We could have a discussion about the meaning of each and every word of these verses...'while they worship Me, not ascribing any partners to Me.' However, at the end of this verse,

God reminds them that if, after they have believed, they associate partners with God, they are sinful (*fāsiq*). A sinner is someone who goes out of the religion.

Our Lord! Make our hearts sincere in all we say and do and let us do it purely for your sake!

Our Lord! By Muḥammad and the Family of Muḥammad, grant us the sustenance of a monotheistic life!

Our Lord! By Muḥammad and the Family of Muḥammad, cleanse our hearts of associating partners with you!

Our Lord! By Muḥammad and the Family of Muḥammad, do not withhold your grace from us. Free the Muslims from delusion, illness, ill-fortune and disorder.

And the enemies of the Muslims–our Lord!–make them busy with themselves.

Divine Promises, Part One

Tuesday 7th Ramadan 1394
24th September 1974

يَا أَيُّهَا النَّاسُ قَدْ جَاءَكُمْ بُرْهَانٌ مِنْ رَبِّكُمْ وَأَنْزَلْنَا إِلَيْكُمْ
نُورًا مُبِينًا (١٧٤) فَأَمَّا الَّذِينَ آمَنُوا بِاللَّهِ وَاعْتَصَمُوا بِهِ
فَسَيُدْخِلُهُمْ فِي رَحْمَةٍ مِنْهُ وَفَضْلٍ وَيَهْدِيهِمْ إِلَيْهِ صِرَاطًا
مُسْتَقِيمًا (١٧٥)

'O mankind! Certainly a proof has come to you from your Lord, and We have sent down to you a manifest light. As for those who have faith in God, and hold fast to Him, He will admit them to His mercy and grace, and He will guide them on a straight path to Him.'
- Sūrat al-Nisā' (4):174–5

In reality, our discussions of faith and belief are merely a preliminary to our main topic to understand what religion is and comprehend the fundamental teachings of religion. And to make us enthusiastic, so that we will pursue knowledge and understanding of the religion with the vigour and earnestness it deserves, we should try to understand the value and quality of faith. It is with this goal in mind that we are discussing faith.

So far, we have touched on two or three issues about faith–two or three fundamental points. These include the fact that faith must come from understanding, not blind imitation. Also, we said that faith must be combined with a sense of moral duty and the performance of right actions. In fact, we said that genuine faith gives rise to this sense of duty and gives life to one's deeds–if it does not, then it is a hollow faith that resides only in the heart but not in the limbs. Also, we said that a true believer is someone who has faith all of the time, not only when it suits him or when it works to his benefit; he is always a believer, wherever he is, at all times, with all people. These are the necessary points that we have covered so far.

Before moving onto the main topic of these lectures–the doctrinal teachings of Islam–there is another issue we must discuss, and that is what we will begin treating today. We will continue this topic tomorrow as well. When I started planning these lectures, I thought that we could finish this topic in a day but, when I got into it, I could see that this is something that would need four or five days to do justice to! So today and tomorrow we will definitely discuss it–assuming, of course, we are still alive!–and, probably, it will not take up a third day. What I want to discuss today is this: In order for us to understand the value and effects of faith, we must make ourselves aware of the promises that God has made to the faithful contingent upon their believing, doing good works and fulfilling their moral obligations. Let us see what God will give to the believer in return for his faith and action. The human being is, by habit, something of a trader. He lives by exchanging with others. So let's see how he trades with God! He believes and, as a result of this belief, feels a sense of moral responsibility towards God but he also wants to know what responsibility God has towards him in return, what promise will God give him? What reward will He offer him? This is something of interest to any believer or anyone who wishes to enter the valley of faith and reside there, and it is something that should give us all a sense of hope!

I have looked at all the verses that discuss faith and the believers in the Qur'an. There are about seven hundred of these in total, discussing faith, the faithful and some of the qualities the faithful must possess. So, I looked at these to see what God says will come as a result of faith. (I am explaining how I went about this so that our dear brothers and sisters who are familiar with the Qur'an can learn how to extract topics from the Qur'an and study them). So I went through these six or seven hundred verses, to see what promises God made to the faithful, what rewards He set aside for them, what outcome they could expect. I saw that there are many! I think there must be thirty or forty things which God mentions in the Qur'an as being the results of faith. A true believer will enjoy these thirty or forty distinctions–and these are not small or insignificant things; they are all things necessary for human happiness and flourishing. Paradise is just one of these thirty or forty things. God promises: 'For such there will be the Gardens of Eden with streams running in them.'[70] This is just one of them.

(If we wanted to study in detail all of these thirty or forty promises and rewards promised to the faithful, as I said before, it would take us at least four or five days to do so! So, we are going to study two today and one or two tomorrow. As for the rest, it will be up to you to study them yourselves.)

What does the human being need in order to enjoy full and complete happiness from every angle? What does it take for a person to be felicitous? When we look at the Qur'an, we see that all the things that man needs to be fully and completely happy are those things which God promises to the faithful. If we look at these rewards that await the believers, we will see that these are things no human can be truly happy without. All of these things are promised by the Qur'an to the faithful for their faith. So, what conclusion do we draw? We conclude that this faith, which in the language of the Qur'an refers to belief accompanied with action, is equal to all of the conditions

70 Q18:31.

necessary for the human being to feel happy and felicitous, from the perspective of all the needs and requirements that a human being might imagine himself to have.

This is not something that comes from a dogmatic understanding of Islam or religiosity. The things that the Qur'an identifies as essential for human happiness are no different to those things that a materialist would identify. Let us look at some of these things and see whether or not it is the case that, were they to be present in a materialistic person's life, that person would be happy. And if they would be, then we can return to the Qur'an and hear God's comforting words, reassured in the knowledge that all of these things have been promised to the faithful–that these are all gifts guaranteed for the faithful–'and God and His Apostle were true [in their promise].'[71] God does not lie in the promises he makes, although this fact depends on the particular way in which we think about religion, as we believe in God.

So what does the human being need? First, he needs to know the destination wherein happiness can be found. He must know where he needs to go. He must know the goal for which he is striving. The end point which he sets off towards at the start of his journey. As well as knowing and understanding the goal, he must know the path he must take in order to reach this goal–the shortest path and the path that will truly help him reach there. Is not the most fundamental element in the human being's journey towards happiness that he knows the destination and goal towards which he must tend? Here, clearly, there is no difference between a materialist and a theist. So, the first thing a human being needs is guidance.

Now, when I say the first thing or the second thing the human being needs, this is not necessarily in a sequence, such that we can

---

71 Q33:22.

dispense with the first thing when we reach the second or vice versa. There are also other things that might come in between these.

Second, the human being needs the veils of ignorance and delusion to be pulled back, along with anything else that keeps his gem of insight and wisdom shrouded in darkness. There are many things that prevent the human being from understanding. The human being's arrogance (*ghurūr*) prevents him from understanding. His ignorance prevents him from perceiving and understanding. Thoughts and superstitions prevent the human being, or indeed a whole human society, from apprehending the truth and understanding it. Tyrannical regimes prevent the human being from knowing and understanding. A variety of veils and barriers, both internal and external, stand between this human being and his using his intellect and wisdom to see, to know and to understand. They want to keep him in the darkness. They want to keep the human being in a dark prison and away from the light of true insight and understanding. And one of the pillars of human happiness is that he must be saved from the darkness of ignorance and from anything that tries to keep him in the darkness of ignorance, so that he can find the light of truth and have a ray of this light shine into his heart. So, first, the human being needs guidance in the sense we have outlined above. Second, he needs light in the sense we have outlined above.

Third, on this long journey towards happiness, a journey which takes him towards that lofty destination and goal, the human being must be free from internal worries and doubts–which are actually more powerful than external factors in blocking his way. Sometimes they stand in your way and tell you: 'We won't let you go any further' but experience and history clearly show that when you stand in someone's way, it makes them even more keen and determined to keep going. If you tell a person they can't do something, they will try harder until they can, until they get past you. This is the case for external obstructions, when something outside of a person's own being blocks their path. However, sometimes, the obstructions come not from outside, but from within the human being. They make him hesitate. They do not block his way–the way is still open! Instead, they sap his strength, his will, his resolve, his ability to strive. This is so much worse than blocking his way. They ask: 'Why do you go? What's the point? You might not make it! There might be danger on the way! Thieves! Wolves! What guarantee do you have? You don't need to go!' This is very devious, because as far as anyone can see, the path is still open. This barrier...this doubt...this worry...is stronger by magnitudes than a roadblock which tells you: 'The way is closed. You may not pass.'

Throughout history, these worries have been there for most of the travellers on the path to happiness and felicity. How they pleaded with Moses: 'We're worried that you've been lied to. That the promise you've been given is false.' The Qur'an says that the pressure and deprivation he faced was so grave that even the best believers were saying: 'When will God's help come?' When? Where? What? You see, even the best of us can fall into this inward hesitation, anxiety or doubt. If the human being wants to be happy...if he wants to reach the end of the path to felicity, one requirement is that he must overcome these worries, these doubts, these feelings of insecurity, this disquiet, this uncertainty. This is one of the things that will take the human being to happiness. On the long road to happiness, he must pass these worries and doubts that are so much more powerful than any physical obstruction. How? Through certainty and security.

In *Duʿā Kumayl*, we recite: 'My Lord! My Lord! My Lord!' (*Yā rabbi! Yā rabbi! Yā rabb!*) 'Make strong my limbs in your service' (*Qaww-i ʿalā khidmatika jawāriḥī*) 'And make steadfast my heart in determination' (*Washdud ʿalā al-ʿazīmati jawāniḥī*). In other words: Give me the strength to make a firm decision, to overcome my weakness, my hesitation, my doubt, my worry and my anxiety. This is a person who can traverse the path to happiness.

Fourth, a person must know that his efforts matter, to have hope that his struggles will take him to where he needs to go. Someone who does not believe that his striving and effort will lead to his destination, will certainly never reach happiness and felicity. He must be sure that what he is doing will bear fruit. He must know that whatever he does will have a positive effect. He must know that every step he takes is bringing him closer to his goal. If you are in the wilderness and you know that home is this way, you know where you need to head. No matter how distant it may be. No matter how alone you are. No matter how far you've fallen behind. Be steadfast! Be brave! Strive! Take courage! Move, and you will reach your goal! On the other hand, if you have lost your way, if you do not know whether you should turn left or right, no matter which way you walk, you will despair. Why? Because you don't know whether your efforts will matter. You fear that instead of taking you closer to home, each step is just leading you further away. So, you go one way. Then you stop, turn around, and come back. You go a different way. Then you come back again. Therefore, one of the conditions necessary for a person to attain happiness when they are on the path, when a person is struggling, when a person is giving their all...one of the conditions is that they must know that what they are doing will bear fruit.

Fifth, that these are all slips and errors that can be made-up for and forgiven. This is very important. Throughout his life, in whatever he is doing, the human being makes mistakes. He slips and does something wrong. If every error or mistake he makes is like a wound that cannot be healed, if it is an act that cannot be made-up for, then the human being will forever be afraid of doing anything lest he make a mistake. He will tell himself: 'I should stay still or else I will make a mistake and that mistake will take me even further from the goal and away from the right path.' He will be forever despairing of the past. Constantly pessimistic about the future. But if he knows that, as long as he tries to atone for his mistakes, these mistakes can be forgiven...that his errors can be overlooked so long as he is regretful of them...if he knows this, then his enthusiasm, his hope, his energy and his determination will grow correspondingly. So, forgiveness (*maghfirah*) and mercy (*raḥmah*) are necessary also.

Sixth–and this is always necessary–he must be sure that there is someone he can rely on. He must know that wherever he is, whatever is happening, there is someone he can call on for assistance. Just like someone who puts a map in his pocket and sets out on the journey. He is taking these roads, he is not making any mistakes, and he is not worried. He knows that if at some point, somewhere along the road, he loses his way and becomes lost, there is a map he can take out and refer to. He can use it to find his way back. Therefore, wherever he is, he has a support and a protection that he can take hold of and make use of.

Seventh, when he faces enemies and threats, he can call on God's assistance and support. This is another condition of finding happiness and tranquillity. Of course, a materialist does not believe in God, so we will not use the name 'God' with materialists. We can say: 'If you are working towards a materialistic goal, or a social goal...if you are struggling for something and you know that there is a force, even a force that is beyond matter or nature, and that force is with you, then what? You have something powerful which you can call upon for help and assistance.' If someone knows this, their eyes will light up and they will tell you: 'Excellent!' How wonderful it is for the human being to have a force that is beyond matter and nature, which will support him against enemies and threats, against their snares, against their deceits, against their violence...and he believes and knows that this supernatural force will help him and protect him. Of course, for a materialist, the name 'God' does not count for much. He does not believe in God, although he may not be certain of this fact either. However, a theist who has certainty knows that there is an all-powerful supernatural force upon which all material things depend, and which has control over all things...see with what speed and enthusiasm he will travel along the path to happiness!

Eighth, to know that he is superior to the enemies arrayed against him. He should know that, ultimately, he has superiority. This has an incredible effect on people–if they believe this, they will actually find it easier to traverse the path.

Ninth, that he will triumph over the opponents who are seeking to thwart his goal and bar his way. If a person makes all of these efforts only to be defeated, this will not bring him happiness. Therefore, one of the most important elements in a person's attainment of happiness and felicity is that they should ultimately succeed. Can it be any other way? Do the different philosophies of this world not strive to succeed? Therefore, one of the key elements that lead to people attaining happiness, whether as individuals, groups or as a society is: when they are facing enemies, they should know that they will triumph.

Tenth, the outcome. After all the hardships, difficulties and adversities a person faces, they should attain their goal and reach the destination. This, in the vocabulary of the Qur'an is called 'victory' (*fawz*) and 'success' (*falāḥ*).

Eleventh, that in every circumstance, whether on the path or at the destination, whether pursuing the goal or after attaining it, a person should enjoy what has been kept instore for him in this world. He should benefit from the blessings of the heavens and the earth, whether the wheat of the ground or the drops of rain from the sky; the provisions of the oceans, the forests, and the mountains; all of the organic and inorganic materials necessary for his existence; and, above all, the source of his perception, intelligence, wisdom, potential and innovation should be opened up to him so that he can make use of all of these. This is one of the most important things that must be present in order for the human being to attain happiness. This includes all the things that a person could possibly think of as being conducive to his happiness and felicity.

Ultimately, after all of these things, which are bound up in the various stages of a person's living, struggling and awakening...after a person has died, after the lamp of their worldly life has been extinguished, after they have outwardly become inanimate, this does not mean that he no longer benefits from these things. On the contrary, this is his first respite, his first moment of reward, the first step of his real life. For a materialist, once you have died, there are only the worldly effects of your efforts that remain–a materialist has no hope of a life beyond this world. Even they say that when you die and leave this world you are at rest. But how can this be without a soul? Don't you see? This is truly the core of human happiness: that once you reach the end of your life and all of your efforts have come to an end, you come face to face with a fitting reward, you enter Paradise and the abode of God's satisfaction.

These are the necessary conditions for human happiness. For a human being to attain felicity...for a human being or human society to be truly fortunate, these are all necessary. Now listen to the Qur'an when it says all of these are promised to a person who has faith–the kind of faith that is accompanied by a sense of duty and good deeds. How can this be? The Qur'an says that all of these elements and factors that are considered essential for happiness and felicity–these and tens of others that we have not mentioned–are all guaranteed by God for the one who has faith. The Qur'an says, 'these are for you.' It promises guidance, it promises light, it promises security and certainty, tranquillity and confidence. It promises that your actions will matter and guarantees that your efforts will never be wasted. And, if we look closely at the past, at history, we will see that this has been true in human affairs. God's practice (*sunnah*) never changes. It is always the same.

Pay close attention to the verses we are studying today in light of the premises we have laid out and explained above. We have taken these verses from all the different parts of the Qur'an today. The first verse is from *Sūrah Yūnus*: 'Indeed those who have faith and do righteous deeds, their Lord guides them by the means of their faith.'[72] So a person who combines his faith with right action, as we have previously explained, has a faith which gives him a sense of moral responsibility and he acts accordingly. When someone does this, the Qur'an says that the Lord will guide him because of his faith. His faith is the reason for him finding the path. Which path is this? The path to the destination, and the path that leads to all the other paths and means of transportation. Some people ask: 'How can we reach the destination you described?' When you analyse this verse, you see that this first step of faith is not merely faith of the heart, as this kind of faith is not accompanied by action. If you do righteous deeds, you are entitled to guidance. And this first step means that the second step will also become clear. As the poet, ʿAṭṭār says: 'The journey will tell you how you need to go!' When the human being is directed towards his goal by faith and follows this faith, the path makes itself clear for him through his faith–'their Lord guides them by the means of their faith'–and the ways open up to them.

In the first step, none of the leaders, the elites, the travellers, or the followers know what the tenth step will be. For example, let's say there is a desert whose length and breadth are ten kilometres or more. On a dark night, lit by neither moon nor stars, you are crossing this desert. All you have with you to light your way is a small torch. Someone tells you: 'You have to go the whole way by the light of this torch.' What would you say? 'This torch barely lights a metre in front of me! Am I supposed to go the whole ten kilometres with just this? How do you expect me to do that?' This is how someone

72 Q10:9.

inexperienced or unknowing might think. How would you answer them? What would you say in response to this flawed logic? Wouldn't you say: 'My friend, doesn't your torch light one metre in front of you? Take a step forward and it will illuminate another metre! This metre is lit up, so go one metre forward. Take a step and the next step will become clear...if it doesn't, then don't go any further. But, if it does, then take another step. And so on, and so on. In this way, your way through the desert will be gradually illuminated and you will be able to go on until you reach your destination!' Is this not so? Is this not the answer? 'Their Lord guides them by the means of their faith'–their faith is the means by which they find their way.

The Qur'an discusses this in several other verses. In one of these, it says that when a chapter or verse of the Qur'an is sent down, the disbelievers, hypocrites, and those who have a sickness in their hearts say to one another: 'Which of you has had his faith increased by it?'[73] Who amongst you gained more faith after hearing this verse? The Qur'an answers them by saying that for those who are truly believers, those who have been converted, this verse and others like it *do* increase their faith. It is the faith of their hearts that leads them to take guidance from its source.

The next verse I want to discuss reads: 'O mankind! Certainly a proof has come to you from your Lord, and We have sent down to you a manifest light.'[74] By this proof and this light is meant nothing other than the Qur'an itself and the teachings it contains, as is clearly demonstrated by the following verse: 'As for those who have faith in God, and hold fast to Him, He will admit them to His mercy and grace, and He will guide them on a straight path to Him.'[75] Therefore, to merely have faith in one's heart is not enough, one must also hold

73 Q9:124. Abdullah Yusuf Ali's translation.

74 Q4:174.

75 Q4:175.

fast to God, meaning one must hold fast to God's religion and walk on God's path. When someone does this 'He will admit them to His mercy and grace, and He will guide them on a straight path to Him.' He will guide them towards him. He will guide them along the right path; the path that is nearest to Him. This guidance is only for the truly faithful. If someone does not have faith, or if they have faith but do not hold fast to God, if they do not act on their duties towards God, then they will not be guided to God. The light of guidance will not shine in their hearts. This is only for the truly faithful.

Another verse is 'As for those who strive in Us, We shall surely guide them in Our ways, and God is indeed with the virtuous.'[76] Those who strive in God's way...and what is God's way? What does this mean? It means those who strive for divine goals, for any goal that God has in this world...and what are those goals? Justice, safety, the devotion of His servants, the growth and development of His servants, the development of the earth, and the development of human hearts, the preparation of this world and the Hereafter for the sake of human beings, the perfection of all beings–these are God's goals. The removal of superstition, the removal of idolatry, the removal of disbelief, the removal of insecurity, the removal of violence and enmity, the removal of oppression and tyranny–these are God's goals. 'And those who strive in Us'–those who struggle for divine goals, who struggle to fulfil the divine plan, who strive for the sake of God's will–'We shall surely guide them in our ways'–We will show them our ways, We will not leave them confused, We will not leave them lost. As ʿAṭṭar said:

'Set out on the journey and do not ask
The journey will tell you how to go!'

'As for those who strive in Us, We shall surely guide them in Our ways'–this is true in all arenas, whether this is understanding religion and religious issues, social issues, or global issues–for anyone who is

76 Q29:69.

pursuing divine goals, whoever takes a step towards these, his next step will become clear to him. The one who strives in God's way for God's goals, will be guided to His ways, which are the ways to human happiness and flourishing. 'And God is indeed with the virtuous.'

These verses from the Qur'an were all about guidance. This is just the first topic. There are still other verses on this which, if we wanted to gather them all together, we could spend three or four days just discussing the theme of guidance!

We said that light is something necessary for human happiness, keeping in mind the explanation that we gave for light above, and light has been promised to the faithful: 'God is the ally of the faithful: He brings them out of darkness into light.'[77] The word 'ally' (*walī*) signifies that God is on the same side as the faithful, and I have given preference to this meaning to those others associated with the Arabic world *walī* such as 'master', 'friend' or 'helper.' This is because *wilāyah* means to be joined with something. When two things are linked together, this is called *wilāyah*. So when we say that God is the *walī* of the faithful, this means He is connected to the faithful. What does it mean to say that God is joined to the faithful? It means they are on the same side. God's enemies are on the other side–opposed to the faithful and opposed to God. Wherever the word *walī* appears in the Qur'an, such as 'and God is the *walī* of the faithful'[78] or when we speak of God's *awliyā*ʾ, the meaning is 'ally'.

'God is the Guardian of the faithful: He brings them out of darkness into light'–there is something that should be clarified here, namely the meaning of 'darkness' (*ẓulumāt*). The word darkness here is actually plural, and it refers to all the different kinds of darkness: to ignorance, superstition, delusion, tyranny, inhumanity...all the things that imprison the human being and his intellect. This is what

77 Q2:257.

78 Q3:68.

darkness means. This is what God guides them out from and into the light–what light? The light of knowledge, the light of wisdom, the light of human values. This is what God does for the true believer. Someone who is not a true believer, who has no faith, who is doubtful and hesitant, who is a disbeliever or a wrongdoer, can never reach this light. That is why the idolater is always perplexed. The idolater is always anxious. The life of an idolater is always paired with confusion. There is no light for him. There is no real knowledge for him. There is no wisdom for him. 'As for the faithless'[79]–what about the faithless (*kuffār*)? The faithless are those who do not value the teachings of religion and reject God's gifts. They are ungrateful (*kāfir al-niʿmah*). Pay attention, because this is the original meaning of the word *kāfir*. A *kāfir* is not just someone who does not accept religion. A *kāfir* is someone who covers a blessing, who rejects a gift. Why do we call someone a *kāfir*? Ok, they reject religion, so why a *kāfir*? Because this religion is a gift from God, and this gift from God is given for the sake of the happiness of this person and all people. But this person rejects it. He does not value it. He is ungrateful for it. Therefore, he is called a *kāfir* or 'ingrate'. 'As for the faithless, their guardians are the Rebels'–their allies are the wrongdoers and tyrants. Those who encourage their faithlessness are their leaders and masters 'who drive them out of light into darkness'–out of the light of knowledge, away from wisdom, to the prison of darkness and ignorance. 'They shall be the inmates of the Fire, and they shall remain in it.'

'O you who have faith! Remember God with frequent remembrance, and glorify Him morning and evening.' And why is that? 'It is He who blesses you, and so do His angels, that He may bring you out from darkness into light, and He is most merciful to the faithful.'[80] This is God's promise contained in the Qur'an.

79 Q2:257.

80 Q33:41–43.

There are several other promises we want to discuss which we will continue with tomorrow, God willing. Of course, we cannot deal with every single promise that God makes to the faithful in the Qur'an, as it would take ten days or more to do justice to every promise and reward given to the faithful in the Qur'an for being truly faithful to God. Therefore, we will cover just a few more tomorrow and, if necessary, we will continue for one more day. Otherwise, tomorrow will be our final discussion on these promises.

Divine Promises, Part Two

Wednesday 8th Ramadan 1394
25th September 1974

الَّذِينَ آمَنُوا وَتَطْمَئِنُّ قُلُوبُهُمْ بِذِكْرِ اللَّهِ أَلَا بِذِكْرِ اللَّهِ
تَطْمَئِنُّ الْقُلُوبُ (٢٨) الَّذِينَ آمَنُوا وَعَمِلُوا الصَّالِحَاتِ طُوبَى
لَهُمْ وَحُسْنُ مَآبٍ (٢٩)

'Those who have faith, and whose hearts find rest in the remembrance of God. Look! The hearts find rest in God's remembrance! Those who have faith and do righteous deeds, happy are they and good is their destination.'
- Sūrat al-Raʿd (13):28–29.

Yesterday, we said that God has promised the truly faithful that He will reward them with all the things they need for human happiness and flourishing. Those things that come to mind when we think about the elements of human happiness–ten or twelve in total–were mentioned and explained in the previous lecture's verse. All of these things appear in the Qur'an as clear and definitive promises to the faithful. Two such things that God promises to the faithful in the Qur'an are guidance (*hidāyah*) and light (*nūr*), and in the previous lecture we looked at these in several of the Qur'an's verses. We are going to look at two further things in this chapter, and we will leave the rest to you to study in your own time based on the arrangement we laid out beforehand: Look at them one by one. Study the Qur'an. Recite the Qur'an. If you know Arabic, then read the Qur'an in its original Arabic. If you don't know Arabic, then read its translation. But, in any case, study these subjects as they appear in the Qur'an.

One of these topics is the reward that awaits in the Hereafter. This is one of the promises given to the faithful in the Qur'an. Read the Qur'an yourself and you will see that throughout its pages, God promises a reward in the Hereafter to the faithful and those who believe and do righteous deeds. Another thing that God promises the faithful in the Qur'an is superiority and victory over their enemies. Read the Qur'an–is there anywhere in it where God tells the faithful that they will defeat their foes? Now you're searching for whether the Qur'an does give this promise to the faithful–that they will be triumphant against their opponents, so long as they believe and fulfil the duties associated with that belief? Does it tell them that in the end they will succeed against their enemies in the way they think they will? Does such a verse exist in the Qur'an or not? Can any of you tell me whether or not there is such a verse in the Qur'an?

'Do not weaken or grieve: you shall have the upper hand, should you be faithful.'[81] Very good. This is one such verse. It says that if you are true believers, then you will have the upper hand–you will have the advantage over your foes. There are several other verses that promise to reward the faithful with certain victory over the enemies that are arrayed against them. 'God has ordained: "I shall surely prevail, I and My apostles."'[82] 'And indeed Our hosts will be the victors.'[83] There are many other verses like these. Keep these in mind when you read the Qur'an and study its verses. Instead of making it your goal to finish a *juz'* or a chapter, make it your goal to understand

81 Q3:139.

82 Q58:21

83 Q37:173.

the Qur'an. As we read in the narrations of the Prophet (s) and the Imams (a), your concern when reciting the Qur'an should not be to get through its parts and chapters as quickly as possible. Maybe you finish it. Maybe you don't. Maybe you just read a single verse. But however much you read, let it be with attentiveness and reflection. See whether the verse you are reading says anything about these promises we are discussing, as these are the essential elements of human happiness and flourishing–does the verse say how you can become worthy of these gifts? Does it help you see whether you will receive them or not? I want you to study the Qur'an in this way.

If God grants me success, perhaps I will be able to translate and explain many verses of the Qur'an to you by the end of the sacred month of Ramadan. For example, let us say I can explain fifty verses, or another fifty or sixty verses on top of that. The Qur'an contains approximately six thousand verses–or even more than six thousand! So I cannot possibly explain them all to you–you must familiarize yourself with the Qur'an. Those of you who speak Arabic, try to make yourself conversant and fluent in the Qur'an. Those of you who do not speak Arabic, try to learn Arabic, the language of the Qur'an. Of course, you should not put off reading the Qur'an or trying to understand it until you have learnt Arabic. No, you should read the Qur'an while you are learning it. At the end of the day, you should find a good translation of the Qur'an and, in my view, there are several good translations of the Qur'an out there. And, when you read the Qur'an, refer to these translations and pay close attention to the meanings of the verses. Look out for the promises we have mentioned here and see which of them you can find in the Qur'an.

Today, I am going to speak about another one of the promises which God has given the faithful in the Qur'an. It is up to you to find and study the remainder of these promises, and I hope you will not leave this until after the month of Ramadan or for a time when you have nothing to do. Tonight. Today. At the first opportunity. At the earliest time possible. Open the Qur'an with this goal in mind, to recite it, to become familiar with it, and make use of it for yourself. The Qur'an is nothing other than the everlasting wellspring of our learning. Whatever we have, we should make use of the Qur'an, and whatever can be a means of our attaining human happiness and flourishing, we must bring forth from the Qur'an. This bright and luminous scripture is already in our hands. What we must do is make use of it.

However, although I am speaking about the Qur'an. I do not mean to imply that only the Qur'an is important to the exclusion of *Nahj al-Balāghah* or the authentic traditions we have from the Prophet and Imams–no. Why? Because we must also make use of *Nahj al-Balāghah* alongside the Qur'an. We must also make use of the authentic traditions from the Imams alongside the Qur'an. However, the Qur'an is a text that is accessible to everyone and whose full and authentic version everyone can have access to and carry with them on their person. We cannot say the same about the traditions or *Nahj al-Balāghah*.

Now, we have said that tranquillity, composure and security–all of which are in the same constellation of ideals–are one and the same thing. By this, we meant that although there are three words, when we refer to the verses of the Qur'an to see what it says about them, we see that tranquillity (*iṭmīnān*) means for our heart and soul to be at peace. What does it mean for a thing to be at peace? What does this expression denote in relation to our hearts and souls? Does it not mean that our hearts and souls do not move or exert themselves in the slightest? Does it mean that our hearts are in a state of half-sleep and half-wakefulness? No, to be at peace is the opposite state of being anxious or perturbed. Being at peace or tranquil is the opposite of being full of doubt.

Imagine there are two people. Both of them are about to take an exam. One has studied hard and revised the subject ten times. He has revised with his friends and committed everything in the textbook to memory. The other one has not even opened the book. Or, if he has, he has only read a little of it. Or, if he has read more than that, he does not have a good memory. Both of them are taking the exam. Do they feel the same way as one another? See how when the first one walks into the exam, his soul is at peace, it is not disturbed, anxious or filled with doubt. He tells himself: 'Whatever the question, I know the answer.' But what about the other one? He is in a constant state of worry, like a boat being tossed between the waves on a heaving, stormy ocean. Sometimes he is thrown this way. Sometimes he is thrown that way. The winds push and pull him in all directions. This is the state of his soul as he walks into that exam hall.

Another example is when someone accused of a crime stands before a judge. In any of history's great social and political events or conflicts, these two states and these two spirits can be observed in one person or one society. This is something you can see for yourself.

Imagine now, that these two are soldiers going to the battlefield. One of them is well-equipped and well-led. He knows that his enemy is weak and that he can rely on his friends and comrades. On top of this, he knows that his side has reinforcements hidden behind a hill, waiting for the signal for the right moment to rush into battle. On the other hand, the other one has no trust in his own preparations, nor those of his leaders, nor those of his comrades for battle. He sees his own side as weak and the enemy as strong. He feels under-equipped while he thinks his opponents are armed to the teeth. Do these two soldiers feel the same as they wait for battle to commence?

These are two examples to illustrate the meaning of 'tranquillity'. I want you to understand what it means for the soul to be at peace. What does it mean for the soul to be tranquil? The first soldier is tranquil. The first soldier's heart and soul are at peace. It doesn't mean that when he arrives on the battlefield, he puts his boots under his head as a pillow, stretches out on the ground and takes a nap–snoring all the while! No, this is not tranquillity. Tranquillity does not mean stopping for a cigarette break in the midst of fighting! Or sitting down and gathering one's thoughts while watching the battle unfold around you. No, not at all. Being tranquil does not meaning ignoring what the enemy is doing. It means not being anxious, not being confused, knowing that the future is clear and that your side will triumph and, for this reason, not being afraid. This is a heart and soul that is at peace! Like a well-laden ship sailing through calm waters on a clear day. This is what we mean by 'tranquillity'. Someone who is not tranquil, who is not at peace. Such a person is like a piece of driftwood bouncing through the rapids of a fast-flowing river. Forever anxious. Forever going this way and that way. So, you see, these are two completely different states of being.

Let me give you another example of tranquillity as we gradually approach the ideal that is being expressed in the Qur'an. From a student taking an exam, to a person accused of a crime standing before a judge, to a soldier on the battlefield. One more example: Someone who has set out on a journey somewhere and is heading towards his destination. There are a hundred reasons that might prevent someone from undertaking such a journey. Fear is one of them–fear, worry, apprehension. Fear might turn a person back. But fear of what? Fear of the hardships of travel. Fear of robbers and bandits. Fears of wolves lying in wait. Fear of getting lost. Ultimately, fear of not arriving at the destination! This is just an idea of the kinds of things that might prevent someone from continuing their journey.

Another is desire. But desire for what? The desire for an easy life. One might think: If I do not take this road, if I don't pursue my goal, then I can relax in the warmth and comfort of my own home and stay here with my beloved wife and children. This is what an ordinary person, a small person, a weak-souled person imagines an ideal life to be. This is what he loves. What he seeks. He will let try his absolute best for this. Clearly such a person is not ready to give this up easily. He wants an easy life. He wants the money of the person who tells him: 'If you stay and don't take that road, this purse of money is for you.' He wants to attain a position in society, so people tell him: 'If you stay put, you'll climb the ladder and, one day, you'll be somebody!' Desire! These are the reasons why a person turns back from the road: fear and desire. And if we ask: 'Fear of what?' We find the fear of a hundred things. If we ask: 'Desire for what?' We find desire for a hundred different things. Seeking a life of ease, seeking comfort, seeking opportunity and seeking benefit are all the same.

Now, let us imagine there is someone who takes a chance and strikes out on his own. He's on the move, but does this mean the obstacles vanish? Does this mean that on the road he is taking there are none of the hardships or troubles he feared? No, they are still there. Pay attention to this! Just because he has set off, does not mean that the path ahead is easy. The same troubles and hardships still lie in wait, and the road is long and winding. Every step he takes is like a thistle, a hook or a chain clinging to his leg, to his clothes, to his hand and pulling him back, dragging him away from the road. He trips this way. He stumbles that way. This thistle catches on his clothing, that chain pulls his leg. This love for his children pulls him back. That memory of the comforts of home weighs him down. He is assailed from all sides by obstacles and he is pulled in every direction. Such a person will become shaken, like that little boat on a raging sea–tossed in one direction and then in another. This person is not at peace.

But let us imagine someone else who when they set off, when they strike out on the path, they have a motivation that makes all other wants and obstacles seem insignificant and small. There is a force within his heart that drives him forward and pushes him harder than the pull of all these little forces; the force of children, the force of one's spouse, the force of one's life, the force of money, the force of status, the force of life...there is a more powerful force that overwhelms all of these and keeps him moving forward. There is a force that makes them nothing. That renders them ineffective.

Tens of magnets may pull a single small body in all directions, but when there is one magnet bigger and more powerful than all of them, it overwhelms their force and pulls this body towards it. When this happens, none of the other magnets have any effect!

Now, when a person sets out on his journey with this force as his lodestar, when he sets out with resolve and a determination to walk the path he has chosen, nothing else can hold him back–not his children, not his wife, not any of the other things that give us a life of happiness and ease, not any of the pleasures we enjoy. Who is this person? This is a tranquil person, a person whose soul is at peace: 'O tranquil soul! Return to your Lord, pleased, pleasing!'[84] The person who can follow God's path to its end, who can reach his intended goal, who is tranquil is someone in a state of peace. This is the true meaning of tranquillity; it means to be moved by a single force: The force of faith. The force of one's connection with God. The force of one's connection with one's destination. When a person is led forward by such a force, all other forces are nullified and reduced to naught. The earth's gravity cannot be compared to the gravity of a mountain. Not even the greatest mountain in the world. It is the earth that moves the mountain, not the other way around. Equally, the rock you hold in your hand cannot compare to the mountain. The mountain has mass, so it exerts a gravitational pull. But this gravitational pull is nothing compared to that of the Earth. Yes, if the mountain was floating in space without any bodies more massive than it nearby, it would attract objects with its gravitational force. But when it rests on a body that is many thousands of times more massive than itself, its attractive force has no effect on objects, as these are all caught up in the gravity of that object.

So, when faith in God inheres in the soul of a human being, it works like a powerful force that moves the human being towards the goals

84 Q89:27.

of faith and overwhelms lesser forces. When someone lacks faith altogether, he is now at the mercy of these forces. But even against a little faith, these forces are almost powerless. Yes, a person might harbour doubts in his heart–something we can see in history from the very earliest days of Islam, which we will discuss. However, as time is short, you should also do your own research and find examples of this so that you can better understand the forces that act on human lives!

Let me now return to defining these two or three terms above. 'Tranquillity'–what does 'tranquillity' mean? In short, we saw that tranquillity means for a person's soul to be at peace and for their heart to be at rest. What does it mean for them to be at peace? Not that they are stationary. Not that they don't move or progress. It means that they are not pulled this way and that way by different forces of attraction, they are not diverted from their goal. The things they love, care for, covet and desire do not rule over them. On the contrary, the gravity of faith keeps them steady, at peace and tranquil. And yet, at the same time, they are moving with the utmost haste towards the goal of humanity and the purpose of creation–this is the meaning of tranquillity.

Second, there is 'composure' (*sukūn*). As in the verse: 'Then God sent down His composure upon His Messenger and upon the faithful.'[85] In five or six places in the Qur'an, God speaks about sending down composure on the faithful. And one of them is the verse that I have just mentioned. This is usually at critical moments, such as during the Battle of Ḥunayn.[86] In this battle, the Prophet's troops were overconfident and expected to win an easy victory. However, as is God's habit, pride goes before a fall. When a people become haughty, they become oblivious and then they will suffer a reversal. So whether as individuals, or as a group, or as a nation, people must always be

85 Q9:26.

86 Which took place after the capture of Makkah.

watchful and vigilant, as the Commander of the Faithful (a) says: 'By God I will not be like the beast that sleeps with a lullaby.'[87] Apparently, hunters would go outside the dens of some animals, like hyenas, and sing a lullaby to them so that they would fall asleep so that they could capture them. Here, Imam ʿAlī (a) says that he is not one who is put to sleep–he is always vigilant. But it is God's practice (*sunnah*) that when someone is not alert and vigilant, he will be struck. So the Prophet's troops became careless on the battlefield. This was not without cause: 'when your great number impressed you.'[88] The Muslims were impressed with the size of their won army and felt confident they would be victorious. 'But it did not avail you in any way'. On the contrary, their overconfidence made them careless and they suffered a reversal at the hands of their enemies. They were not defeated outright, but it was a severe blow and they ran away. Only a handful of steadfast and faithful troops–one of whom was Imam ʿAlī–stood their ground. When the others saw this, they came back. It was then God says: 'God sent down His composure on His Messenger and upon the faithful'.

Another time that God sent down composure upon the faithful was when they renewed their oaths of allegiance beneath a tree at Ḥudaybiyyah.[89] Another time was when the Prophet set out from Makkah for Madinah with the intention of creating a new Islamic society there. This was a dangerous undertaking, as his enemies would surely try to kill him before he reached his destination. The Prophet had given much thought and planning to this because, if the idolaters were to kill him en route, then everything he had struggled

87 *Nahj al-Balāghah*, sermon no. 6.

88 Q9:25.

89 See Q48:18–'God was certainly pleased with the faithful when they swore allegiance to you under the tree. He knew what was in their hearts, so He sent down composure on them, and requited them with a victory near at hand.'

for would be for nothing. He sought refuge in a cave, and it was there that God said that he sent down composure upon him.[90] He reassured him at this stressful and sensitive moment. There are several other instances of this. So a believer is someone who has composure. And, like tranquillity, composure refers to a peace and stillness of the soul–it does not mean that someone is inactive, idle or heedless of what is going on.

Finally, there is security (*amn*). Clearly what is meant here is a security of the spirit, rather than security on the level of society. Security on the level of society means that everyone enjoys a common safety and protection, so that each individual person can exercise their rights. Then there is silence (*sukūt*), but silence by force is not the same as security. Security means that everyone can fully exercise their rights and attain their lawful desires. However, the kind of security we are speaking about here is not the same as the sort that is desirable on the social level. We are talking about security of the spirit, which means not being shaken, not becoming anxious, not becoming fearful, not to be scared or frightened. These are the three qualities that I wanted to define. Now we will consider those verses that talk about these three qualities in relation to the true believers.

In verses 28 and 29 of *Sūrat al-Raʿd*, we read: 'those who have faith, and whose hearts find tranquillity in the remembrance of God.' What puts their souls at peace? The remembrance of God (*dhikr Allāh*). This remembrance of God is the same as that powerful force of attraction we mentioned above. That force that we said renders all other forces null and void is the remembrance of God. Why do we attach so much importance to prayer? Why do we say that if your prayers are not accepted, nothing else will be accepted? Why must we visit Makkah only once in our lives, fast for only one month of the year, and give only a little of our wealth as charity and *khums*

90 See Q9:40–'Then God sent down His composure upon him.'

(and the other acts of worship to roughly the same amount) but we must pray every day? And not just once a day but several times a day or even more? Why? Because, as I have said on other occasions, it is like a dose of God's remembrance for one's heart. The totality of prayer is the remembrance of God. That is why after the Qur'an says 'Indeed the prayer prevents indecencies and wrongs', it adds: 'and the remembrance of God is surely greater'. This aspect of prayer, the dimension of prayer that is concerned with remembering God, is greater still than that which prevents indecency and wrongdoing. This is the greatest quality of prayer. The quality of God's remembrance. Remembering God. Turning towards God. Being ever mindful of God. Knowing God. The mere knowledge of God is sufficient to protect the human heart from anxiety, doubt and worry–from all the other forces that pull it this way and that way–no matter what work it is engaged in, no matter what path it is taking. This heart will find peace through God's remembrance. Like the ballast of a boat, that weighs it down to some extent and, in doing so, keeps it somewhat steady upon the waters. This is what God's remembrance does for the human heart.

'Those who have faith, and whose hearts find tranquillity in the remembrance of God'–whose hearts are steadied by God's remembrance–these people will be guided towards God. How do we know they will be guided towards God? Based on the previous verse: 'and guides to Himself those who turn penitently:[91] Those who have faith, and whose hearts find tranquillity in the remembrance of God.'

Then God says: 'Look! The hearts find tranquillity in God's remembrance!' The remembrance of God possesses this amazing quality. And you can see yourselves how much of an effect such tranquillity can have on a person's success. This is one of the ways in which a believer is distinguished from all other people, because they enjoy this great spiritual power.

91 Q13:27.

The next verse reads: 'Those who have faith and do righteous deeds happy are they and good is their destination.' To do righteous deeds means to fulfil the duties that arise out of faith and accompany it. Happy is their present and blessed is their future. This is one of the conclusions we can draw from the phrase 'happy are they and good is their destination' (*ṭūbā lahum wa ḥusnu maʾāb*). In short, it means that they are in a good state today and they will be in a good state tomorrow as well. Their life in this world is good. Their life in the Hereafter is also good. This is the truth of it: A community of believers, where every believer fulfils their duties towards God, will have a good life in this world and a good life in the next world. Their life in this world is Paradise and their life in the next world is also Paradise. This is one of the verses.

Another passage we should consider from the Qur'an is its account of Abraham's debates with his own people. Abraham was God's intimate friend (*khalīl*) and the proclaimer of divine unity in times long ago. He disputed and argued with his own people and his own nation. They debated with him and he debated with them, responding to the things he said. The Qur'an recounts these debates. It says 'His people argued with him'–Abraham's people started to debate and dispute with him. The Qur'an does not tell us what they said, or how they argued with him, or what points they made. However, it preserves what Abraham said to them in response and, from this, we might be able to guess at what they said in the first place. So let's read Abraham's first response and you can guess what they might have said to him.

'He said: "Do you argue with me concerning God, while He has surely guided me?"'–In other words, he is saying: Everything is clear to me. I am certain about my path. You want to make use of doubts and misgivings, and arguments and disputations to turn me back from my path. But I have already been guided. I have already found the right path. I know what I am doing. 'I do not fear what you ascribe to Him as partners, excepting anything that my Lord may wish', in other words: I only fear God. I fear only what God will put in my path or what He has in store for me in my future. But as for the deities that you set up as partners to him, I have no fear of them. It is clear from this brief statement, and it will become clearer, that Abraham's people had told him: 'O Abraham! Fear these deities of ours, which are God's partners! They will be displeased with you. They will punish you. They will curse you and make your days bitter. There is no escape!' Abraham responded by saying: 'I do not fear them. There is nothing I have to fear from them.' The following verse and the rest of what Abraham says makes this clearer still.

'My Lord embraces all things in His knowledge.' God's knowledge encompasses all things, 'So will you not take admonition?' To take admonition (*tadhakkur*) means to understand or pay attention. Abraham is asking them: 'Won't you take heed? Won't you come to your senses? Won't you pay attention?' And there is yet more to Abraham's discourse with his people. This is just one part.

Next, Abraham says: 'How could I fear what you ascribe [to Him] as partners, when you do not fear ascribing partners to God for which He has not sent down any authority to you?' Here we can clearly see what their argument with Abraham was about. Abraham tells them: 'Why should I be afraid? It is you all who should be afraid! Why should I fear those that you claim have a share in God's dominion, authority, command and creation, when you have no evidence for this, while God has guided me and made this matter clear for me? No, you are the ones who have made partners for God–the Lord of the Worlds–without any evidence, without any logic, without any rational basis–so how is it you are not afraid? You should be afraid, not me!' From this it is clear that in their debate with Abraham they were saying: 'Be afraid! Be afraid!' Now, who is it that Abraham is supposed to be afraid of and why? Of idols of wood and stone, of living persons who have been made into partners, or of both? It is not clear yet which partners Abraham's people are saying he should be afraid of.

Generally speaking, people have set up all manner of partners for God. The Israelites worshipped a golden calf, others worship idols made of wood and stone, Pharaoh and Nimrod claimed to be living gods amongst their people. However, based on what we have said about divine unity it is clear that whether the idol is a golden calf, a wooden carving, a stone statue or a living Pharaoh or Nimrod, all of them lead to the same fire, all of them are part of the same disease–there is no difference between any of them. In any case, Abraham's people told him that he should be afraid of God's partners, but as for whether these partners were humans, jinns, living or dead–we do not know.

'How could I fear what you ascribe [to Him] as partners, when you do not fear ascribing partners to God for which He has not sent down any authority to you?'

Next, Abraham asks them: 'So, which of the two sides has a greater right to safety, if you know?' Me or you? I am more worthy of having safety of spirit. I have no doubts or hesitations–what about you? Abraham tells them: 'My heart is set upon God. I have been guided by God. Which of us is more without doubt? Me or you? You have no basis or evidence for what you do, while for me the matter is clear! Which of these two groups–me, Abraham, or you, the idol worshippers–is more worthy of feeling secure?' Abraham knows God and has come to Him on the basis of understanding and insight. Meanwhile, the idol worshippers have no evidence for their false beliefs. Now, what does it mean when Abraham adds: 'should you know' (*in kuntum taʿlamūn*)? It means the conclusion is obvious. The answer is obvious. It is clear which of the two sides should be worried and which of them should feel secure.

Finally, he says: 'Those who have faith and do not taint their faith with wrongdoing–for such there shall be safety, and they are the guided.'

Recall, when we spoke about divine promises, we said that the first thing the human needs on his journey is to know his destination, the second thing he needs is understanding, the third thing he needs is to be free of doubts and worries–which we discussed above. Now, the fourth thing the human being needs is to know that his efforts matter. His work must be fruitful. What does this mean? This is one of the things that, if the wayfarer has it, he will be more motivated to press on and there is a better chance of him reaching his destination. If he does not have this, he will not travel so quickly and there is a higher probability of him never reaching his destination. It all depends on whether or not he knows that his actions count for something–does he sense that this journey of his, and every step that he takes on it will not vanish, that his efforts will not be in vain, that his movement, his every step will have some effect? Does he know that every step he takes creates a wave that carries him closer to his destination? If he truly believes this, he will press on and move faster. He will work harder. He will be less tired. He will be more at ease as he travels. But if he does not believe this–how terrible! But the true believer is this way. The true believer knows his efforts matter. The Qur'an teaches him this–there are many verses on this topic:

'Indeed God does not waste the reward of the virtuous.'[92]

'We do not waste the reward of those who are good in deeds.'[93]

There are verses like this throughout the Qur'an. There is one instance I want to call attention to in *Sūrat al-Baqarah*, but there are ten or fifteen other instances that you can find throughout the scripture.

92 Q11:115.

93 Q18:30.

The verse I am going to discuss now is about the qibla, or direction of prayer. There is a little bit of history you need to know about the qibla. When the Muslims were in Makkah, before the Hegira (*Hijrah*), they turned towards the Kaʿbah when they prayed. Then, when they first came to the city of Madinah, they turned towards Jerusalem in prayer. This was done at God's command. This was also the direction in which the Jews of Madinah prayed. So the Jews and the Muslims were praying in the same direction. A little while later, a verse was revealed that said: 'so turn your face towards the Holy Mosque.'[94] Once again turn to face the House of God, the Kaʿbah, the Holy Mosque. So, the Muslims started to pray towards Makkah instead of Jerusalem. The change of qibla is discussed extensively at the beginning of *Sūrat al-Baqarah* and there are seven or eight verses in this regard which explain the different dimensions of this. This is mostly beyond the scope of our present lesson.

However, there is one verse which says to the faithful and to the Prophet: 'When you first came to Madinah from Makkah, we told you to take Jerusalem as your qibla in order to see what you would do. Before you became Muslims in Makkah, you revered the Kaʿbah and believed it was holy. After you became Muslims you continued praying towards the Kaʿbah in Makkah. Now that you have come to Madinah, we wanted to make a clean break from the traditions of your forefathers and ancestors and we wanted to see how ready you were to put these aside for the sake of God.' This is a very important point to consider. This isn't directly relevant to our current discussion, but we should think about this all the same. You say you are a believer–are you ready to give up the ways of your forefathers for God? Something which you feel attached to? Something which you respect and revere? Are you ready to put that aside or not? So do not imagine that the prayers you offered when you first came to Madinah and faced the

94 Q2:144.

qibla of Jerusalem count for nothing with Us. Do not think that we will not accept them or that the qibla of Jerusalem was false! Not at all! Whatever you did, all of it, will be accepted. All the efforts you made. All of your struggles for your faith, whether in regard to the qibla or with regard to anything else, are valid and valuable–they will be rewarded by God. However, this period in which you prayed towards Jerusalem was so that we could test you. So, this is the original context of the verse we are about to discuss–let us see how it relates to our present discussion.

God says to the Prophet, 'and We did not appoint the qibla you were following', meaning Jerusalem; so, when was this verse sent down? When the qibla changed back from Jerusalem to the Kaᶜbah in Makkah once more, so that they would pray towards the Kaᶜbah; and why did God do this? 'But that We may ascertain', in other words, to make known 'those who follow the Apostle from those who turn back on their heels.'[95] In other words, it was to see who would follow the Prophet and who still held on to the ways of their forefathers and wanted to cling to the past. It was to separate and distinguish these two groups. God tested them through this change of qibla to see who would continue following the ways of pre-Islamic ignorance. 'But it was indeed a hard thing except for those whom God has guided'–those whose hearts had been guided did not have any trouble with this. They could stomach this change. But those who had not been guided could not.

Next, God says, 'and God would not let your prayers go to waste.' This is the phrase that is crucial to the argument we are presenting here, namely that God will never let your faith count for nothing. That your faith, your works, that whatever you do will not be in vain. That it will not be fruitless. So do not stop. Do not hold back. Your journey. Your every movement. Your every step brings you closer to

95 Q2:144

your goal. It brings you closer to happiness and fulfilment. So your faith is never wasted, for 'Indeed, God is most kind and merciful to mankind.'

Now, pay attention. It is not only this verse but several other verses in the Qur'an that make this promise to the faithful, namely that your works, your faith, your belief and your efforts will not be allowed to go to waste. They are not futile. They are not pointless. What does this mean? It means they will have an effect. It means they will bear fruit. If a believer cultivates this attitude in themselves, it is obvious that the path to spiritual growth and perfection will be easier for him!

Next, we will be looking at divine unity.

Section Two

Divine Unity (Tawḥīd)

Tawḥīd: An Islamic Worldview

Thursday 9th Ramadan 1394
26th September 1974

اللَّهُ لَا إِلَٰهَ إِلَّا هُوَ الْحَيُّ الْقَيُّومُ لَا تَأْخُذُهُ سِنَةٌ وَلَا نَوْمٌ لَهُ مَا فِي السَّمَاوَاتِ وَمَا فِي الْأَرْضِ مَنْ ذَا الَّذِي يَشْفَعُ عِنْدَهُ إِلَّا بِإِذْنِهِ يَعْلَمُ مَا بَيْنَ أَيْدِيهِمْ وَمَا خَلْفَهُمْ وَلَا يُحِيطُونَ بِشَيْءٍ مِنْ عِلْمِهِ إِلَّا بِمَا شَاءَ وَسِعَ كُرْسِيُّهُ السَّمَاوَاتِ وَالْأَرْضَ وَلَا يَئُودُهُ حِفْظُهُمَا وَهُوَ الْعَلِيُّ الْعَظِيمُ (٢٥٥)

'God there is no god except Him–is the Living One, the All-sustainer. Neither drowsiness befalls Him nor sleep. To Him belongs whatever is in the heavens and whatever is on the earth. Who is it that may intercede with Him except with His permission? He knows that which is before them and that which is behind them, and they do not comprehend anything of His knowledge except what He wishes. His seat embraces the heavens and the earth, and He is not wearied by their preservation, and He is the All-exalted, the All-supreme.'

- Sūrat al-Baqarah (2):255.

In a nutshell, what we will be looking at today are the verses of the Qur'an about divine unity (*tawḥīd*). We are going to study the verses and you yourselves can deduce what the Qur'an says with regard to divine unity. First of all, what does it mean? Second of all, what is its practical meaning in human affairs? Of course, you must also remember what we have said previously: The faith in any idea or any principle from the fundamental tenets of the religion must, firstly, be based on knowledge, understanding and awareness, not blind following and, secondly, that faith engenders a moral responsibility on the part of its possessor. Whatever it is we are supposed to believe in must certainly have some practical effect on our lives and behaviours, whether at an individual level or a societal one, whether it pertains to ourselves or to others in society, whether to humanity or to the future of history. Faith, without any doubt, places a responsibility on our shoulders.

With this premise in mind, when we discuss the question of divine unity, it is obvious that this discussion will produce a moral duty. Therefore, the way in which we will approach divine unity is as follows: First of all, we will understand what it is. Secondly, we will see what kind of duty it places on our shoulders. Is divine unity nothing more than understanding without any responsibility attached? Is it simply to know a truth without the knowledge of that truth requiring us to do anything? Or is it something else: Is divine unity the knowledge and understanding of something and, once we have known and understood it, it impels us towards some kind of moral duty or ethical responsibility? This is the question we will be seeking to answer by examining what the Qur'an says about divine unity.

So, the verses we are going to look at in this lecture today will be about divine unity from one perspective. Tomorrow's lecture will look at verses that present divine unity from another perspective. And on each day that follows, the verses we study will open up a new direction for us from which we can approach divine unity. I do not claim that in just a few days, by looking at a few verses of the Qur'an, we can give an exhaustive treatment to divine unity in the Qur'an or in Islam. Without a doubt, anyone who examines this topic more closely, in greater detail and at further length will see that studying divine unity in the Qur'an is like diving into a vast and limitless ocean. But, to the limited extent that these gatherings allow us, we will delve into this topic as best as we are able.

First, I should say that discussing divine unity in the Qur'an and in the manner we intend to, might seem like quite a heavy topic. In fact, it might seem more suitable for a class rather than a sermon. However, I have always wondered why we don't make our religious gatherings more educational, and why shouldn't our sermons be more like a lesson? Why shouldn't we make use of these public religious gatherings, where many people have come together and are ready to sit and listen to a speaker, to present more complex issues that require thought and reflection, just as we might in a classroom? Why must we use these gatherings in the month of Ramadan only to speak about easy topics or tell pleasant stories? Why? Why shouldn't we expect more from our religious gatherings? Why shouldn't we discuss deeper and more advanced topics?

Therefore, my brothers and sisters, I do not know whether in the coming days you will find this topic difficult or not. Perhaps you will or perhaps you won't. But, if you do find it challenging, think of it as something that is important for you to understand. Ponder on it. Study it. Use all of your mental energy and ability to try and grasp this. Remember what we discuss. Take notes. If you find it hard to understand, discuss it with your friends and colleagues afterwards. If this is something you genuinely find unfamiliar to you, please try not to immediately label it as something difficult or hard that you couldn't understand. On the contrary, try to make it something you can understand!

However, as we always say in many lessons, discussions or lectures, we should never expect anyone–not even one person–to accept everything we say completely and utterly. On the contrary, whatever we say here is just food for thought. It is up to you to take whatever we discuss and examine it further, to ponder on it, investigate it and draw your own conclusions, just as the following verse of the Qur'an advises us: 'So give good news to My servants who listen to the word and follow the best of it.'[1]

In any case, we will presently approach divine unity via two avenues–of course, as we discuss the topics, it is possible that other angles will also open up. The first of these is divine unity in the Islamic worldview. Without a doubt, divine unity *is* part of the Islamic worldview, but we want to know what it is and what it means. We want to see how the Qur'an presents divine unity in the Islamic worldview–how does it explain it? The second avenue is divine unity in the ideology of Islam. But before going into these, I will briefly explain what I mean by worldview (*jahānbīnī*) and ideology for those that don't know, as divine unity is at the same time a part of the Islamic worldview, but it is also a constituent of the Islamic ideology which gives life to Islam.

In addition to this, divine unity is part of and made manifest in all of the branches of Islam. Wherever you see any rule, law or moral teaching given in the name of religion which runs contrary to the spirit of divine unity or in which there is no trace of divine unity, you should know that this teaching is not a part of Islam. This is because divine unity permeates through all of Islam's teachings in the same way that a spirit permeates throughout all the limbs of a body. It is like a breeze that wafts through all the rooms of the edifice that is called 'Islam'. It is like the pure life-giving blood that flows through the arteries, veins and capillaries of a person named 'Islam'. You cannot find a single teaching in Islam that does not have its roots in

1 Q39:17–18.

divine unity or that is not a manifestation of divine unity. So, today, we want to discuss divine unity in the Islamic worldview.

First of all, what do we mean by 'the Islamic worldview'? When you as an individual try to make sense of the world and of humanity, you form a certain image in your mind. Perhaps you have never consciously done this, but anyone who thinks about the world, about the human being, about the relationship between the human being and the world, about metaphysical issues, about what lies beyond both the human being and the world–anyone who does this forms a series of images and thoughts in their mind. This is what we call a 'worldview'. It is, quite literally, the way in which you look at the world. And every school of thought has its own perspective, its own conclusions, its own impression of the world. So every school of thought has its own worldview. This is a term that has only entered the Persian language relatively recently. It does not mean, as some suppose, being open-minded or taking a broad view of things, when they say: 'So and so is *jahān-bīn*' (literally 'someone who sees the world'). This is not what worldview means.

In short, worldview can be defined as follows: A worldview is a person's impression of the world, a person's understanding of the world, a person's view of the world or of the human condition. Now, we've said 'a person' but we could equally say 'a school of thought' instead, or 'a path', or 'a religion'–how a society understands the world. This is called a worldview. Islam has a worldview insofar as it has a way of looking at the world. I will briefly explain how Islam sees the world to the extent that this relates to our present discussion of divine unity.

Islam believes that this totality which we call 'the world', from top to bottom, from the tiniest and most insignificant beings to the greatest and most awe-inspiring ones, from the lowliest creatures (or even inanimate objects) to the highest, noblest, wisest and most powerful of them (meaning the human being)–all of it, without exception throughout, submits to a Higher Power, which is the source of its being and the maintainer of its subsistence. Beyond this realm of appearance that you and I see, beyond whatever the most acute vision can perceive, and beyond whatever the most precise empirical science can apprehend–beyond all the phenomena that we can sense and touch–lies a reality that is higher than any other, more sublime than any other, and nobler and mightier than any other, and through whose power all the phenomena of the world came to be. To this higher being, we give a name. We call it 'God'. We call it 'Allah'. Therefore, the world is a reality which, at the very core of its own being, does not exist independently or in of its own self. It did not bring itself into being. It did not come into existence spontaneously. On the contrary, this panoply of phenomena, about which we learn more and more with each passing day as they disclose more and about themselves to us, was created by this Higher Power. It is this power that created the tumult at the heart of the atom and has created many millions of galaxies, of which we have only discovered a few. All of this was brought into being by this higher power. This factory has a maker. This device has a creator. It is no coincidence. It does not exist by virtue of itself. Islam sees the world in this fashion.

These are the elements of the Islamic worldview that relate to the topic of divine unity which we will be discussing bit by bit. That is God, who is above the world and all of its inhabitants; that is Higher Power whom we call 'Allah' and who possesses all good attributes by virtue of His own essence. In other words, this being has knowledge. He has power. He has life. He has will. And He has whatever springs forth from these attributes. His life is not derived from anyone or anything else. His knowledge is not learnt from anywhere or by any means. And so on for all of His attributes.

He is the Master of the cosmos. Who are the denizens of this cosmos? What are the atoms of the universe in comparison to Him? When He created these atoms, did these atoms gain an independent existence in the same way as when a mother gives birth to a child, the existence of her child becomes separate from her own? No, this is evidently not the case. On the contrary, these atoms need God not only for their creation but for each and every moment of their continued existence. They depend upon His power and His will. Everything–even the atoms–serve God. All of the beings of the cosmos are His creations, His servants and at His disposal. He can do with them as He pleases. He created each and every one of them according to a specific plan. Each of them was brought into being according to a precise order and set of laws. These laws of the universe that science today is uncovering all point to the existence of a cosmic intelligence. The discussion of God's existence is beyond the scope of these lectures, but there are many excellent books out there dealing with this topic, which I advise you to go and read.

At the same time, however, it is worth mentioning what some scientists have said in this regard. Scientists, not philosophers–scholars of empirical sciences, who carry out experiments and work in laboratories. There is a book, which has been translated into Persian, called *The Evidence of God in An Expanding Universe*[2], in which forty modern American scientists say that, based on their research into the laws and phenomena of the cosmos, they believe that God exists. They say that they see evidence of a finely tuned cosmic order that permeates the structure of the universe and, based on this, this world is created and has a creator. So, to sum up, all the beings in the cosmos are God's servants, they are brought into being by Him, all of them are disposed to His will, and in the grasp of His power. The human being is one such being.

This is divine unity in the Islamic worldview: It means that the world has a creator and a maker or, to put it another way, it has an immaterial spirit. The world has a creator and all the components of

2 Authored by John Clover Monsma and published in 1958.

this world are considered to be at His service and under His dominion. This is divine unity in the Islamic worldview. So, when a Muslim looks at the world through the lens of Islam, he does not see this world as something independent or self-sufficient. On the contrary, He sees it as something that is essentially dependent upon a Higher Power. But, so what? What effect does this have? Actually, it has a tremendous effect. In our forthcoming discussions on divine unity, it will become clear what effect this particular worldview and understanding of the human condition has on the way in which we configure our lives.

And, when we refer to the verses of the Qur'an about the Creator of the cosmos, we see that the Qur'an says exactly this. Here, we will look at two particular extracts from the Qur'an. The first is a well-known verse from *Sūrat al-Baqarah*, known as *Ayat al-Kursī*[3]–the first part of *Ayat al-Kursī* is about this topic. It begins: 'Allah, there is no god except Him'–'Allah', there is no single translation which does justice to the meaning of this name, but what is 'Allah'? God. Who is God? That being whom 'there is no god except Him', there is none worshipped save Him. The word 'god' (*ilāh*) means 'that which is worshipped' (*maʿbūd*). 'God' means any being which the human being venerates as holy and sanctified, any being to which he surrenders his will, that which he sees as the most important thing in his life, or that which he sees as a source of blessings for himself. This is what the Qur'an calls a 'god'. That is why a person who sees his own desires as the most important thing in his life is said to have taken them as a god.[4] Someone who allows the affairs of his life to be directed by a vain and tyrannical person, is said to have taken Satan as his god. Someone who blindly follows the traditions and customs of his ancestors has made those traditions and customs into his god. Whenever a human

3 Q2:255.

4 See Q25:43 and Q45:23–'Have you seen him who has taken his desire to be his god?'

being submits to something without question and allows it to govern his life, he has made that thing into a god.

So when we say, 'there is no god except Him'–there is none worshipped except Him–what does this mean? Does it mean there is nothing worshipped in this world except God? There are thousands upon thousands of things that men worship in this world! There were three hundred and sixty of them housed in the Kaʿbah alone before the Prophet came–three hundred and sixty different idols. There are at least as many living idols in this world who rule over other human beings. So how can we say there is no god except Him!? Therefore, when we say, 'there is no god except Him', this means there is no *real* god except Him, there is none *worthy* of being called 'god' except Him, and there is no *true* god except Him. In other words, if you give anyone divinity–in the sense that we have defined it above–or take anyone as an object of worship except Him, you have sinned. You have gone against the truth, because there is no one in existence worthy of being worshipped or called 'god' except Him.

'Allah, there is no god except Him'–what is this Allah, 'the one true god', like? We are given some of His qualities: 'the Living One' (*al-ḥayy*)–all are dead, everything else is dead. Only He is alive. This is obvious in the case of inanimate objects, but even living things are dead compared to Him. Living things which at one time were nothing, then came to be, then will again return to nothing...living things whose life is always under threat...living things whose life might be snuffed out by the slightest thing...how can we call such things 'living'? The truly living is the one who lives eternally, who is life itself, who bestows the gift and blessing of life upon other creatures–the truly living is God. 'The Living One.' Then, 'the All-sustainer'–the One who subsists and causes others to subsist. The One whose life is eternal, everlasting and without end. The One by whose life all other living things are live. And, if He were not to exist or if He were not to will it, no living thing would remain in the world–'the All-sustainer.'

'Neither drowsiness befalls Him nor sleep'–he does not need rest, let alone sleep. What does this mean? It means that He is never heedless or unaware, not even for a second. Not even for a moment. Other beings–false gods–are sometimes (or even always) heedless. When they claim to know things or to possess special insight, this is always false, for they are–in fact–overwhelmed by heedlessness and ignorance.

'Have you not regarded those who have changed God's blessing with ingratitude, and landed their people in the house of ruin? Hell, which they shall enter, and it is an evil abode!'[5] Imam al-Kāẓim (a) recited this verse for Hārūn al-Rashīd. It says that those who deny God's blessings will take themselves, their people and their followers to the house of ruin and nothingness. And where is this house of ruin and nothingness? It is Hell! They go to Hell themselves, and their followers are taken to Hell with them. The Imam recited this to Hārūn and said: 'This is about you.'[6] Now, if Hārūn was not heedless, then why would he lead his followers into Hell? Therefore, it is clear. All gods beside God are overwhelmed by heedlessness.

The one who is never overcome by heedlessness, He is the true ruler of the cosmos. That is God. 'Neither drowsiness befalls Him nor sleep.' It appears that 'drowsiness' (*sinah*) means to doze or nap lightly, while 'sleep' (*nawm*) means a heavy sleep. This verse negates both states from God Almighty. The question is, why does the Qur'an mention this here? Below, we will see why. It is because every remark about divine unity (*tawḥīd*) and every point about divine unity either serves to negate divinity from everything other than God or to highlight the deficiencies and shortcomings of everything besides God. The general rule is that whatever is affirmed for God is negated from those who claim divinity besides Him. Whatever is said about divine

5 Q14:28–29.

6 See *Tafsīr Nūr al-Thaqalayn*, commentary on Q14:28.

unity, it is those things that must be reflected in the practical life of those who believe in monotheism and worship God. All the qualities and subtleties of divine unity must be made manifest in the life of the monotheist person, as we shall see in later chapters. Therefore, 'the Living One, the All-sustainer' is an allusion to the heedlessness, slumber and unawareness of the false gods and their worshippers.

'Neither drowsiness befalls Him nor sleep. To Him belongs whatever is in the heavens and whatever is on the earth. Who is it that may intercede with Him except with His permission?' In other words, there is no other power whom we can call upon, even as an intercessor to mediate with God on our behalf, that is independent of God. Even if there is someone who can intercede on the behalf of others, this too is only by God's leave. The prophets who intercede, and the saints, the Imams, the righteous, the faithful and the martyrs who intercede with God on behalf of others–they cannot do so unless they have God's permission first. They do not offer anything to mankind that God does not offer through them. Therefore, they do not represent powers independent from God's power, nor are they a court of appeal which can override God's judgements. Even if God has bestowed special affection and grace on some of His servants, they remain God's servants–nothing more.

'Who is it that may intercede with Him except with His permission? He knows that which is before them and that which is behind them, and they do not comprehend anything of His knowledge except what He wishes.'

See how the whole cosmos is divided into two levels. One level is the level of God. The other level is the level of all other beings. In this latter level, all of the atoms of the cosmos are the servants of God, and they all share the same rank. What I mean to say is that, at the level of servanthood, there is no distinction between any two beings in this universe. Insofar as all beings are servants of God–insofar as they are under God's power and in His grasp–they are all the same. All of them! Even the greatest beings in the universe, the mightiest and most important human beings in history, including the Prophet of Islam, *insofar as they are God's servants*, are the same as all the atoms of the cosmos! To the extent that those atoms are under God's dominion, the Prophet of Islam is also under His dominion. It is not the case that prophets have special ranks–that they are great persons, because they are great, because they are special, because they are God's beloved, because they are dear to God–it is not the case that they have a power that is independent of God. On the contrary, they are servants who act in complete submission to their Lord, no matter how great or important they might be. During *tashahhud* in our daily prayers we say: 'I bear witness that Muḥammad is His servant and messenger' (*ashhadu anna Muḥammadan ʿabduhū wa rasūluh*). Notice that we place 'servant' before 'messenger', which means that first and foremost–before any other rank or status–the Prophet is God's servant.

'His seat [of power] embraces the heavens and the earth, and He is not wearied by their preservation, and He is the All-exalted, the All-supreme.' What do you understand from this verse overall? By this, I mean you should focus on the verse's basic meaning while putting aside its subtleties and finer points, of which there are many, because you or I might grasp one or two of these, while tens (or even hundreds) of others lie hidden from the understanding of all but God's most elect servants. For instance, with regard to the phrase 'Allah, there is no god except Him', Imam Zayn al-ʿĀbidīn grasps some subtle and precise elements of the verse that you and I will miss. So, putting aside these points, putting aside any social or doctrinal issues that might be contained herein, what is the overall impression that this verse leaves on us?

In short, what does this verse tell us about Islam's view of God? It tells us that throughout existence, there is a power named 'God'–a transcendent locus of knowledge, power and life–and, in contrast to this awesome and limitless power, stand all other phenomena in the cosmos. Without exception, every other being stands in a state of neediness and a state of servanthood towards this power. There is no distinction between any of the denizens of the universe with regard to their status as servants of this power. From the tiniest particles to the greatest galaxies, from the righteous to the wicked, from the lowest creatures to the highest humans–all, without exception, are in a state of utter submission towards that Absolute Existence, or whatever other formula you wish to use to express this reality.

However, being cognisant of this fact has consequences for our understanding of the Islamic ideology, for our understanding of Islam's practical blueprint for society. Let me give you an example so that you know we are not engaged in merely abstract theorising: When we know that all human beings are completely and utterly equal in relation to this Higher Power, it makes no sense to build a statue in the likeness of a Roman emperor for people to bow down in front of. We would say: Why? What is the point of such a thing? Is this great emperor not one of God's servants? If so, then why are you bowing before him and venerating him like a god? Is there some other level of being beneath that of God's servants? Aren't both you and he on the same level? So why do you behave like this?

You see, if we looked at the world in this way, with this worldview, then what becomes of the emperors, kings, noblemen to whom throughout history had millions upon millions of slaves and servants bound to their will? Who could say: 'I am of a different makeup to ordinary people. I am different. I am superior. They must bow down to me. I must place my foot on their necks. I was made to rule and command. They were made to serve and obey. I was created noble and fortunate. They were created ill-fated. I am the servant of a superior God and they are the servants of an inferior one. Just as the Israelites used to say. They would say: Our God is the God of the cosmos, Yahweh, and Yahweh has chosen the Israelites as His people and blessed them more than anyone else. Similarly, Hinduism says that society is divided into four classes, and each class has a particular deity, and each class has been created from a different source. By contrast, what does Islam say? Islam's pure monotheism says that all contingent beings–everything that exists besides God–have come from the same source, from one origin, from one power, who created them and shaped them. All of them are servants of this power. All are captives of this power. All must obey this power. No one has the right to place his head beneath the foot of another, nor does anyone have the right to place his foot on the neck of another. In other words, no one should consider himself innately superior to anyone else. Why? Because both the rich and the poor, the mighty and the weak, the high and the low, are servants of the same God and there is no difference between these servants in their innate human dignity.

'To Him belongs whatever is in the heavens and whatever is on the earth. Who is it that may intercede with Him except with His permission?' Who is closer to him? Who has any power against him? Who is capable of claiming their independence as a being when confronted by His being? That's right, 'except with His permission'– there are intercessors, but only those whom he has permitted. He never permits the tyrants to intercede, but he permits the Imams to do so. He never grants those who sow corruption the proximity and permission that intercession brings, but rather grants this to the prophets, the saints, the righteous, the martyrs and those who have attained a high rank in spirituality; those servants who have lived bitter and toilsome lives in this world, but whose spirits are strong; who strove to fulfil their moral duties; who endured hardship and difficulty in order to do the right thing; such people as these can intercede with God. And the reason why they can intercede with God is because they worked harder in his service, because they saw themselves as under God's power more than others did. No one served God at the time of the Prophet like the Prophet himself did. No one served God at the time of the Commander of the Faithful as the Commander of the Faithful did. No one served God at the time of Imam Zayn al-ʿĀbidīn as Imam Zayn al-ʿĀbidīn did. It is because the Prophet was the best of men, because ʿAlī was the best of men, because Zayn al-ʿĀbidīn was the best of men that they can intercede–not because any one people is better than any other people! It is because they served God more than they enjoy a higher status in His eyes. It is because they served God more that they are better. So, in a general sense, this verse–*Āyat al-Kursī*–means that when they stand before the Lord of the Worlds, all beings, all creations–the whole cosmos!–is in a state of submission and obedience to Him. And whoever wishes to be closer to Him should strive to serve him better. This is the first verse.

The next verse is in *Sūrah Maryam*: 'They say, "The All-beneficent has taken a son!"'[7] Different religions have claimed this in various ways: The Christians in one way, the Jews in another, the idol-worshippers of the Quraysh and the Arabian peninsula in another way still, and idol-worshippers elsewhere in a way of their own as well. Some say that He has daughters. Others say that he has a son. Some say He has sons and daughters. Some say He has one. Others say He has many. Some say He has a whole family! 'They say, "The All-beneficent has taken a son!"' Why have they said that God has a child? Pay attention to this point: The claim God has a child, which was made by Christians, Jews and idolaters, essentially means that amongst the creatures of this world and the denizens of the cosmos, there is a person or persons whose relationship with God is not one of a servant to a master–do you see?–but of a child to a parent. He is the master's *son*, not the master's servant, even if he is not the master himself.

According to the Qur'an, the Jews said that the Prophet Ezra was the son of God.[8] This would mean that if all of the beings of the cosmos

---

7 Q19:88.

8 See Q9:30.

were the servants of God, Ezra is excluded from this category. He is not one of God's servants, but rather God's son and God's beloved. The Christians say the same thing with regards to Jesus. The idolaters said that Lāt, ʿUzzā and Manāt were God's daughters.[9] The ancient Greeks and Romans believed that the gods had many offspring. In reality, what these worldviews do is they take the two levels we have established–God and His servants–and made them into three levels: God, His servants, and His children. This verse in *Sūrah Maryam* negates this worldview. Now let us turn to what follows:

First, God says: 'They say, "The All-beneficent has taken a son!"'

Then he says: 'You have certainly advanced something hideous!'[10] See what God says about this? What a horrendous thing you have said! What a dangerous belief you have presented!

He continues: 'The heavens are about to be rent apart at it, the earth to split open, and the mountains to collapse into bits that they should ascribe a son to the All-beneficent!'[11]

Clearly this is a very important issue. God is not prone to emotional overreaction when confronted with bad words and deeds. However, whatever God gives to people as a system of belief works to bring about the fulfilment of the divine goals for Creation. Conversely, those beliefs God negates as corrupt are those which lay down the roots of corruption in human society. Believing that God has a son, in the same way as a king has a prince, is to believe in an intermediate level of existence between God and humanity, to believe in something half-divine and half-human, and this has serious negative repercussions for human society. However, these consequences can only be uncovered gradually through an exploration of the concept of divine unity. But, in short, such beliefs often serve as a pretext for turning

---

9 See 53:19–20.

10 Q19:89.

11 Q19:90–91.

people away from being servants of God and making them servants of someone else.

'It does not behoove the All-beneficent to take a son. There is none in the heavens and the earth but he comes to the All-beneficent as a servant. Certainly He has counted them and numbered them precisely.' This is the second verse I wanted to discuss.

Now, to sum up: What have we covered in our discussion today? We asked what was the meaning of divine unity (*tawḥīd*) in the Islamic worldview, and we studied divine unity as one of the fundamental constituents of this worldview. Tomorrow, God-willing, we will study divine unity as a constituent of the Islamic ideology: We will see what the difference between the two is. This is a preliminary to that. This is a foundation for that. The Islamic worldview is this: The world, the cosmos, existence is such. Now, let us see what message this conveys to us? What are we supposed to do with this knowledge? What is Islam's plan for our lives? What is it to put divine unity into action? This is divine unity in the Islamic ideology.

Outcomes of Understanding Tawḥīd

Friday 10th Ramadan 1394
27th September 1974

وَمِنَ النَّاسِ مَنْ يَتَّخِذُ مِنْ دُونِ اللَّهِ أَنْدَادًا يُحِبُّونَهُمْ كَحُبِّ اللَّهِ وَالَّذِينَ آمَنُوا أَشَدُّ حُبًّا لِلَّهِ وَلَوْ يَرَى الَّذِينَ ظَلَمُوا إِذْ يَرَوْنَ الْعَذَابَ أَنَّ الْقُوَّةَ لِلَّهِ جَمِيعًا وَأَنَّ اللَّهَ شَدِيدُ الْعَذَابِ (١٦٥)

'Among the people are those who set up compeers besides God, loving them as if loving God but the faithful have a more ardent love for God though the wrongdoers will see, when they sight the punishment, that power, altogether, belongs to God, and that God is severe in punishment.'
- Sūrat al-Baqarah (2):165.

The theist says that beyond what we see lies a reality higher and greater than the world of perception and that, were this reality not to exist, none of the phenomena we perceive would have ever come to be. On the other hand, the materialist says no, on the contrary, we can only believe in or affirm that which we can see, empirical scientific investigations have yielded no trace or evidence of this being that you believe in. This debate between theists and materialists is dealt with fully in the works and discussions dedicated to this topic.

What we believe is that materialists today–not historical ones who lived, died and turned to dust many centuries ago, such as Democritus–even if they claim that God does not exist and that there is no reality beyond the world of matter, actually express this position out of intellectual and spiritual frustration with the theistic school of thought. When they argue that it is only possible to build a modern world, govern the human race, establish justice and efface divisions under the auspices of a single materialist school of thought, it is in this sense that they are turning away from the theistic school of thinking–not because they believe God does not exist. If we look closely at the thinking of some of those today who were converted to this view fifty or sixty years ago, we see that this is the case. It is not because they have anything against God, or that they have any convincing intellectual argument that God does not exist, to reject God or to deny Him. No, this is not usually how such people argue their case. After all, there is no argument *against* God's existence now and there never has been. You cannot find anyone who says: 'God does not exist and here is the proof.' You cannot find a single person who claims this! Amongst all the materialists of the world, from the earliest days of human history until now, you cannot find anyone who says they have proven that God does not exist. Instead, what they say is that it has not yet been proven to them that He *does* exist, or they do not accept that the arguments for His existence work. The Qur'an alludes to this with the phrase 'and they only make conjectures',[12] as they cannot provide any evidence to deny God's existence.

Therefore, they do not reject God on the basis of any philosophical arguments advanced by the materialist school of thought. Instead, what the materialist school claims is that it is best suited to managing the affairs of the human race and governing the world. This is a social ideology: Materialists say that they are best able to put a stop

12 Q45:24.

to injustice, they are best able to end inequality and division, and they are best able to end tyranny once and for all. They argue that religion is incapable of achieving these ends. Why do they say that religion cannot accomplish this? Because they do not know anything about religion–in the everyday sense of the word–except what the masses believe, except the traditional blind faith that they see all around them. In short, they know nothing about true religion. If you ask them: 'What is religion?' They will name some practices and say: 'This is religion.' They will say: Religion is a drug. Religion is a tool of the oppressor. Religion cannot help the downtrodden. So leave it!

Of course, when a person is confronted by this logic, the correct response is to say: 'You're right! If you find a religion that helps the oppressor, that supports the tyrant, that never gives aid to the oppressed, that never helps the downtrodden, that whether now or in the future does not alleviate an ounce of human suffering–then, on our behalf, if you find such a religion, no matter where it is, reject it. Do not accept such a religion for even a moment! This is because, if a religion is from God, it will not be like this: God did not send religion without any rhyme or reason! On the contrary, there are ways to identify a truly godly religion: It has certain features and characteristics–it meets certain criteria! If a religion meets these criteria, we accept it. If it does not, we do not. When we speak about the prophethood of our Prophet–God willing–we will discuss this point in more detail.

The Qur'an says: 'Certainly we sent Our apostles with manifest proofs, and We sent down with them the Book and the Balance.'[13] In other words, God sent the prophets to mankind with clear evidence and gave them a collection of ideas and an array of practical tools, tools which would allow them to judge between people in their daily disputes and disagreements. Why did God do this? Notice He

13 Q57:25.

says 'Our apostles' (*rusulanā*), not just one prophet: Not just Moses, Jesus or the Prophet of Islam. 'We sent Our apostles'–God sent all the prophets with this goal, with this ideal, with this purpose. What was this purpose? 'So that mankind may maintain justice.' So that people may have a fair and just existence in this world. If you see a religion that opposes this general philosophy of divine religions, then you should know that it is either not originally from God or it has been corrupted by people. If you see someone walking in the opposite direction to God's prophets and messengers, know with certainty that this person has not received God's revelation. This much is clear.

So, O materialist! O you who say that religion cannot possibly govern human societies! I ask you: Which religion? The religion of Islam? The true Islam? The revelation of Muḥammad (s)? The way of ʿAlī? You believe that these are incapable of the governance of human affairs? Ok, then prove it. Where is the evidence for this? When Islam came and erased division, when Islam rejected class divisions, when Islam established an equitable division of wealth amongst the people, when it improved people's standard of living and provided them with opportunities for growth, when it took the reins of power out of the hands of tyrants and handed them to the just divine law, when it raised up the oppressed, the downtrodden, the slaves, when it took people who were willing to commit the worst outrages for vanity or wealth...when Islam took this abased human and ennobled him, dignified him, and bestowed upon him the best human and moral virtues–all of this, under the auspices of a single wise and just order. So where is your proof?

The Prophet did not just educate individuals. He did not take people one by one and sit them down and utter slogans to them until they became good, until they became human–this is not how he did it. He was not a preacher–he did not just sit and preach to people. This wouldn't have had any effect. On the contrary, he created a social order. He laid down solid foundations for an Islamic society at a time of ignorance and formed them according to a particular plan and shape. Then, through this framework, he brought people forth. He brought humans forth. It was in this way that he made humans humane. So, if you say that your ideals are not aligned with the religion of Islam–meaning the true religion of Islam–when it has these features, when it has elevated mankind with justice and safety, when it has looked after the fundamental needs of the human being–this is unfair in the utmost.

If a thinker grew up in an outwardly Christian environment and knew nothing of the religion except corrupt practices like the selling of indulgences or the false forgiveness of sins, perhaps he had the right to form this opinion of religion. But you, who live a hundred, or eighty, or fifty years after him, at a time when Islam is more or less showing its true self, and producing the most wonderful and dignified manifestations of humanity the world has seen, you do not have the right to say the same thing about Islam as he does about Christianity. If this is what you mean to do, then this is being intellectually dishonest.

On the other hand, if you say that surface religions, false religions, religions with a pleasant exterior but a corrupt core, religions which promote indolence, subjugation, prejudice, division and conflict... the kind of religions that tell the poor if they are not wealthy, if they do not have money, they should not strive to better their lot in life. While, at the same time, they tell the wealthy to give a little of their riches to the church or this holy man and, in return, all of the sins they committed in amassing this money will be forgiven. If this is what you mean by 'religion' then we agree with you, and both of us are following what the Qur'an says: 'O you who have faith! Indeed many of the rabbis and priests wrongfully eat up the people's wealth, and bar from the way of God.'[14] Notice that they do not just consume wealth,

14 Q9:34.

but they actually hold people back from growth and development. This is what the Qur'an says, and this is what you say. Therefore, we are in agreement with one another! Any religion that behaves in this way is not a true religion. When a religion is like this, those who have no religion are better off without it! This is why sometimes it is those who have no faith who refuse to aid the wrongdoing and oppression of others, while these kinds of pseudo-religions become a tool, a stick, and a weapon in the hands of the oppressor.

So, to sum up, the doctrine of divine unity is the answer to a question: Does God exist or not? Is there anything beyond the material world? Is there a higher power or not? As a response to this question, the theist says one thing and the materialist says another. This is the root of the conflict between the two schools of thought, on which a multitude of works have been written. However, to delve further than this is beyond the scope of this lecture. For our present discussion, what we have already said suffices as a preamble.

Now bear in mind that if we cannot cover the entirety of this topic in one lecture, that's OK, because there will be further lectures in which to discuss it. Tomorrow, God-willing, we will go into more detail. But before going into detail, you must first grasp a general overview of the subject and that is what we are presenting now.

Onto the next point, something that everyone must consider when discussing topics of Islamic thought is that when you discuss something like divine unity, you should not discuss it as the answer to a dry theoretical question: This is something which knowing it or not knowing it has a direct impact on one's life, because it is something fundamental and determinative. Let me explain what I mean by this.

Let us say you are travelling somewhere. You have a companion with you to keep you company and, as the two of you drive, you talk about things. You say 'The soil on either side of the road appears barren, nothing can grow here.' He says 'On the contrary, the soil here is perfect for growing such and such a crop.' You say one thing, he says another. You bring your evidence, he brings his. Now, how important is this discussion? You are travelling. Your car goes at seventy miles per hour down this road. Now is not the time to stop and test the soil, nor is it the time to buy a plot of land along the road for you to come back and toil on, nor is it the time to gather evidence and expert opinions to support your position. This discussion has no relevance for you! It is an answer to a question, nothing more. Even if you somehow managed to prove that the land is barren and will not produce crops, or your companion proved the opposite, that it is fertile ground for growing certain crops, what difference would it make to your journey? Would you see any change in your life as a result? If you prove that the land is barren, it is not like your friend will say: 'You're right. It's barren. We should turn around and go back!' Because this question has no relevance for you. By the same token, if your travelling companion convinces you it is fertile, you're not going to suggest that you stop to offer two *rakʿats* of prayer on this rich soil! It's an irrelevant question. It doesn't matter which one of you is right, or who makes the better case for his opinion, the outcome will have no bearing whatsoever on your journey, on your future, on your friendship, on anything whatsoever. So this is one kind of discussion, one kind of question, and one kind of answer.

On the other hand, let us say the two of you are driving the same car down the same road but your friend turns to you and says 'I think the road we are on is taking us north.' When your destination is supposed to be south! You might say, 'No, this road leads south.' Again, he says one thing and you say another, and you start to debate which of you is right. If he turns out to be right, you need to turn your car around and go back because otherwise you're going to be heading the wrong way! On the other hand, if you turn out to be right, you have to continue going the same way down the road. In fact, maybe a little faster now that you're sure you're heading in the right direction. Now, this disagreement between the two of you has a number of effects.

First of all, the driver is going to apply the brakes and slow down a bit so you can get your bearings and work out whether or not you're going the right way for your destination. This question and answer and debate will produce a result that has a definitive effect on what you are doing. The discussion of divine unity should be seen in this way, and not in the way of the previous example.

The way in which an ordinary person, or a person who does not have any social responsibilities, or who is not committed, might discuss divine unity differs from the way in which a committed and sincere person should approach this question: Does God exist or not? OK, He does, now what? Or He doesn't, then what? What effect does this have on my life, what difference does it make for the social order? How should it be changed in light of this knowledge? If God exists, then what would become of capitalism or the superpowers that dominate the world? If someone is made president of a country and he believes in God, how would he behave? If he doesn't believe in God, how would he behave? Would it make a difference either way? The kind of belief in God that has no effect on the global economic and social order belongs to the same category of belief as believing that a certain plot of land is barren or fertile–it has no use for us. It has no impact on the world. If a country's political leader believes in God but belief in God, for him, means nothing more than answering an abstract theoretical question, then what use is this? When believing in God or being a monotheist has an effect on a political leader, on an ordinary person, on a society, or on an entire nation–this belief in God is useful; in fact, it is necessary, for it is alive. This belief in divine unity is important because of the effects it produces in the world, because of the social order it promotes, and because of the way of life it engenders. We must understand divine unity in order to address *these* issues, and this is what makes divine unity essential for modern living.

Sometimes, we imagine *tawḥīd* to be something that we only need to make clear to ourselves in our minds. When it comes to real life, this belief in divine unity has absolutely no bearing on what we do. In fact, even if this belief in divine unity might have an effect on the lives of some individuals, it never affects the life of the society as a whole. I might believe in God, but I own the same wealth, drive the same car, work for the same company, in the same factory, with the same relationship to employees, and the same relationship with the land as I would have if I didn't believe in anything at all. Let us imagine that in one of the world's great capitalist economies, there are two capitalists, two great businessmen, two captains of industry. And let us imagine that one of them believes in God, while the other is a materialist. What difference do we expect to see in their respective behaviours? Now, the person who believes in God might go to church on a Sunday and may perhaps even tithe some of his wealth so that he might be absolved of his sins and smooth his path to Paradise, but what practical difference will this make in his life? In the conditions of his factories? In his relations with his employees? In his relations with other people? In his relationship to his wealth? In the way he obtains his wealth and spends it? If the answer is 'none' then what is the difference between this belief in divine unity and idolatry?

The kind of belief in God to which Islam calls people, is the kind of belief in God that goes beyond the answer to a question. So, what is it? *Tawḥīd* in Islam is an inspiration for the kind of society that we wish to build, the direction we want this society to take, and the goals we want it to reach. This extends to people's moral duties, their duties towards God, their duties to one another, their duties to society, and their duties to all the other beings of the cosmos. This is the true meaning of belief in God. Just as A leads to B, and B leads to C, and so on until we reach Z. Divine unity does not mean to say that God is one, not two, full stop. Yes, God is one and not two, but what that *means* is that whether with regard to yourself as an individual or with regard to society as a whole, no one except God has the right to issue commands.

When we say that there is only one God, not two, this means that whatever we or anyone else has at their disposal belongs to God and that we have only been entrusted with it for a brief time. Who is ready to be a monotheist under these conditions? All your wealth is borrowed–all of it is on loan. If a friend entrusted some money to you, what would you do? You certainly wouldn't give it to anyone else without his permission. Give ten *tumāns*[15] of it to that child, to that old man, to that stranger, to that friend...put ten *tumāns* in that charity box...burn ten *tumāns*! Would you do any of this without permission from the money's rightful owner? Would you give yourself the right to dispose of this money with which you have been entrusted as you please? Of course not! A tradition says: 'All wealth belongs to God. He has entrusted it to people.' This is the logical corollary of *tawḥīd*.

If this is the kind of divine unity you believe in, then all sorts of class differences and divisions in society would be utterly meaningless to you. A society with upper and lower classes, with haves and have-nots is not a truly monotheistic society. Divine unity tells us: 'All of you are from Adam and Adam is from dust.' Your closeness to God and your priority with Him comes only from your Godwariness (*taqwā*) and nothing else; whoever best observes God's commandments is higher. Otherwise there are a thousand reasons within any given society for why divisions should exist. If you complain about someone's behaviour only to be told that he belongs to a special class of people with their own rules, this shows you have a society in which there is a division between the elite and ordinary people and, moreover, that the elite believe that they are entitled to be treated differently to everyone else. In a society where God's servants are not all on the same level and some are servants of others, this is not a society built

15 Currency in Iran.

upon *tawḥīd*. When *tawḥīd* is implemented in a society, all of God's servants are treated equally. What does this mean? It means they are all first and foremost God's servants, as we discussed yesterday. All the denizens of the cosmos, whether human beings or other kinds of beings, are servants under His dominion and all share in the same relationship of servanthood towards Him. As we said yesterday, in this framework, no one is God's child, spouse or partner and, therefore, no one is outside the sphere of His servitude. When everyone is a servant of God, it is meaningless to speak of one group being different to the rest, or to have a different kind of chain around their necks! To be a servant of God means to be free from serving everyone and everything besides God–one cannot simultaneously serve God and serve something else.

The representative sent by the Muslim armies to the imposing palace of the Sassanid Shah was a shabbily dressed Arab whose clothes were so threadbare that, had you wanted to put a value on everything he was wearing, you would not have given him a penny in exchange for it. He entered the extravagant palace of a king who had thousands of servants to wait on him and surrounded himself with generals and courtiers dressed in finery. Do you think this Arab man was afraid? Do you think he had any hesitations? Far from it. Normally, when an ordinary person is confronted by a powerful figure, they are overawed. They feel insignificant and if they want to approach such a person, it is with humility and fear. Do you think this is what happened on this occasion? Of course not! As he approached the throne of Yazdegerd in order to deliver his letter, it seems the Shah did not move to receive it. Instead his servants came to take it from the hand of the Arab. But he refused to give it to them, saying he was only to deliver it to the Shah himself. Of course, the Shah did not rise from his throne to receive the letter in person, so the Arab was forced to approach until he was standing beside the throne and could deliver the letter by hand. The Shah asked him: 'Why have you come?' The response the Arab gave is worthy of being engraved on a golden tablet and displayed in front of all humanity, so that they might know the slogan and ideal of Islam. He said: 'To free mankind from the service of servants that they might serve God.'

What does it mean to serve servants? Let me give another example from history. In one of the wars between Rome and Persia, when one of the Achaemenid kings gave the order for his soldiers to assemble, an old man approached the king and said: 'Your majesty! I have three sons who will fight for you, but please leave this one with me for I am old and frail. Permit this one to stay with me rather than come with you.' He was sent away without anything being promised to him. The next day, as the soldiers marched out and reached the city gates, the three brothers saw the fourth brother had been drawn and quartered, with his body parts displayed either side of the gates to serve as a warning to others who would ask their sons to be spared from fighting for Darius. This is what real slavery is. When people in a society do not even have the right to voice their requests, let alone make demands. When people have no right to call out for justice or stand up against division. When people have no right to want freedom for themselves and must accept the suffocating oppression as the natural and proper condition of human beings. When people live in such a society, this is the severest, ugliest and bitterest form of slavery. This is the worst form of slavery. Why? Because it is the most insidious kind. When you go and kidnap an innocent person, shave his head, and then sell him in a faraway land, this is something you have done clearly and openly–he knows he is a slave. But, when you covertly play with people's thoughts and emotions–when you manipulate their free will and decisions, you have enslaved them without them even knowing that they are slaves!

So the Arab messenger told Yazdegerd that they had come to free them from serving servants. In other words, he was saying: 'To free people from serving you, O Yazdegerd!' To free them from serving your governors, your nobles and your generals, no matter where they are. Then, once they are freed, what should they do? They are no longer the servants of Yazdegerd, so how should they live? Are they left to their own devices? No, they should be God's servants. To be a servant of God is to be free, to be dignified, to be on the road to human flourishing and perfection, to be free to make use of the means of human flourishing to any extent that they desire. This is what an Islamic society looks like. In an Islamic society, people serve God rather than the powerful. Even when Islamic society went astray in history, when it was no longer one hundred percent Islamic, it still reflected these values. Even in those years when the Muslim armies conquered Iran, the effect of the values of the Qur'an and the Prophet's teachings on the people was there. A governor would ascend the pulpit and said: 'If I go astray, correct me!' A Bedouin sitting at the foot of the pulpit stood up and said: 'If you do not do right and you go astray, I'll correct you with this sword of mine!' Did the soldiers and police come and chop off his head? Did they arrest him and throw him in prison for sedition? Did they take him away and make him disappear? Not at all, for he had said something that was both correct and logical. Freedom does not mean to be left to one's own devices, it means to follow a law that is humane and fair and which, both in the human soul and in human society, does not let a person bow to any man–not even his ruler. If the ruler speaks from God, with divine inspiration, then he is an Islamic ruler and his words are to be accepted because they are right. But if he speaks without divine inspiration, then his words are to be rejected because they are wrong.

'To free mankind from the service of servants that they might serve God, and from the narrowness of this world that they might enjoy its breadth and the breadth of the Hereafter.' In a society where people live without a correct worldview, no matter which way they look, they see only this world and its trinkets. No matter which way they look, they see only enjoyments and opportunities for selfish pursuits. Whatever they see, they see only through the lens of base animal desires and temporary material benefits. In the society ruled over by Yazdegerd, not everyone was happy with Yazdegerd–there were many unhappy with him. However, this discontent was tempered by their short-sightedness. Because their horizons were so narrow, they feared that if they made their displeasure known, they would lose what little good they had of this life. They would lose out on two more morsels of food, two more days to live and wander the streets, and because they placed such a high value on these trivial things, and loved this short life of theirs so much, they were not ready to risk it for freedom, for dignity, or for virtue. Why? Because their vision was narrow. Because their world was constrained.

But when a person becomes a Muslim, everything is a means for him–a means for what? A means to reaching a wider world–I do not say 'a better life after death'!–a world of thought and vision in which a person's own vision is made broad through God's ample generosity. Everything is a means for a person to use in order to attain God's satisfaction. The life of this world, its wealth, its trinkets, its loves... none of these have intrinsic value. It is only when they are used in God's way (*fī sabīlillāh*) that they acquire value. However, when this love, this wealth, this position, this life, this child, this honour, this status is not used in God's way or to fulfil one's moral duties, it has no value whatsoever. This world and the Hereafter are closely connected in Islamic thought. For a Muslim, this world does not have an end. But for someone who serves other servants and is a slave to false gods, this world is limited and narrow. But for the Muslim, it is wide and expansive. Death is but a gate and, when we look through this gate, we see gardens, orchards and whole worlds on the other side. A Muslim knows that there is something beyond this world, just beyond the gate. Therefore, death is not something that troubles him.

These are all manifestations and dimensions of *tawḥīd*. However, we must discuss *tawḥīd* in a much more systematic and precise way, and we will–if God wills!–in the coming days. Today, I just wanted to offer a general introduction. In reality, this has been an overview–a preliminary to a proper discussion of *tawḥīd*. However, there are other dimensions and angles we have yet to consider and I hope that we will be able to do them justice in the coming days. In any case, this was one aspect of *tawḥīd* today, which is a reflection of the teachings of the Qur'an and the divine religions.

With regard to the verses we looked at, it is very interesting to see how *Āyat al-Kursī* is almost a slogan for *tawḥīd*. Perhaps this is the reason why it is recommended to be recited on so many different occasions, so that this slogan of divine unity will always be fresh in a person's mind and so that, just as it describes God, it will be ever-living and always-subsisting therein! The verse I introduced in today's lecture is also from *Sūrat al-Baqarah*; it provides a visualisation of the Day of Judgement which is deeply connected to the matter of divine unity:

'Among the people are those who set up compeers besides God'–meaning they take up partners for God, whether these partners are human or otherwise–'loving them as if loving God'–here, the Qur'an opens a parenthesis, because it is not talking about love. However, it is talking about their love in relation to God, so the Qur'an opens a parenthesis and remarks: 'and those who believe have a more ardent love for God', in other words the true believers love God more than all this world of appearances, more than all the things that attract human hearts, more than all false gods, more than the god of ego and desires; more than all of the objects of worship that are set up above human societies, if you are a true believer, you love God more.

'But the faithful have a more ardent love for God though the wrongdoers will see, when they sight the punishment, that power, altogether, belongs to God, and that God is severe in punishment.'

Suddenly, the Qur'an paints for us a scene from the Resurrection: When all the creatures are brought back to life and gathered together on the Day of Judgement–the disbelievers, the wrongdoers, those who have served other gods, God's own servants–and all the beings present on that day (whether we know them or not), all of them are gathered together. All the means of divine punishment and divine mercy are visible to them–we cannot even conceive of these here and now; we cannot comprehend anything about the next world while we are in this one. However, at a basic level, we can understand that there are means for punishment and immiseration, and that everyone is present seeing them–the good and the bad. Suddenly, the tyrants and wrongdoers realise that all power on that day belongs to God.

This is something amazing! In this world, look around: Everyone appears to have some measure of power. Everyone can do something. People in higher positions in society have more power, but even those on the lower rungs have *some* power. Everyone has some degree of ability and power. Everyone can do something–especially the tyrant who has power over everyone else. The wrongdoer who serves the tyrant–who is himself a tyrant by extension–also imagines that he has power, because he is connected to someone with even more power. He is like a fox that has tied its tail to that of a camel! This is how this world is. However, on the Day of Judgement, when everyone is assembled, everyone who looks will be able to see clearly that they have no power, no authority, and no ability whatsoever. All power is in God's hand: '"To whom does the sovereignty belong today?" "To God, the One, the All-paramount!"'[16] And so, when the wrongdoer–whether he is a wrongdoer because he wronged others or because he wronged himself–looks around, he is awestruck! All of these words, these claims, these vanities, these palaces, these lives...all of them are nothing now. No one can do anything here!

---

16 Q40:16.

In this midst of this striking scene, two groups will be visible; one group worshipped the other group in that they obeyed them unconditionally and unquestioningly. On the Day of Judgement, these two groups will face one another and argue together. 'The wrongdoers'–who we said are those who served other than God, which is how some of the classical Shīʿī commentators on the Qur'an interpreted this phrase–'will see, when they sight the punishment'–what will they see? '*That power, altogether, belongs to God and God is severe in punishment.*' And what will happen when they see it? The answer is implicit: They will regret their past behaviour. They will grieve for their treatment of others, for oppressing and tyrannising them, because on the Day of Judgement they realise that their power is gone. But, if they really have any insight, they will see that even in this world they did not have any power. 'When those who were followed will disown the followers and they will sight the punishment'–this is when someone like Yazdegerd will say: 'O God! O my Lord! Those who you saw serving me in my worldly life, I have nothing to do with them! You must not think I have any connection to them, they who took me up as a partner to You! They were wrong to make anything Your partner and I want nothing to do with them!' Imagine how his subjects must feel upon hearing this? We gave up our world and our afterlife for this crook! And now, on the Day of Judgement, he says he has nothing to do with us! What is this verse saying?

'When those who were followed will disown the followers', the leaders will repudiate those who followed them, 'and they will sight the punishment while all their means of recourse will be cut off, and when the followers will say, "Had there been another turn for us, we would disown them as they disown us [now]!" (As they disown them today, on the Day of Judgement.) Thus shall God show them their deeds as regrets for themselves, and they shall not leave the Fire.'[17]

17 Q2:166–167.

And this is the lesson we find in this verse, namely that those who served masters other than God in this world and let themselves be made slaves to them, who accepted something that was against *tawḥīd*, the Qur'an considers them followers of the wrongdoers and therefore, deserving of punishment.

Worship Belongs Only to God

Saturday 11th Ramadan 1394
28th September 1974

هُنَالِكَ تَبْلُو كُلُّ نَفْسٍ مَا أَسْلَفَتْ وَرُدُّوا إِلَى اللَّهِ مَوْلَاهُمُ
الْحَقِّ وَضَلَّ عَنْهُمْ مَا كَانُوا يَفْتَرُونَ (٣٠) قُلْ مَنْ يَرْزُقُكُمْ
مِنَ السَّمَاءِ وَالْأَرْضِ أَمَّنْ يَمْلِكُ السَّمْعَ وَالْأَبْصَارَ وَمَنْ
يُخْرِجُ الْحَيَّ مِنَ الْمَيِّتِ وَيُخْرِجُ الْمَيِّتَ مِنَ الْحَيِّ وَمَنْ يُدَبِّرُ
الْأَمْرَ فَسَيَقُولُونَ اللَّهُ فَقُلْ أَفَلَا تَتَّقُونَ (٣١)

'There every soul will examine what it has sent in advance, and they will be returned to God, their real master, and what they used to fabricate will forsake them. Say, "Who provides for you out of the sky and the earth? Who controls [your] hearing and sight, and who brings forth the living from the dead and brings forth the dead from the living, and who directs the command?" They will say, "God." Say, "Will you not then be wary?"'

- Sūrat Yūnus (10):30–31

As we have said previously, doing justice to the topic of divine unity in the Qur'an requires an exceptionally long and detailed discussion. It is perhaps the topic dealt with at greatest length and in most detail by the Qur'an itself, even more so than the topic of prophethood (*nubuwwah*), which the Qur'an treats at length, all while presenting stories and accounts from the lives of the prophets as a means of delivering moral lessons to its audience. This is because the topic of prophethood ultimately rests on that of divine unity, God's existence and, in particular, the negation of idolatry and polytheism. Therefore, there is arguably no other topic dealt with in so many ways in the Book of God, both in terms of the tone adopted when discussing it and in terms of the number of verses addressed to it. Therefore, taking into account the scope and detail of this topic in the Qur'an, we will confine ourselves here to discuss a few key issues in light of a handful of verses we have selected for this purpose–it is not possible for us to touch on every single issue related to divine unity in the Qur'an in the course of these lectures.

In our mind, it seems that if we accept that divine unity is not only a way of looking at the world or an impression we have formed of reality, but also a framework for action or an *ideology*–something we have elucidated to some extent in previous lectures–or, to put it another way, if we accept that *tawḥīd* is a system of belief that necessarily leads to the existence of certain moral duties and responsibilities for the human being, we must ask the following: Can we find these duties, which are lay at the heart of the doctrine of divine unity, laid out for us in the form of clear articles, paragraphs and headings in the Qur'an and the traditions of Islam, which we can then follow line-by-line, chapter-by-chapter? I implore you, brothers and sisters, those of you who have some prior understanding of this topic–which I think most of you have–please pay close attention to what I am saying and ponder on it so you can grasp my meaning properly.

To reiterate, what I am asking is this: If *tawḥīd* is a doctrine that necessarily engenders certain duties, responsibilities and obligations, which are placed upon the shoulders of the one who believes in it, then this person must find out what these duties are! Is the person's responsibility, in sum, to accept this belief with their heart, mind and tongue? Is the belief *itself* a duty? Or is this duty something whose domain lies beyond the heart and mind but rather pertains to one's personal conduct? For example, when someone believes in divine unity, this belief places a series of obligations on his shoulders, such as the fact he must pray, that he must invoke God's name at the beginning of everything he does, that he must only slaughter a sheep in the name of God, and so on–is this the extent of these duties? Or, is it something more than this? Does divine unity place responsibilities not only on the individual believer but on the society of believers as a whole–responsibilities which address the most important, universal and fundamental issues of any society? Like what? Like government. Like economics. Like international relations. Like relations between members of the society–the fundamental principles that govern the life of any human society! We believe that the responsibilities created by *tawḥīd* and placed upon the shoulders of the believer are of this kind–that these responsibilities extend to every aspect of society and deal with its most fundamental issues.

I just want to say one thing so that, once we get into the meat of the discussion and start dealing with more specific issues, we can always understand the difference between the constitution of a society founded on the principle of divine unity and that of a society not founded on the principle of divine unity. It is not the case that if a law is enacted in a society of divine unity, that if the same law or ten others like it are enacted in another society, those laws are necessarily *tawḥīdī* as well. No, the configuration of a *tawḥīdī* society is such that all the elements of that society and all of its organs are founded on the principle of divine unity and true monotheism. Any society not organised in this way is utterly different. And, in a word, this is what we are going to discuss today: the social order of divine unity.

The social order or societal configuration of a *tawḥīdī* society is something utterly distinct and different from–and, sometimes but not always, implacably opposed to–that of a non-*tawḥīdī* society. This is what we want to discuss. As, when it comes to the core of the social system and the organs of society, there are discussions and debates which we can attempt to understand with the help of the new terminologies spreading through the world today (and even more so, with the help of the Qur'an and the collections of traditions). This is our overall topic.

To be more precise, however, what we want to do is view divine unity as a treaty made up of individual articles and examine each of these articles one by one. What articles does the treaty of *tawḥīd* contain? Just as when two groups, sides or individuals have held negotiations with one another, they produce a binding document detailing what each side must do in the form of a compact or treaty. In this case, it is the believers of the world who have a treaty with their Creator–they are obliged to God to undertake the articles contained in this treaty.

The first article in this treaty is expounded clearly by the verse we want to discuss today. Based on the principle of *tawḥīd*, people do not have the right to make anyone or anything other than God the object of their worship and obedience. This is the first article in the treaty of divine unity. However, when we say 'anyone' or 'anything', this gives this article a very broad scope. So let us see what we mean by the terms, 'worship' and 'obedience'.

God says in the Qur'an: 'Did I not exhort you, O children of Adam, saying, "Do not worship Satan. He is indeed your manifest enemy!"'[18] I have explained the meaning of 'worshipping Satan' in other discussions, elsewhere. Satan here does not necessarily refer to Iblīs or some malevolent force that you cannot see or touch but that follows man wherever he goes. The meaning of 'Satan' (*shayṭān*) is much broader than this. 'Satan' denotes any baleful power that exists outside of the human being. An evil power, but only one that is outside of a person's own existence. This is what 'Satan' means

18 Q36:60.

here. Just as the lower self (*nafs*)–which is the partner of Satan, his servant, and one of the tools at his disposal, could be defined as follows: Evil forces that exist *within* the human being. The self which prompts man to evil (*al-nafs al-ammārah bi-al-sūʾ*) and Satan–one is a power inside the human being, one is a power outside of him. These two powers corrupt a person, lead them astray and cause them to become fallen in nature. Satan refers to anything that is outside of your own being that tries to lead you away from perfection, to prompt you to commit evil, to kindle wrongdoing; the thorns, wolves and thieves that lie in wait for the unwary travel, or that which calls these harmful beings–this is Satan. When we speak about the Prophet and prophethood in a later lecture, we will see that all the prophets whom God sent had enemies in the form of Satans from amongst the jinn and men.[19] However, we will also look at these enemies and see who exactly they were–what kind of people were they? Which groups and classes in society did they belong to? So, 'Satan' in this sense is very broad indeed!

'Do not worship Satan'–what does this mean? It means do not serve, obey or do as bid by these evil forces. This is the meaning of divine unity. Of course, I do not mean that this encapsulates all of divine unity in every aspect, as there are other dimensions to it which we must also discuss, but this is one of the core elements of *tawḥīd*: to not obey, to not serve, to not take up these burdens.

There is a tradition that pertains to a number of topics, including this one. It is narrated from Imam al-Bāqir in our reliable collections of traditions, one of which is *Uṣūl al-Kāfī*. It is a *ḥadīth al-qudsī*, meaning that God is meant to be the speaker, which reflects what we have just been saying. It reads: 'I will surely punish every flock in Islam who believed in the authority of any tyrannical leader who was not

19 See Q6:112: 'That is how for every prophet We appointed as enemy the devils from among humans and jinn'.

appointed by God, even if this flock were righteous and pious in their personal conduct. And I will surely forgive every flock in Islam who believed in the authority of any just leader appointed by God, even if this flock were wrongdoers and sinners in their personal conduct.' The general meaning of this tradition is that obeying any power not appointed by God as God's representative, obeying any centre that does not receive inspiration from the centre of Divine Power, is either on the verge of idolatry or idolatry itself; this is the case even if the people who are tested in this manner and who go astray in this manner are otherwise good and pious people in their personal conduct. This test is so important that God will deprive those who fail of His mercy and kindness. He will punish and chastise them!

Why would God do this? Because obeying someone or something besides God, serving anything besides God, contradicts the very purpose for which God created the human being. It runs contrary to human flourishing and growth. It deprives the human being of his freedom and his wisdom–the freedom and wisdom he needs to attain the apex of his existence. If this freedom is not there, then the human being is a prisoner bound in fetters, who cannot take flight towards perfection, who cannot reach the destination for which God created him–he cannot grow, he cannot develop. He is like a plant strangled by weeds. He is like a plant held back from growing and flourishing. And when a plant cannot grow, it will not flower, and it will not bear fruit. And what use is a plant that cannot bear fruit? Why should such a plant exist? Was it not planted in the orchard in order to bear fruit? So obeying someone or something other than God is something which harms the human being. In any case, there are numerous verses of the Qur'an dealing with this.

As I was scanning through the Qur'an, I found the verses we will be discussing today. Now, let us get to the point of the lecture and examine these verses. We must make ourselves familiar with the tune of *tawḥīd* in the Qur'an. Unfortunately, when it comes to learning about Islam, we often find ourselves far from the Qur'an or we are taken in by all manner of nice-sounding beliefs that are prevalent amongst people but lack any real basis. Worse still, these are often accompanied by superstitions and falsehoods. This means that these beliefs crumble when they are exposed to the waves of materialism. And, if we are not taken in by such beliefs, we sometimes end up at the opposite end of the spectrum and find ourselves obsessed with abstract arguments that are not only lacking in spirit but lacking in any practical upshot in the realm of divine unity.

How many abstract, philosophical discussions there are that have no practical use! Do you see how much the theologians discussed divine unity, and yet all of these discussions came to naught–none of them led to the creation of a society oriented around the principles of *tawḥīd*. If you spent a hundred years discussing an issue directly related to people's lives, is it thinkable that these discussions would have no practical effect on their lives? A hundred years of dry discussions which seem interesting and intellectual on the outside but are really empty and devoid of useful content–they have no relation to objective reality or to people's lives. This is what the theologians spent centuries locked in discussion about. Now, when we want to create a new kind of life for human beings–a life centred around divine unity–we refer to their discussions, and what do we find? We find that these discussions are of no use whatsoever to us. They are ossified. All of these debates and discussions, now that we want to apply them to the outside world, what use are they? On the other hand, if we refer to the Qur'an and study *tawḥīd* from the Qur'an, we see that it presents different aspects and angles of the edifice of divine unity to us. In its hundreds of verses, we see it has given us the best and clearest explanation. When we turn to the Qur'an, that is when we see what it means for a human being to live a *tawḥīd*-oriented life. That is when we see what it is for a human being to be a true monotheist.

Now, as I was saying, we will look at one or two verses now, but you must find others by yourself and ponder on them.

God says about the Resurrection: 'On the day when We gather them all together, We shall say to those who ascribe partners [to God], "Stay where you are–you and your partners!" This is said in a tone of a rebuke and reprimand. 'Then We shall set them apart from one another'.[20] Here, on a basic level, you can understand that these partners are *persons* that people took up as partners besides God. Now, on the Day of Resurrection, Hubal won't be resurrected because he was never alive–he was a stone idol, not a person! You wouldn't tell a stone idol: 'Stay where you are!' You wouldn't tell Manāt, ʿUzzā or Lāt either–even if their idols were in the form of a human being or an angelic being. These are not the partners being referred to in the current verse. Not the idols of the pre-Islamic Arabs, or of the pagan Greeks or Romans, nor the idols of the Hindu religion–no, what the present verse is addressing are those human beings who were taken as equals or rivals to God. They are the ones who will be told to stay where they are!

So, the command for them to stay where they are makes clear that those things worshipped alongside God have no power on the Day of Resurrection! What effect do you think this will have on that day? It tells us that whatever people imagine to be an equal or a rival to God–it doesn't matter whether by an Arab, an Iranian, a Roman, an Ethiopian, an Indian, an Egyptian–its position on the Day of Resurrection will be like this. It and its followers will be detained to one side by the divine command, by God's reprimand and by His power.

'Then We shall set them apart from one another, and their partners will say, "It was not us that you worshipped."' See how the ones they worship respond like one who stands accused of a crime who will

20 Q10:28.

do anything to escape the charge he faces. Just as we saw in the verses from yesterday's lecture and as we can see elsewhere in the Qur'an: 'Those who were abased will say to those who were arrogant, "Rather [it was your] night and day plotting, when you prompted us to forswear God and to set up equals to Him."'[21] See how those who went astray and those who led them astray will turn on one another on the Day of Resurrection? Those who associated partners with God and ascribed others as equals to Him want to free themselves from any association to these partners by any means necessary. They say: 'I worshipped you instead of God and look at the calamity it has brought down on me!' On the other hand, those who were worshipped and served in this world try to deny any knowledge of this and disown those who followed them and worshipped them. They say: 'It was not us that you worshipped! God suffices as a witness between you and us. We were indeed unaware of your worship.' This is what those worshipped besides God will say.

'There every soul will examine what it has sent in advance'–on that day, a person will examine their own deeds that they did in this world–'and they will be returned to God, their real master, and what they used to fabricate will forsake them'–there will be no trace of it. Anything in the human heart that could motivate someone to obey something other than God will be forgotten. All the excuses and pretexts they offered for serving something other than God, that they thought would provide a way out for them on the Day of Resurrection, will be taken away from them. Think of all the time people spend in thought in order to contrive excuses for themselves to associate partners with God, to invent valid-seeming reasons for the things they did. On the Day of Judgement, when they enumerate their excuses–first, second, third, fourth, fifth!–they will see for themselves that these are empty, false, nothing. 'And what they used to fabricate

21 Q34:33

will forsake them'–another possible interpretation of this phrase is that in this world the human being imagines that there are things that support him in this world, and he worships them as a result–he obeys, serves and feels a sense of attachment to them. But on the Day of Resurrection, all of these things that he thought provided him with a means of support or protection will vanish. The poor soul! 'And what they used to fabricate will forsake them.'

See how the Qur'an develops its arguments? Sometimes, it straightforwardly affirms its point. Other times, it does not make an explicit argument but lays the groundwork for the human being to draw his or her own conclusion. In these verses here, God wants to establish clearly that only God should be worshipped and obeyed.

'Say, "Who provides for you out of the sky and the earth?"–who sends the life-giving rains from the skies and brings forth sustenance from the ground–"Who controls hearing and sight"'–do not imagine that 'hearing' (*samᶜ*) simply means your ear, that would be *udhun* in Arabic; here, God is speaking about the power of hearing. The two are not the same: If someone has his ear cut off, for example, you wouldn't say he had his hearing cut off! So the organ is not the same as the sense. The same is true of 'sight' (*baṣar*); this has a broader meaning than just the organ of seeing (the eye) as it denotes the power of sight. Your eye is something physical. Sight is something immaterial. And, even if the Arabic word *baṣar* can also be used for the eye (unlike *samᶜ* for the ear), you would not say that one's *baṣar* has gone blind, bur rather than his eye has gone blind. 'Who controls hearing and sight'–who has power over these senses of hearing and seeing? In reality, this verse is referring not only to physical sight but also to *insight* (*baṣīrah*)–the power of thought and reflection–as it is asking the human being to think and give an answer to this question.

'And who brings forth the living from the dead'–the outwardly living from the outwardly dead; a woman dies while pregnant for example, but her unborn child lives. A living child is brought forth from a dead mother. This is one possible interpretation. Another possibility is that from human sperm and eggs–neither of which are capable of living by themselves–a fully-formed living human is brought forth. Or, from the earth, which contains thousands of minerals that are essential for life while being dead itself, God brings forth living organisms like you. Does the human being contain any material not taken from the earth? So, God 'brings forth the living from the dead' in several observable ways. 'And brings forth the dead from the living'–a living woman might miscarry her child; or a bad person with a dead spirit might come forth from a good person with a living spirit. These are the sorts of interpretations and readings that a human being might think of. In any case, all of these serve to demonstrate God's complete power. He brings forth something living from something dead, and something dead from something living–this shows He has power over everything; all power belongs to Him.

'And who directs the affair?' The affairs of the cosmos: Who gave the earth its gravity so that man might live upon it? Who endowed its lands, its seas, and its mountains with all the materials he needed to live? Who gave the human being the power to extract them? Who set in motion the sun, the moon, the stars and all the galaxies of the cosmos and gave them this wonderous order and arrangement? Who placed the moon at just the right distance from the earth for human beings to live–such that if it was closer, life would not be possible as the tides would overwhelm the land and if it was further away, life would not be possible as water would not stay on the surface of the earth and would be absorbed by it? Who made the sun and placed the earth at the ideal distance from it in order for life to flourish, so that it is neither too hot nor too cold for us to dwell upon?

Now, what should we say about God's artistry and power? When we look at all the books written by the scientists of the world in the last century that are so numerous and so replete with knowledge that if someone wanted to stand here and simply relate their contents to you, it would take days for him to do so. So 'who directs the affair?' If we want to think and reflect and give an objective, unbiased answer, what would we say? 'They will say, "God!"' This wonderous order we perceive in the material cosmos is from God and God alone. It is His power on display as the planets orbit the sun. Whatever we see, whether we see it with our eyes or with our scientific equipment, and whatever we cannot yet see but will come to see as science improves and the state of our knowledge expands, is all a manifestation of God's power and wisdom. 'They will say, "God!"'

Ok, so the answer is God. Now the Qur'an tells the Prophet–who God sent to bring glad tidings to mankind and lead them towards perfection–to take them by the collar and 'Say, "Will you not then be wary?"' In other words, will you not fear this all-powerful God, whose might is displayed through His creation? Will you not be wary of worshipping or serving other than Him? Will you not be wary of associating partners with Him? If it is He who directs the material cosmos, why do you think anyone other than Him governs the moral cosmos? Consider the verse: 'Blessed is He in whose hands is all sovereignty, and He has power over all things. He, who created death and life that He may test you [to see] which of you is best in conduct.'[22] How does this verse begin? 'Blessed is He *in whose hands is all sovereignty*'–sovereignty means governance, it means power. Which power? The power to create *and* the power to legislate. Both are in his hands. Why should the being who created the physical universe not also hold sway over the moral universe? If this authority is given to anyone else, that being is also a creation of God. When God is the one who made the laws that govern the cosmos, why should the laws that govern society and human behaviour be devolved to the authority of those who are incapable, whose intellects are imperfect, whose knowledge is incomplete, whose will is weak? Why should

22 Q67:1–2.

this power be given to mere mortals? Why doesn't God direct human society? Why doesn't God provide us with laws? Why does God not provide us with a system that protects us? A system of leadership and governance? Why does He not appoint a leader? Why does He not give us a representative from Himself to guide mankind's limited intellects? 'That, then, is God, your true Lord. So what is there after the truth except error? Then where are you being led away?'[23]

A few verses later, God tells the Prophet: 'Say, "Is there anyone among your partners who may guide to the truth?"'[24] God tells the Prophet to ask them this in order to teach them and guide them–do they have anyone who guides them to what is true and good and right? Now, I think it is clear here that he is not talking about their idols of wood and stone, as not even the idolaters expected their idols to guide them. After all, how can they guide anyone? So it is clear that this verse is not talking about the idols. Instead, it is talking about those who have power in their society, whether worldly power or religious power. For example, like Pharaoh or a religious scholar, or anyone who holds such a position.

'Say, "Is there anyone among your partners who may guide to the truth?"' Do any of these so-called partners or rivals whom you have ascribed to God have the ability to guide people to the truth? What was the idolaters' answer when the Prophet asked them this? They might have said: 'Yes, those whom we have chosen are true. They are walking embodiments of the truth! Guidance is nothing–they do more than just guide!' That is why the Qur'an does not record their answer because, whatever it might have been, it was wrong. They were wrong to claim that the partners they associated with God had the power to guide people. So the Qur'an tells the Prophet to answer them: 'Say, "God guides to the truth"', God is the One who guides and

23 Q10:32.

24 Q10:35.

leads humans and intellects towards the truth. Why? Because God is the one who created the truth, God is the one who knows every aspect of the truth, and God summons mankind to follow the truth. Anyone who opposes God automatically opposes the truth and calls people to other than the truth! Therefore, it is only God who can bring people to the truth.

So, now it has been established that it is God who guides people to the truth and that the so-called rivals people associate with God cannot do this, the Qur'an tells the Prophet to ask: 'Is He who guides to the truth worthier to be followed', this is a conclusion that can be drawn by man's God-given intellect and intelligence, 'Is He who guides to the truth worthier to be followed, or he who guides not unless he is guided?' Who should we follow? Should we follow God who created the truth and guides towards the truth? Or should we follow someone who, even if he wanted to reach the truth, must himself be guided and led to the truth by another? That would be the blind leading the blind! He wants to guide others but he himself must be guided in turn–someone needs to come and guide him!

Now, who is this we are talking about? This partner who has been associated with God whose ability to guide people is being debated in these verses, what kind of being is this? Is this verse talking about idols and holy cows and the people who worship these? Is it talking about the idols that the polytheistic Qurayshī and non-Qurayshī used to worship? Is it talking about the sacred fire of the Mazdeans or the Zoroastrians? Or the statues inside the temples and gods of ancient Greece and Rome? Clearly, it is not talking about any of these! The only sort of beings which we can say are capable or incapable of leading others, or who need to be guided by others, are human beings who are claiming some position of authority, who are claiming they can lead others to happiness. But the Qur'an says that it is God who can lead humanity to happiness. It is God who can show humanity the way to the spring of truth. It is God who can guide man to the truth. Those who have nothing in of their own selves cannot do this. 'Is He who guides to the truth worthier to be followed, or he who is not guided unless he is shown the way? What is the matter with you? How do you judge?' In other words, why do you not think and ponder? How do you allow someone other than God to claim this authority? This is one aspect of *tawḥīd.*

Refusing to worship false gods. 'False gods' are those people who claim divinity and sanctity for themselves. They are living, breathing idols. And they have existed throughout human history. Refusing to worship false gods, whether they dress themselves in the cloak of faith–like the rabbis and priests–or in the robes of worldly power–like the tyrants and princes–this is the meaning of *tawḥīd.*

God addresses the People of the Book through the Qur'an to refuse to obey any authority except God: 'Say, "O People of the Book! Come to a word common between us and you: that we will worship no one but God, and that we will not ascribe any partner to Him, and that we will not take each other as lords besides God."'[25] Ponder on this until tomorrow, when we shall continue our discussion.

25 Q3:64.

Service Belongs Only for God

Sunday 12th Ramadan 1394
29th September 1974

أَفَغَيْرَ اللَّهِ أَبْتَغِي حَكَمًا وَهُوَ الَّذِي أَنْزَلَ إِلَيْكُمُ الْكِتَابَ مُفَصَّلًا وَالَّذِينَ آتَيْنَاهُمُ الْكِتَابَ يَعْلَمُونَ أَنَّهُ مُنَزَّلٌ مِنْ رَبِّكَ بِالْحَقِّ فَلَا تَكُونَنَّ مِنَ الْمُمْتَرِينَ (١١٤)

'[Say,] "Shall I seek a judge other than God, while it is He who has sent down to you the Book, well-elaborated?" Those whom We have given the Book know that it has been sent down from your Lord with the truth; so do not be one of the sceptics.'
- Sūrat al-Anʿām (6):114.

However much we might try, we can have never said enough about divine unity. Firstly, because it is the foundation of our faith. Secondly, because it is the most important guiding principle of our behaviour as individuals and as a society. Thirdly, because even the Muslims do not know much about it–or anything at all, for that matter! When we were children in school, we were taught that God is one and He is not two, but the sad fact is that most believers do not learn anything correct about the many different facets of *tawḥīd* until they are at an age when they are getting ready to leave this world. Hence, when there is a topic of such importance and people know so little about it, one can never have spoken enough on it!

It so happens we can see this reflected in the Qur'an itself, as it speaks about divine unity in a variety of contexts and in a number of ways. Even taking several more days to expound upon this element of Islamic thought would not do it justice, so I will try to provide a general overview of it through a discussion of some verses and examples from the Qur'an. Today, in particular, I would like to focus on another element of *tawḥīd*, which I briefly alluded to yesterday but which I would like to give a fuller explanation of now.

God says in the Qur'an: '[Say,] "Shall I seek a judge other than God, while it is He who has sent down to you the Book, well-elaborated?" Those whom We have given the Book know that it has been sent down from your Lord with the truth; so do not be one of the sceptics. The word of your Lord has been fulfilled in truth and justice. Nothing can change His words, and He is the All-hearing, the All-knowing. If you obey most of those on the earth, they will lead you astray from the way of God. They follow nothing but conjectures and they do nothing but surmise.'[26] We will give a brief explanation of this in a moment. Then, a few verses later, He says: 'Do not eat of that over which God's Name has not been mentioned, and that is indeed transgression. Indeed the devils inspire their friends to dispute with you; and if you obey them, you will indeed be idolaters.'[27]

With these verses in mind, I would like to call attention to the fact that there are two kinds of worship (*ʿibādah*). The first kind, which is the more common one, is that man worships something he recognises as being holy and possessing supernatural power–it is for precisely this reason that people have worshipped idols throughout history and, at first glance, this appears to be the proper meaning of worship. When we say that it is obligatory to worship God, a similar idea of holiness and spiritual greatness comes to mind. For example,

26 Q6:114–116.

27 Q6:121.

Christians consider Jesus and his mother, Mary, as holy figures. They bow down and pray before icons and statues representing these figures. This is the common understanding of worship.

Meanwhile, there is another idea of worship–or perhaps more accurately, another dimension of worship–which is employed throughout the Qur'an. If someone worships someone or something else in the sense that we are about to explain, then this too would count as worshipping something other than God. In short, we will show that worship is not merely to venerate or sanctify something as holy, to bow down to it, to prostrate oneself in front of it, to outstretch one's hands in supplication to it, or to raise your voice in praise of it. Worship is more than just this. There are other things a person can do that can be called worship, not only by us, but by the Qur'an. Therefore, we can see that in the lexicon of the Qur'an the concept of worship is much broader than what we imagine it to be and it is up to us to uncover this broader concept of worship in order that, should we desire to worship God and avoid worshipping other than Him–in other words, if we want to *practice* the principle of divine unity in how we live our lives–then we should be careful of unwittingly worshipping something besides God in the second sense of the word. Most of the monotheists in the world, while never bowing down or glorifying anything or anyone other than God, have nevertheless worshipped something besides God in thought, practice, heart and spirit–this is in the second sense of worship.

So, what is this other concept of worship? It is something very simple and easy to understand. It is obedience. To obey someone without question or reservation is to worship them. If one person obeys another so utterly and unconditionally that they follow their every dictate in their lives, in their own person, in their own behaviour, without any hesitation, they have worshipped them. Where is our proof for such a claim? We base this claim on the Qur'an itself. The Qur'an uses the word 'worship' (*ʿibādah*) in the sense of obedience (*iṭāʿah*). When ʿAdī ibn Ḥātim al-Ṭāʾī–the son of the proverbially generous Ḥātim al-Ṭāʾī–came to Madinah and became a Muslim, the Prophet began to recite the following verse of the Qur'an because he saw ʿAdī wearing a crucifix around his neck: 'They have taken their rabbis and their monks as lords besides God, and also Christ, Mary's son; though they were commanded to worship only the One God.'[28] When ʿAdī heard this verse, he turned around and said: 'O Prophet of God! This is not so. When have we believed rabbis and monks to be lords besides God? When have we worshipped them?' ʿAdī objected to the Prophet about the verse–why? Because in his mind, worship meant what it means to you right now. When someone tells us a person is worshipping, we imagine him raising his voice in prayer and bowing down in veneration, whether physically or in his heart. This is how ʿAdī ibn Ḥātim understood worship. So, when he heard the Qur'an saying that these people took up their priests and scribes to worship as lords in place of God, this seemed patently incorrect, so he spoke up and said this is not what they do. After all, even today, when do you see a Jew worshipping a rabbi or a Christian worshipping a priest?

In response, the Prophet told ʿAdī ibn Ḥātim words to the effect that yes, they do not bow down to their priests and rabbis, but they accept whatever these tell them without hesitation or reservation: 'but they permit that which is forbidden and forbid that which is permitted.' Perhaps you wanted to understand the truth of the matter, but you accept whatever they told you without question. This is worship. This is what it means to make someone or something a lord besides God. The same explanation can be found in a tradition from Imam al-Ṣādiq (a) in *Tafsīr Nūr al-Thaqalayn* about the verse I quoted above.

In the language of the Qur'an, worshipping any being other than God, be it a political authority, a religious authority, an internal to the

28 Q9:31.

human being such as the ego or one's own desires; be it something outside the human being, if not a political or religious authority, then a woman, or someone who they admire, or a friend; worshipping any of these means obeying them. Giving anyone or anything other than God your unquestioning obedience means to worship it.

Here, I would like to mention a tradition which shows that this Qur'anic idea is found throughout the sources of Islam, especially Shiʿa ones. There is a narration from Imam al-Jawād (a), in which he says: 'Whoever pays attention to a speaker has worshipped him.' See how much broader the scope of worship is compared to what we imagine? Not just to obey someone, but to attend to them with one of our senses is to worship them. OK, now you might say: 'Does that mean we shouldn't listen to things which are good and right?' That is why the narration continues: 'So, if the speaker was speaking from God, then the listener has worshipped God.' In other words, if the speaker who caught the attention of your senses was speaking from God, then when you turn your heart and mind, and your thoughts and spirit towards him, you are worshipping God. On the other hand, it goes on: 'And if the speaker was speaking from the tongue of Iblīs, then the listener has worshipped Iblīs.' So if the speaker was speaking against the logic and philosophy of divine thought, he was speaking from the tongue of Satan, and if you are listening attentively to him, then you are engaged in worshipping and obeying Satan. In other words, he himself is a devil. He is not Satan's representative, or Satan's mouthpiece, he is a devil in the sense that we described previously. He is a devil in the Qur'anic sense of the word.

So, obeying something in this way, even if it is not a political or religious authority, without question or reservation, is tantamount to worshipping it. If someone wants only to worship God and nothing else–meaning they want to be a true monotheist–then they must only give their full and unquestioning obedience to the Lord of the Worlds, to God Almighty. One of those things which, if you follow it, you have worshipped it is the law. One of the things which, if you follow it, you have worshipped it is the social system. One of the things which, if you follow it, you have worshipped it are customs and traditions. So which law should we follow? Does this mean we should break the law of the land? That we should not observe our people's customs and traditions? That we should not follow the social system where we live? Of course not. What it means is that we should strive to ensure that all of this conforms to God's will so that, when we do follow these things, we are actually engaged in the worship of God.

Do you see how broad our horizons become? Do you see how historical issues can give meaning to human existence? Every prophet who came to mankind came with the idea of *tawḥīd*. This is what we will find explained by the Qur'an when we begin our discussions of prophets and prophethood. All of God's prophets came to make people believers in one God. What does it mean to believe in one God? It means to be freed from the shackles that bind people to worshipping things other than God. The Qur'an itself says this. See the verse: 'and relieves them of their burdens and the shackles that were upon them.'[29] This is the mission of the prophets.

When we look at divine unity through this length and with this goal in mind, we see that it is more than an abstract belief; it is an idea and a principle that is supposed to be applied in our daily lives, within a social order, to direct all human affairs, to tell people how to live in human societies. See how different this idea of *tawḥīd* is from the *tawḥīd* of saying 'God is one but not two.' This is the true meaning of *tawḥīd*.

Now, there are so many verses I have found in the Qur'an which deal with this idea and to try and explain them fully, it would take five or six pages in which to do so. So, instead, I will present two examples that clearly show that obeying anything other than God

29 7:157.

is to worship it and that true divine unity–which is the spirit and foundation of the religion–means that the human being obeys only God with all his heart and soul, who follows God's directions, and who strives for the sake of God. There are just two examples I will use to elucidate this matter, then it is up to you to do more research into this and look for this idea in the Qur'an.

Refer to the Qur'an. Try to understand the Qur'an. Do not be someone who needs me to explain all the verses to them. You should familiarise yourself with this bottomless treasure and ocean without a shore. I always say this because, whenever I don't, I feel like there is a weight of responsibility upon my shoulders. First, I feel that it is my duty to encourage you to refer to the Qur'an. This limitless ocean without a shore. As a poet once said: 'It is the sea no matter from which direction you approach it ' (*huwa al-baḥr min ayyi al-nawāḥī ataytahū*). Anyone who sits down with the Qur'an for a while will benefit from it. No matter how you approach it, if you are able to understand its language, you will benefit from it and the more you refer to it, the more enlightened and aware you will become. In *Nahj al-Balāghah*, it is related that the Commander of the Faithful (a) said: 'No one sits with this Qur'an save that when he gets up he has more or less: more guidance or less blindness.'[30] Pay attention to the words Imam ʿAlī uses here at the beginning of his statement: 'no one sits with this Qur'an'–the language tells us that this is a universal rule; it includes everyone. So, whoever sits with the Qur'an will receive any increase in guidance or a decrease in his blindness, in the sense of spiritual or intellectual blindness. I say this as a reminder to all of us.

Why do I mention this reminder? Because, brothers and sisters, we know that there are many snares–limitless, in fact–set to keep us away from the Qur'an, which are still used until today. One of these snares that we hear repeatedly nowadays by some ignorant persons

30 *Nahj al-Balāghah*, saying no. 14.

is that no one but the Infallibles (a) can understand the Qur'an–only the Imams can understand the Qur'an. The only thing I can think of to say about this claim is what the Commander of the Faithful (a) said when he heard the slogans of the Khawārij: 'A true statement with a false meaning' (*kalimatu ḥaqqin yurādu bi-hā al-bāṭil*). On one level, this statement is true, but not in the sense intended by those who utter it–their interpretation of this principle is truly harmful. Yes, of course, the Imams (a) have complete knowledge of the Qur'an, as we would expect! They with their pure spirits and lofty intellects are fully versed in the intricacies of the Qur'an. They are walking embodiments of the Qur'an. Each and every one of them is a living Qur'an. There is no dispute about this. However, just because the Imam (a) has full knowledge of the Qur'an, this shouldn't be taken to mean that no one else can understand any word of it. It is true that the Imams (a) know the Qur'an better than anyone, but the people who say this do not intend to raise the Imams up, they intend to push others down by keeping them away from the Qur'an. There is no difference between this and someone who says: 'If prayers are what my master ʿAlī offered [in terms of quality], then there is no need for me to pray!'

This is their logic. They say that if the Imams understood the Qur'an, then why should anyone else open it? Woe upon you! What a shame it is that these people deprive themselves of the wisdom of the Qur'an. But an even greater shame is that, not content with their own ignorance, they want to make others ignorant too! They keep themselves thirsty and do not let any other thirsty person drink from the cool spring of the Qur'an's knowledge. They turn away from the Qur'an and try to turn other people away from it, with all manner of excuses and pretexts. They will do anything to stop people from understanding God's words. Brothers and sisters, you know that today more than ever before it is our duty to refer to the Qur'an. As the Prophet himself once said: 'When the tribulations cover you like the blackness of a dark night, then hold on to the Qur'an!' Is now not that time? Do we not see tribulations covering us like the darkest of nights? Are not the winding roads lost to us in the gloom? Are we not beset by brigands and thieves from every direction? So, who should refer to the Qur'an? Who is this saying of the Prophet for? Do you think this is for the time when the Imam of the Age (aj) will come? No, for he is the speaking Qur'an. It is today, in his absence, that we must refer to the Qur'an. And the first step to benefitting from the Qur'an in this way is *understanding* the Qur'an.

There are two excerpts from the Qur'an I have found that are related to our discussion today. If you look, you will find ten more. I strongly advise you, dear brothers, that those of you who can understand the Qur'an–meaning you can understand its apparent meanings–that you study the Arabic and Persian translations side by side and pay close attention. Those of you who cannot, must make yourselves able to do so. Study Arabic, learn the Qur'an, attend lessons on the Qur'an, make yourself familiar with the Qur'an, consider the Qur'an as your friend. Every day that you spend without familiarising yourself with it–in fact, every moment you spend without doing so–should be a cause for regret!

The first excerpt is from *Sūrat al-Anʿām*. Here, you must pay close attention to the way in which the Qur'an speaks. The Qur'an is not like an ordinary book where you can go to a certain chapter for the meanings of obedience and worship. The Qur'an is a holy scripture–the way in which it addresses its audience is loftier than that of an ordinary book. For the Creator of the World, all beings are alike. That is why when there was an occasion that needed revelation, revelation was sent in the form of a verse. You must study the expressions, allusions, sentences, style and context of the verse.

The Qur'an says: 'Shall I seek a judge (*ḥakam*) other than God...?' Commentaries on the Qur'an say that the word *ḥakam* means judge. It can also mean ruler. Someone who people turn to for a ruling (*ḥukm*), meaning someone to whom they turn for a command, or whom they approach for a judgement is called a *ḥakam*. God is both the best judge and the best ruler. Commandments must come from God–'Look! All creation and command belong to Him'.[31] It is He who creates, and it is He who commands. So, 'shall I seek a *ḥakam* other than God...?' Shall I seek a judge, a commander or, a ruler other than God? 'While it is He who has sent down to you the Book, well-elaborated (*mufaṣṣal*)'? *Mufaṣṣal* means God has sent it down without any confusion in its discussions, and without mixing it with anyone's speech aside from God's. *Mufaṣṣal* can also mean fully explained and expounded.

'Those whom We have given the Book know that it has been sent down from your Lord with the truth; so do not be one of the sceptics.' This is addressed to the Prophet–lest you doubt! Lest you be sceptical! You know that this book has come to you from your Lord, you know that God has given these revelations to you and you are aware, you are informed. So do not doubt, be certain.

'The word of *your* Lord has been fulfilled in truth and justice.'[32] 'Fulfilled' means that it has been finished. It is done. It cannot be undone. God's command was that a series of prophets should come and gradually lead mankind towards their destination. Then the last prophet comes and leads them to a wide horizon, to a limitless field. He gave them whatever they needed to grow, develop and make this journey, so that the human being could continue his journey into infinity; 'and to Him do we indeed return.'[33] God's command, His decree, His word has been fulfilled in full and cannot be taken back. 'Nothing can change His words'–or commands–'and He is the All-hearing, the All-knowing.' He hears even your innermost needs and

31 Q7:54.

32 Q6:115.

33 Q2:156.

he knows what is best for you. Therefore, it is He who must guide you and create a programme for you to follow.

'If you obey most of those on the earth'.[34] Do you see how the Qur'an prepares the minds of its listeners to receive its message? In the first sentence of the first verse, it discusses God's judgement and authority, as He is more entitled to pass judgement and issue commands than anyone else. In the second verse, it discusses how God's religion and commandments cannot be undone–no matter what the enemies of His religion and those who obstinately reject it might say or do, God's command has been fulfilled completely. In the third verse, it says you should not obey your or anyone else's wants and desires, but only God: 'If you obey most of those on the earth, they will lead you astray from the way of God. They follow nothing but conjectures and they do nothing but surmise.' People act on the basis of suppositions and guesswork. Those who fashion ways of living and bid others to follow them–are they certain about the way they have chosen? After a few decades their ideas will be shown to be false. They do not have certainty, for 'they do nothing but surmise.' They create abstract theories to govern human beings and human societies, but God does not govern by theory, but rather with the fabric of reality itself; with knowledge and wisdom–in the truest sense–God leads mankind to the right path. 'Indeed your Lord knows best those who stray from His way; and He knows best those who are guided.'[35]

'Eat from that over which God's Name has been mentioned, if you are believers in His signs.'[36] Here, a listener might be surprised. After the Qur'an mentions all of these general principles: Do not obey the majority of people, do not follow guesswork, conjecture, or theories,

---

34 Q6:116.

35 Q6:117.

36 Q6:118.

your Lord's command with regards to prophethood and religion has been fulfilled by the Final Messenger and cannot be changed. After everything it has said, suddenly now it tells its listeners to eat from that over which God's Name has been mentioned. For example, a lamb which has been slaughtered with God's name being invoked. But this is a particular issue of practice. A person might find this to be a very striking transition; what does this particular issue have to do with what we just discussed? Let us look at this for a moment. Now, what I am about to say is my own impression of this verse. I cannot give you copper-bottomed proof that what I am about to say is the case. However, there is room for us to reflect on the meaning of the verses we are studying and to ask: what is the relation between them?

First, for God, who is above this world and beyond the comprehension of human beings, as we have said, all issues are the same. For God, general issues pertaining to human beings are no different from particular ones. They are all the same to him. For God, everything is one. For the Creator of the World, whatever is conducive to human happiness is all part of a single command. It does not matter whether this command is about a particular matter or issue, whether it pertains to a single person, or whether it is general and universal and pertains to the entirety of humankind. This is first.

Second, let us understand the proper significance of how we slaughter an animal. What does it mean that the name of God must be invoked while slaughtering an animal for someone to eat? Well, whenever idol-worshippers, pagan tribes, or those nations who do not share a belief in divine unity wanted to do something significant, they would invoke the name of their deity. A Christian might say, 'In Christ's name', for instance. You also know that the idols of this world and the powers of this world are forever trying to put their name on everything. Every action that does not begin in the name of God is naturally done for someone or something other than God. When you do something for money, for your own desire, or for any motivation like this, you do it in the name of that thing, with that thing in mind. No matter what it is you are doing, it is automatically directed towards whatever you invoke when you do it, whether out loud or in your mind. When you do something with money in mind, you direct that action towards money and from start to finish, that act is about obtaining money–there is no reason save money for which you are performing that action. By the same token, when you do something in the name of God, when you undertake something with God in mind, then this act is directed towards God, which means it will be done according to God's commandments and laws. The Qur'an says that even when we want to slaughter an animal for food, we should do so in the name of God. Think on this: Your most urgent necessity and your most basic need is food. And this food must be obtained 'in the name of God'–which means it must be *for* God. In other words, even when you are filling your stomach, you should do this for God. This is because filling your stomach is not the principle upon which you act–God is the principle upon which you act. Therefore, if there came a time where you felt that filling your stomach would take you further from God, then you would forgo this–you wouldn't fill your stomach; you'd choose to remain hungry. In fact, you would rather die hungry than turn away from God. Why? Because even if it is necessary for your survival to fill your stomach, your stomach is not the principle upon which you live your life. That principle is none other than God. This is the lesson we are taught by invoking God's name when slaughtering an animal, or when we invoke God's name as we place a morsel of food in our mouths.

Whatever you want to do–begin it by saying *bismillāh*. Even something as routine as eating food. Begin by saying 'in the name of God'. Even if you want to be intimate with your spouse, begin by saying 'in the name of God.' Whether you are entering a room, leaving a room, going out somewhere, at home, in your place of work–whatever you are doing, say *bismillāh*. Why? What is the significance of this? Because it reminds you that whatever you are doing in your life, whatever need you are looking to fulfil, even if these are just your basic needs, you must always follow God's commandments and do things for the sake of God. 'Indeed my prayer and my worship, my life and my death are for the sake of God, the Lord of all the worlds.'[37] Abraham says that all of this is for the sake of God, the creator and director of the cosmos. 'He has no partner'[38] in any sphere of my life, not only in my prayers, but even in the food I eat–in my every movement, my every effort, God has no partner. If my being is a kingdom, it is entirely under the rule of God and His commandments. Even if you want to slaughter an animal to eat, you must do it in accordance with God's commands–this is true *tawḥīd* in practice. On the other hand, a pagan of the Qurayshī tribe will slaughter an animal one way, a disbeliever from another people will slaughter it in another way. When they slaughter an animal, eat food, live their lives, open their shop, not only do they not do this in God's name, they do it in the name of other things and other gods.

Think of slaughtering this animal as a symbol. When you invoke the name of God as you slaughter a sheep, think of this as symbolic. Even though slaughtering an animal is a ritual practice and, as discussed in jurisprudence, you must invoke God's name to perform this slaughter properly and render the meat permissible to consume. This is the ruling. But, just imagine that this *bismillāh* is a symbol–a symbol of all the basic needs that a human being experiences in his life. When you slaughter a sheep, you must invoke God's name. Why? Because even in the most basic, the most fundamental, the most primary of your needs, it is for God's sake that you seek to fulfil them. In this way, when you eat a piece of bread to sate your hunger, you eat it for God. You sate your hunger and strengthen your body for God. Now, clearly,

37 Q6:162.

38 Q6:163.

any strength the human body gains for the sake of God will also be used for the sake of God. This is the logical conclusion–as surely as two plus two makes four. See the wisdom behind this?

'Eat from that over which God's Name has been mentioned, if you are believers in His signs. Why should you not eat that over which God's Name has been mentioned, while He has already elaborated for you whatever He has forbidden you, excepting what you may be compelled to [eat]. Indeed many mislead [others] by their fancies, without any knowledge. Indeed your Lord knows best the transgressors.'[39] So, according to this verse, the transgressors are those who lead others astray without having any knowledge themselves.

'Renounce outward sins and the inward ones'[40]–there are acts which are clearly problematic and whose ill consequences are obvious to all. For example, everyone knows that it is wrong to murder someone or to take a life without justifiable cause. The sinfulness of this act is self-evident. On the other hand, there are acts which are sinful but whose sinfulness is not immediately apparent. There are many things which people do not comprehend the gravity of; speaking without knowledge, following others without knowledge, taking the name of God lightly, obeying someone other than God, fulfilling the commands of someone other than God–these are the kind of things people do not imagine to have any serious consequences, or even to be necessarily wrong, even though these are sins. But, God tells us to avoid both of them: 'Renounce outward sins and the inward ones. Indeed, those who commit sins shall be requited for what they used to commit.'

'Do not eat [anything] of that over which God's Name has not been mentioned, and that is indeed transgression (*fisq*)'[41]–*fisq* means 'to

39 Q6:118–119.

40 Q6:120.

41 Q6:121.

go out' of one's faith. This shows how important it is to remember God and to invoke God's name!

'Indeed the satans'–this is the verse we want to focus on. All the verses we have read so far are beneficial, but this is the point that they have been building-up to. God says: 'Indeed the satans inspire their friends to dispute with you; and if you obey them, you will indeed be polytheists.' The satans and the poles of wickedness provoke their friends, their allies and helpers into arguing with you. What is your duty towards these friends of the devils? 'And if you obey them, you will indeed be polytheists'–do you see? It is very clear: You will be a polytheist. An idol-worshipper. Therefore, obeying Satan, which means to obey the poles of evil in opposition to God, the All-merciful, or to obey the allies of Satan, meaning those who are under his influence and who are his instruments, will definitely make you an idol-worshipper.

This is one of the key verses we wanted to examine. The next is in *Sūrat al-Shuʿarāʾ*. This is one of the most interesting and powerful expositions we find, whether in the Qur'an or the traditions, on the topic of the Resurrection. When you want to make something tangible for your listener to the extent that it affects the very depths of his soul, you should show him how that thing appears on the Day of Resurrection and how this reflects its reality in this world. This verse is a prime example of this technique. God says, 'and Paradise was brought near for the Godwary'.[42] Notice that although God is speaking about the Resurrection, which will happen in the future, He is using the past tense. This is because, in Arabic, when you want to speak about a future event that is sure to happen, you express it in the past tense. For example, see the verse: 'The Hour has drawn

42 Q26:90.

near and the moon is split.'[43] This verse means 'the Hour *will* draw near and the moon *will* split.'

'And Paradise was brought near for the Godwary, and Hell was brought into view for the misguided'.[44] The misguided (*ghāwīn*) are those who have gone astray, as in the phrase 'these are the ones whom we have misguided'.[45] It will be said to them: 'Where is that which you used to worship besides God?"[46] The ones who have gone astray will be asked where the things and people they worshipped besides God have gone? Where are these poles towards which you directed your every effort and every waking moment? Notice that the Qur'an uses the word 'worship' (*taʿbudūn*) here. They used to worship these things or these people. But now let us see what it is they used to worship to better understand what the Qur'an means when it uses this term.

'Do they help you, or do they help each other?'[47] From this we can see that the things these people worshipped are things in need of help. Therefore, they must be other human beings. These are not idols of wood and stone, but of living flesh and blood. 'Then they will be cast into it on their faces they and the misguided'–the ones who went astray and sought corruption, and the ones they worshipped–'and the hosts of Iblis all together'[48]–anyone who worked for Iblis in any way, shape or form, who did anything to lead others astray. On the Day of Resurrection, all of these will be sent to Hell. That is their destination and place of return.

---

43 Q54:1.

44 Q26:90–91.

45 Q28:63.

46 Q26:92–93.

47 Q26:93.

48 Q26:94–95.

'They will say, as they wrangle in it', when they go to Hell, they will blame one another for their fate. The leaders will blame the followers. The followers will blame the leaders. The followers will say: 'You led us astray! You forced us to follow you!' The leaders will say: 'It was your choice to follow us. No one forced you to follow us!' However, even though they were in a clear and grave error, they claim they did not understand that they were astray; even though if someone has the slightest presence of mind, they know which way is right and which way is wrong, 'by God, we had indeed been in manifest error'. Anyone with the slightest sense knows where danger lies and knows the outcome he risks by following a course of action. If we gave it the slightest thought, it would have been clear to us, and yet we still go astray!

'By God, we had indeed been in manifest error'. What was this manifest error? 'When we equated you with the Lord of all the worlds!'[49] We should have feared God but, instead, we feared you. We should have listened to His commands but instead, we feared yours. We should have striven to move towards Him and enter his proximity. Instead, we strove to keep you happy. We should have sought our daily sustenance from God. Instead, we sought it from you. 'We equated you with the Lord of all the worlds! And no one led us astray except the guilty. Now we have no intercessors, nor do we have any sympathetic friend. Had there been another turn for us, we would be among the faithful.' From here onwards, God is speaking directly again: 'There is indeed a sign in that; but most of them do not have faith.'[50] Notice how in these verses, the ones speaking are those who worshipped other people. So, whoever we follow, we are in fact worshipping them in the sense of worship described here. Here, those expressing regret followed their leaders instead of God

49 Q26:97–98.

50 Q26:98–103.

and sought from them what they should have instead sought from God. Instead of avoiding that which should have been avoided for the sake of God, they followed the whims of these leaders. And this is the result!

Tawḥīd and the Abolition of Social Classes

Monday 13th Ramadan 1394
30th September 1974

مَا اتَّخَذَ اللَّهُ مِنْ وَلَدٍ وَمَا كَانَ مَعَهُ مِنْ إِلَٰهٍ إِذًا لَذَهَبَ كُلُّ
إِلَٰهٍ بِمَا خَلَقَ وَلَعَلَا بَعْضُهُمْ عَلَىٰ بَعْضٍ سُبْحَانَ اللَّهِ عَمَّا
يَصِفُونَ (٩١)

'God has not taken any offspring, neither is there any god besides Him, for then each god would take away what he created, and some of them would surely rise up against others. Clear is God of what they allege!'
- Sūrat al-Muʾminūn (23):91.

If you remember, we said that if we consider divine unity (*tawḥīd*) as a practical doctrine which gives rise to certain duties, we inevitably find ourselves encumbered with a series of moral duties. We must, as a matter of priority, understand what these duties are. However, we also said that these duties are not restricted to the individual or to the personal aspects of human existence, but that most, if not all of these duties have a strong social element–to the extent that they concern the fundamental structure and system that governs society. In other words, when the principle of *tawḥīd* is introduced to a society, the first effect it has is to reorient and reorganise that society so that it is in harmony with this key doctrine. It is only after this step that we turn towards the doctrine of prophethood (*nubuwwah*) to see what duties a human being has as an individual within this *tawḥīd*-oriented social order.

In any case, we must know and understand these duties, which we said were contained in the 'treaty of *tawḥīd*'. We said that divine unity is a treaty between us and God, containing articles that we are expected to fulfil. Therefore, if we are truly to live as monotheists, we must familiarise ourselves with these duties. And the first of these duties is to worship and serve only God. This is the first duty of *tawḥīd*. We looked at a number of verses that illustrated this and explained their contents. Today, we will look at the second duty that divine unity places upon our shoulders. A *tawḥīd*-oriented society, a *tawḥīd*-oriented individual and a *tawḥīd*-oriented world can all be identified through this quality, and that is the abolition of social classes.

With this short phrase, the details of which we will come to, you can clearly grasp the general contours of a *tawḥīd*-oriented society. It is a society without classes. It is a society in which groups of human beings have not been separated from one another in light of the rights and standards that God has endowed them with. All human beings in such a society dwell in the shelter of one law for all. All follow the same path, and all have access to the same rights and possibilities as one another. This is the society which *tawḥīd* presents to us in terms of how social classes are arranged.

When we look at history, we see that the differences between social classes have been a major source of suffering across human societies. This is not only the case in backwards or developing societies, in societies which are far from civilisation–it is something visible even in those societies which were the cradle of human civilisation, which were shining beacons of enlightenment and progress. In fact, it was in these societies that such class distinctions often took on their most ugly and bitter forms–as the pages of history bear witness to. In fact, one of the greatest crimes of human history has been nothing other than dividing people into classes. What does it mean when we say 'dividing people into classes'? It means that even though people live together in the same society, they are not treated alike in that society. One group are destined to be poor and deprived, are destined to serve others, but are forbidden to raise their voices in protest at their lot in life. Another group are set apart to be prosperous and powerful, to live lives of enjoyment and pleasure, able to make use of the very best things that their society and civilisation has to offer, without anyone to tell them otherwise.

A prime example of this can be found in Indian society. You know that India was the cradle of the Aryan civilisation and the Aryan race since they had been city dwellers and had formed a nation. They say that the Aryans came from the northern regions and Siberia and they split into two groups, some went towards India and some went towards Iran and the people who were in India formed a civilisation sooner than those who moved and lived in Iran.

India is home to one of the oldest civilisations in the history of the world, and to one of the most rigid social hierarchies as well. Originally, there were four castes arranged in a hierarchy, with one caste beneath all others, and hundreds of minor castes in between these four major ones. Those who are interested can find the details of this in books about the religions of the world–and I would advise them to spend some time contemplating on the difference between this and the kind of society the Qur'an envisages. People were divided into these four castes. The first and highest were the priesthood–or Brahmins–then, second, there were the warriors and princes. However, there were often conflicts between these two castes and, at one time, we are told that it was the princes who ruled. However, due to a variety of factors, the priesthood was able to gain a monopoly on knowledge and spiritual authority, relegating the princes and warriors to the level beneath them.

After the second caste, came the level of the farmers, labourers and craftsmen. The priests and the princes did not produce any goods for society–after all, what does a priest do aside from reciting a few prayers and invocations and clapping his hands together? And what does a prince do other than owning more land or wealth than others? On the other hand, labourers and farmers were the ones who worked the land and its resources and produced things. This was the work of the third caste. Finally there were the ordinary people, not belonging to any of the above castes, who would have had ordinary occupations in society. Beneath all four of the castes was a fifth class, who were seen as inferior to all the other castes and ritually impure. Hence, they were called the 'untouchables'. This arrangement was not only confined to the ancient world–it has a long history. A history that has gone on right down to the present day. As anyone who has studied the history of India will know, this practice remained unchallenged until very recently. It was Gandhi who stood up to this and tried to eradicate it. He said: 'What is this untouchability?' The first Prime Minister of India, Nehru, was himself a Brahmin from both his mother's and his father's sides. However, because Nehru was strongly opposed to the caste system, he did not like being reminded of this fact. However, the reason that I mention this is not because I want to discuss history, but because I want to point out that almost fourteen hundred years after the Qur'anic message of *tawḥīd*, there are still people living in the shadow of a rigid system of social classes.

Now, let me explain a little bit more about the social classes of India. There were four main castes and according to John Boyer Noss who has written on the history of religions, within each of these, were tens or hundreds of others. For centuries, if two people were from two different castes, they could not marry. In fact, they could not even talk, or touch one another, sit together, walk together, be friends with one another or anything of this sort. It was as if an invisible wall separated them. Why should this be the case? What does a priest have that a farmer does not? Or that this trader does not? What natural superiority has a prince over a commoner? Do you know how they would answer this question? They would say: 'It's none of your business! They were created this way by the gods. They were made into two groups by a higher power, not by human decisions and agreements!' They will say that when their supreme deity, Brahman, wanted to create, when he wanted to create human beings, he made the priests from his own head, he made the warriors and princes from his hands, he made the farmers from his arms, and he made the ordinary people from his feet. As for the untouchables, they were not made from Brahman at all. They were not made from a pure source. In fact, they are not from the chosen race at all. Then, if the fourth caste were made from Brahman's feet, what right do they have to consider themselves equal to the priests who were made from his head? They will be told they were made from a different substance. That one group are from a higher and nobler origin and, as a result, deserve greater respect and reverence. Their gifts are natural and innate. Their power and wealth are essential to them. It is their right. Meanwhile, the poverty of the lower castes is also natural, innate and essential to them. It too is their right.

Now, ask yourself: In such a society, is there ever going to be any possibility of extirpating social divisions? Is it even conceivable that social classes should disappear from such a society? How could they? Which person could overturn such a society? Would someone from the highest caste come and say he is renouncing all of his rights and benefits for the sake of God? This seems unlikely. More likely is that the deprived and the downtrodden castes will raise their voices and demand their share of what the higher castes have and complain of the inequality they are suffering. But even then, this probably won't happen. Why? Because even the lower castes believe that this is what the gods have ordained. When someone believes it is good and natural for him to be poor because that is the way the gods have made him, it is impossible that he should hope for anything different, or that he should demand the rights which he has been told are not appropriate for him by virtue of his essential nature. He will say: 'This is my due! What the gods have ordained, none can undo!' He will say he was made this way. This is his fate. He cannot change his stars. When you take a black piece of cloth to the ocean and wash it–will it ever come back white? If black is its natural colour, no matter how much you wash it, it will not change! You can wash all the dust and the dirt from it, but it will only become blacker as it becomes cleaner. People believe this as though it was a fact of nature and it is this belief that perpetuates this grave wrongdoing throughout human history.

And yet, there are reformers. They come and they change the way people think. Pay attention to this point. There are reformers who first come and change the way people think. They change the culture of a society. They come and say: 'This way of thinking is wrong. These ideas have the wrong foundation. These beliefs make people accept oppression!' And this is how the world changes: Reformers come and change ideas. We shouldn't say that we are going to change people's circumstances, or that we are going to change the structure of society, and then people's way of thinking will change. No, reformers come and change people's thoughts first. This is *our* history, by the way–the history of the East. Those who say otherwise do not seem to have studied the history of the East very closely–they have focused on Europe's history instead. When you look at the east, whether India, China, Iran or Egypt, you see that religious and spiritual reformers come and the first thing they do is to change how people think. They change the dominant philosophy in people's minds. And once they have changed the way people think, the foundations are ready for a new social order, for a new way of doing things, to replace the unjust social order that came before. This is what we see in history.

If you study history, you will see that India was like this, Iran was like this, Egypt and China were like these. Wherever there was a civilisation, this was the course it took. In what sense? In the sense that people said that mankind were created in two different groups, from two different sources, with two different natures, and for two different purposes–or more than two!–and, for this reason, people living in the same society should not enjoy the same rights as one another. They should not be treated as equal or the same, and whoever claims otherwise is clearly in error. This is how these societies were structured.

Then Islam came and said that there were no gods or children of gods–there was only God. It said that those who thought that there were two gods, or that these gods created two groups of human beings with two different sets of qualities and propensities, were wrong. Instead, it said: There is only one God. He created the cosmos in its entirety. The cosmos and its inhabitants are in the grip of His power and dominion. And He created everyone equal. Therefore, everyone is from a single source, from a single substance, of a single nature and with a single root. There are many verses of the Qur'an which say this, for example: 'O mankind! Worship your Lord, who created you and those who were before you'[51], today, we will look at some of these verses and explain their meaning.

According to Islam, all human beings come from a single source and a single origin. Everyone comes into the world the same way. Each and every person is capable of ascending towards the limitless horizon of perfection. All people can become better, and better, and better still. This is the potentiality found in everyone. However, take note that there are still beings who occupy a higher position than ordinary human beings, and these are the prophets and Imams. They are excluded from our present discussion. When we say that all people have the capacity to strive towards perfection, this does not mean that they can become a prophet or an imam through their efforts

51 Q2:21.

and spiritual struggle. This is something else entirely. How a prophet becomes a prophet or an imam an imam is a discussion whose full treatment we must postpone until another occasion. However, to give a brief overview, the prophets and Imams are people who enjoy some special abilities not granted to all human beings. They have qualities that ordinary people lack. They are also very few in number. They are the exception, rather than the rule. However, they are still human beings and come from the same origin and share the same basic characteristics of other members of their species. In a poem attributed to Imam ʿAlī (a), he says: 'Their father is Adam and their mother is Eve' (*abūhum Ādam wa al-ummu Ḥawwāʾ*).

In short, it is an Islamic principle that the human being is taught in the light of *tawḥīd*, that there should be no social classes in human societies. The kind of society that Islam wants to create is not a society divided into different groups and ranks, with some enjoying more rights and others enjoying fewer. An Islamic society is not one in which we say that human beings are from two or more different sources or origins. An Islamic society is not one where a person is said to be created from dust and another one formed out of light. Their flesh is one and the same. Therefore, when we speak about divine unity, we are talking about more than just monotheism–when we say that there is one God and that this God is the sole creator and director of the heavens and the earth, this necessarily implies the abolition of all social classes within human society.

However, one might object to our argument by saying that not all social class systems are as rigid as the one you have described in India. It is not the case that they all share the same social philosophy: on the contrary, there are many human societies and nations that say all men are created equal, while distinct social classes continue to exist in practice.

Look around at the world today, especially the capitalist world, and especially the wealthiest nations of the capitalist world–you can clearly see that class structures exist in such a society. However, no one in these societies would ever claim that workers and managers are created from two different substances or come from two different sources! No, they would not say that the founder of such and such great company was created one way, and that the worker in such and such a mine was created another. On the contrary, the owner of the factory draws up a contract with his employees, and it is this contract that creates these two classes within a society. However, in practice, there is only a little difference between this and those who believed that different castes of people were made from different substances or brought forth from different sources. This is because the result of a caste-based society and a capitalist society is virtually the same: A small group enjoys limitless resources, while the majority has virtually nothing. A small group monopolises almost all the wealth in the world, while the masses labour day and night just to feed themselves and their families.

This too is a form of social class–one that is observable almost everywhere in the world today. In fact, I would argue that this form of social class is even more harmful and pernicious that the caste system of ancient India. At least in the caste system, they said: 'Yes, you and I are made from two different substances. We are two different species!' On the other hand, today they say: 'We are all brothers and sisters. We are all equal! We will protect your rights!' But, in practice, we see that this is not the case. In practice, there is one rule for the wealthy and another for everyone else. In theory, when we look at the laws of a capitalist country, we see a kind of equality between people: Anyone who commits this crime will suffer this punishment, no matter what their social class. In practice, however, looking at the enforcement of these laws, we see this is not the case. We see that class makes a difference on how the law is applied to you. And thus, we see that the class system is alive and well in the developed world, just as it was in ancient India. The majority of the benefits are reserved for an exceedingly small number of people, while the majority remain deprived. And the most important thing these people are deprived of is a proper understanding of the world.

Islam sets out to abolish all of this. When I looked through the Qur'an to see which verses dealt with the issue of class differences in society, I saw that there were a great many! Here, I am only going to present a few.

God is the one and only Creator, Sustainer and object of worship for all humanity. This is a basic Islamic principle. There is only one being who created all others–God. You might say: So? What difference does this make? It makes a big difference! If we said that there were two creators, this would give rise to a dualistic philosophy and a dualistic society. The first effect this dualistic worldview would have on a society is that it would legitimise the existence of two distinct groups of people–one for each creator. When we say we believe in one God, this necessarily means that all the people of a society are equal–they are a single group and of a single class. No individual is innately superior or inferior to any other. Pay attention to this: When we say we believe that there is one God, what does this mean? That there is one God instead of two? No, it means more than this. It means that all of God's servants are on a single level, not two levels! This is one of the constellations of ideas associated with the basic monotheistic principle that there is one and only one God, and He is the Creator of all: All of God's servants are equal, why? Because they are all at the same level, why? Because God is one and His creation is one.

But could this God love one group of people more than another group after He created them? [As the Qur'anic verse states,] 'The Jews and the Christians say, "We are God's children and His beloved ones."'[52] The Qur'an responds to these claims, by asking: 'Then why

52 Q5:18.

would you kill the prophets of God in the past?'[53] If you were God's children and beloved ones, then why did you kill His prophets and messengers? Why did you kill people who believed in Him? When the Jews and Christians claim that God has chosen them to the exclusion of all others, Islam responds by saying that they are mistaken. Elsewhere, the Qur'an says: 'Say, "O Jews! If you claim that you are God's favourites, to the exclusion of other people, then long for death, should you be truthful!"' If you are truly God's beloved and God's chosen, then long for death. Leave this life behind and go to God who you say has chosen you for Himself! But the Qur'an observes, 'yet they will never long for it.'[54]

Once again, God is the Creator, Sustainer and object of worship for all. This is an extremely important point, because if the creator and the object of worship for all is one, then all people are naturally equal with one another, as all people are made from the same substance. Let us focus on this word 'substance' for a moment: From the material point of view, the point of view of the body, all human beings are made from the same stuff. No one has a physical trait that grants them any more rights than another person. Pay attention to this point: I am not saying that no person has anything to render them better than another, as some people are clearly endowed with abilities that others lack. Some people are naturally intelligent. Others are naturally stronger. Others are naturally weaker. Some are naturally thinner. Others are naturally more beautiful. These differences exist, but what Islam says is that none of these physical differences should be the basis for any legal difference between people. It is not the case that just because someone is physically stronger, they should have more rights than those who are weaker–never! It is not the case that just because a child is born into an influential household,

53 Q2:91.

54 Q62:6–7.

he should be given any more than any other child–never! If Islam opens a school, this school is there for all children; if Islam gives lessons, these lessons are for all children; if Islam gives a person the ability to work and earn a living, or to strive for a better life, it gives everyone this ability.

An Islamic society, ruled by an Islamic government, that lives in the shade of Islam's commandments, is not one where people need some kind of connections to study, to find work, to understand something, to earn a living, to be employed–even at the highest levels. An Islamic society is not like this. The field is open for all. There are a million ways for a million people to follow. Everyone can make use of these to achieve their own material and spiritual goals. There is no problem with this–the way is open for all. This is unlike societies which are not *tawḥīd*-oriented. This is unlike ignorant social orders, where all the doors are opened for some people, and the ways are all closed and blocked-up for others. This is not how an Islamic society should look.

In an Islamic society, even the highest ranks of the social order are open to everyone. Look at the Prophet's companion Bilāl who became the muezzin for the Prophet's Mosque. This was a position of considerable social importance at that time. Not everyone could become a muezzin. Even though as a freed African slave, Bilāl would have been seen as inferior in pre-Islamic Arabian society, in Islamic society, a freed slave could reach the highest ranks. Salmān the Persian is another example: As a non-Arab, he too would have occupied a lower rung on the social ladder in the pre-Islamic era, because the Arabs saw themselves as superior to all other peoples. Not only was Salmān not an Arab, he was also a stranger to Arab society. He had most likely learnt Arabic by living with the Arabs for many years, but he probably could not speak it as well as they did. Nevertheless, he was made the governor of a territory within the Muslim lands. And there are many other examples like this.

This reflects the fact that according to Islam, no one is made better than anyone else. No one has any rights on the basis of their individual differences, even if these individual differences do exist between people. Every position in society is open to people on the basis of their own efforts and abilities. The only exception, of course, are those positions of authority and leadership to which people are directly appointed by God but, as I have said, we will deal with these later. The whole world belongs to God and all people stand in need of Him. Everyone must supplicate to Him. Whatever anyone receives is only from Him. Everyone must turn to Him with their palms outstretched. Therefore, everyone is equal.

Imam al-Sajjād (a) was the descendant of the Prophet, of Fāṭimat al-Zahrāʾ, of the Commander of the Faithful, and of Ḥusayn ibn ʿAlī (peace be upon them all), but he still had to suffer trials and tribulations in this world. He still had to depend on God in all of his affairs. And a person with no connection to the Holy Household of the Prophet is in the same position in relation to God as the Imam was. Meanwhile, Imam al-Bāqir (a) and Imam al-Ṣādiq (a) both performed manual labour in order to earn a living and provide for themselves in this world, just as an ordinary person would have had to do. Imam al-Ṣādiq relates that the Commander of the Faithful (a) also used to perform manual labour, even though he commanded a position of power and respect in society. At the time of the Prophet, one of his top military leaders and someone who fought in almost all of his major battles, was the Commander of the Faithful. This great warrior and leader would work the earth, would tend orchards, carry water and the like. Do you see? If you want to earn money, you must work. If you want to learn, you must study. If you want to get somewhere in society, you must strive for it. And the door of effort is open to everyone–anyone who works hard will get somewhere.

This is the logic of Islam which is displayed throughout the Qur'an in numerous verses. Now, let us refer to the text of the Qur'an and ponder on the meaning of its verses, lest we become like those described in the verse: 'Do they not contemplate the Qur'an, or are there locks on the hearts?'[55] The first batch of verses I would like us to look at today are from *Sūrat al-Muʾminūn*, verses 84 to 91.

'Say, "To whom does the earth belong and whoever it contains, if you know?"'[56] This verse tells the Prophet to ask the idolaters, who believe that their gods each control different parts of the world, to whom does the entirety of the world belong? 'They will say, "To God."' The idolaters of Makkah believed in God and said that their idols were their intercessors with Him. 'Say, "Will you not then take admonition?"'[57]

'Say, "Who is the Lord of the seven heavens and the Lord of the Great Throne?"'[58] Then the Qur'an tells the Prophet to ask them who directs the seven heavens and the Great Throne. What is the meaning of 'throne' (*ʿarsh*)? What are these seven heavens? I've discussed some of these meanings elsewhere, but these are not relevant to our present discussion. There are different opinions, but we will have to discuss these at another opportunity as they are not important at the moment. 'They will say: "To God."' So they acknowledge that God's power extends throughout the heavens and the earth. 'Say, "Will you not then be wary?"'[59] Will you not fear this God? Will you not think and act in accordance with His commands and revelations to you?

'Say, "In whose hand is the dominion of all things, and who gives shelter and no shelter can be provided from Him, if you know?"'[60] Then God tells the Prophet to ask them who has absolute authority

55 Q47:24.

56 Q23:84.

57 Q23:85.

58 Q23:86.

59 Q23:87.

60 Q23:88.

over all things? Someone who has power at his disposal will have power over his own body. He has power over his own home, as he can move one brick from here to there. This is the extent of his authority. He can take two pieces of iron and fuse them together or break them apart. This is the extent of his power. But what about someone who has power over all the atoms of everything? Now, this is being that has *true* authority! The movement of the very particles of the cosmos is by his command. The growth and flourishing of plants, animals and humans, and all the movements that take place within them. Everything that exists is in His grasp. Everything is under His control. That is God. 'In whose hand is the dominion of all things', who is it that holds power and authority over everything, 'and who gives shelter and no shelter can be provided from Him?' This means that no one can keep anyone else safe from God. Imagine that a Christian sins against God and seeks Jesus's protection against God, and that Jesus protects him from God–is such a thing possible? Of course not. It is God that gives protection and shelter to each and every being, to each and every person, and against Him no shelter can be given. 'If you know?' (So who is it that fits this description?) 'They will say, "To God."' They will admit that everything is in God's hands and that He protects and nothing can protect against Him! 'Say, "Then how are you being deluded?"'

See how the Qur'an deals with those who have been led astray? When someone is deluded like this, they remain heedless. But the Qur'an always wants to rouse people from their state of heedlessness. It does not want them to remain deluded. It wants to open their eyes. The Qur'an is sure that if people opened their eyes and saw things clearly, they would agree with what it says. Today, I say the same thing to you. If people in the world today opened their eyes, they would govern the whole world according to what this Qur'an says. If they opened their eyes! As no one will accept the ignorance or delusion being offered by deceivers when they see the world clearly.

'Rather We have brought them the truth, and they are indeed liars.'[61] God says He has made the matter clear for them. He gave them the truth. But in spite of this, they still make excuses and offer lies. 'God has not taken any offspring, neither is there any god besides Him.'[62]

Notice how this is where God offers His main argument, even though the verses that came before were also pointing to this fact. How do we know that God has no offspring and that there is no god besides Him? The Qur'an answers: 'For then each god would take away what he created', so if there were many gods, then each god would keep his own creation to himself. In other words, there would be differences, there would be different classes of people. When the Qur'an says each god would take away what he created, this means he would gather it together and, in doing so, destroy the unity and harmony that underlies the creation as we see it; the creation of both the world and of humanity. If there was a god of light and a god of darkness, and a god of humans, a god of the elite, and a god of the poor, then creation would fall apart into a hundred pieces, with one for each god. On the other hand, according to the worldview of divine unity, creation is one contiguous and harmonious whole. All beings, whether humans, animals, mountains or stars–all of them without exception–are bound together and unified. 'For then each god would take away what he created', if there had indeed been another god, then each god would have had his own creation, 'and some of them would surely rise up against the others' and seek superiority. 'Clear is God of what they allege!'

The next set of verses I would like to discuss are verses 21 and 22 from *Sūrat al-Baqarah*: 'O mankind! Worship your Lord, who created

61 Q23:90.

62 Q23:91.

you and those who were before you, so that you may be Godwary.'[63] This means that worshipping and serving God causes you to attain Godwariness (*taqwā*). In other words, worshipping God engenders a state of being in the human spirit in which a person is protected from sinning. Therefore, a society in which everyone is first and foremost a servant of God is a society in which Godwariness exists in abundance. There is no shortage of Godwariness, unlike today!

'He who made the earth a place of repose for you',[64] notice how the Qur'an describes everything as being for everyone's benefit. What does it mean when the Qur'an says something was 'made for you'? It means it is for everyone! 'And the sky a canopy, and He sends down water from the sky, and with it He brings forth crops for your sustenance.' He sends rain to bring forth fruits and vegetables for *your* provision, not only the provision of a special class of people who can give a share of it to you as charity. No, it is for everyone. If this is the case, 'So do not set up equals to God, while you know'. Do not set up a second god as a rival or equal to God by dividing human beings into two or three or more groups: everyone is one group.

Next, let us look at verse 13 of *Sūrat al-Ḥujurāt*, which is very well-known amongst people: 'O mankind! Indeed We created you from a male and a female'.[65] Notice how this is addressed to everyone ('O mankind!') and it says that they all came from one man and one woman; all of them came from a single couple. There is a poem attributed to the Commander of the Faithful, in which he explains this:

'Mankind are all alike in their image
Al-Nās min jihat al-timthāl akfāʾ-u
For their father is Adam and their mother is Eve'
Abūhum Ādam wa al-ummu hawwāʾ-u

63 Q2:21.

64 Q2:22.

65 Q49:13.

All are the same and equal with regard to their origin and creation. 'And made you nations and tribes that you may identify yourselves with one another.' So, tribes and nations exist so that we may know one another (this is something that would benefit from further explanation, but we must leave it for another occasion due to time constraints). 'Indeed, the noblest of you in the sight of God is the most Godwary among you.' This is Islam's final word on the abolition of social classes; nobility comes from *taqwā* and nothing else. Nobility does not come from one's social class, from one's family or from one's lineage. However, there is an even more interesting and significant point that the Qur'an is making here, namely that even those who have more *taqwā* and are, therefore, nobler than others, do not enjoy any special rights or privileges as a result of this. It is not the case that the most Godwary of people receive more money or have the right to do things that others do not or have access to facilities in society that others do not. Not at all–it is not like this! 'Indeed the noblest of you in the sight of God is the most Godwary among you' and while *taqwā* has some impact on one's place in society (for example, some duties require the person to be recognised as possessing *taqwā*), this does not change a person's status before the law. 'Indeed God is the all-knowing, all-aware.'

The next verse I would like to discuss is verse 70 from *Sūrat al-Isrā*ʾ: 'Certainly We have honoured the Children of Adam, and carried them over land and sea' (by multiplying their modes of transportation). The verse then carries on to say 'and provided them with all the good things'. This, combined with 'and carried them over land and sea' might point to relations between different people as if a person cannot move from one place to another, there is no possibility of them forming relations with other people and, where there are no relations between people, no society can form. So, unless God carried human beings across land and sea to connect them with one another, they would have remained divided and scattered. 'And provided them with all the good things, and given them an advantage over many of those We have created with a complete preference.'[66] Who are these that God is speaking about here? Who has He ennobled? Who has He provided with all the good things? Who has He favoured over many of the creatures? The answer is humanity as a whole–all human beings, and not merely a special class or group of them.

O Lord! By Muḥammad and the Family of Muḥammad, let us hold fast to the Qur'an in this world and the Hereafter.

By Muḥammad and the Family of Muḥammad, O Lord! Grant us abundant good from studying the Qur'an!

66 Q17:70.

The Psychological Effects of Belief in Tawḥīd

Tuesday 14th Ramadan 1394
31st September 1974

الَّذِينَ اسْتَجَابُوا لِلَّهِ وَالرَّسُولِ مِنْ بَعْدِ مَا أَصَابَهُمُ الْقَرْحُ
لِلَّذِينَ أَحْسَنُوا مِنْهُمْ وَاتَّقَوْا أَجْرٌ عَظِيمٌ (١٧٢) الَّذِينَ قَالَ
لَهُمُ النَّاسُ إِنَّ النَّاسَ قَدْ جَمَعُوا لَكُمْ فَاخْشَوْهُمْ فَزَادَهُمْ إِيمَانًا
وَقَالُوا حَسْبُنَا اللَّهُ وَنِعْمَ الْوَكِيلُ (١٧٣)

'Those who responded to God and the Apostle [even] after they had been wounded-for those of them who have been virtuous and Godwary there shall be a great reward. Those to whom the people said, "All the people have gathered against you; so fear them." That only increased them in faith, and they said, "God is sufficient for us, and He is an excellent trustee."'
- Sūrat Āl-i ʿImrān (3):172-173.

So far, we have discussed a number of topics connected to the effects that belief in *tawḥīd* has on the fabric of human society and the form which it bestows on a human society where it is present. Many other topics yet remain to be discussed. One of the most important of these is the effect that belief in *tawḥīd* and the worldview of *tawḥīd* has on the economic affairs of a *tawḥīd*-oriented society. This is an important paragraph in the treaty of *tawḥīd*! This is something that requires considerable research and discussion, and it is not something that can be undertaken in public lectures such as these. However, we can briefly allude to this topic through the verse: 'and give them out of the wealth of God which He has given you.'[67] So give to the poor and the needy when they have need. This reflects how the *tawḥīd*-oriented worldview sees worldly wealth. However, if we want to use the various verses about money and wealth to develop a *tawḥīd*-oriented economic policy for Islamic society, this is a topic that must be dealt with in an academic or scholarly setting. For this reason, we will not be discussing it here.

Another reason is that we have more essential topics to discuss in the field of the fundamental doctrines of Islam and Islamic ideology. These present lectures will, assuming God grants us the life and the opportunity, continue until the end of the Month of Ramadan. Clearly, if we want to discuss every aspect of this topic, we will not reach our conclusions before the month is out. So these are two issues that we will have to pass over in briefly our lectures.

While the topic we will be discussing today is still about *tawḥīd*, it is strongly related to the first part of this series of lectures, that dealt with faith, belief and the promises given to the faithful in the Qur'an. Faith (*īmān*), as we said there, means a belief that leads to action and which gives rise to moral responsibility. However, we said that faith must always be on the basis of knowledge and understanding–it should never be blind or unquestioning faith–and, at the same time, it should not be merely a verbal profession of faith, without any righteous acts to back it up. This is what we discussed previously. The doctrine of *tawḥīd* is a part of faith, as it is a belief that leads the believer to act, and a belief that is based on knowledge and understanding. Belief in divine unity means that the believer must shoulder a heavy moral

67 Q24:33.

responsibility. Indeed, it is the heaviest and most momentous of beliefs in Islamic and religious ideologies. The commitment to *tawḥīd* by a believer in reality is basically a commitment to create a *tawḥīdī* world. It is a commitment to efface all the effects of polytheism from society. This is the duty created by *tawḥīd*.

Let me just mention a brief point here for those of you who are familiar with the Arabic language. The word *tawḥīd* belongs to the morphological form of *tafʿīl*. If you ask any student of the Hawzah what the linguistic meaning of this word is, they will tell you: 'to make something one.' *Tawḥīd* is derived from the root *waḥdah*, meaning 'oneness'. When you conjugate *waḥdah* in the form of *tafʿīl* to produce *tawḥīd*, it means 'to make something one.' In other words, to make many gods into one God. Therefore, to make a society which is not *tawḥīd*-oriented into one which is. This means taking an idolatrous mind or an idolatrous heart and making it a monotheistic mind or monotheistic heart. *Tawḥīd* in the sense of 'making one' is, in its entirety, concerned with a moral act. The word itself implies a sense of duty and a sense of obligation. The etymology of this term is a fact which, upon close examination, will help you better understand the whole concept that it represents.

So, believing in *tawḥīd* is a major part of faith and it embraces a serious moral obligation, to the extent that no other Islamic or religious doctrine, or even non-Islamic social doctrines, approach the seriousness of *tawḥīd*. For example, eliminating poverty from society is a duty, redistributing wealth in any society is a duty that a particular philosophy or school of thought might demand from its followers. Putting an end to wars is a duty which a school of thought might undertake to fulfil, or which a follower or followers of that school might take up themselves. However, when we look at *tawḥīd* in the truest sense of the word–when we say that *tawḥīd* means not only to make God one, but to establish a divine government, a divine society, a divine law or a divine way of life, this embraces all of the duties we just mentioned, even those which other philosophies or schools of thought might share in common with ours. Do you see how momentous the duty of *tawḥīd* is when we look at it in this way?

So, *tawḥīd* is faith, founded on understanding, accompanied by a moral duty, a moral duty which underpins all other religious and non-religious doctrines, and which is more momentous, more definitive and more comprehensive than any other duty. This is *tawḥīd*. And if believing in *tawḥīd* means this and it is a real and true belief, then we can look at this faith and see what effect it has. What effect does this practical doctrine have on the psychology of the one who believes in it? What effect *should* it have and what effect *will* it have? This is a separate topic altogether. Let us see what effect this belief will have on this person's spirit and mind when they believe in *tawḥīd*, when they believe that God is one and apply this belief to every conceivable angle of human existence.

There are two reasons why it is worth having such a discussion. First, because this will increase our familiarity with *tawḥīd* from a different angle: We will understand what *tawḥīd* means as a spiritual and psychological teaching. This way, if we meet someone who interprets *tawḥīd* as a kind of spiritual opiate to put people to sleep, we can tell them they are mistaken, that this is not the proper understanding of *tawḥīd*, and offer them a correct interpretation. So, we will know *tawḥīd* better. This is first.

Second, we will each be able to see whether we are true believers in *tawḥīd* or not. It will give us a criterion by which to recognise the effects of belief in divine unity on our own hearts and souls. How do I know that I believe in *tawḥīd*? How do I know that this belief has really rooted itself in my spirit, in the depths of my being, and that it has had an effect on me? When I know what the psychological effects of *tawḥīd* should be, it is like knowing what the effects of a medicine should be. When I know this, I can look and see whether this effect is there or not. I can see whether I have taken the right medicine or whether I have been given a placebo? Did the physician give me real medicine or just sugar pills? If I see that these effects are not there in my own being, I will know that I've been given a placebo. That this medicine was fake. Because, if it was genuine medicine, then I should be experiencing its effects in myself. Now, we could spend a great deal of time discussing the various psychological aspects of *tawḥīd*, so what I will be presenting here today is just a summary in order that in tomorrow's lecture, we can begin discussing prophethood.

So, let me summarise the psychological effects of belief in divine unity in just a few sentences. A true believer in *tawḥīd* will experience a number of spiritual effects as a result of this belief. First, he will be broad-minded and farsighted in how he sees the world. A believer is cured of narrow-mindedness and short-sightedness. He will not say: 'I was defeated in this arena' or 'I was beaten in this confrontation' or 'all this effort was a waste.' He will not be so short-sighted as to say these things. He will know that the idea of divine unity extends throughout the full length of not only his life, but human history as a whole, and what is ten, twenty, fifty or even a hundred years compared to all human history? It is but a minute, a fleeting moment, and nothing more. To put it another way from another perspective, a believer does not only see things in terms of material issues and physical needs. He sees beyond this. When a true believer sees himself, as well as his material needs, whether these needs are in the tens or hundreds, he also recognises the greatest and most urgent human needs. His mind and senses are not completely absorbed by lowly physical needs like those people who are inwardly fixated on this world, even if they make an outward show of godliness and piety–they are actually imprisoned in materiality. When a believer in divine unity looks, he sees the future stretching out before him to infinity. Just as I said in an earlier lecture, a believer does not believe in the end of the world. This is because the end of this world is the beginning of another world. This life and the life that follow are but a single scroll. Death is not a wall to the believer. It is not the end of the road. Rather, it is a bridge that must be crossed in order to reach a world that is broader and more magnificent than this one. This is one of the unique features of *tawḥīd.*

For someone who does not believe in *tawḥīd*, every sacrifice, everything given in the service of higher human principles, all of it is lost with his last breath. On the other hand, for the true believer, his last breath is but the beginning of a new and broader life in a more magnificent and glorious environment. If a materialist is extremely altruistic, he is ready to lay down his own life in a limited set of circumstances, even though this means he is reduced to nothing. On the other hand, if a true believer wishes to sacrifice himself, he is like a moth to the flame–he has no thoughts of his own benefits. In fact, even if he doesn't want to sacrifice himself it is still easier for him than a materialist who does, because he does not believe that death reduces him to nothingness, because he knows that there is more to reality than just this world. There is a life awaiting us beyond this life.

Another effect that belief in *tawḥīd* has on the psychology of a believer is that it causes fear to dry out and shrivel up–this is very significant. At several places in the Qur'an, as we will see today, God tells the faithful 'Do not fear them but fear Me!'[68] Belief in divine unity removes all fear of others from your heart because God tells you: If you want to fear someone, fear Me! And someone who fears God fears nothing else. Someone who is a true believer in *tawḥīd*, who recognises God's awesome power, has no fear of anything. If, when I ponder on this and reflect on my own self, I see that there is fear there, I must remind myself that it is this fear that causes people to lose this world and the next. It is fear of poverty that causes people not to spend for God, it is fear of persecution and harm that causes people to stay quiet when all matter of crimes, injustices and

68 Q3:175.

humiliations are being heaped upon them. The fear that they might not be able to live another day or two in this world! And what kind of life is this, to be lived in fear? Fear of losing this lowly life for which there is no guarantee that it will last more than another day or two! Fear of losing this worthless life is what causes a person to end other lives, to make social life bitter or to take it away altogether. Even a person's ambitions are borne out of fear, and the fears are at the root of every misery in this life. If you look at the length and breadth of human history, you will see the reasons for the fact that the supporters of the truth were always in a minority, and what kept them as a minority. What things caused people who knew the truth to turn away from it, when those that knew what was right did not act upon it. What things caused people to commit the worst crimes, when you see people dirtying their hands with such acts. Usually, if you study all of this closely, you will see that all of this comes from fear–from *fear*!

When the Islamic society, as you all are well aware, lost its way and went into decline, why was it that Muslims could not hold onto the real Islam? That they could not keep hold of the gifts God had given to them freely? I say this because it was the first generation who sacrificed, but it was the second generation who reaped the rewards. So why was it that they could not maintain these? Was it any reason other than fear? Who amongst the people did not know the kind of man that Muʿāwiyah was? Of those who were around the Commander of the Faithful, who listened to what he said, who benefitted from his presence, who did not know? In the Hejaz, was there anyone that did not know Muʿāwiyah ibn Abī Sufyān? Was there anyone who didn't know ʿAbd al-Malik ibn Marwān? Was there anyone who didn't know the character of the Umayyad house, who could not see with their own eyes? Who had not experienced it themselves? Who had not understood the words the Qur'an and the Prophet had uttered about them, nor seen the testimony of history against them, nor had been touched by their acts? Everyone knew exactly who they were! So why did no one raise their voice? Was it for any reason other than fear? This was why they surrendered to him. This is why they cooperated with him. This is why they danced to his tune–fear. Nothing but fear. This fear extended from the lowest ranks of society to the highest, even to some well-known figures who people were hoping would stand up to Muʿāwiyah, although they never did.

ʿAbd Allāh ibn ʿUmar was one of these figures. In his time, he was a symbol of quiescence, meekness who rejected the truth. ʿAbd Allāh ibn Zubayr was another one who rejected the truth but, when you look at a figure like Ibn Zubayr, you see he is to be much preferred to ʿAbd Allāh ibn ʿUmar. It was ʿAbd Allāh ibn ʿUmar who, after ʿUthmān was killed, did not pledge allegiance to the Commander of the Faithful. Why did he not pledge? He said it was because the affair was not clear for him. So he exercised precaution and did not pledge allegiance to ʿAlī. Out of religious precaution, he did not pledge allegiance to the Commander of the Faithful! Because, in his own words, in his own mind, this was not something that all the Muslims had agreed upon. Now, even if you don't have any personal ambitions, and if you are not afflicted by any diseases of the heart, have you not heard the words: 'Do not be afraid on the path of guidance by the meagre number of its people'? And even if you have not heard these words of Imam ʿAlī, have you not heard something to this effect in the words of the Prophet and in the verses of the Qur'an? Do you not understand that the path of God, the right path, the path of guidance, does not swerve because of numbers? Do you not understand that you should not turn aside from the path just because you see there are few people here and more people over there? You should only see whether or not it is guidance. This is an important Islamic principle for how we should live our lives: Do not look at what others are saying or doing. Do not concern yourself with what the majority–who are trapped in their own ignorance–are doing, or what they are doing it for. But because

ʿAbd Allāh ibn ʿUmar did not grasp this important principle, and because he did not apply it in his own life, he turned away from the Commander of the Faithful and failed to pledge allegiance to him.

Years later, the Commander of the Faithful (a) was martyred. Muʿāwiyah ruled for many years. This same ʿAbd Allāh ibn ʿUmar knew Muʿāwiyah very well. He was a close associate of his. And even if he did not know what kind of person he was at first, he certainly came to know it later. Then came the rule of Yazīd. The three years of his reign are like a black stain on the history of Islam. Marwān ibn al-Ḥakam succeeded Yazīd for a short time, before his son ʿAbd al-Malik ibn Marwān took over for him. For the entirety of this time, for the reigns of all of these tyrants, ʿAbd Allāh ibn ʿUmar was in the city of Madinah, in the middle of the debates and discussions, with history unfolding all around him. He was not uninformed. He was not unaware of what had happened and what was happening to Islamic society. It was not the case that he did not know who these men were. He knew exactly who the Umayyads were and what they were like. At the same time, Ḥajjāj ibn Yūsuf al-Thaqafī, the enforcer and executioner of the Umayyads, came and recaptured Makkah when ʿAbd Allāh ibn Zubayr led a rebellion in the city. ʿAbd Allāh ibn Zubayr rose up in opposition to the Umayyads and fought doggedly against the armies of the Umayyad Caliph, ʿAbd al-Malik ibn Marwān, which had been hard marched from Syria. Ḥajjāj ibn Yūsuf won the war because he was more brutal than anyone else. That is why the Umayyads sent him to Hejaz. He set up catapults on the mountains around Makkah and bombarded the city. Even the Kaʿbah was not spared. Many people were killed. ʿAbd Allāh ibn Zubayr was slain and his body was put on display.

Ḥajjāj ibn Yūsuf sat in his command tent writing a report of his conquest of Makkah to send to Damascus, which was then the capital of the Caliphate. ʿAbd Allāh was amongst the people of Makkah as they came in groups to pledge allegiance to Ḥajjāj ibn Yūsuf. It was not the case that people did not know who Ḥajjāj was–they knew exactly who he was. It was not the case that they thought he was a good and pious Muslim–they knew he was a cruel and ruthless general in the service of a wicked tyrant. They knew all of this, but because he had defeated them, because he held the power, because if people did not pledge allegiance to them he would have their heads cut-off as punishment–because they were *afraid*, these people came in groups to pledge allegiance to Ḥajjāj. ʿAbd Allāh ibn ʿUmar was one of these thousands who came out of the city to Ḥajjāj's encampment to do just this. As he approached, he said: 'Tell them that ʿAbd Allāh ibn ʿUmar has come!' He thought that he would receive a formal welcome and be well-received. What he did not grasp was that the nature of power is one of indifference to those who lack it. He thought that because he had once helped and advised Muʿāwiyah, and because he had not supported the Family of the Prophet, now the Umayyads recognised his worth. He did not realise that these were men who would bite the hand that fed them. He came and said: 'I am ʿAbd Allāh ibn ʿUmar.' They told Ḥajjāj: '"ʿAbd Allāh ibn ʿUmar is here.' He said: 'Tell him to come inside.' He came in but Ḥajjāj did not make any move for him. He did not show him any respect. He didn't even look up from his papers to see him or to greet him. ʿAbd Allāh ibn ʿUmar said: 'Commander, give me your hand that I might pledge allegiance.' Who is speaking here? ʿAbd Allāh ibn ʿUmar is saying to Ḥajjāj that he wants to pledge allegiance. This is the same ʿAbd Allāh ibn ʿUmar that out of 'religious precaution' did not say to ʿAlī ibn Abī Ṭālib: 'Give me your hand so that I might pledge allegiance.' He tells Ḥajjāj: 'Give me your hand that I might pledge allegiance.' Do you know what Ḥajjāj says in response? 'My hand is busy writing. You can pledge allegiance to my foot!' So he pledges allegiance to Ḥajjaj's foot. This is what a lowly person does: For the sake of two more days in this world, to go on living in this state of abasement, to live in a way without dignity in this world or the Hereafter, to go on living by eating a few morsels of illicit provisions, to go on living in a way that will not bring them closer to God but only closer to Satan. For two more days like this, a person is willing to come to Ḥajjāj and pledge allegiance to his foot. Why? What other reason could there be besides fear?

That is why there are supplications narrated from the Prophet's Household (a) specifically for the month of Ramadan–and I strongly encourage you to read the supplications narrated from the Imams and ponder on their meaning–in which these psychological issues and issues relating to the human spirit are often mentioned. In one of these supplications, Imam al-Sajjād–who would teach people through his supplications–says: 'O God! Grant me a long life'.[69] This is one sentence from his supplication that I would like to explain to you, first so that you will understand why supplication is considered so important, so that perhaps those of you who are less inclined towards supplication or do not know much about it, will perhaps give it more thought. Second, so that those who are against supplication altogether will understand what it is they are against, and will see that there are teachings and ideas latent within these supplications for their benefit.

Imam al-Sajjād says: 'O God, grant me a long life so long as my life is dedicated to your service!' (*Allāhumma ʿammirnī mā kāna ʿumrī bidhlatan fī tāʿatik.*) Notice that he does not just ask for a long life–he does not ask to live a hundred or a hundred and twenty years for no reason–he specifies that he wants a long life so long as this life is spent in the service and worship of God! A long life spent striving hard, spent doing righteous deeds, that is what he wants. He does not want a long life of idleness and leisure. 'O God, grant me a long life so long as my life is dedicated to your service! So, when my life becomes a pasture for Satan, then take me unto you.' Now, you must remember what we said about the meaning of this word, 'Satan'–you will recall we said

69 See *Duʿā Makārim al-Akhlāq.*

that this name refers to all malign forces, anything that would lead the human being and humanity down the path of error, sinfulness and corruption. So what the Imam is saying to God here is: 'Whenever You see my life has become a pasture for Satan, when you see it has become a tool for the benefit of Your enemies, when you see them using me for their own propaganda, when you see them using me for their own benefit, when you see them taking advantage of my ignorance, or of my delusion, or of my pride, whenever you see that I am of more benefit to the bad than I am to the good, whether I know this or not–then I have become a servant of Satan, a pasture for Satan, so take me unto You as I do not want to live such a life!' This is the meaning of his prayer!

Now if you say these words to God with sincerity and from the depths of your soul, being aware of its true meaning and significance, how do you think you would live? This is a supplication which has been given to us by the Imams to teach us that death would be better than a life which profits the wrongdoers and the enemies of God.

So, why should you fear death, O ʿAbd Allāh ibn ʿUmar? Give up this appearance of life! What has Ḥajjāj to give you? Your life? The life that you cannot be sure will go on for more than ten minutes after you give him a humiliating pledge of allegiance or ten years? And what sort of life would it be even if you were to live ten more years? Let Ḥajjāj take such a life from you. Let him put an end to it. Don't you see the misery that awaits you in this world?

ʿAbd Allāh ibn ʿAbbās is another historical example. He lived and died most miserably. He too abandoned ʿAlī, Ḥasan and Ḥusayn. Hence, I believe that people like ʿAbd Allāh ibn ʿAbbās and ʿAbd Allāh ibn ʿUmar were not truly believers in *tawḥīd*. Or else they would not have accepted to live like this.

The most important psychological effect that belief in *tawḥīd* has on the soul of a person who is setting out on the path of God, the path of duty, the path which leads to the purpose of his existence, is to make him unafraid of the enemies he will face on this path. I will not say that he never feels fear, or that he will never tremble, no–only that he will not be driven by fear and anxiety. He will not be held back by fear from following the path of God. Such fear will not exist in him: the kind of fear that prevents a person from behaving virtuously, the kind of fear that lays the foundations for treachery, the kind of fear from which springs the worst crimes and immoral acts. *Tawḥīd* puts this fear aside.

The verses from the Qur'an which I would like to discuss with you today are from two parts of the Qur'an, one is from *Sūrat Āl-i ʿImrān*, as we mentioned ad the beginning. Then, I would like to discuss a few verses from *Sūrat al-Raʿd*.

If we look at verse 172 from *Sūrat Āl-i ʿImrān*, what does it say? 'Those who responded to God and the Apostle [even] after they had been wounded–for those of them who have been virtuous and Godwary there shall be a great reward.'[70] Now, there are several preliminary points that we must mention from the preceding verses as we read this one. 'Those who responded to God and the Apostle', what does 'responded' (*istajābū*) mean here? It means that they answered the call of God and the Prophet, and they answered it with action. They did not just answer affirmatively in their hearts to God's command, no; they set out with the Prophet of God! And when was this? At one of the most difficult and critical moments in the Prophet's mission, they answered the call. This was when they were wounded in battle–'after they had been wounded'–after they had been injured in the fighting–'for those of them who have been virtuous and Godwary there shall be a great reward.'

This verse refers to the Battle of Uḥud. As you will recall, during the battle of Uḥud some of the Muslims turned tail and ran. The Prophet called out to them to stand and fight, but they were afraid, so they did

70 Q3:172.

not listen to his words. However, there were some wounded soldiers who heard the Prophet call out, and they answered his call. At Uḥud, some reports state that Imam ʿAlī suffered as many as seventy-one wounds on his body. In any case, he was badly wounded. So were many other of the Prophet's companions, although perhaps not as seriously. Some of these responded to the call of God and the Prophet, while others did not and ran away. This verse explains what reward lies in store for those who did not turn and run but stood their ground and answered the call. The Qur'an continues to describe them: 'those to whom the people said...'. Pay close attention to the universal import of these verses. Do not limit them only to the Battle of Uḥud. Although these verses are about events at the advent of Islam and they were revealed in response to specific circumstances, we should not restrict the ideas contained in these verses to these specific contexts. And what concerns us most about these verses are their ideas. What do the verses want to say to us today?

There is a point which I have often made: Sometimes in the context of a story in the Qur'an, there is a phrase or sentence connected with that story which reveals a universal Islamic principle. Pay attention to this. For example, in the story of the Prophet Noah, when Noah boards the Ark, he brings his family and dependents with him, as well as his followers, the faithful and those who were with him. Everyone else was left exposed to the flood waters with nowhere to go: The waters were rising, and the waves were heaving all around them. They were going to drown. Noah had a son who was not a believer. He did not board the Ark. And while this may appear to be an ordinary story, it contains many important ideas and principles for us to reflect upon.

The Prophet Noah lived an extremely long life, he told his son: 'Come and board the Ark or else you will drown!' His son replied: 'No, I will not board the Ark and I will not drown. I am going to climb to the top of that mountain. I don't need you!' While they were speaking, a wave came between them and, after that, Noah could no longer see his son. That was the end of it. Of course, as a human being, Noah is grieved–he had lost his son, after all. He calls out to God, upset, and says: 'My Lord! You promised me that my family would be saved! My son is one of my family!' To this, God responds: 'He is not of your family. Indeed, he is [personification of] unrighteous conduct.'[71] Here, we will not focus on the meaning of 'unrighteous conduct', but there is one phrase in particular that I want to look at (and there are still many others we could examine in this story), namely 'He is not from your family' (*innahū laysa min ahlik*). This illustrates a universal Islamic principle and important moral teaching: Two brothers who do not think alike are like strangers to one another, but two strangers who think alike are like brothers to one another. In this case, the father and the son thought differently to one another. One believed in God, the other disbelieved. One was on God's side, the other was on Satan's side. A father and a son like this are not from the same nation, let alone kin or family, as one another. From the viewpoint of Islam, relations of family and blood are second to relations of thought and faith. This is an Islamic principle.

When we study the traditions of the Prophet and his Household, we find much evidence to support this principle. There is a narration from one of the Imams which reads: 'A believer is the brother of a believer, but not through his father or mother.' In other words, you could be a million miles apart from your own blood brother, but closer than a blood brother to a believer that lives on the other side of the world. This is because you think alike, because you are on the same side, because you share the same faith. This is an Islamic principle. So, pay close attention to the stories of the Qur'an and ask yourself what message they hold for us in the present day, what principle, idea or historical reality do they expound that could be repeated in

71 11:46

a hundred other places? Now, let us return to the verses about the Battle of Uḥud:

'Those to whom the people said, "All the people have gathered against you; so fear them."'[72] The people told them that everyone is against you, they are plotting and working together to bring you down, so you should be on your guard! This is given as well-meaning advice to the faithful. But, when the faithful receive this well-meaning advice, what is their response? 'That only increased them in faith'. First of all, it made their faith stronger. The plots of the enemies made the faith of the believers stronger! How interesting! Then what? The verse continues, 'and they said, "God is sufficient for us, and He is an excellent trustee."' Second, they entrusted their affairs to God.

'God is sufficient for us, and He is an excellent trustee.' What does 'God is sufficient for us' (*ḥasbunā Allāh*) mean? There are several ways of understanding this and all of them are correct. It could mean that God's help is sufficient for us. It could mean that God will use all the forces of nature to aid us because we are on the side of truth. It could mean that even if we are not successful in this world, God will be pleased with us and that is sufficient for us. Any of these interpretations or others would be correct. 'God is sufficient for us, and He is an excellent trustee. So they returned with God's blessing and grace, untouched by any evil. They pursued the pleasure of God, and God is dispenser of a great grace.'[73] These people who received God's blessings and were not harmed in the slightest were happy and rejoicing. Why were they happy and rejoicing? The Qur'an does not tell us precisely what happened with them, but it makes no difference, however this happened, whether they became martyrs on the battlefield, or they returned home safely to the city of Madinah, it is all the same. If they returned home, they returned

72 Q3:173.

73 Q3:173–174.

home triumphant, victorious and, ultimately, unharmed, because any wounds they suffered in battle would be soothed by their return home to their families. 'So they returned with God's blessing and grace'. And if they were slain in battle and martyred, then they returned *to* God's blessing and His grace; a blessing and grace that has no limit, that never ends, where no harm or unpleasantness will ever afflict them again; a rest without disturbance. 'So they returned with God's blessing and grace'.

'That is only Satan frightening his followers! So fear them not, and fear Me, should you be faithful.'[74] This verse is one to be remembered and pondered upon. It says that it was Satan who frightens his own followers by telling them: 'All the people are plotting against you, they are scheming to bring you down, they have gathered their forces, the hypocrites have joined forces with the idolaters of Makkah, they have their swords hidden and lying in wait to strike you!' These thoughts which frighten you 'that is only Satan frightening his followers!' The one who frightens you is God's enemy, Satan, and only Satan should be afraid. What about you? Will you fear the words of Satan? Will you be one of those who become afraid? What sort of person will you be? He can only frighten his friends. If you are frightened, that is because you are his friend. If you are not his friend, you will not be frightened. Do you see how this short verse is so full of meaning and significance? 'That is only Satan frightening his followers! So fear them not, and fear Me, should you be faithful.' God says: If you want to fear something, fear me. Obey my commands and fear my punishment, if you are truly believers!

Then, God tells the Prophet: 'Do not grieve for those who are active in unfaith; they will not hurt God in the least: God desires to give them no share in the Hereafter, and there is a great punishment for

---

74 Q3:175.

them.'[75] God wants to deprive them of their share in the Hereafter. As time is short, we will have to forgo our discussion of the other verses. However, what we have covered is sufficient for the topic of fearing God verses fearing Satan.

75 3:176.

Section Three

Prophethood (Nubuwwah)

The Philosophy of Prophethood

Wednesday 15th Ramadan 1394
1st October 1974

هُوَ الَّذِي بَعَثَ فِي الْأُمِّيِّينَ رَسُولًا مِنْهُمْ يَتْلُو عَلَيْهِمْ آيَاتِهِ
وَيُزَكِّيهِمْ وَيُعَلِّمُهُمُ الْكِتَابَ وَالْحِكْمَةَ وَإِنْ كَانُوا مِنْ قَبْلُ
لَفِي ضَلَالٍ مُبِينٍ (٢) وَآخَرِينَ مِنْهُمْ لَمَّا يَلْحَقُوا بِهِمْ وَهُوَ
الْعَزِيزُ الْحَكِيمُ (٣)

'It is He who sent to the unlettered [people] an apostle from among themselves, to recite to them His signs, to purify them, and to teach them the Book and wisdom, and earlier they had indeed been in manifest error. And to others from among them [as well] who have not yet joined them. And He is the All-mighty, the All-wise.'
- Sūrat Jumuʿah (62):2-3.

There are several issues surrounding prophethood that we will be examining in the light of the Qur'an's verses. But first it is worth remembering, brothers and sisters, that Prophethood is one of the fundamental teachings of almost all religions. We cannot simply say that it is a fundamental doctrine of the faith. By this, I do not mean to deny that it is one of our *uṣūl al-dīn*, but rather to say that it is *the* fundamental doctrine of any faith. After all, religion without a belief in some kind of prophethood is utterly meaningless. A religion (*dīn*), by definition, is a programme, a path, a school of thought based on a message brought from God. This requires that there be a messenger who brought this message from God in the first place. Therefore, prophethood is an essential component of religion as a category. It is what makes religion *religion*. So, when we discuss the doctrine of prophethood, it must be with this fact in mind.

With regard to prophethood, there are a number of topics that are traditionally covered by texts on this subject. What I will do here is select one of these to discuss in a slightly different perspective based on the verse that we recited at the beginning of this lecture. On the whole, prophethood (*nubuwwah*) is traditionally dealt with in theological texts. However, our view is that while these texts contain many important discussions, it is not necessarily the case that these discussions will be useful for people today looking to improve their knowledge of the religion. Many things that scholars say might be correct, insofar as a few sentences might express a general teaching that has been derived from many years of study and research, however of all the correct things that scholars have said, we must look to see which are necessary today? And of all the things that are necessary for us to discuss, which is the most pressing? We should begin with the most urgent issue first and, only having addressed this, move onto other issues in order of importance, until we are only left with discussions that, while correct, are of low importance for the needs of our time.

For example, when talking about prophethood, we can talk about the extent to which a prophet is a possessor of divine knowledge or of secular learning. This is a discussion within theology. Or, we might want to discuss whether or not the Prophet of Islam was able to read or write, as per the verse: 'You did not use to recite any scripture before it, nor did you write it with your right hand, for then the impugners would have been sceptical.'[1] Now, when the verse says that the Prophet did not recite scripture or write any of it, was this because he lacked the ability to do so? In other words, was it because he was illiterate by today's standards? Or not? Could it be that he was able to read and write but simply did not do so? This is yet another discussion. Alternatively, we might ask what was the religion of the Prophet before he was chosen as a prophet of God? Yes, all of these are questions we *could* ask had we the inclination, but which of these, if any, are *necessary* for us to know? The answer is none of them. Not one of them.

Yes, once someone knows everything about prophethood and religion, there is no problem asking such academic questions: For example, what was the religion of the Prophet before he was chosen? But right now, when we know so little, when our society has yet to grasp the basic meaning of prophethood, of someone being sent a message from God, of the purpose of God sending messengers in the first place, and of the way in which prophecy and prophethood function, how necessary are such academic discussions? Muslims do not know the purpose of Muḥammad's mission or what he was sent to accomplish, and this is the cause of our miserable state today. Because, if we truly grasped what his mission was, we would be pursuing it right now. So, when we are ignorant of the fundamentals of prophethood, of the basics of prophethood, what use is there of delving into secondary issues or trying to answer academic questions about it? That is why in these lectures we will not be addressing prophethood in the way that theologians have typically addressed it in their works. If you are interested in the traditional approach to prophethood, you can go and read it from their books directly. That is not to say that their discussions are not useful or in some sense necessary, only that they

1 Q29:48.

are less useful and less necessary than the topics we intend to cover in these lectures. Hence, we will not be touching on these.

The first issue I want to address with regards to prophethood is the philosophy of prophethood. Why should we have prophets? Why should God appoint someone to guide other human beings? Can the human being not guide himself? Is not human knowledge and learning up to the task? What use is a prophet? Why do we need someone to bring us knowledge of the unseen? This is the question we must first address because, if we do not know the philosophy behind prophecy, then all of the other topics we might discuss with regard to prophethood will lack a foundation–they will hang suspended in mid-air! Therefore, the first thing we must find out is: What is prophethood *for*? And this is what we are going to be addressing today.

In short, the answer to this question is as follows: The human being's innate senses, instincts and intellect are not sufficient by themselves to guide him to his goal. There are beings for whom their senses suffice. There are living creatures, for example, that need only their senses to fulfil their purpose in life–their outward senses. Then there are other animals who, in addition to their outward senses, have also been endowed with instinct to guide them, such as honeybees, whose instinct tells them to visit flowers, collect nectar, bring it back to the nest, and store it in hexagonal cells according to a certain arrangement. There are queens and guards that perform their own specific duties. How do bees know to do this? Did all the hives of the world send representatives to a world bee congress to decide how they should construct their hives? Did they debate about the relative merits of triangular, hexagonal or octagonal forms for their rooms? Did they carry out scientific studies, draw up proposals and hold a plebiscite on the final plan? No, they just followed their God-given instincts, as their Creator intended. 'And your Lord inspired the bee: "Make your home in the mountains, and on the trees and the trellises that they erect. Then eat from every kind of fruit and follow meekly the ways of your Lord.'"[2] This was God's revelation to the bees–revelation not in the sense that the bees were sitting and waiting for Gabriel to descend to them with God's message, but in the sense that God endowed them with this instinctive knowledge of how to build a hive, and how to gather nectar, and how to live together. This is instinctive, which means that the bees have no say in the matter–their instinct drives them to live this way. It is their innate nature to make their houses in this form, in these locations, to seek out these kinds of plants and to gather their nectar. If a bee did not follow her instincts, going to poisonous plants instead of the flowers, the other bees would not allow her to return to the hive. So bees live entirely in accordance with their instincts.

So instinct is sufficient for the bees. The Belgian author, Maurice Maeterlinck, spent many years studying and pondering the lives of bees, ants and termites–and wrote two books about them. No one is happy to find termites in their home, but these termites do amazing things. They build their nest in a specific form and arrangement, and this form–like the hives of the bees–has remained virtually unchanged since the time of prehistory. If you went and studied an ancient beehive or termite mound and compared it to one today, you would see that nothing has changed. There is no spiritual or intellectual progression amongst honeybees, termites or other creatures like this. Whatever receives revelation through its own nature, whatever is guided by its instincts, whatever is led by the form in which it was created, will perform its function to the best of its ability so long as nothing prevents it from doing so. Therefore, it has nothing but instinct.

Human beings also have instincts which they rely on, but less than the honeybee. When we are born into this world, we are very much alike these creatures, in that we are driven by instinct to suckle

2 Q16:68–69.

at our mother's breast for nourishment. No one teaches us how to suckle at the breast, so this is instinctive. However, once we reach the age of childhood and older, this tool we call instinct grows weaker and becomes less useful. At the same time, we develop something more powerful and more influential called the intellect, which takes the place of instinct and allows us to learn. For instance, it is not your instinct that teaches a shopkeeper to go and open his shop at a certain time of day, to answer his customers in a certain way; for a student to study in a particular manner or a teacher to teach. These are not instinctive. These are things we learn through the use of our intellects. Our intellect enables us to learn how to live in this world in a variety of ways.

Now, the question we must ask is whether this intellect, this human capacity for thought, is sufficient by itself to guide you to happiness? Can the intellect be enough to guide mankind? Well, what does intellect say? If it thinks, without prejudice or bias, it will say no. Just as a judge might declare himself unable to adjudicate a case, a sound and impartial mind will say that it is unable to guide humanity independently. Do you want proof of this fact? There are two arguments we have for this. The first argument is that the human intellect is limited and finite, while human needs are unlimited and infinite. How can a finite intellect comprehend these infinite needs in order to fulfil them properly, let alone to provide a system of laws to regulate them? The human intellect cannot accomplish this. It is not strong enough, not capable enough, not mature enough to fully comprehend all the pains of human existence, let alone to cure all of them!

The second argument is that if we look at the facts of history and science, does it seem that the intellect is capable of achieving this goal we seek to set for it? Did lofty intellects like those of Socrates, Plato and Aristotle suffice to guide mankind? Plato was a great thinker. He would ponder, study and discuss. One result of his philosophising was that he devised the image of a perfect society–the *Republic*–but this perfect society could not exist beyond the confines of his own mind. It could never be put into practice. Go and read the *Republic* today and you will see that it would be an unacceptable and farcical thing if we were to implement it today.

Do you see how different philosophical and intellectual schools confront against one another? Do you see how so long as the human species has no connection to a higher power or principle, it cannot possibly find its way to happiness? This is the meaning of prophethood: That the human being needs a higher power to provide him with a deeper and more profound form of guidance than the guidance of sense, instinct or reason. How will this guidance work? Will it compete with your senses? Will it go against your instincts? Will it discard your intellect? Of course not! This guidance is there to direct your intellect, to nurture and train it, to unearth it and bring it forth into the light.

The Commander of the Faithful, in truth, was not only the Commander of the Faithful. He was also the teacher of humanity. In *Nahj al-Balāghah*, he says that God sent the prophets in order to call human beings to maintain the pact of their innate nature (*fiṭrah*), to remind them of the divine blessings they had forgotten, and to unearth the buried treasures of their intellects for them (*wa yuthīrū lahum dafāʾin al-ʿuqūl*).[3] The prophets came to unearth the human minds, intellects, understandings, senses and societies which had been buried by tyrants such as Nimrod and Pharaoh. Pharaoh did not want people to have intellects, because he did not want them to think for themselves, because if they thought for themselves then his reign would be at an end. This is something we will discuss in greater detail in the coming lectures on prophethood, God willing. Pharaoh didn't want people to use their minds, so he tried to bury them–how

3 *Nahj al-Balāghah*, sermon no. 1.

did he bury them? We will discuss this too, God willing. In any case, the prophets came to unearth these buried treasures, to remove the dust from them, and to return them to their rightful owners.

So prophets were not given the power of revelation in order to fight with the intellect. Those who imagine that religion is in conflict with reason either do not understand religion or lack reason. Someone who has an active mind, someone who uses their mind and has studied the religion, will know for sure that religion has no conflict with human reason or learning and never will. What religion says is understood by a sound intellect. There are ignorant people who, in the name of defending religion, say things like: You shouldn't ask 'why' about religion. You shouldn't ask for proof in religion. You shouldn't bring philosophy into reason. They think that using one's reason diminishes religion. But they must learn that this is not the case. When the true religion is placed side by side with a complete intellect, neither one of these has any conflict or contradiction with the other. Today, great human minds understand the meaning of divine unity, of prophethood, of prayer, of fasting, of charity, and of the other rulings of the religion.

It is through our scientific research and collective experience as human beings that we have come to understand the many harms that alcohol has on the human body, on the human mind, and on human society as a whole. So why should we hesitate to say the verse aloud: 'Indeed wine, gambling, idols and the divining arrows are abominations of Satan's doing, so avoid them'.[4] Why don't I mention this verse of the Qur'an? Why don't I argue on the basis of what human understanding has grasped in this field? Why don't I say this is the work of Satan, meaning those satans who give this to you, and those satans who consume it–why don't I raise my voice, knowing all that I do?

4 Q5:90.

Someone might argue against this with the saying of Imam al-Sajjād (a): 'God's religion is not found through the intellects' (*dīn Allāh lā yuṣābu bi al-ʿuqūl*). However, this actually means something else. This means that God's religion cannot be discovered through intellectual processes. What do I mean by this? I mean that if you did not have a narration telling you that the *ẓuhr* prayer consisted of four *rakʿat*s, you could not deduce using reason alone that this prayer consists of four *rakʿat*s. If the Qur'an did not tell you the times of prayer, then you could not use your own mind and reason to work out when the time for prayer should be. ('Maintain the prayer from the sun's decline till the darkness of the night, and the dawn recital. Indeed the dawn recital is attended.'[5]) To know these sorts of things, you must be told by either a verse of the Qur'an or a tradition from the Prophet or Imams. In other words, this has to come to you by way of revelation. This is what Imam al-Sajjād means in the aforementioned narration. It does not mean that we cannot understand the teachings and rules of the religion with the aid of our intellects, as some ignorant people claim in the name of 'defending the faith', saying: 'Don't philosophise about the religion!' Why not? Why shouldn't we explain the religion? However, as I always say, whatever we understand is not even a fraction of the complete knowledge of the faith. Whatever I can utilise or explain is much less than everything that exists out there. There is no doubt about this. However, I say something, then someone comes and adds something else, then another person comes and adds still more. When you study history, this is what you see: After two hundred or five hundred years, people have gained a deeper understanding of the faith. They are much more convinced of their faith than the time when these ideas were first propounded!

Therefore, the religion sent by God did not come to suppress the intellect. It did not come to abrogate reason or to cast thinking out

5 Q17:78.

from human affairs. So why did God send religion? To guide the intellect, to take it by the hand. The intellect is there, but when the intellect is beset by desire, it cannot judge impartially. The intellect is there, but when ambition is by its side, it cannot see clearly. When some personal goal is next to it, it cannot understand properly. Religion was sent to defend the intellect from desires, ambitions, passions and fears. It strengthens the intellect and supports it so that it can understand properly. When you look at Islam, you see that from the beginning to the end, it is full of mention of the intellect! How many examples can we find in the Qur'an? How many times does God say: 'Will you not apply reason?' (*afalā taʿqilūn*)? How many times does God say 'Will you not think?' (*afalā tatafakkarūn*)? How many times does God say that the creation of the world contains 'signs for those with intellects' (*la āyātin li 'uli al-albāb*)[6]? How many times do we read in a narration that 'God has two authorities over mankind' (*inna lillāhi ʿalā al-nās ḥujjatayn*)–one being the Prophet and the other being the intellect? How much more could possibly be said about the intellect in the scriptures of Islam?

In short, what I want you to understand is the following: First, the human being, without the guidance of revelation, without him hearing God's message, cannot attain happiness for himself. Second, that when revelation comes, it does not overthrow man's reason, nor does it suppress his instinct, nor does it tell him to ignore his outward senses. On the contrary, revelation strengthens and directs his outward senses, his human instincts and his power of thought. It refines them, purifies them and leads them by the hand. This is the function of revelation and the philosophy of prophecy.

Because this is the case–because we are imperfect beings, because our own knowledge and vision is not sufficient to guide us, we need help from the unseen world. This is how God's assistance comes into

6 Q3:190

play: It does not mean that when I am hungry, I should wait for God to give me bread. Or that when I see injustice, I should do nothing and wait for God to intervene. Or that I do not perform my duties as a Muslim, that I do not enjoin the good and forbid the evil, that I do not walk the path of God, but instead wait for God to come and do all these things!

God says in the Qur'an: 'Did you see him who denies the Recompense? That is the one who drives away the orphan and does not urge the feeding of the needy.'[7] And elsewhere He says: 'They will answer, "We were not among those who prayed. Nor did we feed the poor...and we used to deny the Day of Recompense."'[8] These verses characterise the deniers of the Day of Judgement as those who neither feed the orphans nor encourage others to feed them; on a deeper and more profound level, they do not think of those less fortunate than themselves, nor how to eradicate hunger and poverty from the society in which they live–the people to whom this verse applies don't take any practical steps to alleviate the suffering they see around them, but instead wait for an invisible hand to fix things for them! I think if such a hand does exist, it would first strike these deniers on their heads for their falsehoods! Yes, there is a hidden hand at work in the cosmos because, as we have said, such an unseen force is necessary to guide mankind. But that hand is called prophets and prophethood! The core of prophethood is that it guides human beings and, as I have said above, it works with their intellects to do this.

This potentially raises a number of other issues, which I will briefly summarise here. One is: Now that we know what it is for, what exactly *is* prophethood? What does it mean for someone to be 'sent' as a prophet? How does this work? These are some of the discussions that surround prophecy that we will not discuss.

---

7 Q107:1–3.

8 Q74:43–44, 46.

On the other hand: What is the starting point of the prophets' missions? How do they begin to reform society and help people? What is the nature of their mission? Where does their mission end? Do they plant the seed and leave? Is that it? When a tyrant cut off the head of John the Baptist, was that the end of the matter? Was prophethood at an end? Or is this not the case? Is there another purpose? Another end towards which they strive? The Qur'an discusses these topics and we will look at them in the coming lectures. On the philosophy of prophethood, what we have said so far is sufficient.

The verses we have on this topic are extremely thought provoking and profound. At first, when I was planning this lecture, I thought I would recite the first of today's verse and explain it detail. Then, I saw that if I want to explain it in full, I would not have time to say everything else I wanted to cover on prophethood today and it would take me another day or two to cover it. I cannot explain the full meaning of this verse in the time we have. It is very interesting, but I will leave it to you to read it and ponder on it in your own time. Here, I will just give the briefest of explanations.

God says in the Qur'an: 'Mankind were a single community'.[9] Commentators on the Qur'an have spilt much ink debating over the meaning of this verse. Mankind were a 'single community' (*ummatan wāhidah*). Was this a desirable state of affairs for God or an undesirable one? No matter which way you interpret this statement, the other side will have an objection. Some say that 'mankind were a single community' refers to the fact that they lived in a state of 'primitive communism'. However, there is no evidence for this interpretation aside from the fact we have a term called 'primitive communism', and the Qur'an does not say anything more on this, unless we take 'mankind were a single community' to refer to a time that human beings lived in a state similar to the way animals might; an unclothed

9 Q2:213.

herd living in the wilderness, using stone tools and hunting for food and sometimes hunting one another. Could this be what it means? No, we should never try to make the Qur'an agree with whatever other theories we have. We should simply read the Qur'an and try to understand what it is saying to us. If we can understand its meaning, we have done something quite artful indeed! We do not need the make the Qur'an agree with other theories or terminologies in order to take it seriously. It is already worth taking seriously on its own terms!

'Mankind were a single community' could be interpreted in a number of ways. There are two readings in particular that we will pay attention to, which we take from the work of Ayatollāh Ṭāliqānī's *Partovi az Qur'ān* ('A Ray of Light from the Qur'an'). 'Mankind were a single community' means that people were all in the same condition as one another, both in terms of their needs and in terms of their innate potential. All human beings are alike in terms of their needs and what they are able to do, and the social reality has always been like this. All human beings have an intellect with the power to think and to reason, and all human beings have their internal and external senses. All human beings feel hunger, all human beings feel thirst, all human beings experience sexual desire, all human beings want a home, all human beings what clothes–and so on. Everyone's needs are equal, and everyone's potential is more or less the same. Of course, a person who has been given a better upbringing or education will display more of their potential, but this is another topic. Someone born into an aristocratic family, who was given a personal tutor from the time they were six or seven years of age, will easily be able to acquire new languages with which to speak. On the other hand, the child of a labourer who lives in a village will be barely able to speak Persian by the time they are six or seven years of old, let alone any other language! This does not mean that the first child had any more potential than the second, only that those around him were better able to bring that potential forth, while the potential of that second child remains dormant and undiscovered. Consider the following analogy: If a country has deposits of mineral wealth that are far richer than those of its neighbour, but these remain undiscovered while those of its neighbour have been found and utilised, whether to light homes or power cars, everyone will have heard of its neighbour but not of it, even though it might have more wealth beneath it than its neighbour. The same is true of people who have not yet had the opportunity to develop their God-given talents.

Therefore, by nature, humanity was a single nation–with similar needs and potentialities, as we explained. 'Then God sent the prophets', amongst these human beings that were similar to one another, God appointed messengers. This means that the Creator of the Universe made one person higher, stronger, deeper, more passionate, and with greater potential than all others and chose this person to be His representative. To do what? 'As bearers of good news and as warners'. What was the good news that these prophets brought? They brought good news of Paradise, good news of happiness in this world, good news of a virtuous society, good news of security, peace and comfort, good news of the end of poverty, despair, fear, insecurity and ignorance. They brought good news! Ultimately, they brought good news of the establishment of a virtuous government and a society that suited the human being and, after that, of going to Paradise and being attached to the satisfaction of God. But they also brought warnings: They warned people about the fires of Hell, they warned them about the narrowness of the 'Bridge to Heaven', they warned people about the vicissitudes of this world, they warned them about the demons of ignorance and poverty, they warned them against falling into the pit of corruption, and they warned them against squandering their God-given potential as human beings. They brought warnings!

'Then God sent the prophets as bearers of good news and as warners, and He sent down with them the Book with the truth'. But that is not all, they did more than bringing good news and warn. They brought something else too: A book from God. They were sent a book with the truth and which was in accordance with the truth. There are several ways in which we could interpret this word, 'truth' (*ḥaqq*), but we do not have time to discuss all of the possibilities. In short, whatever is in agreement with the innate nature of the cosmos, whatever is conducive to the natural order of the universe, this is what we call 'truth'. Whatever is in harmony with the innate nature of the human being and the nature of the world in which he dwells, is also called 'truth'. The scripture brought by the prophets is also true, because the natural path for the human being to take is that of his innate nature (*fiṭrah*), which leads him and helps him on the journey towards perfection, and the Book of God helps the human being on this journey and guides him towards his destination.

'And He sent down with them the Book with the truth, that it may judge between the people concerning that about which they differed'. He sent this book to settle the disputes that came about between people. But people will always argue; it is human nature to disagree and dispute with one another. Disagreement is a good thing, because disagreement leads to growth. The Book is sent to judge between people, to settle their disputes, to adjudicate in the matters they disagree regarding. What do we understand from this? We understand that the rule of the prophets–the rule of any individual prophet–is never tyrannical. On the contrary, it is a government founded upon law, founded upon scripture. When a prophet comes, he sets right society, so that the true ruler of that society is none other than that scripture–namely, the law!

'That it may judge between the people concerning that about which they differed, and none differed in it except those who had been given it'. The ones who differed concerning the Book were none other than those to whom it had been sent. What does this show us? It shows us that distortion and falsification existed in all divine religions concerning the teachings of their prophet after he left them. When the prophets came, they brought a scripture, a law and a school of thought. Then those whom they bestowed this knowledge upon disagreed about it. Meaning what? Meaning that some interpreted it correctly while others did not. Therefore, there are people who claim to follow a religion and speak about it, but they do not speak the truth: this shows that a certain amount of distortion exists within the divine religions.

'After the manifest proofs had come to them, out of envy among themselves. Then God guided those who had faith to the truth of what they differed in, by His will, and God guides whomever He wishes to a straight path.'

So what have we covered so far? We have explained the philosophy of prophethood and seen that it is a common principle shared by virtually all religions in some way, shape or form. In fact, we have seen that it is the foundational principle of religion as, without some form of prophethood or revelation, there is no religion to speak of, as religion is something that comes from God and the way in which we receive a message from God is through revelation, which is the keystone of prophethood.

The Mission of the Prophets

Thursday 16th Ramadan 1394
2nd October 1974

اقْرَأْ بِاسْمِ رَبِّكَ الَّذِي خَلَقَ (١) خَلَقَ الْإِنْسَانَ مِنْ عَلَقٍ
(٢) اقْرَأْ وَرَبُّكَ الْأَكْرَمُ (٣) الَّذِي عَلَّمَ بِالْقَلَمِ (٤) عَلَّمَ
الْإِنْسَانَ مَا لَمْ يَعْلَمْ (٥) كَلَّا إِنَّ الْإِنْسَانَ لَيَطْغَى (٦) أَنْ
رَآهُ اسْتَغْنَى (٧) إِنَّ إِلَى رَبِّكَ الرُّجْعَى (٨)

'Read in the name of your Lord who created; created man from a clinging mass. Read, and your Lord is the most generous, who taught by the pen, taught man what he did not know. Man indeed becomes rebellious when he considers himself without need. To your Lord is indeed the return.'
- Sūrat al-ʿAlaq (96):1-8.

Today, we are going to discuss the changes that take place in the person of a prophet and in the world around him when God selects him to serve as His representative on earth. However, our focus will not be so much on the internal or psychological changes that a prophet experiences, although this is one aspect of it that I will touch upon when I shed light on prophethood through interpreting one word that is found throughout the Qur'an and in religious language which reveals much to us about the nature of prophethood.

As you know, when the Qur'an speaks about the Prophet, it speaks about his appointment or *biʿthah* ('raising up'). The Qur'an says: 'Certainly We raised an apostle in every nation.'[10] God raised Abraham, Moses and other prophets. What does it mean for God to 'raise up' a person? What is the relationship between this raising up and prophethood? That is the question we will seek to address in our lecture.

The Arabic word *biʿthah* means 'to raise up'. What does this mean? It means to quicken something or awaken it from dormancy. A man lies sleeping in his grave for hundreds of years as his body decays but when God brings his body back and awakens him from his slumber, we say God has *raised him up*. 'This is the Day of Resurrection (*yawm al-baʿth*, literally 'Day of Raising Up').'[11] A person might be asleep in his home or even asleep as he goes through the motions of his daily life. His energies and efforts are not directed anywhere contrary to the flow of the society in which he lives. He is like a piece of driftwood floating in the current of his social existence, carried in whichever direction society takes him. When this person comes to his senses and emerges from this state of indifference, he realises that that there is nothing inevitable about this path or natural flow. He realises he does not need to be content with this. He does not need to passively accept this. He can take another path–a path that will lead him towards human happiness and flourishing. When the mind of a human being awakens, that is when you witness real effort, real movement. And when this happens, you say that this person has risen. When you wake from sleeping, we say you have risen. When you get up from your slumber and begin to move about, we say you have risen. This is the meaning of rising, and this is what *biʿthah* means.

10 Q16:36.

11 Q30:56.

As we already mentioned, the Day of Resurrection is also called *yawm al-baʿth*, or the Day of Raising. The Resurrection is, of course, when the dead are raised up alive and brought forth from their slumber. It is a day of movement; a day on which human beings, from the moment they emerge from their state of heedlessness until their final destiny is decided, will always be striving, scrambling and moving. Prophethood shares something in common with this idea of Resurrection–for it is the revival of the soul.

I want to present the subject of prophethood to you in a completely new way. Some people think prophethood is like a preacher coming to a city to teach its inhabitants a little bit about the religion, or like a scholar sitting to answer people's questions, or like a lecturer standing up in a meeting to deliver a speech on a particular topic. That is how people usually imagine a prophet to be–like a pious religious scholar in the midst of some people. We imagine that, sometimes, people respect him because they are good, and we call them believers. And we imagine that, sometimes, people disrespect him because they are bad, and we call them disbelievers and idolaters. This, in general, is how we imagine prophethood to be.

However, when someone becomes a prophet, they undergo a kind of transformation. In fact, we must say they undergo two transformations. First, the being of the prophet undergoes a kind of resurrection–a metamorphosis in the core of his own self. He is changed–brought forth from slumber as a raising up of spirit takes place. This is a resurrection within him. A resurrection in his own heart and mind. Through this process, God awakens all of his potential, like a spring from which there erupts a million streams, with all this water having been contained beneath the ground until just a moment before. Once this transformation has taken place and the prophet is now utterly under the influence of divine revelation–once this spring has burst forth from the depths of the prophet's heart–he now takes his message to the people. The waters of revelation flow out from him into the fabric of society and the transformation that began in him now ripples out to his environment, to his people, to his community, to his nation. The resurrection that took place in his heart is mirrored in an even more magnificent resurrection in his society. Through his efforts, the transformation in his heart brings about a transformation in society and a true 'raising up' takes place. Therefore, we can see that from every aspect, prophethood is a kind of raising up or resurrection–whether in the person of the prophet himself or in the society to which he has been sent.

What was the prophet before he became a prophet? There are two points that apply to all prophets before they were chosen by God. First, even though a prophet has not yet been raised up, he nevertheless displays considerable potential as a human being–much more than those around him. He is both mentally and physically very able. His readiness for this spring of revelation to burst forth from him is not comparable to other people. His readiness to worship God and to serve God is to the extent that cannot be conceived in other people. All of the other potentialities that lay dormant and buried in other people are already present and visible in him. He has reached the apex of the arc of 'to God we belong and to Him we return' (*innā lillāhi wa innā ilayhi rājiʿūn*). In other words, he is a true servant of God and he has embodied the moral qualities of God.

Why should this be more in him than anyone else? Is God showing favouritism towards him? Is God mistreating His other creatures? This is a separate issue. However, the short answer is as follows: It is this way because the prophet must be ready to bear the burdens of being a prophet. He must be ready to endure the hardships associated with this role. Being God's representative on earth is not an easy thing. Carrying the divine message to mankind and turning an ignorant society into a *tawḥīd*-oriented one is not easy. This is a momentous undertaking and one that ultimately not all people could bear. Who could accomplish this? An ordinary human being? Or does it require someone who, based on the conditions of his environment, family, and society, enjoys a greater potential? Who, because God recognises this potential and sees that it will help this person achieve his mission, pours out His grace and kindness upon him, who nurtures him and chooses him, so that he can carry this heavy burden? Ultimately, if God's messengers did not carry this burden, you and I would not be able to carry ours, and our work in this world would be left unfinished. The work of men like Gandhi and Patrice Lumumba would be left unfinished. The work of Socrates, Plato and Aristotle would be left unfinished. There must be someone strong enough to carry this burden–the burden of the divine message, of prophecy, of 'raising up' or whatever other name we would give it–and this is not a simple thing to achieve. There must be someone amongst humankind who has this potential. So this is the first point: before he is a prophet, a prophet is someone who has potential and abilities beyond those of an ordinary human being.

The second point is that a prophet, before he is chosen and made a prophet, lives amongst the people and interacts with them normally. He is not necessarily someone who spends his days thinking about what he must do to change society. Perhaps he is unhappy with the way society is–he almost certainly is. He is an intelligent person who is unhappy with the divisions he sees in society, from the ignorance he sees in society, from the poverty he sees in society, from the injustice he sees in society or–to put it in Islamic terms–from the *jāhiliyyah* ('ignorance') of the time in which he lives. However, this is all. He is not actively planning to stage a revolution to overthrow the existing social order.

Consider Moses. He grew up in Pharaoh's household. He had all the benefits of being a Prince of Egypt. Then once, in the marketplace, he struck down an Egyptian official who was mistreating an Israelite, and he was forced to flee. Then, after years of working for the Prophet Jethro, he receives a revelation from God and is made His prophet.

Then, when he returned as a prophet and was asked why he struck down that man, he said: 'I did that when I was astray.'[12] What does he mean by this? It means that he had not yet found the right way to oppose the direction society was taking under Pharaoh's rule, not that killing one of Pharaoh's officials was a grave crime, not at all. What he means by this is that when he did that, he was not someone following a specific ideal–he was not following the right way to bring about change. He was just one person amongst many. He followed the same path as everyone else. He did his best as an ordinary person amongst other ordinary people. Now, however, he has returned as a changed person. Now, he is leading a movement to change society entirely. In other words, he is now a person 'raised up' in society. Since when? Since his *biʿthah*. Since he was 'raised up' as a prophet.

We can see the same about our own Prophet (s) in the opening verses of *Sūrat al-Ḍuḥā*.[13] Now, there are many narrations about these verses, but these are interpretations (*taʾwīl*) rather than explanation (*tafsīr*), as they go beyond the apparent meaning of the words. This indicates that the Imams have derived something more from the verse than its apparent meaning. This does not mean that the Imams wish to interpret the verse in a way that goes against its apparent meaning–the apparent meaning is always preserved and has its place–only that they wish to draw out non-apparent aspects of the verse: Things that, when you or I look at the verse, we would not grasp by ourselves, which is why the Imam wishes to teach them to us. This is the meaning of *taʾwīl*.

The chapter of the Qur'an begins by swearing an oath: 'by the morning brightness'.[14] And this oath is something meaningful in itself. It is an oath sworn by a particular time of day. Perhaps this

12 Q42:25.

13 See Q93:1–8.

14 Q93:1.

contains an allusion or intimation for the audience, as the rest of the verses clearly concern the sending of the Prophet. 'The morning brightness' (*ḍuḥā*) symbolises the new light dawning across the horizon of the world with the appearance of the Prophet of Islam and the advent of a new divine message for mankind. Next, the Qur'an adds: 'by the night when it is calm'.[15] Now, it swears by the night, when the sky is completely dark. 'Your Lord has neither forsaken you nor is He displeased with you'.[16] It seems that when the Prophet began receiving revelations, there was a period of time in which the revelations stopped. So, after the spiritual excitement felt by the Prophet upon his meeting with Gabriel, he underwent a dark night of the soul, in which he received no new revelations. This saddened him greatly. How long did this interval of silence last? Some say that it was forty days. Some say more–to the extent of two or three years! Then came relief in the form of *Sūrat al-Ḍuḥā*, which gave hope and good news to the Prophet with the words: 'Your Lord has neither forsaken you nor is He displeased with you, and the Hereafter (or the future) shall be better for you than the world (or the past).'[17]

'Soon your Lord will give you [that with which] you will be pleased.'[18] There is a narration about this verse which says the thing that will please the Prophet is the power of intercession (*shafāʿah*). This is correct, as the power of intercession is one of the things that God granted the Prophet and He granted it to him to the extent that he was contented. However, even in this world, God gave the Prophet enough for him to be pleased: He gave him the power to guide others, to establish an ideal society, to defeat his enemies and liberate lands,

15 Q93:2.

16 Q93:3.

17 Q93:3–4.

18 Q93:5.

to guide the new Islamic society towards perfection–these are the blessings that God granted His prophet.

Then, God asks: 'Did He not find you an orphan, and shelter you?'[19] God found an orphan, a nobody who had no shelter, and He gave him shelter. This orphan had no father, for his father had died before he was even born. His mother died shortly after. His grandfather died a few years later. He would have been utterly alone in the world, had his grandfather, Abū Ṭālib, not taken him in. In this rhetorical question, God is telling the Prophet: 'You began life as an orphan, but We were always watching over you, We looked after you with Our kindness and Our mercy!' This is supposed to give the Prophet hope. It is meant to remind him that God's protection and shelter is always with him, from his childhood until now, with the heavy responsibility of prophethood weighing upon his shoulders. So, God says, do not be afraid. Do not worry. Do not imagine that God would ever leave you. God would never leave you, not after He has brought you all this way.

'Did He not find you astray, and guide you?' There are also several narrations about this verse, although some of these are also weak and others have been mixed with remarks by commentators on the Qur'an. God says: 'Did He not find you astray, and guide you?' But this does not mean that the Prophet was astray in his ideas or his spirit. It is far more literal than this: It means that when he was a child, he became lost as he wandered in the hills surrounding Makkah, but God guided his grandfather to be able to find him. On another occasion when he was lost as a child, a woman found him. Alternatively, the verse could be read as saying that the people of Makkah did not know who you were, until God guided them to you. These are the different meanings given to the verse. Now, we do not reject any of these out of hand–pay close attention to what I mean by this–as all of them are possible and, if we find narrations that are genuinely authentic about

19 Q93:6.

any of these readings, we accept them without hesitation. Perhaps the narrations we have about this verse are weak, and perhaps they are strong, and if any of the strong narrations on this topic reflect any of the above readings, then of course they are to be accepted. However, even though all of these narrations are possible and we accept them on the basis of authentic narrations, they do not properly reflect the apparent meaning of the verse–although this does not mean we should reject them, either.

Now, the apparent meaning of the verse clearly states: 'Did He not find you astray, and guide you?' What does it mean to say that the Prophet was 'astray' (*ḍāll*)? Does that mean he was an idol-worshipper before He was a prophet? Of course not! Does it mean that he was someone who was misguided? Of course not! Does it mean he was a sinner? Definitely not! So what does it mean? It means that this straight path which was shown to you through you being chosen as a prophet was not previously available to you. Could it mean anything other than this? Were these teachings, these laws, these concepts, these ideas which the Prophet received via revelation, which were made clear and manifest to his pure heart, something he had in his possession before God selected him and raised him up as a prophet? Certainly not! So this is the meaning of being astray which reflects the apparent meaning of the words of the verse and, once we have this apparent meaning, there is no problem with us also applying the verse to being lost amongst the people of Makkah, being lost in the hills around Makkah, or being lost searching for a sheep that wandered off, as we find in some verses.

Next, God asks: 'Did He not find you needy, and enrich you?'[20] What does this verse refer to? With the previous verse, we saw that the Prophet was lost or astray even as he moved amongst the ordinary people and lived in society, even if he was not happy with

20 Q93:8.

the conditions he witnessed there: For example, the occasion on which some of the notables of the Quraysh badly mistreated a poor man's servant girl, and the other wrongs he saw all around him. As a result, he joined the 'pact of the virtuous' (*ḥilf al-fuḍūl*). And, while he lived as an ordinary person, he still never associated any partners with God, or made any offerings nor showed any reverence for the idols, and he never allied himself with the rich and powerful. Instead, he lived as a noble and decent member of that society. So, whatever the Prophet did before he became a prophet of God, was within the normal bounds of the society in which he lived.

So the Prophet lived as an ordinary person of virtue and decency until, one day, he receives revelations from God. This produces a profound transformation in his being and his character. This transformation was so powerful and strange that it even appears to have had an effect on the Prophet's physical being and psyche. When the Prophet was in the cave and the first flicker of revelation was kindled in his heart, he saw a heavenly messenger telling him to read (*iqraʾ*, 'Read'!). Now, either the Prophet could not read anything or did not have anything to read, so he said: '*Mā aqraʾ*', which could mean either 'I cannot read!' (in which case the *mā* is for negation) or 'Read what?' (in which case the *mā* is an interrogative). Then the first verses of the Qur'an were revealed to him: 'Read in the name of your Lord who created; created man from a clinging mass. Read, and your Lord is the most generous, who taught by the pen, taught man what he did not know.'[21] The flame of revelation was lit within the soul of the Prophet and a great change took place. This thinking person–this virtuous person–underwent a complete transformation. He was raised up. He was not the same person as he was before. Muḥammad was no longer the Muḥammad of one moment ago. He was not the same being as he was an hour before. He was now something else. He was

21 Q96:1–5.

of a different substance entirely. First, being chosen as a prophet brought about a complete transformation of his own inner being, and once this was accomplished, he was now ready to transform the world around him. If he had not changed, he could not change the world. This is an important lesson for those who follow the Prophet: As long as they have not changed, they cannot change the world around themselves. As the Sufi poet, Jāmī says:

An essence that has not been granted existence from the Giver-of-Existence,
How can it become a giver-of-existence to others?

You, who did not give rise to your own existence, who has yet to make use of this outpouring of grace and blessings from the light of the Creator, who has yet to leaven his spirit with it, what do you have to offer people? You must first be burning yourself before you can set the cold black coal ablaze!

So the Prophet was first set ablaze himself. He was first transformed and changed in his own being. He first felt the quickening of the Resurrection in his own heart. Only then could he bring new life to the world. He became a person who was ready to surrender his life but never his ideals. Could it be any other way? This was no joke. Was it a joke when they tortured Bilāl to within an inch of his life? But though they whipped him again and again under the burning sun, he would call out: 'He is one, one, one–there is only one God!' By saying these words, it was as though he was calling out for his own death. It was no easy thing for the Prophet to raise up men like this. By himself, the Prophet could not make an Abū Dharr, a Bilāl, a Miqdād, or an ʿAbd Allāh ibn Masʿūd. No, first the Prophet needed to be changed himself. Do you see now what the revelation did to the Prophet? Do you see what it demanded of him?

Another verse I would like to look at today are the verses of *Sūrat al-ʿAlaq* that we mentioned above. This chapter begins with the words:

'Read in the name of your Lord who created',[22] this represents the beginning of a sequence of phrases. The first thing that a monotheistic person like our Prophet, who never worshipped idols, will recognise that draws his heart towards God is perhaps the simplest of all truths–that of creation. 'Read in the name of your Lord who created', all creation belongs to Him. So, everything you see is a manifestation of His power.

Once this idea has crystallised in a person's mind, he goes a step further. He goes a little higher than creation: 'Created Man from a clinging mass', what is it that distinguishes the human being from any other creature? The human being does not begin his existence as aware of himself or his surroundings. In a street, a car passes by. A person passes by. You ride in a car. Ten people pass by. Ten trees pass by. What is the difference? If you don't pay attention, trees and people can seem very much alike as you pass them by! But the human being is a very special kind of being–he is higher, superior. People who do not think might never work out the difference between a human being and anything else, because a thousand people mean no more to them than a thousand ants. And just as you might dispose of a swarm of ants without a second thought, so too would some people cast aside a crowd of humans just as easily. But we don't want anything to do with such people.

Now, at first glance, it might not be clear why a human being is any more important or any better than anything else in the cosmos. But what about when you really pay attention? Then what? You see that there is indeed an important difference between human beings and other things–a profound difference! What is it that separates the human being from everything else? The power of thought, of intellect, of knowing universal truths, of deriving general laws from particular instances! This is not something a tree can do, or a rock, or any other

22 Q96:1.

animal. Invention, innovation, discovery–if the human being could not invent, then the human race as a whole would have remained forever the same and unchanged in its circumstances, like everything else (just like the example of the honeybee which we gave yesterday). The human being is distinguished because he has the power of will, of decision, of choosing what it is he wants to do. This is unlike all other creatures who can only follow their instincts: Whatever their instincts tell them to do, they follow. There is no want. No wish. But the human being can act against his instincts. It is human instinct to eat food. It is human instinct to sate one's sexual desires. Are these not instincts? And yet, you can find human beings who never once in their life act on their sexual urges–not even once! This is because human beings can deny their instincts. They can work on themselves. There are human beings that can sustain themselves for days with just one almond, without eating anything else. So it is only the human being that can choose to ignore his desires and his instincts.

In short, it is the human being's power of thought, choice, will and innovation that renders him different from all other creatures. There is nothing else in existence that rivals the human being in this way. Scientists have more or less come to this conclusion as well, that the human being is unique amongst species in this regard. They do not say that the human being is not an animal, but they recognise that only the human being possesses certain qualities. And all of these qualities we find in the human being are the result of God's outpouring of His spirit upon him; it is the manifestation of God's spirit in the human being: 'and breathed into him of My spirit'.[23]

So, the Prophet realises that there is something higher still than mere creation, and that is the creation of the human being, the creation of reason, the creation of thought and understanding. And from whence do these come? 'From a clot' (*min ʿalaq*), what a journey

23 Q15:29, 38:72.

it takes from a clot to a fully formed human being! 'What hath dust to do with the Lord of Lords?' How can something inert and unliving be transformed into a thinking being? To be transformed into a person like Socrates, into a thinker, a philosopher, a prophet! How is this possible? Is there any other explanation save that it is the work of the Creator? 'Created Man from a clinging mass.' Our Prophet, at the very beginning of his revelation, was made aware of this extremely profound realisation. See how God wishes to bring about a complete transformation in his being? He wants to shoe him in steel and place a steel rod in his hand, so that he can go forward, so that he will never again know the meaning of tiredness. The first step of this process of transformation can be found in these words.

'Created Man from a clinging mass', from a clot of blood! 'Read'! The command repeats, because God is even greater still, 'and your Lord is the most generous'.[24] Why is He the most generous? 'Who taught by the pen'.[25] Now the Qur'an speaks to the Prophet of the education of the human being. As you all know, if there was no pen, there would be no writing and, if there was no writing, there would be no progress for the human race. The means by which one generation can pass its knowledge on to the next, and that generation can pass its knowledge on to the next, so that each new generation can utilise the collective learning of the human species and draw on the experience of earlier people is only through the pen. If the previous generations had not written down their scientific researches and their discoveries, then we would not have had access to them, and we could not have made use of them. If Avicenna had not read the books of Aristotle, Avicenna would not have become Avicenna, who rose even higher than Aristotle! If Shaykh al-Anṣārī or Mīrzā Shīrāzī did not have the books of jurisprudence of Shaykh al-Ṭūsī or ʿAllāmah al-Ḥillī, and

24 Q96:3.

25 Q96:4.

the knowledge and ideas that they contained, they would have never been able to become two of the most outstanding jurists to be seen for centuries. This is self-evident. If a person has five *tumāns*, and he gives these to another person, who adds five *tumāns* from himself, making ten, and gives this to a third person, who adds five *tumāns*, bringing the total to fifteen *tumāns*. This makes the third person the richest of the three, but where did these fifteen *tumāns* come from? If it was not for the first person in the chain, would there be fifteen *tumāns*? If there was no second person, would there be fifteen *tumāns*? Absolutely not, the third person would only have the meagre five *tumāns* with which he began. The sum of human experience and discovery which is passed on to subsequent generations accumulates like these fifteen *tumāns*. But what is the means by which it is handed down? By what device are we able to accomplish this? By writing. Writing with the pen.

Therefore, teaching the human being with the pen is an act of God even greater than creation itself! 'Read, and your Lord is the most generous, who taught by the pen, taught man what he did not know.'[26] These are the blessings which God has bestowed on the human being. The human being should give thanks for these! When God taught the human being, when God showed the human being the right path, when He gave the human being the pen, when He gave the human being intelligence and knowledge, the human being should always be going higher and higher and never, not even for one moment, going backwards or descending, for therein lies human misery. Is this not so? The following verse gives the answer, almost as if it anticipates the question: If God created man, taught man, gave man the pen, cared for man and ennobled him–if God did all this for the human being, then the human being should never be miserable, never lost, never corrupt, never astray. Is this not so?

26 Q96:3–5.

No, it is not as we think. What is the state of humanity today? 'Indeed man becomes rebellious when he considers himself without need.'[27] It is the recalcitrance of the human race, their arrogance and their pride that has led them to rebel against the All-merciful and to fight one another. This is the source of all human misery. These tyrants will not let humanity be guided. The wrongdoing, vainglorious and arrogant ones do not want mankind to make the most of its God-given blessings, or for God to educate them as He wills, or to lead them to flourish as He wills. This is because they see themselves without need, so they become arrogant and rebellious. They turn aside from the path of God. But you see, God is still sending prophets to remind people of His kindness, of His generosity, of His teaching, of the fact that God is the Creator, of the fact that it is God who teaches mankind, of the fact that God is the most-generous, of the fact that the human race has yet to achieve its full potential. And the fact that they have not is the fault of the rebellious ones.

They are rebellious because they think they do not need anyone else. They amass wealth, hoard treasure, pile up money and make men bow their heads to them. When this happens–when ungodly powers are brought into this world–that is when the human race will not reach its destination. This is the inspiration God sends to His Messenger at the very beginning of his mission. This is the flame that God lights in his heart.

It is not as we imagine. Do we expect the human race will become enlightened? No! 'Indeed man becomes rebellious when he considers himself without need. Indeed to your Lord is the return.'[28] But will these rebellious ones have a successful outcome? No! They will go back to their Lord. The outcome is with God. The ultimate end is towards God and with God. The way that God, the Creator, has laid

27 Q96:6–7.

28 Q96:8.

down is the way that mankind must follow. There is no doubt that humanity will reach its destination: 'Indeed to your Lord is the return.'

There are many other issues worthy of discussion that arise from this chapter. Do you see the realities it contains about our Prophet, and the transformation that took place within him, and the transformation that he was ultimately able to bring about in the world?

Finally, I would like to discuss some of the verses in *Sūrat al-Najm* which also refer to this transformation within the soul of the Prophet. There are, of course, many other chapters and verses which also address this but which we do not have the time to mention here. However, I will briefly mention and discuss the meaning of these verses.

'By the star when it sets: your companion has neither gone astray, nor gone amiss.'[29] According to many of the commentaries, these verses relate to the Night of the Ascension (*laylat al-miʿrāj*). However, they are also related to the changes taking place within the Prophet and the state he enters when receiving revelation. This chapter was revealed after the Night of Ascension; when the Prophet tried to tell people about this, they refused to listen to him. This is the context of the verses. 'Nor does he speak out of desire: it is just a revelation that has been revealed.'[30]

'Taught him by One of great powers, possessed of sound judgement'.[31] 'Sound judgement' (*mirrah*) means wisdom and discernment. Commentators on the Qur'an say that this refers to the Angel Gabriel, as the Prophet relates whatever Gabriel says to him, and Gabriel relates whatever God has told him. So it is through

29 Q53:1–2.

30 Q53:3–4.

31 Q53:5–6.

Gabriel that God teaches the Prophet. 'He settled',[32] the revelation was given to him and he rose to his feet.

'While he was on the highest horizon',[33] 'highest' (*aʿlā*) here means the supreme horizon. 'Then he drew nearer and nearer'.[34] Perhaps we can explain this as follows: 'while he was on the highest horizon' means that before he became a prophet, he was at a higher level compared to those around him, and it was being at this highest level and enjoying superior potential that meant he could be chosen as a prophet. 'Then he drew nearer and nearer', based on the reading we have just given, the Prophet drew nearer to God, then nearer still as a result of his worship and spiritual exercises, and as a result of his meditation and contemplation, and as a result of the grace that God bestowed upon him. His spirit came nearer and nearer to God until it was ready to receive revelation. Some have suggested that the sentence 'he drew nearer' (*danā*) is actually referring to Gabriel drawing near to the Prophet, and 'and nearer' (*tadallā*) refers to Gabriel reaching him. In other words, Gabriel came nearer and nearer to the Prophet in order to grant him revelation. In any case, there is no real difference in significance, but I believe that the first reading is closer to the apparent meaning of the verse.

'Until he was within two bows' length or even nearer'.[35] The Prophet came closer and closer to God until the distance between him and his Lord was two bows' length or less. Now, do not think that 'two bows' length' means physical distance, with each bow length being about a metre, so that the Prophet was two metres from God! Where is God in the first place such that the Prophet could be two metres away from him? No, this is a symbolic reference, a metaphor if

---

32 Q53:6.

33 Q53:7.

34 Q53:8.

35 Q53:9.

you will. He came closer, not in physical distance. 'Two bows' length' (*qāba qawsayn*) means he came very, very close to God; so close that there was almost nothing between the Prophet's spirit and God. Closer than any human being ever has been to God or ever will be.

'Whereat He revealed to His servant whatever He revealed. The heart did not deny what it saw.'[36] What the heart of the Prophet witnessed; it saw truly. It did not deceive. It did not err. 'Will you then dispute with him about what he saw?'[37]

These are the verses I wanted to discuss from *Sūrat al-Najm*. So, this was the inner transformation that the Prophet underwent, which changed the Prophet's path, gave a new hue to all of his activities, and led him to undertake a determined struggle. A struggle for what? A struggle to bring about a transformation and a resurrection in the fabric of human society. After he was transformed, he strove to transform society. This is the mission of the prophets and the very reason for which our Prophet was sent.

36 Q53:10–11.

37 Q53:12.

The Prophetic Resurrection of Society

Friday 17th Ramadan 1394
3nd October 1974

وَنُرِيدُ أَنْ نَمُنَّ عَلَى الَّذِينَ اسْتُضْعِفُوا فِي الْأَرْضِ وَنَجْعَلَهُمْ
أَئِمَّةً وَنَجْعَلَهُمُ الْوَارِثِينَ (٥) وَنُمَكِّنَ لَهُمْ فِي الْأَرْضِ وَنُرِيَ
فِرْعَوْنَ وَهَامَانَ وَجُنُودَهُمَا مِنْهُمْ مَا كَانُوا يَحْذَرُونَ (٦)

'And We desired to show favour to those who were abased in the land, and to make them imams, and to make them the heirs, and to establish them in the land, and to show Pharaoh and Hāmān and their hosts from them that of which they were apprehensive.'
- Sūrat al-Qaṣaṣ (28):5–6.

One topic that arises out of these verses and the verses of *Sūrat al-Ṣaff* is a topic which can best be described with the title which I have given this lecture: 'the Prophetic Resurrection of Society.'

What I want to discuss in this lecture is the meaning of 'the Prophetic Resurrection of Society'. We have covered some of the preliminaries necessary for understanding this in previous lectures, where we said that the 'raising up' (*biʿthah*) of a prophet means bringing about a transformation within his very soul and a redirection of his efforts that begins with the flame of revelation being lit within his heart. A prophet is a servant chosen by God, who has been endowed with special potentialities not granted to others, whom God entrusts with the momentous duty of being His representative on earth and the conveyer of His message to mankind. Once this servant begins receiving divine revelations, the very core of his being is forever altered, and he is forever transformed. Before he became a prophet, this person lived as a virtuous but ordinary human being in his society, and he followed its course. Once chosen, however, his being and his social orientation are irreversibly changed. When a person receives revelation, they are no longer the person they were yesterday or even two hours before. Authors who do not believe in the Prophet of Islam–including orientalists, not all of whom necessarily have an agenda, although many do–suggest that before declaring that he was a messenger from God, the Prophet must have spent his days studying and contemplating and that this is what brought about the transformation of his character. However, this theory does not match the apparent situation of the Prophet and is, in fact, entirely false.

It was not through meditation and reflection that the Prophet was transformed and began preaching the message of Islam. On the contrary, when he was raised up as a prophet and charged with his mission, this represented a complete break with his past self. This is not only true of our Prophet but of all the prophets of God in history. Moses was on an ordinary journey with his wife and child when, on a dark night and in the middle of the wilderness, he had an encounter with God that changed him, and he began to receive revelations. He forgot everything else. When Moses received his divine mission, he became a different Moses to the Moses he had been just a moment before. Something had changed inside of him. His soul was in motion in a way it had never been before. Someone who claims that prophethood has nothing to do with God or the unseen world is simply repeating the claims of orientalists, who base their theories on limited research and information.

In any case, the 'raising up' of a prophet refers to a transformation, change, alteration or, to put it another way, resurrection in the being of the person who has been chosen by God to serve as his mouthpiece. When this transformation has taken place, the role of the prophet begins, namely, to take this inner transformation and realise it in the external reality. To mirror the change within the prophet's spirit in the fabric of the social reality. And this is what we mean by 'the Prophetic Resurrection of Society'. We will discuss this topic in today's lecture before moving on to other aspects of prophethood tomorrow. There are still some very important issues to cover in this regard. For example, tomorrow we want to address the goal of prophethood and divine messengership. What is the purpose of this social resurrection that the prophet is sent to bring about and what methods does the prophet use to achieve it? We will discuss this in the following lecture or lectures. There are still other issues beyond this that I would like to touch on, if God grants me the opportunity to do so.

As for the subject of this resurrection that we are positing for the Prophet, what can we say? Today, when we use the term *inqilāb* ('transformation'), this has taken on a new meaning in the modern lexicon (that of 'revolution'). This is a very meaningful term. However, it should be clear that what we are talking about is a major change at the very foundations of society. This does not necessarily refer to a contentious, violent or bloody event. It is possible that this change could occur peacefully and through dialogue, or through struggle and conflict (especially if there are powerful forces resisting this change). It is possible for there to be violent events leading to an '*inqilāb*'. However, the word does not contain such a definition, and it can also happen peacefully.

If we wanted to give a very simple analogy for the meaning of *inqilāb*, consider this mosque in which we sit, it has a particular structure and architecture. The walls, the doors and the foundations all have a specific layout and placement. Now, imagine if we wanted to change this mosque into an apartment complex: We would need to completely change the architecture. Tearing down some walls, putting up new ones. Closing up some doors, opening up new ones. We may even have to modify the foundations to support the new structure we wish to erect. Now imagine that instead of an apartment complex, we decided to build a bank, or a wedding hall, or a house for a single family–then what? We would have to make completely different changes to the architecture of the mosque to accommodate the building's new function. We couldn't simply repaint the walls and say that it was something else. No! Because each of these buildings that we might want to erect in its place has its own particular layout and design according to the function that it is supposed to serve. A mosque is designed to serve as a place for Muslims to gather and to worship. A bank has a completely different purpose! Therefore, if we ever wanted to change this mosque into another kind of building, we would have to make some fundamental changes. This is the meaning of *inqilāb*. It means changing the building, starting from the foundations: completely changing its structure, its design, the placement of its load-bearing walls, its divisions, and so on, so that it becomes a *completely different building* to what it was before.

Now, imagine a society of, let's say, fifty-thousand persons, or five-hundred-thousand persons, or fifty-million persons. It doesn't matter how many: A society is a collection of people who live together and co-operate with one another according to a general programme or plan, all walking a similar path. Yes, there are different parts of society, but they are all moving in the same general direction. They are a unit. A single society. This society, which may contain fifty-thousand, five-hundred-thousand, five million or fifty million souls, could fall into one of two general categories of society, although there are sub-categories within these two.

Generally speaking, there are two possible ways in which a society can be organised. One of these is that of these fifty-thousand or fifty-million souls living together in a geographical region, there is a class of people–a minority–who govern, give orders and hold authority over the rest of the society. They are the ones who direct the activity of the society as a whole. They are the ones who legislate the laws that govern people in the society. And, if people act against their wishes, they punish them severely. If they criticise their rule, they will silence them using various means. If society suffers a catastrophe of some kind, they will use this catastrophe to their advantage, even if this is to the detriment of the other members of that society. If it so happens that a tribulation befalls this society, it is the ordinary people who will be left to suffer, while these elite use their positions to protect themselves. This is one kind of foundation for society–whether or not this society contains any class differences or not.

If we imagine a society in which there are class differences, this means a society in which people are not seen as equal before the law, nor have equal access to the benefits and facilities of that society, nor a roughly equal standard of living. There will be one group that enjoy more privileges and benefits and better lives as a result, and who have the right to order others to do their bidding, and another group who are compelled to serve this elite group, to obey their orders, and to submit themselves to them. If such a society exists, this is what we call a class-based society. In this society, the economy is also class-based. Government is also class-based. Even the constitution is class-based. This is one kind of society.

Now let us imagine another kind of society for these fifty-thousand or fifty-million souls: If it is not to be like the first type of society we outlined above, then how is it to be? This would mean that no individual in this society has the right to make demands of any other individual–not only is there no class of individuals above all others, but also there is no individual higher than any other! You cannot find a single person in such a society who, if asked 'Why did you commit such and such an act?', would answer: 'Because I wanted to.' There is no 'because I wanted to' in this society. No one has any right to rule over anyone else, to dominate anyone else, or to deprive anyone else of their rights. Everyone is equal before the law. No one is any lower, worth any less, or any less deserving of justice than anyone else. All fifty million people follow the same rules and laws and submit to a single higher power. And who is this higher power? It is God.

So, there are two basic ways in which we can design the structure of society. In one such scheme, the majority of people are effectively the slaves or prisoners of others. Meanwhile, in the other scheme, no one needs to submit to anyone else, nor be held prisoner by anyone else, because everyone is a servant of God. With the first kind of society that we imagined, we saw that its economy would work primarily for the benefit of its ruling class, its government would fulfil the wishes of its ruling class, its constitution and laws would be drafted to safeguard the interests of its ruling class–or those allied with them. Conversely, in the second kind of society–a society that is not driven by class divisions, in which no one has the right to boss anyone else around, or dominate anyone else–the economy is run for the benefit of all, the government acts for the benefit of all and is accountable to all. The constitution is for everyone and the law is for everyone. Most importantly, whatever is good, is good for everyone and whatever is bad, is bad for everyone. In such a society, everyone has a share. This is Paradise on earth.

As we have seen, there are two basic ways in which we can structure society, and we have explained some of the features of each. These two kinds of society can be observed throughout human history. Now, we will only pass over this briefly, as this is an exceedingly complex and detailed discussion, which touches on numerous religious and social issues, and these gatherings are not the right forum to give a full account of this. This is because we all enjoy different levels of knowledge and understanding, and what is important in these lectures is for all or most of you to grasp the main points I am raising. Furthermore, it would take many hours for us to deal with this topic exhaustively. Therefore, what follows should be seen as a basic summary, which you can go and do further research about should you desire.

So, there are two kinds of society: One is a class-based society in which there is wrongdoing, oppression, inequality, exploitation, division and domination. The other is a society which is classless: There is justice, humanity and freedom in such a society. I place special stress on this idea of freedom, because there are societies which claim to be classless, in which nobody is the servant or slave of anyone else, in which all are equal and all benefit equally, but which are actually lacking in freedom. In any case, you can see that both of these systems exist in the history of mankind.

Societies of the first type are those in which discrimination prevails. They are the societies founded by emperors and despots. Societies of the second type are those in which freedom and humanity prevails, where there is no division or discrimination. These are the societies which were founded by the greatest of God's prophets. Now you're wondering: 'Did the prophets found societies?' To which I say: 'Yes, the prophets founded societies!' In the Qur'an we find numerous examples of the kinds of societies that the prophets founded. Look at the stories of Solomon, Ṭālūt, Moses and his leading the Israelites to the holy land after freeing them from their enslavement in Egypt–after he led them out of Egypt, where did he want to take them? He wanted to take them somewhere where he could create a just and virtuous society. These are topics which we might touch on tomorrow and the day after. However, for our present discussion, this brief summary will suffice.

In short, there are two kinds of society. Both kinds have existed throughout history. The intellect clearly recognises which of these is bad and sees that this has always been instantiated in the ungodly political regimes of world history. The intellect also recognises which of these is good and sees that this has always been instantiated in the virtuous political orders of world history–meaning the prophets. The prophets were sent to their individual societies in order to do what? They were sent to transform societies from the first kind of social order into the second kind of social order. This is the very essence of our topic today.

Usually, when we think of the prophets, we imagine them differently. People think that the prophets came to a society like a wise and generous philosopher–a mountain of knowledge and wisdom–who came to society, rented a house and sat in a corner so that people would come to him and hear what he had to say! They think that a prophet is this sort of person. Imagine that a prophet is sent to a particular society, as Abraham or Moses were, and takes up residence in a house, where he sets aside an hour of the day for meeting believers and non-believers alike. Whoever comes to him, he enjoins them to good and forbids them from evil. He tells them to fear God and proves that He exists. He discusses. He makes some of them better people. Then he leaves this world behind. This is how people imagine a prophet to be.

But this is not how a prophet is! When a prophet is sent to a society, this means he is chosen and–as we explained above–transformed through a resurrection of his spirit. He is a radically different person, the leader of a movement, who never stops and never rests. His mind and soul are aflame. He takes one look at society and sees that the whole edifice needs tearing down and rebuilding: The whole social structure is wrong, because the architecture goes against the very essence of human nature. He sees that it must change. He sees that the structure must be transformed. What does this mean? It means he sees that this society is class-based, that it is rife with division, injustice, wrongdoing and inhumanity. Therefore, it must be rebuilt and reordered into a society that is oriented towards *tawḥīd*.

And what is a *tawḥīd*-oriented society? We looked at this in our discussions of divine unity. We said that true *tawḥīd* means the abolition of all social classes. True *tawḥīd* means the power and governance of God. True *tawḥīd* means that everything–whether the law, traditions, treaties, manners, culture–must be inspired by God. True *tawḥīd* means that everyone is a servant of God alone–they do not serve anyone or anything else. Being servants of God makes them free from serving all others. When a prophet enters society with this ideal, with this thought, and with this goal, this class-based society will be transformed. It will be brought down and ruined, and a classless *tawḥīd*-oriented society that is utterly free from tyranny and under the rule of the Creator will be formed in its place. This is why a prophet is sent.

To give an example of similar individuals who were not prophets, I could refer to some figures who will be well-known to anyone who is well-read. By this, I do not intend to draw a comparison between religious and non-religious figures, but only to illustrate the kind of work the prophets came to achieve. Such a person enters society to bring about change, not to bring about bloodshed. They do not come to fight and kill. They do not come in order that people lose their lives. This is not the case. As I said before, the word '*inqilāb*', the word 'change', the word 'transformation'–none of these necessarily imply a violent event. Yes, bloodshed could occur, as it does in everyday life also, but it could also not. What was the First World War about, ultimately? A man assassinated an archduke. The bloodiest conflict in human history, which caused untold destruction, was set in motion by a single gunshot. So yes, a transformation of society could result in bloodshed, but it also could not. There is nothing inherently violent about a revolution.

For example, when Moses came to Pharaoh and told him that he should not sit upon his throne, that he should not enslave the Children of Israel, and that he should not divide society into different classes, if

Pharaoh had responded: 'You're right. We need to change things. Tell me what to do!' then Moses would have set about changing society like a great architect, without a single drop of blood being spilled! It is from those in power that violence plays a role in the prophetic transformation of society. The Qur'an says: 'How many a prophet there has been with whom a multitude of godly men fought.'[38] That is why the doctrine of holy struggle (jihad) was promulgated: Because the ruling class, the ones against whom the revolution is directed and those who stand to lose the most in the event of its success, are not ready to let it happen. Otherwise, had they truly understood, had they–like so many other men of wealth and power throughout history–suddenly experienced a change of heart and submitted to the truth, and come down from their high places, then there would have been no need to fight whatsoever.

Therefore, when a prophet enters a society, it is for the sake of bringing about this transformation. The Prophet comes to make change. What does change look like? What does he do? For example, in the society of pre-Islamic Arabia, the Prophet came and asked why all the wealth in this society should be concentrated in the hands of a select few. Why should servants and slaves be subject to the whims and desires of the elite? Why should the weak be at the mercy of the wicked, like Walīd ibn Mughīrah, Abū Jahl, or Abū Lahab? Why should there not be equality between people?

As the saying goes: 'People are equal like the tooth of a comb.' If you look at a comb, do you see how each of its teeth are level with one another? How there is not a single one that stands above the rest? All are equal. All are at one level. All are one size. All are one form. They are all the same–and beautiful! Humanity is like this. 'People are equal like the tooth of a comb.' This is the call of our Prophet: 'All of you are from Adam, and Adam is from dust!'

---

38 Q3:146.

That man of influence who sits in his mansion on a certain section of Makkah, who must eat well and drink well, for whom people do business, who owns slaves and workers and makes use of them, and who rules over the city, this man of influence with this description is no different to the lowliest servant in his house. There is no difference between them. In terms of the basic substance of humanity, they are utterly like and without any distinction. So why should one enjoy such wide power and influence, while the other barely has enough to eat? The field should be open for everyone to participate in society. This is the call of the Prophet.

In all of the societies where a prophet appears, it is with this call and this mission: A prophet comes to reform society, to change it from its form, which is wedded to inequality, wrongdoing and tyranny, into a new form that is balanced, beautiful and just. This is one issue. 'The Prophetic Resurrection of Society' means this. Every prophet sent to a society came to achieve exactly this, as you know. Meanwhile, there was not a single prophet who came just to sit in the corner and discuss the vagaries of everyday life with people.

Now, the greatest of the prophets–who are known as 'those endowed with firm resolve' (*'ulu al-ʿaẓm*)–were the axes of the divine transformation of society. Other prophets either came to follow the path trodden by these great messengers, or to complete the work they began, or to bring their plans to fulfilment, or to safeguard the gains of their revolution. Just as the successors of our Prophet, after he passed away, took up his work after him–this was the role of the Commander of the Faithful, the work of Imam Ḥusayn, and the work of all the Imams. And, after the Imams, it became the task of the scholars of Islam. Ultimately, today it is the work of the Imam of the Age (aj).

Another point about this resurrection of society that we should pay attention to is why it was necessary in the first place. You might ask: What was the problem with pre-Islamic Arab society? Why couldn't it remain in place? Could it not be made into a fairer social order? This prophet who came had to put himself through fire and water and make great personal sacrifices in order to change his society for the better–why did he have to do this? Why couldn't he have left things the way they were? What was wrong with the natural order of things? Might, after all, makes right–so let the victors enjoy their spoils. Those who are downtrodden are downtrodden because they were beaten. So why should the Prophet work so hard to change this?

This is an important question. Now, you will tell me that no one asks this question but, even if they do not ask it aloud, they still might ask it of themselves, so it is a question that must be answered. The explanation is as follows: A prophet does not move without a destination in mind. He did not go through fire and water for no reason. On the contrary, he looks at the social reality of his own day and age and sees that it is one in which falsehood predominates, and one which goes against the nature of the human being and the nature of the very cosmos itself. So, he wants to replace falsehood with truth and redirect society towards the path of humanity.

Truth and falsehood–these are two words you find mentioned throughout the Qur'an. The confrontation between truth and falsehood is embodied in tens of its verses. But what are truth (*ḥaqq*) and falsehood (*bāṭil*)? Let us try to understand what these terms mean. We have said that the human being is a creature that travels through the world with such and such a shape and appearance. However, the human being has certain features, abilities and needs which are unique to himself. This world in which the human being lives out his days also has certain features and characteristics, and it is moving towards the end for which it was created. This world that you behold with your two eyes–all of it is related. Its sun a million miles away. Its humans. Its plants. Its animals. Even though none of these appear to be connected at first glance, from the perspective of someone who knows God and worships Him, there is an indivisible unity at the core of all things. The whole cosmos is one thing. All of its parts are parts of a single body. And like a single body, it is moving with all of its parts in unison. This is the nature of the world we inhabit.

In the human being, we see that the stomach performs one function, the eye performs one function, the liver performs one function, the brain and nerves perform one function, but when you put all of these functions together, you find they have one thing in common. What is that thing? That they all contribute to the life of this human being, to his movements, to his efforts, to his continued existence in this world. The sum of all the motion you witness in the cosmos, whether it is on a grand scale or a microscopic one, when you put it all together, you see that the whole universe is moving as one. All of the other denizens of this cosmos which exist alongside the human being, which either lack awareness or free-will, have no say in the direction that they travel. They go with the flow of the universe. It is only the human being that has free will. It is only the human being that can choose to do his own thing, to separate himself from the cosmic sequence of events, to turn around and walk the other way. It is only the human being that can choose not to follow the cosmic procession, which we said is heading towards a single destination. Everything else that exists, if it can be taken out of its natural state or diverted from its natural heading, it is only by virtue of human interference with it. It is the human being that discovers uranium and, instead of using it to treat a thousand illnesses, turns it into a bomb with the capacity to kill millions. Uranium does not make itself into a bomb; it merely follows its natural course. It is not LSD that, instead of being a medicine to cure sickness, is instead made into a drug to intoxicate youngsters. It is not the fault of LSD how it is used. It is not the fault of the matter. Rather, it is the fault of the human beings that choose to use it in this way.

In this procession that we have described, of which the sun is one member, of which the earth is another, of which the cosmos and all of its countless denizens are members, all are following their natural path. There is only one kind of being–this devil, this agent, this free-willed entity–that sometimes diverts these things from their proper path. Uranium follows its natural trajectory. LSD follows its natural trajectory. Morphine follows its natural trajectory. Morphine–which should be used entirely for the purpose of helping humanity can instead be used to immiserate humanity. A foodstuff which should give life to mankind, is instead used to bring death to mankind. It is not by its own choice that it does this. It is the human being that diverts it from its proper course. It is only the human being that has this ability.

Because the human being has this ability and because the human being has free will, the human being has the power to change and, because he has the power to change, there must be a law to guide him and direct him to the right path, to tell him how to join the cosmic procession towards God. And also, a law to warn him that if he leaves this path, he will have left the cosmic procession. In short, what does this mean? It means that the human being needs a system of law to bring him into harmony with the rest of creation. And what do we call this law? What is its name? Truth (*ḥaqq*). This is what truth means. It is the law that is in harmony with the very nature of the cosmos itself and, because it is in harmony with the cosmos, it is also in harmony with human nature. The human being, after all, is a part of the cosmos which he inhabits. And, because the human being is one part of this greater whole, and because this law that is promulgated in order to guide him is in harmony both with his nature and the nature of the cosmos as a whole, it leads him to a good life.

What, then, is falsehood (*bāṭil*)? Falsehood is that course, law and path whose promulgation goes against the nature of the cosmos and of the human being. It is that which is created by the tyrants, devils and those who wish to lead others astray. The prophets always brought truth in order to extinguish falsehood. In the society which

Pharaoh presided over, people were divided into different social classes, and society was structured in such a way that one class ruled over the others and tyrannised them for the benefit of itself. This situation, this system, and this structure of society was one that was founded on falsehood. The prophets came to tear down this edifice of falsehood. They came to reduce it to dust and to establish truth in its place. Therefore, the Prophet put himself through fire and water for the sake of the truth. The truth is what he spoke, and the truth is what he desired. It was for the sake of the truth that he endured trials and ordeals. It was for the sake of establishing truth in the place of falsehood that the prophets struggled unceasingly, never flagging in their cause, never forgetting it for one moment, never resting and never diverting. It was a matter of establishing truth in the place of falsehood–this is the proper analysis of the prophetic function.

To sum up what I have said so far: The prophets came to overthrow a regime that was class-based, tyrannical, exploitative and inhuman. And all of these qualities are best summed up by the name 'ignorance' (*jāhiliyyah*). Therefore, the prophets came to overthrow the regime of ignorance and establish a divine regime in its place in the form of a *tawḥīd*-oriented society. They wanted to create a society that was under the authority and governance of God, rather than subject to the whims and desires of men. This is what the prophets were supposed to achieve. The prophets came to replace an incorrect social order with one that was good and right. Their slogan of divine unity was also for this purpose. Their struggle against tyranny and false gods was for this purpose. It was also for this reason that the tyrants sought to suppress them. Perhaps, in the course of these lectures, we can discuss the different classes of people who fought against the prophets and the reasons for their opposition to them.

The verses we are about to discuss from *Sūrat al-Qaṣaṣ* illustrate this situation perfectly; Pharaoh's regime of ignorance and the Pharaonic society he presided over, and the social order which Moses wanted to establish in its place. These two opposing sides could not be more clearly defined and, therefore, God gives a promise to those who follow Moses' example. He promises that, ultimately, it is God's will that the followers of Moses in this world, meaning the supporters of divine unity, should be successful in their endeavours. The reason for this is clear–this is yet another topic that we will gradually address, namely what is the final goal of prophethood? To what end will the prophets be victorious and why? They will be victorious because their struggle aligns with the nature of humanity and the cosmos as a whole. This is summed-up nicely in the verses below:

'Ṭā, Sīn, Mīm'.[39] This is the sequence of letters at the beginning of *Sūrat al-Qaṣas*. There have been many theories about the significance of these sequences of letters at the beginning of different chapters of the Qur'an, and commentators have expended much energy discussing them. However, this has little to do with our current discussion. 'These are the signs of the Manifest Book. We relate to you some of the account of Moses and Pharaoh in truth for a people who have faith.'[40] Notice that the Qur'an says it will recite *some* of the account of Moses and Pharaoh. This is because the Qur'an's approach in relating such accounts from the lives of the prophets is to focus on a particular aspect of the story in order to make a particular point, rather than relating the entirety of the story in full detail. Here, the Qur'an mentions a brief excerpt from the story of Moses in order to deliver a particular message, namely about the triumph of truth over falsehood. However, we are not going to deal with all of these parts of the story in our discussion today.

God says He wants to recount a relevant part of the account of Moses and Pharaoh 'in truth' (*bi al-ḥaqq*)–meaning in accordance with the truth, as it really happened, not as a myth or a legendary

39 Q28:1.

40 Q28:2–3.

account–'for a people who have faith'–to benefit those people who truly believe. In other words, God says: What we are about to relate to you is not something idle or useless, on the contrary it is extremely effective and useful for the faithful who are around you. When they hear this story from this point of view, they will grasp God's way of doing things in this regard and, as a result, they will see what it is they need to do. In short: 'Indeed Pharaoh tyrannized over the land'.[41] Pharaoh sought dominion over the land and raised himself above it. He sought to gain [what is known in Arabic as] (*ʿuluww*) which means to raise above. What does this mean? It means that against the context of the equality of all human beings, he suddenly rose up, sat himself on a pedestal, and set himself above all others. In other words, he set himself above equality and gained superiority over other human beings.

'Indeed Pharaoh tyrannized over the land'. He raised himself up and established dominion over it 'reducing its people to factions'; in the new order, he was at the top of the hierarchy, but he also divided those beneath him into different groups and levels. Some were closer to him, such as Hāmān and others similar to him, then there was a level beneath them, and a level beneath them, and so on and so forth, until the lowest level, 'abasing one group of them'. So, as well as dividing society into different groups, there was one group in particular that he 'abased' (*yastaḍʿifu*, from *istiḍʿāf*), meaning that he made them a special target of his oppression and cruelty. However, the word *istiḍʿāf* means more than just oppression, although this is certainly a component of it and peoples who are abased are also oppressed. However, to be abased also means to be made weak, to be denied opportunities, to be deprived of power. So he not only oppressed them, he rendered them unable to resist his oppression, 'abasing one group of them', he made one group, one class of people in particular weaker than

41 Q28:4.

all the rest and rendered them impotent. In short, they were denied every opportunity and every benefit accorded to other members of that society. Now, if you study the way in which a society functions, especially in the developing world, you will understand this easily. In such societies, all the means of advancement and development are monopolised by a small group of people and no one outside of this group is permitted such opportunities. It is as if they cannot breathe without the leave of those who rule over them. Their growth, if they grow at all, is entirely for the benefit of their rulers–they are utterly exploited–'abasing one group of them.'

And how were they abased? 'Slaughtering their sons'. They did not allow their youth to become numerous because they feared a rebellion amongst their slaves, and they knew that if such a rebellion were to occur, it would be led by the youth. And, because in those days, women were not as involved in social issues as they are today and sons took on the most important responsibilities, they focused on oppressing the sons of this abased class. There are some reports and traditions which say that amongst the youth, there were still young men like Moses appearing and it was, of course, one of these, Moses himself, that came and changed the world. A priest foretold that a child would be born into this world, fitting this description, whose name is Moses, that would put an end to Pharaoh's rule. Whether or not Pharaoh believed this prophecy, he was a shrewd man and he understood that it was the young men of the Israelites who posed the greatest threat to his rule. He feared the appearance of a young man such as Moses, who would be driven by his great altruism to oppose his rule. Therefore, in order to forestall the appearance of such a young man, Pharaoh ordered the sons of the Israelites to be slaughtered.

'And sparing their women'. Pharaoh did not kill the women of the Israelites, either to promote immorality and vice, or so that they would be forced to marry outside of the Israelites. In other words, the daughters of the Israelites could not marry their sons, as these had been slaughtered, so then they would be forced to marry Egyptians and have Egyptian children. This would integrate the Israelites with Pharaoh's society by destroying their communal identity. As I have said on other occasions when discussing some of the verses of *Sūrat al-Baqarah*, consider the fact that, by some accounts, the Israelites were enslaved and oppressed by the Egyptians for hundreds of years and yet, in spite of this, they were able to hold fast to their ideals and their faith.

So, the battle lines are drawn between the two sides. On the one hand there is Pharaoh, whom the same verse of the Qur'an describes, saying: 'Indeed, he was one of the agents of corruption.' In other words, he was a corruptor of human nature, a corruptor of society, and a corruptor of the world. In *Sūrat al-Baqarah*, we read: 'And if he were to wield authority, he would try to cause corruption in the land, and to ruin the crop and the stock, and God does not like corruption.'[42] What sets apart the likes of Pharaoh is that he sowed corruption in the land and brought about ruin, he did everything he could to stand in the way of growth and human flourishing, so that whatever development did take place was distorted and diverted from its proper course.

Now, on the other hand, what about truth? What is God's will? What is it that God does in these circumstances? 'But We desire'–this is God's cosmic will (*irādah takwīniyyah*)–'to show favour to those who were abased in the land'.[43] Notice that God does not say, 'We desired' (*aradnā*), in the past tense; He does not say He desired this only at the time of the Israelites enslavement in Egypt. No, He says this in the present tense, showing that this is something continuous and unceasing throughout human history. In other words, God *always* desires to show favour to those who are abased, to the underclass, to

42 Q2:205.

43 Q28:5.

the downtrodden and oppressed, and to save them and bring them out of their abasement–'and to make them leaders'–to take them from being followers in their society and make them into leaders and rulers–'and to make them the heirs'–so that they will inherit all the good things in this world. This is God's will.

'And to establish them in the land, and to show Pharaoh and Hāmān'[44]–because these are the representatives of the ruling class; of course, although Pharaoh was from the ruling class, he was the highest member of this class, almost in a class of his own and even the other members of the ruling class such as Hāmān, were under his control. Hāmān, meanwhile, was the representative of the class directly beneath Pharaoh, who placed their power and abilities at his disposal. The Qur'an uses the term 'elite' (*mala'*) to denote this class, and we will discuss them further at a later point, God-willing. 'And their hosts', their soldiers, those who fight for their cause and serve them without necessarily enjoying all of the benefits that they do, 'from them', the abased and downtrodden , 'that of which they were apprehensive', meaning what Pharaoh and Hāmān feared would happen, namely that the downtrodden would rise up against them and seize power from them. After all, in any society, the downtrodden and dispossessed usually make up the majority. This too is a manifestation of God's will.

Then, the Qur'an turns to other matters which demonstrate God's power: 'We revealed to Moses' mother, "Nurse him"'.[45] There is another verse in *Sūrat al-Ṣaff* which also shows how the divine system triumphs over the ignorant system, although this is beyond the scope of our present discussion. What we are interested in, however, is how when a prophet emerges, he stands up to an ignorant system, shows people a divine and *tawḥīd*-oriented system, and then strives to

44 Q28:6.

45 Q28:7.

establish this new social order in place of the existing one. Replacing the order of falsehood with the order of divine truth.

The Goals of Prophethood

Saturday 18th Ramadan 1394
4th October 1974

لَقَدْ أَرْسَلْنَا رُسُلَنَا بِالْبَيِّنَاتِ وَأَنْزَلْنَا مَعَهُمُ الْكِتَابَ وَالْمِيزَانَ
لِيَقُومَ النَّاسُ بِالْقِسْطِ وَأَنْزَلْنَا الْحَدِيدَ فِيهِ بَأْسٌ شَدِيدٌ
وَمَنَافِعُ لِلنَّاسِ وَلِيَعْلَمَ اللَّهُ مَنْ يَنْصُرُهُ وَرُسُلَهُ بِالْغَيْبِ إِنَّ اللَّهَ
قَوِيٌّ عَزِيزٌ (٢٥)

'Certainly We sent Our apostles with manifest proofs, and We sent down with them the Book and the Balance, so that mankind may maintain justice; and We sent down iron, in which there is great might and uses for mankind, and so that God may know those who help Him and His apostles in [their] absence. Indeed God is all-strong, all-mighty.'
- Sūrat al-Ḥadīd (57):25.

In our discussion of prophethood (*nubuwwah*) we came to the conclusion that when a prophet is chosen by God as His messenger, he undergoes a transformation within his own being and, when he brings his message to his people, he brings about a transformation within the fabric of society that is a reflection of his own inner transformation. He causes a profound change in the social structure. Today, we want to grasp what is the purpose of causing this change? We will examine this question in a general sense that encompasses the missions of all the prophets of God. This issue is not only relevant to our overall topic from a number of angles, it is actually essential to it. What mission does a prophet follow? What goal does he pursue? What does he want to achieve?

The primary goal of any prophet is one thing and one thing only. However, the path that leads to that goal comprises a number of other intermediate goals for this prophet to achieve, and of these there is one which this prophet feels is more important and pressing. Now, the primary goal of all of God's messengers can be summed up in a few words: The prophets came to this world in order to guide mankind upwards and towards the perfection for which they were created. As a creature, the human being is endowed with numerous latent potentialities, he has countless abilities and energies, all of which enable him to become something higher, nobler and greater than what he is in appearance.

Fundamentally, from the moment a person is born, from the moment that a world exists for him, he is on a journey towards perfection, and forever in a state of growth and development. This is clearly visible with regard to the physical existence of their body. A new-born babe lacks many of the physical features possessed by an adult: A new-born lacks teeth, a strong jaw, a firm grip, the ability to walk...even its internal organs, such as those of its digestive tract, are not fully mature when it comes into this world. All of this means it cannot immediately live like an ordinary adult human being. Its brain and nervous system are still developing. But, after some time has passed, the child begins to develop all of these faculties. Nothing is added from outside that is not already there. That baby's little jaw grows stronger, its tiny hands learn to grip things tightly, those little legs which could not carry its weight become stronger and steadier, its nervous system develops, and its brain which at one point could not hold the most basic thoughts now becomes able to understand the most important and complex questions of its existence. Nothing is added to this child from outside. This all comes from within. These are all the child's latent potential and unrealised abilities which, with the passage of time and the fulfilment of the necessary conditions, blossom in this child and become visible. A child has the potential to speak, and later acquires the ability to do so. A child has the potential to think, to understand and to learn, and will grow to do all of these things. Therefore, from the moment he comes into this world, the human being is forever growing and moving towards perfection. Things which were not but came to be, could not but then became able, which had no intellect but then came to acquire one, lacked experience but later gained it–they all belong to this category.

In matters pertaining to the human body, as all of you have seen and understood just now, we find that the human being is always growing. In other words, he is always increasing what he has and gaining things which he previously did not. But this is also true in matters which pertain to the moral and spiritual life of the human being. There is a whole world of potential which is hidden deep within the human being. We could compare the human being to a rich mine buried deep below the ground which, when it is mined, is seen to contain wonders but, so long as it remains buried, there is naught but dirt and dust.

Let me give you an example for this sort of thing. The human being is like one of the mosaics you find around a water cistern. When they want to make a mosaic, the first thing they do is create a template on which to lay the tiles. They spread out their material to make a flat surface. If you were to see this template before the tiles were laid, you would not see any trace of beauty or finery therein. You would just see a thick, dark and unattractive surface. However, when it is time to polish the surface, they use special tools or their hands to apply friction to it. Then, you see that this dark matter becomes bright and clear as they polish it–and there are many things which appear dark, but when they are exposed to friction they become transparent–but also, more than this, you see that there were things in this matter which you had no idea even existed. As they polish the outer layer you see that this contains beautiful stones of many hues, intricate patterns and bright colours, and that all of these were hidden in the dark matter. You could not see what this matter contained, and you might never have thought that this was something that could be used to make something beautiful. But, once this surface has been scrubbed, you see the beautiful stones it contains. Now you can see the beautiful sections of mosaic–the beauty that was previously hidden. The great potential that hides within the human soul is very much like the stones you find hidden in the dark matter of a mosaic before it is scrubbed to reveal their beauty.

The human being that you see is like an uncut, unpolished stone you find in the street somewhere. This small child that still cannot speak has nothing special for anyone, aside perhaps for its mother and father. But, as you can see, there is a wealth of treasure buried within this child's soul. He has deep reserves of special qualities. There is beauty there that is waiting to be discovered. There are potentialities there waiting to be unlocked. As the poet Saʿdī once said:

'Just as a bird takes flight, you must leave behind
The fetters of desire and soar with wings of humanity.'

This is a truth that has been expressed in speech and verse by mystics and poets alike since long ago. They say that man is a resplendent being, for man is higher than the angels and archangels. The human being contains an overflowing spring of goodness, beauty and potential that needs only to be brought forth into the world. In short, each human is ready to flourish, to grow and to ascend towards perfection. And the real goal of the prophets is to guide the human being on this journey. This is what we find described in the Qur'an with words such as 'refinement' (*tazkīyah*) and 'education' (*taʿlīm*). The prophets came to expunge the negative traits from human beings, to lead them away from following their desires, to save them from a way of living that was merely animal. As Rumi remarked:

'O you wolves who tear at the shirts of Josephs
Awaken from this heavy slumber!'

Those who have the appearance of humans while having the character of wolves, those who give pleasant smiles while acting like monsters, these people cannot be called 'human'. A person who enjoys shedding blood, a person who delights in inflicting death and destruction on others, who is not saddened by seeing the ordeals of his fellow men, who remains unmoved by the suffering of others, this person is not a human being regardless of appearances to the contrary. Is he very smart? Is he very wealthy? Is he very powerful? Is he very well-presented? He could be all of these, but none of these add up to a human being. Knowledge, wealth, power, presentation–humanity is something else entirely.

The prophets came to purify the human being. You will find no trace of animal behaviour in the preaching of the prophets. You will find no sign of animal level of existence in the lifestyle of the prophets. All you will find there is the pure light of humanity. And this is one of their greatest miracles.

When people think of prophetic miracles, they imagine displays of supernatural power and demonstrations of impossible acts. They imagine prophets causing walls to crumble or trees to grow. Granted. The prophets certainly performed miracles comparable to these–there is no doubt in this regard–but the greatest miracle of the prophets was something else entirely: The creation of a virtuous human being. In all earnestness, what miracle could be greater than this?

There might be someone who may be committing every criminal and immoral act imaginable. But upon being polished by the message of Islam, i.e. by that tool that the Prophet uses to polish the human soul, this man is suddenly and utterly transformed, the same person who yesterday would not hesitate to do wrong and whom no one would expect to become a paragon of virtue.

What kind of person was Abū Dharr before Islam? Abū Dharr was a rough desert nomad who had no regard for humanity whatsoever. Was this not so? He was the sort of person that you would not care if ten thousand people like him were to be killed in an earthquake. He was a man who did not understand and did not *want* to understand. There was not a grain of compassion in his persona. There was not a shred of interest in virtue. He was a wild-looking figure who had grown up in the harsh landscape of the Arabian desert. If you saw him, would you have any sympathy for him? If a great moral teacher saw him, would he have hope that such a man could change? People who call themselves moral teachers or reformers tend not to have much concern for men like Abū Dharr. They prefer to work with people who recognise their importance and harken to their words–people who are already educated and thinking.

However, the Prophet of Islam was able to take this rough unpolished stone that was Abū Dharr and, through the polish of revelation and preaching, make a human being. And not just any human being–a human being who displayed every possible moral virtue available to man! This is the Prophet's greatest miracle. To make a man who puts aside all ego and selfishness–which is the axis round which most men's lives turn–and is willing to sacrifice everything for the cause of truth. Could you find such a person under normal circumstances? We want everything for ourselves and the things connected to ourselves: our business, our title, our children, our name and, of course, our own persons. Abū Dharr sacrificed everything he had–everything that went back to his own self–for the sake of God and for the sake of the Prophet, to walk the path that was laid out before him. This is what it means to be human. A human being with those qualities is transformed to a human being of this type. What is capable of effecting such a change? The revelation and preaching of the Prophet.

From this dull stone the Prophet made a glistening jewel. This is the purpose of prophethood–to transform mankind.

Yes, it is of the utmost importance to set up the proper social order. It is essential to have a system that brings freedom and prosperity to all. However, when discussing this, we must also ask that, once we have a society in which there is freedom and prosperity combined with social justice and class differences have been eradicated, and people are living and growing-up in such a society–what then? What comes next? What goal do materialist philosophies assign the human being who lives in an ideal society? What is the purpose of humanity? Human beings struggle and sacrifice in order to create a free society, but once they have it, what comes after? What do we do with this freedom now that we have it? For instance, when you build a mosque, there must be a purpose for this mosque after it has been built, so that when construction finishes people will come and pray, or listen to sermons, or something of this kind. It is meaningless for us to build a mosque, with all the money, time and effort that goes into this, only for the mosque to remain unused! Why did we build this mosque? What do we do now it is finished? Would we say: Nothing, we just wanted to build a mosque! This would be absurd! And yet, this is exactly what materialist philosophies say about the creation of a just and fair society.

Materialist philosophies say that we should develop the world, eliminate poverty, uproot ignorance and build a better society–a human society, a society in which there are no class divisions, in which there is no division or exploitation. Great! But once we have it, what are human beings supposed to do in it? Materialist philosophies do not have an answer to this. What is to become of humanity in such a society? No answer. Are people just meant to eat and sleep? Are they just meant to have an easy life, and that's it? Are we to struggle and sacrifice just for people to have an easy life, meaning to eat and sleep with ease? Is that all we want? This is where materialist ideologies ultimately fail.

Theistic philosophies, on the other hand, say that there is a further goal to be achieved. There is a higher goal for which the creation of a just social order is a prerequisite. And that is to elevate the human being. In fact, it is to make men into human beings. A man is not the same thing as a human. A man is a creature that walks on two legs, but a human is something more. To become human, a person must realise their latent potential and acquire virtue. Now, you might ask: Then what? To which the answer is: There is no 'then' because the human being is limitless and God is limitless, and so the journey is never-ending. 'To God we belong and to Him we return.' When the human being sets out upon the path of perfection, there is no end to this road. This is the idea that lies at the core of monotheism and all the world's great religious traditions. The human being is forever ascending onwards and upwards. The human being is forever climbing to new heights. There is no end. And it is for this idea that the prophets were sent.

The prophets came to save mankind from vice, degeneracy and ignorance, from these latent potentialities remaining hidden. They came to make real human beings. This is the primary goal of the prophets. This is what the Qur'an tells us on numerous occasions, as we have seen in the verses we have already mentioned in this series. 'God certainly favoured the faithful when He raised up among them an apostle from among themselves to recite to them His signs and to purify them, and to teach them'.[1] So, the prophets came to enhance the human being, to adorn him with virtue, and to purify him from vice. This is the goal of the prophets. That is why our own Prophet is narrated to have said: 'I was sent to perfect the best of morals.' This is first.

1 Q3:164.

But there is an even more important point to consider. We have all heard the first point on many occasions and some of us love to repeat it over and over because, if the mission of the prophets was only a question of moral refinement and development, someone could say: 'We know where to go and we've understood what we must do, so stop stirring up trouble and give up fighting. Instead, let's go to that monastery and live as monks. We will spend all of our time purifying ourselves and becoming better people, and we will save ourselves. Then, if someone comes to us and is receptive, we can teach him how to do the same, and we'll make him a better person too!'

This attitude is often used an excuse for being lazy, quiescent, saving one's own skin and choosing the path of least resistance. Because it can be used to excuse these traits, we find it repeated often. Such words please people, they please rulers, and they please those who bear the responsibility of educating and guiding the people. Moral refinement is something straightforward and easy to preach. It does not bring you into conflict with others. You just need to gather a few people, tell them some nice stories, make them a little less selfish, and say that you've helped them on the path to spirituality and moral refinement! It is also easy for people, or at least it looks easy for them (when in reality, it is not)!

That is why I say what we have said so far is uncontroversial and well-known. However, the question is this: How did the prophets elevate people and inspire them to virtue? What did they do? Did they go and speak to people one by one, take them by the hand and lead them to a corner, a mosque or a school in order to teach them and educate them? Did the prophets sit in a hermitage and wait for people to come to them, like the ascetics and mystics of this world? Did people look at their spiritual state and decide to become just like them? Or were the prophets like the philosophers of the world–did they open a school, set up a blackboard and call people to come and learn from them? Is this how the prophets were? Or not: The prophets did not believe in educating only the individual. They did not believe in making people into real human beings one at a time, like you might imagine Socrates and Plato did. Do you think Abraham, Moses, Jesus or our Prophet sat in a school and waited for people to come to them? They were not like this, and neither were the Prophet's successors. It is an error to imagine, as some people do, that Imam al-Ṣādiq (a) just sat atop a pulpit and preached to his four thousand students, as some people unthinkingly suppose. Because Ibn ʿUqdah counted some four thousand individuals as students of and narrators of traditions from him, some suppose that these four thousand people came and sat at his feet while he narrated traditions, answered legal questions and delivered moral exhortations from the pulpit!

But this is not the case for Imam al-Ṣādiq or for his grandfather, the Prophet of Islam, or for any of the prophets who came before him in this world. This was not their way. It is not the job of the prophets to open schools, deliver sermons or educate individuals. The prophets have just one answer to the question: How to make a human being? How to educate a person in accordance with the proper divine paradigm? They have one answer: By creating an environment that is conducive to this, a healthy environment, an environment in which people can grow and learn. That is all. They say that it is not possible to do this on an individual basis, one person at a time. Instead, you must make a factory. If you want to change a whole society one person at a time, you will die before you accomplish this. Instead, you must change society in order to change its people. There must be a system, an assembly line that makes people in the desired fashion. That is all.

The prophets say that the human being is like a fruit tree (let us say a date palm or an orange tree). These fruit trees grow and give fruit in certain specific conditions that are appropriate to them (such as a warm climate). Date palms typically grow in the south of Iran and in some Arab countries. And they produce a sweet and delicious fruit in these climates. Why? Because these fruit trees thrive best in an environment which has a certain range of temperature, humidity and precipitation, and in a soil which has a certain mineral composition. There are other conditions too, and these conditions are best fulfilled somewhere like Khuzestan. These conditions are not met in Mashhad! Now, if you go and bring a thousand date palms and plant them here, where neither the air, nor the water, nor the soil is conducive to their growth, what will happen?

No, if you wanted to grow dates in Mashhad, you would have to bring a date palm (or an orange tree) and plant it in your house's garden and then keep close watch over it. You'll have to fertilize and water its soil. This takes a lot of work but, if you're lucky, after a while it will give you one or two unripe dates. Now, you could do this–but why would you? If you wanted to grow dates, you would do it in an environment that was conducive to date palms, where you didn't have to constantly monitor them to keep them healthy, where you wouldn't have to expend all that effort for one or two dates. Is it not more reasonable that, instead of growing date palms one by one in an inappropriate climate, to grow them in the right climate? If you can create an environment in which date palms will flourish by themselves?

Clearly, if you wanted to make the right environment though, this too would take a lot of work and require a great deal of effort before you could reap the rewards! It definitely requires more effort than growing a single date palm, but consider the results this effort will yield. Here, you are expending all this effort for one person, for an individual, whereas there, you are expending that effort for a society, for a system, which will affect millions of people and their descendants too. This is the work of the prophets.

It is of the utmost importance that we understand this point properly if we are to be true followers of the prophetic path. This is something we need to ponder on, as it is not always easy to grasp. To that end, we must refer to the verses of the Qur'an, to the lives of the prophets, to the traditions we have on the subject of prophethood. We must study these sources in detail and reflect: Do not accept this hastily. Do not reject this hastily. A topic of this importance deserves time and consideration. Many people will object to what I have said. Some will not understand that the prophets wanted to create an environment that was conducive to spiritual growth, preferring to imagine that they went to people one by one in order to guide them, even though this sort of work is beneath the lofty status of God's messengers on earth.

When we look at the Qur'an, we can understand how the prophets answered this question of how to make a human being? Meaning how to elevate and nurture a human being. Their answer to this question was that we need to create a godly society, a *tawḥīd*-oriented society, an appropriate environment in which to produce true human beings. And not just one, or ten, or even a thousand human beings individually, but rather in groups, in the guiding light of Islamic teachings.

'When God's help comes with victory, and you see the people entering God's religion in throngs.'[2] Now, in the pagan environment of Makkah, the Prophet was forced to guide people one at a time. This is because, in order to create this better society or a system of guiding others, there must be a number of close disciples, a vanguard who were handpicked by the Prophet. There is no contradiction between this and the general scheme of the prophets. In order to lay the foundations of the new kind of society he hoped to create, the Prophet had no choice but to preach to people one by one. One of these was Abū Dharr. Another was ʿAbd Allāh ibn Masʿūd. And so on, and so forth. In this way, he guided one or two hundred people in Makkah. These would be the foundation of the new society–a society built on *tawḥīd* and submission to God. What an effort it was for the

2 Q110:1–2.

Prophet to guide all these individual people, what a struggle, and what sacrifices it demanded from him!

Fathers forbade their sons from listening to him and those sons who had worldly ambitions did not follow him or heed his words. Anyone who inclined towards him in the slightest was harassed and persecuted by the pagans of Makkah. This is what the Prophet was up against in his home city. However, this all changed when he took his mission to Madinah. There, he was able to create a godly and *tawḥīd*-oriented society, with himself at its head, governing by the laws and commands of God. It was at this time that God told him: 'When God's help comes with victory, and you see the people entering God's religion in throngs.'

To sum-up: The prophets had two major goals. Their fundamental goal was to make people into human beings, to save people from their vices and to adorn them with virtues. In short, to make human beings *humane*. This was their highest goal. However, there was another goal which was a preliminary to achieving this one, namely, to create a *tawḥīd*-oriented society that is governed by a godly system of government and ruled by God's laws. This also was the goal of all the prophets. If anyone imagines that God's messengers did not have this goal, they need to pay closer attention when studying the Qur'an, the traditions and the lives of the prophets.

Here, we will discuss two sets of verses from the Qur'an, but there are many more in which God makes this clear. It is up to you to go and investigate further and ponder upon their meaning.

The first of these verses is from *Sūrat al-Ḥadīd*: 'Certainly We sent Our apostles with manifest proofs'. The words of the prophets and the evidence they bring is extremely clear. It is something that anyone capable of thinking or reflecting will be able to understand. 'And We sent down with them the Book'. What is 'the Book' (*al-kitāb*)? On many occasions, we have said that the Book is the totality of the teachings and ordinances that constitute the very foundations of the religion. The lessons and doctrines of the religion–this is the Book. It encompasses the full ideology of the religion. If we wanted to sum up the meaning of 'the Book' using a term that is widely-used today by contemporary schools of thought, we would say that it means 'ideology', meaning the fundamental principles of the religion, the pillars of its thought, and the basis for its practical doctrines that have a tangible and foundational role in its constitution.

In addition to the Book, God also sent 'the Balance' (*al-mizān*)–what is the Balance? A measure? A scale? Does it mean that every prophet who came brought a measure with him under his robes? Of course not. The Balance refers to the means by which balance and harmony in society can be achieved. This is the meaning of the Balance in the Qur'an. It is the means by which justice can be brought about in society. We will see that this refers to society. If the Prophet was not supposed to lead a community or create a new society, why would he need a balance? Why would he need something that is a means of instituting fairness and equality? So what is this means that the Prophet was given for creating a just social order? The tools of divine judgement–this is one–the laws governing judgement and settling disputes in society, the means to implement the laws, a guarantor of their implementation–all of these are things that 'the Balance' could denote. There are laws, a guarantor that these laws will be implemented, and witness to see them being implemented. Just as we see today in democratic nations, we see that the state implements the laws of the society. In nations where there is a state, a parliament, a legislator, and implementor of them, this implementor of laws is the executive that supervises society as a whole. It is possible that 'the Balance' refers to this executive power.

When we look at the traditions concerning these verses, we see one of the interpretations given to the term 'the Balance' is that of the

Imam.[3] I believe this is an absolutely correct application of this verse's meaning. The Balance is the Imam because the Imam is the one who separates truth from falsehood in society. It is he who must make the lines clear. It is he who must bring about justice and equality in society. Why? Because he is the ruler of the society. However, some people might misinterpret the meaning of this tradition. We have nothing to do with these erroneous interpretations–we understand its proper meaning to be as we have stated above. The Imam is the Balance. He is the criterion. Good and evil are measured according to him. The proper ways are applied with him. In addition to this, it is he who oversees society to ensure that people do not overstep the boundaries of justice and equality, and he supervises the implementation of the divine law. This is what the narration emphasises. Therefore, as we have said previously, the Balance is the means by which justice and equality can be realised in society. And this is one of the things that the Prophet was sent with.

So why do we do this? What does the Book need the Prophet for? Why did we need the Prophet at all if there is a book? Why does there need to be a balance? Why does there need to be a book? The Qur'an answers: 'so that mankind may maintain justice'–so that people can live just lives in an environment of justice. So that people can establish a just way of living. This is one meaning. However, there is another meaning too: So that the human being will stand on the basis of justice and live according to the principle of equality. Now, these two meanings sound very similar, but if you pay close attention you will see that they differ subtly.

'So that mankind may maintain justice', so that people can live in an environment of justice, in a just society governed by a just system. This is why the Prophet was sent. So, why did God send messengers? To set up a just system of government. They came to

3 See *Tafsīr Nūr al-Thaqalayn*, on verse Q57:25.

make the world a place of fairness and justice. They came to make society and government just and fair. This is why the Prophet came, because it is only within a just society and a just social order that the human being can find the opportunity to grow and flourish.

Then, God adds: 'And We sent down iron'. That's right! Through speaking and preaching, people set up a just society. Is that all? Let us assume that they manage to do this, do you think the devils, wolves and thieves will leave this just society standing? That is why God sent iron–so that people could defend their most dearly-held values. When we look at the traditions, we see that when the Imam read this phrase ('And We sent down iron'), he said: 'It means weapons'. So, you see, God mentions weapons alongside the preaching of His prophets. As well as the Prophet's mission to teach people, as well as the idea to create a *tawhīd*-oriented and God-oriented society, God mentions weapons and the power to overcome one's foes. 'In which there is great might and uses for mankind, so that God may know'. Of course, God *does* know. When the Qur'an says 'so that God may know', this means 'so that *it may be known*'. 'Those who help Him and His apostles in [their] absence', those who help Him and His apostles in the unseen, with faith in the unseen, or without seeing it, they have not seen God and some have not seen the Prophet, but they believe in Him and they help the Prophet. 'Indeed God is all-strong, all-mighty.'

Now look at the ends of these verses and see how meaningful they are: 'Indeed God is all-hearing, all-knowing', 'Indeed God is all-strong, all-mighty', 'Indeed God is all-forgiving, all-merciful'. This choice of words is not a coincidence; they have not been chosen purely because they rhyme–as they might have been in poetry. These endings to the verses are each chosen according to the meaning of the verse which they follow and which they are supposed to complement. Do you see? Look at the present verse: 'Indeed God is all-strong'. So do not think that the prophets came but were not able to create these societies that we sketch out, that they could not establish justice amongst people, no. God, the One who sent them, is all-mighty. Do not fear those who fight against God's messengers and prophets, for God is 'all-mighty' and cannot be defeated. That is the meaning of 'all-mighty' (*ʿazīz*)–the one who defeats others but cannot be defeated himself. An idiomatic translation of this term might be 'unconquerable' or 'triumphant'. So God is all-strong and unconquerable.

As for the verse I want to discuss from *Sūrat al-Aʿrāf*, it comes after Moses' conversation. We mentioned some of the preliminary points about these events but now we want to focus on a verse that will make this clear.

It is the speech of a believer or a group of believers with God. What do they say? Pay close attention to this verse: 'And appoint goodness for us in this world and the Hereafter, for indeed we have come back to You.'[4] God responds to them: 'I visit My punishment on whomever I wish'. However, God's will is not something arbitrary or pointless. He does not just decide to punish someone for no reason. No, the will of God follows standards and criteria which He has laid out. God punishes sinners and evil people. 'I visit My punishment on whomever I wish, but My mercy encompasses all things. Soon I shall appoint it for those who are Godwary and give the zakat and those who believe in Our signs'. And who are they? 'Those who follow the Apostle, the unlettered prophet'.[5] There is disagreement about the meaning of 'unlettered' (*ummī*) in 'the unlettered prophet' (*al-nabī al-ummī*). Some say that 'unlettered' means someone who was illiterate, while others say it means someone who was from the masses, or someone who is only connected to his mother (*umm*), who has not been influenced by any particular culture. Some say that *ummī* means someone from 'the Mother of Towns' (*umm al-qurā*), meaning Makkah. In any case, our concern is not with these interpretations of the word *ummī*,

4 Q7:156.

5 Q7:157.

only that the people God is talking about are those who follow this unlettered Prophet, 'whose mention they find written with them in the Torah and the Gospel'. These two scriptures foretold the coming of the Prophet. How did they describe him in their predictions? 'Who bids them to do what is right', to those virtues which are known by human reason (*'aql*) and nature (*fiṭrah*), 'and forbids them from what is wrong'. Those things which are alien to human reason and nature. 'Makes lawful to them all the good things'–because every good thing is found in the religion–'and forbids them from all vicious things'–meaning he withholds unclean things from them; this is how an Islamic society should be.

In an Islamic society everything that is good for the human being, whether for his mind, heart, spirit or body, should be readily available to all. Knowledge, education, piety, wealth–whatever is beneficial for the human being–should be there for him. Conversely, whatever is bad for the human being should not be available to anyone. 'And forbids them from all vicious things', whether by keeping it out of their hands, or by implementing laws that do so.

'And relieves them of their burdens'. One of the qualities of the Prophet is that he unburdens the people from the burden of ignorance, the burden of false traditions, the burden of inhuman systems and social orders, the burden of tyranny, dictatorship and exploitation. Whatever the burden, he lifts it from their shoulders. 'And the shackles that were upon them'. What shackles are these? Were there literal shackles upon the feet of the Makkans when the Prophet came to them? Were their collars and chains hung round their necks? Were they all prisoners? Clearly, these were not literal metal shackles or chains. So, what were they? I want you to think about this and work it out for yourself. What were the fetters that bound the Makkans? What were they enthralled to? To cruel traditions, ignorant superstitions and man-made customs. 'And the shackles that were upon them—those who believe in him, honour him, and help him and follow the light that has been sent down with him,' (meaning the Qur'an) 'it is they who are the felicitous.' It is they who will reach their destination as human beings!

The First Note of the Prophetic Call

Sunday 19th Ramadan 1394
5th October 1974

وَلَقَدْ بَعَثْنَا فِي كُلِّ أُمَّةٍ رَسُولًا أَنِ اعْبُدُوا اللَّهَ وَاجْتَنِبُوا
الطَّاغُوتَ فَمِنْهُمْ مَنْ هَدَى اللَّهُ وَمِنْهُمْ مَنْ حَقَّتْ عَلَيْهِ
الضَّلَالَةُ فَسِيرُوا فِي الْأَرْضِ فَانْظُرُوا كَيْفَ كَانَ عَاقِبَةُ
الْمُكَذِّبِينَ (٣٦)

'Certainly We raised an apostle in every nation [to preach:] "Worship God, and keep away from the Rebels." Then among them were some whom God guided, and among them were some who deserved to be in error. So travel over the land and then observe how was the fate of the deniers.'
- Sūrat al-Nahl (16):36.

In today's lecture, we will be attempting to answer the question: What was the first note of the prophetic call? In light of what we have already discussed in the previous lectures, those of you who have been paying close attention will have a thorough understanding of what the prophets were sent into this world to do, what their mission is, what goal they are supposed to achieve, and how they are supposed to go about it. (If this still isn't clear, go back and review the previous lectures. If it still isn't clear after that, then I'm afraid it is because I have done you a disservice!)

So to recap, we have so far answered the question: What is the mission for which the prophets were sent? What good was this mission, and how were they supposed to go about achieving it?

Today, we are going to discuss the following: The mission which God sent His greatest messengers into this world to achieve–namely to create a *tawhīd*-oriented government, society and social order, to destroy the ignorant and idol-centric order, and to bring about a resurrection in the very fabric of society–from where was this all supposed to begin? What was the starting point? This is an exceptionally important question. And it applies not only to the prophetic mission, but to any significant activity that an individual, a group or a society is about to undertake–whatever path they are about to follow, whatever programme they are about to implement. This issue might come up for a group of people, a handful of individuals bound by a common idea or a common outlook on life, for an entire nation, or even for a solitary individual. Whatever they may believe, whatever they are going to do, there is one inescapable question that must be answered as a basis for all future action, namely: Where do we begin? The starting point is very important.

If the proper starting point is chosen, then the probability of the planned actions achieving their desired goals increases severalfold. On the other hand, if a poor starting point is chosen, this does not necessarily mean that the plan will fail or not yield any tangible results–perhaps it will!–but what it does mean is that this will be all the more difficult. This is why the starting point is so important, because the success of so much else could depend on it. Therefore, we must ask this question about the mission of the prophets–whence were they supposed to begin?

Why does this matter? Because it is only by answering this question that we can properly evaluate the prophets' actions. If we want to completely understand their mission and their activities, then we must first understand where this mission began. What was its starting point? This will also be instructive for us; in that it will allow us to draw lessons about what we must do in the present day. If we see that the prophets always followed a particular approach or a specific method in their activities, this can be most instructive for us, because we say that we follow the wisdom of the prophets and uphold their school of thought. So it is useful from a number of angles to answer this question.

When we talk about the starting point of the prophets' mission, we are talking about the very core and kernel of what they stood for. At the beginning of their revolutions, when they sought to bring about a resurrection of faith in society, they never resorted to flattering people. They did not spend time making people happy by telling them things they liked to hear or by adopting pleasant-sounding slogans, and only beginning to divulge their core message once they had gained sufficient support. No, from the very beginning they were straightforward and honest about what they wanted to achieve. And what was that? This goal was *tawhīd*.

As we have already explained in our previous lectures, *tawhīd* is the essence of the prophetic school of thought. *Tawhīd* and knowledge of the Divine are the very basis of all human spiritual growth, which is the ultimate purpose for which the prophets were sent. For them, *tawhīd* means creating a divine atmosphere and a godly society. This is a society that is governed by a just social order, without classes, without exploitation, without tyranny. In other words, the prophets were sent to create precisely such a system, in order to give rise to an environment that was conducive–as we said yesterday–for human flourishing and growth.

Tawhīd is the essence of the prophetic school of thought. It is what guarantees the fulfilment of the ultimate purpose of the prophets: Belief in divine unity, in the existence of God and the absolute oneness of God, and the creation of the environment necessary for human growth, to create a place in which human beings can be made human. Divine unity is the highest and most visible slogan for the prophets, because a *tawhīd*-oriented society is one in which only God is worshipped and revered above all others. No one is treated as divine except God. In a *tawhīd*-oriented society, no being other than God has the right to place moral or legal duties on anyone else. No being other than God has the right to demand the obedience of other beings, not even the Prophet–not even the Prophet, *who is God's appointed representative on earth!*

Consider the verse: 'And when God will say, "O Jesus son of Mary! Was it you who said to the people, 'Take me and my mother for gods besides God'?" He will say, "Immaculate are You! It does not behoove me to say what I have no right to [say]. Had I said it, You would certainly have known it: You know whatever is in my self (*nafsī*)"'.[6] Jesus will say that he would never teach people such a falsehood or say anything about God except the truth.

Another verse that is relevant in this regard is where God says that no prophet has the right to tell people to be his servants: 'It does not behoove any human that God should give him the Book, judgement and prophethood, and then he should say to the people, "Be my servants instead of God!"'[7] Of course, it is clear that no prophet would ever explicitly tell people to serve him and obey him unquestioningly! What this verse means is that no prophet has the right to tell people to obey his own commands without question or condition. In other words, this is the sole province of God Himself. Now, consider the following: When this is the case with the Prophet, when God's most excellent and outstanding servant does not have the right to take up the reins of power, when the messenger who is bringing God's

6 Q5:116

7 Q3:79.

revelation to mankind does not have the right to tell people to do as he says without regard to God's wishes, the moral duty of all other people is clear! The tyrants and bullies who have, throughout history, burdened humanity with their dictates, are the exact opposite of *tawhīd*. *Tawhīd* rejects everything they stand for. The meaning of *tawhīd* is this. And if someone does not understand *tawhīd* properly or they have not studied it in sufficient depth, they will almost certainly be unable to grasp this. This is one of the clearest manifestations of *tawhīd* we find presented in the Qur'an: *Tawhīd* in worship and *tawhīd* in obedience–something which we touched on in our lectures on the meaning of *tawhīd*. So, when the prophets entered their societies, they proclaimed the slogan of 'there is no god but God' in order that friends and foes alike could know what they stood for. Pay attention to this! This is an incredibly important point.

Its importance lies in the fact that there was a sensitivity and understanding amongst people at the time of the prophets that is not found in later generations–like me and you today–what is the reason for this? When the prophets came, from the moment they set foot in their societies as prophets, they made it apparent who their enemies were and who their friends were. From the moment the Prophet emerged from the Cave of Hira and descended from the Mountain of Light and set foot on the barren plains of Makkah, which were devoid of not only vegetation but virtue too, he proclaimed the message of divine unity. And from this moment, the polytheists opposed him. However, opposition takes many forms. At first, the Prophet's opponents came into view–they knew from the very outset of his message that they had to crush him–and they were clearly visible to all. Just as anyone who was part of that class of people that would eventually accept his message, the greater their awareness and understanding, the sooner they understood the importance of what he was saying and the sooner they joined him.

Therefore, from the very beginning of our Prophet's mission, his friends and supporters–those who he had come to aid–knew who they were; equally, his enemies–those who he had come to overthrow–knew who they were. Both groups knew what the Prophet's message and mission were to be in this world–both knew what he had come to say and do. And this is a message that we today still have not fully understood. I do not mean to say that what I am telling you in these lectures has never been said before, only that there are many issues I am explaining that have not been discussed enough. In any case, this is something we must focus on. This is something I must show to you. That I must prove to you: namely, that the Arabs of pre-Islamic Arabia knew as soon as the Prophet came what he had come to accomplish.

Today, the core of our topic is that the essence of *tawhīd* is the negation of any authority apart from the authority of God. Abu Lahab understood this from the very beginning. Walīd ibn Mughīrah al-Makhzūmī understood this. Abu Jahl understood this. All the leaders of the Quraysh understood this from the very beginning of the Prophet's mission. They knew that saying 'there is no god but God'–that there is no object of worship besides God–is not merely a theological doctrine. On the contrary, it is also a social doctrine. It is a doctrine that spelled the end of Umayyah ibn Khalaf, the end of Walīd ibn Mughīrah, the end of ʿĀṣ ibn Wāʾil, and the end of all the leaders and chieftains of the Quraysh. They understood this straight away. And because they understood this, they opposed it with all their might.

Do you think that the reason the disbelievers of the Quraysh opposed the Prophet–and indeed led the opposition to the Prophet in the Arabian Peninsula–was anything other than the fact that they recognised the danger that his message posed to their social and political authority? Do you think they loved their idols? Do you think they believed so strongly in their gods? Have you ever seen the ruling classes of any society at any time as true believers in their religion, for their sacred things, to the extent that they were willing to sacrifice anything for this? It does not matter what their particular religion or faith, experience shows that this is almost never the case. When you are someone like ʿĀṣ ibn Wāʾil, or Umayyah ibn Khalaf, or Wālid ibn Mughīrah, the only thing you really worship is yourself–not idols of wood and stone. The reason why they are upset that the Prophet is challenging these idols is not because they believe in those idols, but because this challenge threatens to upset the social order over which they preside and from which they benefit. It is not because their faith was so strong. Yes, they had some belief, they felt some sense of tribal loyalty, but most of all they were loyal to their own power.

The saw that divine unity would lead to destruction of the palaces of authority and leadership they had built-up for themselves. They saw that the rejection of their gods and idols–meaning the creation of a *tawḥīd*-centric society–would mean that only God would have the power of rulership and the claim of obedience over people.

They saw that divine unity would mean that all people were equal before God. They understood that in such a society there would be no divisions, no class differences and, therefore, the end of the exploitative social order from which they directly benefitted. They understood and it is *because* they understood that they were not prepared to allow such a social order to exist and that they opposed the Prophet. They were no different from Pharaoh. They were no different to Nimrod. They were no different to the Pharisees of the Israelites at the time of Jesus. They were no different to the peoples of ʿĀd and Thamūd. Their case was no different to the case of all those who opposed the prophets, whose stories appear in the Qur'an. The Prophet enters society and proclaims: 'There is no god but God'. This is the first thing a prophet says. And as soon as he utters these words, society begins to divine into those who are for and against his message. There are always those who oppose him, who are against him and want to put an end to him.

So the first note in the prophetic call–the starting point of any prophetic mission–is the proclamation of divine unity. Political parties and schools of thought in this world which have no connection with God or religion have led people astray with false-promises and nice-sounding slogans. For how many years have people been appeased with empty dreams. But in all these cases, we see the real goal of these parties and schools of thought was not what they promised the people. By contrast, from the moment the prophets came to mankind, they spoke directly and truthfully. From the very beginning of their mission they said: 'This is what we want to do.' They said the same thing to the people at the top of the social order as they said to the people at its bottom. They said: 'We want to bring those on top down, and raise those at the bottom up, so that everyone is equal!' This is what they said from the beginning.

But why does this matter? Why should prophets not be like politicians? Why shouldn't they first win people over with promises and slogans and telling them things they like to hear so that they can attain their goal. Where is the problem with this? The problem with this is that, as we said before, faith must be based on reason and understanding. Religious belief will be useless if it is based on blind-following or ignorance. No, what religion wants is that anyone who joins it, anyone who sets foot in its arena, to know what its aims are from the outset. Even the uneducated nomads of the Arabian Peninsula, when they came to the Prophet and converted to Islam, they knew exactly what the Prophet wanted to do. They were not following him out of ignorance. They understood his mission. And that is why they were willing to endure all manner of hardships for him. This is why the Companions were willing to suffer for their faith, because they understood what this was all for! Whenever we study conflicts and battles throughout human history, we see that if a person does not know what he is fighting for, he will tire and fall at the first sign of difficulty. This is human nature!

Imagine you see a group of people who are walking excitedly in the street. You don't have anything to do so you join them. You see they are going somewhere. Now, you've walked a little way with them, you should ask yourself: 'Why am I walking? Where am I going?' If you walk for an hour or an hour and a half with them, where does it end? The very thought of this will make you feel tired. They know where they are going–maybe they're on a journey somewhere and they need to catch a bus, so they're walking quickly so that it doesn't leave without them. Or maybe they want to go to a particular shop to buy a particular item. They know what they are doing, so they won't tire until they reach their destination. Or they will feel tired, but they will push themselves to keep going because they see the value of the goal they are pursuing. You, on the other hand, have no idea why they are walking so purposefully through the streets. You don't know what their goal is. You've just started following them because you were bored and without anything better to do! Now, you've walked a little way, but as soon as you think to yourself: 'Why am I doing this? What is it for? Who am I doing this for?' You will feel tired and want to give up. This is true for anyone who isn't acting on the basis of insight and understanding.

This is why we see, at the time of the Prophet, youths were willing to turn their backs on the things that mattered most in their lives in order to follow him, and people were willing to give up lives of ease and comfort to follow him. Look at Yāsir and Sumayyah–the parents of ʿAmmār ibn Yāsir–and how they were willing to give up all the comforts of this world and even their own lives. What gave them the strength to do this? It was the fact that they believed in God and the Prophet on the basis of insight and understanding.

There is a biography about ʿAmmār and his parents written by the famous Egyptian author Taha Hussein.[8] There are one or two errors,

8 See Taha Hussein's, *al-Waʿd al-Ḥaqq*.

but overall it is an excellent book. When you read it, you see how this faith had penetrated the hearts of these men and women because of the depth of their understanding and comprehension. ʿAmmār's parents were the first martyrs of Islam–do you think they would have endured all they endured if their faith had not been based on knowledge and understanding?

The reason for this is that all the divine religions begin by making clear what their mission is–they do not hide anything from people. This is why people join the movements of the prophets: It is because they understand what the prophets have come to do, not because the prophets are telling them what they want to hear. It is the exact opposite of how we treat religion in the world today. The way we practice our religions today makes thinking or trying to understand something into a crime! Isn't it interesting how some religious people and some anti-religious people today reach the same conclusions about faith? A religious person and an anti-religious person both agree that faith means believing without understanding, that religion means closing your eyes and your ears, that religion means never thinking. Outwardly, we religious people say that the foundations of our religion are logical, that we cannot blindly follow someone else in our fundamental beliefs. But do we dare not to follow? Do we dare to question any of our fundamental beliefs? Try to deviate even slightly from you've been told to believe and see how quickly someone cuffs you on the ear! No, religion for us means that everyone should close their eyes and ears, that everyone should stop thinking and just blindly follow a single path! We're told that in the practical aspects of the religion (*furūʿ al-dīn*) we must refer to an expert, so we think that in every aspect of the religion we need to do the same, when actually the opposite is true–completely the opposite! The truth is one-hundred-and-eighty degrees in the opposite direction from this!

So, faith is fundamentally something that must be founded on knowledge and understanding. No one should be told: 'You should believe *now* and then go and do your research!' Never! This has no place in genuine religion. Even if you say you believe, as long as your heart has not accepted it and your mind does not understand it, you do not really believe! And even if you say you don't care, you accept the religion without understanding it, religion cares and the religion does not accept *you* unless you understand it–not until you know what it is you believe and why you believe it. That is why religion places such a high value on learning and thinking. That is why religion says a person who has understanding and awareness has such a high status in the eyes of God. That is why it wants everyone to turn towards God on the basis of understanding and knowledge. And this is the ultimate goal of the prophets, from beginning to end!

There are several other conclusions we can draw in this arena. Firstly, as we have just discussed, the religion of Islam believes that faith must be based on reason and understanding and does not accept unthinking followers. Secondly, the followers of the prophets, those who considered themselves the recipients of the prophetic legacy, were not just scholars–of course, scholars are the inheritors of the prophets–but all the theists in the world are, in a sense, considered inheritors of the prophets. Anyone who follows the path of divine unity and takes *tawḥīd* as his constitution, this person is a follower of Abraham, Moses, Jesus and all of the prophets of God. So where do the successors and inheritors of the prophets want to begin? What is their starting point? This is arguably an even more relevant and important question than where the prophets themselves started from!

Why is it that today, when we talk about religion, we do not begin with divine unity? Why? This is a question we must ask! Is this not the case? Why is it that when we talk about religion, we rarely speak about *tawḥīd*? Why is it that when we want to give faith to people, to society, or even to the whole world, we do not begin where the prophets began? We want the people of this world to believe in the religion of Islam, and yet we take an approach not taken by the prophets of God! We should be talking about *tawḥīd* in the same way that the prophets themselves did. If we cannot bring about this same resurrection of faith on a global and international scale–which is not, mind you, an easy thing to do–we can at least say on a global level what the mission and goal of the prophets was. This is what we should be saying, so why aren't we?

Why is it that religious preachers, instead of beginning with the topic of divine unity, in thought and in practice, instead go to secondary or tertiary issues for their lecture topics? This is something very noticeable in the world today and something we should be concerned about. Usually, we are told: 'If you have a problem with religious preaching, why don't you go and talk to the preachers about it?' The answer to this is, where do we find these preachers? Those whose style and contents we are criticising, where do we find them? And how likely is it that our advice will be heeded if we go to them?

However, I will tell you this. Those of you who are gathered here–most of you know me. You know how I think, you know what my opinions are. For some of you, this might be something new you are hearing in this gathering, but most of you have been listening to me for quite some time, whether in this mosque or that. So you know that I believe strongly in the importance of religious preaching–in fact, I believe it is fundamental to our faith, just as I believe our scholars (*rowhāniyyūn*) are fundamental to our faith and necessary for it. I believe in this very strongly. The term '*rowhānī*' is not really the proper word for it, but this is what everyone calls our scholars. In any case, I believe that if there were not these scholars, and if there was not this institution of scholarship and learning in Shiʿa Islam, we would be in an even more dire situation than we find ourselves now. Ultimately, there must be a group of people who devote themselves to understanding and explaining the teachings of Islam. Now, a youth, or a businessman, or someone else who is not a specialist in Islamic scholarship might devote time to thinking, researching and explaining–in speech or writing–the religion, and he does this for the sake of Islam, in order to preserve and protect the religion. However, this is not something he is always doing. He is what we would call an 'amateur', but we also need a professional. There must be someone who is a specialist in these topics, and it is these people that make up the Shiʿa institutions of scholarship and learning.

Therefore, their existence is essential for all of you gathered here. I am not just saying this because I am one of them–this is a matter of simple fact. There must be someone who is a scholar. This is the greatest necessity of all. However, we as ordinary worshippers must also give ourselves the right to tell those who are following the path of scholarship what it is we expect them to focus on. And there are many scholars who will listen to you and act on what you tell them. However, there are also others who will never accept that what they are doing today is anything different from what the Prophet was doing; that their starting point is anything other than that of the prophets. They believe that whatever secondary or tertiary issues they are discussing are equal to or even more important than *tawḥīd*–more important than explaining the Qur'an, the fundamental doctrines of Islam and other Islamic teachings.

These preachers are ready to spend hours talking about the angels Nakīr and Munkar when they come to your grave: How will they look? Will they stand on the right or left side of you, or right in front of you? What are they? Questions knowing or not knowing the answers to does not make one iota of difference to whether someone is a Muslim or not, or to whether they are fulfilling the obligations of Islam. There are many issues like this. These preachers are happy to talk about the things we are supposed to believe in according to the religion, but they are never ready to discuss the doctrine of *tawḥīd*, or the role *tawḥīd* plays in shaping society and the political order. Do they have anything to say about this? What I believe very strongly is that this topic should be our highest priority.

A lesson that we can draw from the work of the prophets and the starting point of their mission is that our starting point must be the same starting point as theirs. Even if we cannot bring about the resurrection that the prophets intended to bring about, we can at least say what was their resurrection, what was their goal, what was their methodology–this we can do. Unfortunately, if we speak about the Prophet at all, we tend to focus on tertiary aspects of his life and mission. For example, we might say: 'Do you know? The Prophet didn't have a shadow!' Or we might mention the tradition narrated in the *Khiṣāl* of Shaykh Ṣadūq which says that when the Prophet was walking, he could always see what was behind him! However, Sadūq himself remarks on this tradition, saying it means that the Prophet was so wise, so perceptive and so careful that he was like a person with eyes in the back of his head! Some people stumble through the streets, while other people make gestures and grimace at them–they go on for an hour without realising a thing. On the other hand, there are those who are so perceptive, so careful and so aware of their surroundings that they notice the slightest movement and pick up on the subtlest hint. This tradition is saying the Prophet was one of these clever people. This is not what I'm saying–this is what Shaykh Sadūq, Muḥammad ibn ʿAlī ibn Bābawayh al-Qummī, is saying: A scholar of traditions from one thousand one hundred years ago. One of the greatest scholars of the Shiʿa. Someone whose books, even though they were written a millennium ago, are still well known and relied upon now: *ʿUyūn Akhbār al-Riḍā, Ikmāl al-Dīn, Man lā yaḥḍuruhu al-faqīh*...the list goes on: *al-Khiṣāl, al-Amālī*...tens of books that we are still printing today, books which are part of the canon of Shiʿa Islam! This is the view of this great scholar. Now, it does not concern me at this moment whether his interpretation of the tradition is correct or not...what does concern me is that there are other scholars who are ready to debate about it, they are ready to critique it, to compare it to the views of other scholars about this tradition and subject it to careful analysis. On the other hand, if we were to ask why did the Prophet of Islam come in the first place? What was the Prophet's viewpoint when it came to educating the human being? What did the Prophet say about governing human society? Is it enough to be a good individual, or must we work to make a good society as well? Regarding these questions, such scholars have nothing to say. These questions don't even cross their mind–this is the problem.

The Muslim world today does not have the luxury of deferring these questions. There is no time. Our patient is on his deathbed. The hour is late. Today, we must focus on our priorities–to delay for even a moment is to court disaster. Our time is too precious to waste.

What we should be delaying are those hair-splitting theological debates about secondary and tertiary questions of faith. These must be put-off until the day when we have nothing else to do, or at least when we have fulfilled all of our primary obligations. It is up to you whether you accept this advice or not, but at least we have made you aware of the facts. And the best person is he who hears advice and reflects on it.

Therefore, we said that the starting point of the prophets' mission is divine unity. We have already presented evidence for this from the Qur'an. One is the verse from *Sūrat al-Naḥl*: 'Certainly We raised an apostle in every nation', and what did this messenger preach? 'Worship God, and keep away from the Rebels.'[9] This is the first thing that the prophets told their nations. This is the first lesson. And it is a lesson we have yet to fully grasp–worship God and keep away from the Rebels (*ṭāghūt*).

A rebel (*ṭāghūt*) is anything that competes with God. Anything that opposes God or resists God's command–no matter what it is. Sometimes, this rebel is none other than yourself. As the saying goes: 'Your most implacable foe is the self you find between your own two

9 Q16:36.

flanks.' Sometimes that foe is your own vanity and pride. Sometimes that foe is your daily and nightly desires. Sometimes ambition is a person's *ṭāghūt*. A person's arrogance is his *ṭāghūt*. Other times, *ṭāghūt* can be a power from outside the human being–this covers a wide scope of possibilities! In any case, when the Prophet came, he told people to follow God and not the Rebels. The first principle he called people towards is to serve God and avoid the Rebels.

'Then among them were some whom God guided, and among them were some who deserved to be in error. So travel over the land and then observe how was the fate of the deniers.' See what happened to those who went astray, who denied the Prophet and who rejected his guidance. Go and see for yourself the fallen civilisations and ruined cities: Go and see what became of Babylon, Assyria and Chaldea. Go and see how nothing but ruins and lines in the history books remains of them. Go and see what became of the Egypt of Pharaohs, whose society was destroyed. This is what the Qur'an says: Go and see what happened to the peoples and nations that did not listen to the words of the prophets. Go and see how they faded into nothing! There is nothing miraculous about these examples, although many prophets also performed miracles and called down divine punishment, and there were peoples who were destroyed so quickly that they left virtually nothing behind–such as the people of ʿĀd, who suffered divine punishment, and others who suffered destructive winds, earthquakes, floods and were destroyed by God's power!

However, in general, the rule that operates in this world is as follows: Any society or nation which does not take the path of divine religion or follow its teachings will eventually disappear. By this, I do not mean that all of its people will die–when a nation disappears this means that its national institutions disappear; they will be absorbed by and subsumed into those of another. In other words, the nation will lose its identity. Tell me, today, where are the Chaldeans? What has become of this great civilisation? Where did it go? Does any trace of it remain? 'Then observe how was the fate of the deniers!' This is what *Sūrat al-Naḥl* says. Now, let us turn to *Sūrat al-Aʿrāf.*

Sūrat al-Naḥl says: 'Certainly We raised an apostle in every nation...'. On the other hand, *Sūrat al-Aʿrāf* mentions different prophets one after another: 'Certainly We sent Noah to his people.' And what was the first thing he told his people? 'He said, "O my people, worship God! You have no other god besides Him."' Meaning no genuine god besides Him. 'Indeed I fear for you the punishment of a tremendous day.'[10] But his people rejected his message and then a sequence of events transpired which led to the flood–the specifics of this are not our concern here–and then came ʿĀd.

God says: 'And to [the people of] ʿĀd, Hūd, their brother. He said, "O my people, worship God! You have no other god besides Him. Will you not then be wary [of Him]?"'[11] The people of ʿĀd are an ancient people–perhaps even a pre-historic people–whom have not yet been clearly identified. They came after the flood, and they appear to be the people God describes as: 'And you hew houses out of the mountains skilfully.'[12] Perhaps these are a people from the end of the Stone Age that some archaeologists have described. In any case, they are a very ancient people and they had a prophet by the name of Hūd sent to them. Like Noah, he told them: 'O my people, worship God! You have no other god besides Him.'

Incidentally, can you see how flawed the idea is that monotheism and religion in general developed gradually, in accordance with the human being's surroundings and because of his ignorance of how the world works? Some sociologists say that all early peoples were polytheistic. How bad it is for someone to speak of things which they have no knowledge. It is like someone trying to describe the mosque

10 Q7:59.

11 Q7:65.

12 Q26:149.

in which we are sitting if he has never once been here. Just think, if someone were to say: 'The Imām Ḥasan Mujtabā Mosque is in such and such a shape, with marble walls and chandeliers, and with such beautiful inscriptions and patterns all over!' He has never seen the Mosque, he has only heard that a lot of people go here, so he imagines that it 'must' be like this, based on his own imaginings. But for all he knows, this mosque might not even have walls–let alone patterns on them! (*Laughter of audience*).

In a subject such as sociology, when someone speaks without carrying out real research, the result will be as laughable as this. Equally, they try to explain human history without studying an important part of that history. They speak about religious and spiritual phenomena, without looking at what historical religions say. Now, this religion that might have existed tens of thousands of years ago–or only seven or eight thousand years ago if we believe those narrations that say this is when Adam descended to earth! These historians give an overview of history that says first there was polytheism, and then monotheism came along. However, we see the opposite to be the case, that in ancient times there was monotheism, which polytheism came along and displaced.

In any case, Hūd asks his people: 'Will you not then be wary?' He wanted them to understand and accept the principle of divine unity. But then a debate took place between him and his people. The Qur'an says: 'The elite of his people who were faithless said, "Indeed we see you to be in folly, and indeed we consider you to be a liar."'[13] These are just some of the accusations which are always levelled at those who call people to the truth. And this is an important topic within prophethood–something that perhaps we can dedicate a lecture to: What were the typical slanders and accusations that the disbelievers

13 Q7:66.

directed at the prophets? They said: You are a foolish person. They accused him of being ignorant.

'He said, "O my people, I am not in folly. Rather I am an apostle from the Lord of all the worlds."'[14] In response to their accusations and slanders, he continued to speak the truth. 'I communicate to you the messages of my Lord and I am a trustworthy well-wisher for you.'[15] He tells them that he only wants what is good for them. He is calling them to believe in God and *tawḥīd* because he wants them to succeed. 'Do you consider it odd that there should come to you a reminder from your Lord through a man from among yourselves, so that he may warn you?'[16] In other words, are you surprised that an ordinary person, who looks like you and who dresses like you, should be chosen to bring you a message from God? 'Remember', see how he calls their attention to a matter of history? 'When He made you successors after the people of Noah', who had been sinful, 'and increased you vastly in creation.' By giving you might and power. 'So remember God's bounties so that you may be felicitous.'[17]

'They said, "Have you come to [tell] us that we should worship God alone and abandon what our fathers have been worshiping? Then bring us what you threaten us with, should you be truthful."'[18]

'He said, "Punishment and wrath have already come upon you from your Lord. Do you dispute with me over names which you have named-you and your fathers?'. You want to argue about these names which you made-up and which you gave power to 'for which God has not sent down any authority?'[19] Which God has not given any power

14 Q7:67.

15 Q7:68.

16 Q7:69.

17 Ibid.

18 Q7:70.

19 Q7:71.

to, or for which there is no proof. This is because 'authority' (*sulṭān*) could mean power or it could mean evidence, and both meanings can apply here. So, one way of reading this verse is that God has not provided you with any indication for the validity of these gods you worship. Another way of reading this is that God has not given any power to them–so they cannot do anything. 'So wait! I too am waiting along with you' for God's punishment.

Opposition to the Prophetic Mission

Monday 20th Ramadan 1394
6th October 1974

وَكَذَٰلِكَ جَعَلْنَا لِكُلِّ نَبِيٍّ عَدُوًّا شَيَاطِينَ الْإِنْسِ وَالْجِنِّ
يُوحِي بَعْضُهُمْ إِلَىٰ بَعْضٍ زُخْرُفَ الْقَوْلِ غُرُورًا وَلَوْ شَاءَ
رَبُّكَ مَا فَعَلُوهُ فَذَرْهُمْ وَمَا يَفْتَرُونَ (١١٢) وَلِتَصْغَىٰ إِلَيْهِ
أَفْئِدَةُ الَّذِينَ لَا يُؤْمِنُونَ بِالْآخِرَةِ وَلِيَرْضَوْهُ وَلِيَقْتَرِفُوا مَا هُمْ
مُقْتَرِفُونَ (١١٣)

'That is how for every prophet We appointed as enemy the devils from among humans and jinn, who inspire each other with flashy words, deceptively. Had your Lord wished, they would not have done it. So leave them with what they fabricate, so that toward it may incline the hearts of those who do not believe in the Hereafter, and so that they may be pleased with it and commit what they commit.'
- Sūrat al-Anʿām (6):112–113

We said that prophethood is a social resurrection and that one of the principles of this resurrection is the abolition of social classes, in the sense of there being a class made up of the weak, exploited and dispossessed, and another made up of the rich and powerful who exploit them, and the creation of a new social order on the foundation of divine unity.

It is not only the teaching of Islam, but the teaching of all the divine religions, that even the weakest person should be able to obtain his legitimate rights. It is inconceivable, under an Islamic government, in a society founded on the precepts of *tawḥīd*, that even the weakest should be denied their rights. That is why we read in a tradition: 'No nation is sanctified unless the weak can claim their rights without stuttering.' In other words, if you find a society in which the weakest member cannot demand his rights without fear from the most powerful member, especially when the latter is in a position of importance or influence, then you should know that this society is not flourishing or successful. This means that if the weak member of that society tried to claim his rights, he would stutter out of fear–this is no good. When someone is in their own home, do they feel any shame in going to the kitchen to find food for themselves? Of course not! What Islam teaches is that the situation in any society should be the same. All the members of the society should have an equal share in the benefits of that society. In other words, each and every member of an Islamic society has the same rights as the ruler of that society, just as was the case with the Commander of the Faithful (a), and those rights must be respected to the same degree too!

Even those in the highest ranks of a society should not be allowed to push ordinary people around. Even after Islamic society diverted from its proper path–from the guidance of the Imams after the Prophet–this principle was still observed. If the son of a governor whipped an Arab in the desert, the Arab could, in theory, go all the way to the Caliph in the capital and lodge a complaint against this person. The Caliph would write a letter summoning this governor and his son. He would not tell him just to send his son so that he could make excuses, like saying he was ill–no, he told the governor himself to come. And this actually happened on one occasion! So, when the governor and his son presented themselves to the Caliph, he would ask them why they struck this Arab? The son might say: 'Does he have any proof?' The Caliph would answer: 'His proof is that he came all this way to see me and lodge a complaint! Where would he find a witness in the desert? If you hadn't struck him, he would never have thought to come all this way to complain!' So, the Caliph orders the governor to lay down on the floor to be whipped. The son stands up and objects: 'You're going to whip my father?' The governor–who was none other than ʿAmr ibn al-ʿĀs stands up and says: 'Why am I being whipped? My son is the one who committed the offence!' The Caliph answered: 'Because your son was only able to commit this offence by using your power and authority! If you had no power or if he didn't have your protection, he would never have struck this Arab in the first place!' Now remember, this is not from the time of the Prophet or the Commander of the Faithful. This was during a time when the Muslim nation had strayed from the path of God. This was when a person ruled as caliph who we do not accept as a legitimate caliph. And yet, this principle still applied–the most powerful people in society were accountable to even the weakest!

So, this is what an Islamic society looks like. Now I mention this story for a particular reason and that is in today's discussion I am not going to draw any conclusions–you are. You will arrive at the point of today's topic before I do.

This is the kind of society that Islam and all other *tawḥīd*-oriented religions want: A society in which there is no tyranny, no exploitation, no gross inequalities of wealth, no class divisions. The Commander of the Faithful (a) was expressing exactly this viewpoint when he said: 'I have never seen copious wealth without there being unpaid dues beside it.' If wealth was divided equally amongst people, there would be no one as wealthy as Rockefeller! The reason when men like these have so much wealth in the first place is because they have taken not only their own fair share, but the fair share of tens of millions of others! That is what the Commander of the Faithful meant when he said: 'I have never seen copious wealth without there being unpaid dues beside it.'

According to the logic of *tawḥīd*-oriented religions, an Islamic society or an *ideal* society should be one in which there is no exploitation and no bullying. And even if someone wanted to bully others, he would not be allowed to do so. If someone wanted to sow class divisions into a society governed by an Islamic system, he would not be allowed to do so. Why? Because the Islamic system is the one instituted by the Prophet. Look at the stitching in the clothes you wear: These clothes could be tattered and torn and full of holes, but those stitches will not come apart. The same is true of the threads that the Prophet stitched into the ideal Islamic society: The maker of this society is none other than the Messenger of God. It is a divinely-oriented and divinely-made society. When such a system exists, it prevents wrongdoing, exploitation, and tyranny. It is not the government of one man or one group of men over others. It is a society that God says how it should be structured: It is not founded on ignorance or superstition. In this society, people are made to think. It is necessary that they should all find the path of God and when they have found it, they must follow it.

In this society, everyone is expected to stand up for the rights of the weak, the dispossessed, and the oppressed. In this society, no one can say they only care about their own interests, about their own problems, about their own work. No one can say they are too busy to worry about others. This is because they are all together as one. They are all parts of a single whole. They are all organs of a single body. If this is the case, could they ever say such a thing? There is no laziness in this society. There is no disunity or difference in this society. There is no superstition or blind obedience to anyone in this society. This is the society that the Prophet wanted to create. Pay close attention here! Keep in mind the kind of values that the

Prophet wanted to instil in this society through God's revelation to him. The most fundamental feature of this society–the bedrock upon which its entire structure rests–is knowledge and understanding, justice and equanimity, equality and the absence of class divisions, the abolition of exploitation, hoarding and tyranny, the abolition of partisanship in the name of falsehood and the establishment of partisanship for truth and truthfulness. These are the values that the Prophet stood for in society.

Now let us turn to the main point I want to focus on in this lecture: If a prophet enters an ignorant society and proclaims his message, announces his mission and explains what kind of society and world he wants to create–if he tells the people how he wants to organise society–who will oppose him in an ignorant society?

Since I've already described the kind of society that this prophet wants to create, it should be obvious what kind of people will oppose him. His foremost opponents will be the people who benefit from these class divisions. The people who benefit because they are able to exploit others. Because they are able to utilise other people's labour for their own ends unjustly. Now, if you make everyone equal, who will they have to exploit? Who will they have to use? So, the exploiters of class divisions will oppose a prophet.

The second group of people who will oppose this prophet in his mission to create a new kind of society are those who have become wealthy under the old order. Those who have amassed their riches from others: They take a little from this shopkeeper or that and put it in their bottomless purses. These are the ones who create interest-based institutions so that they can profit from loaning out their money to others and, in doing so, benefit from all trade and economic activities without having to do anything themselves. Is this not the case? When someone earns a living through business, why should only a percent of his earnings belong to him and a percent to this bank or that? When someone has to pay interest on a loan, they are no longer just working for themselves!

When you have a usurious system like this in society, it means that everyone in society is paying interest, and a small group are amassing wealth. In other words, all the business people–in fact, the whole economy–is structured for the benefit of usurious institutions and the people who own them. Now, if you come to a society where being wealthy is revered above all other things, where usury is considered noble, and where someone is making money without needing to produce anything, and a prophet or reformer comes and says that usury is forbidden, it is clear that someone who benefits from usury and charging interest is going to oppose that prophet! So, this is the second group.

So as well as those who benefit from class divisions and usurious practices, another group who will oppose this prophet are the tyrants and autocrats. This is because when the principle of 'no god but God' truly enters society, this means this society has no Pharaohs: Either they must leave the society, or they must submit to being equal to all of its other members. This is the social manifestation of 'no god but God.' And when a society is founded and raised up on this principle, the head of that society is God, not Pharaoh. God is the one who rules, not Pharaoh. Not Nimrod. Not Muʿāwiyah. Therefore, it is clear that Pharaoh, Nimrod and other tyrants like them will do everything in their power to snuff out the prophetic message. So, these are another group opposed to the prophets.

Yet another source of opposition to the prophets are the priests and rabbis; those who control people's beliefs and ideas. The clergy preserve their own social position through the religious teachings they disseminate to the people. On the other hand, if people were taught the truth–if they were taught things that would awaken their minds, make them think and enlighten them–then the clergy would lose their positions of privilege, their spiritual leadership, and the material benefits that go along with this. Throughout history, the priests and rabbis have done everything in their power to keep people ignorant. When Jesus came, he did not have to fight the Roman Emperor–he had to fight the Jewish priests! Who were the people that didn't want the teachings of Jesus to take root amongst the Israelites of that day and age? It was the priesthood, even though it was the very same priests who recognised Jesus for who he was!

So at the advent of Islam, who was it that opposed the Prophet's mission? Who was it that wanted to snuff out his movement? It was those people who stood to lose the most if the Prophet was allowed to come and spread his teachings amongst the people, to enlighten their minds and open their eyes, to free them from superstition and ignorance. It is obvious that where there is Islam, there is no room for the fables and myths of Kaʿab al-Aḥbār or ʿAbdullah ibn Salām. When the light of truth and guidance shines into human minds, it banishes the shadows of superstition and ignorance. This is because a prophetic society is one founded on knowledge and understanding–on learning and free-thinking–it is a divine and *tawḥīd*-oriented society. Hence, when the first notes of the prophetic call ring out, the first groups who sense the danger to their own positions and privilege are the priests and rabbis–those who depend on keeping people in the dark so that they can control them. For them, the Prophet is a threat to their power. In fact, anyone who holds power in a society, whether this is religious power or political power, will see the Prophet as a threat.

This calls to mind the letter that Imam Zayn al-ʿĀbidīn (a) wrote to Muḥammad ibn Shihāb al-Zuhrī, that we have mentioned previously and the full text of which can be found in the book *Tuḥaf al-ʿUqūl*. When we read the contents of this letter today, and when we study our history and see how political and religious authorities have used their power to oppress people, to exploit their potential and to deprive them of their rights, we realise that the Imam was explaining something that we have only just been able to understand today with the gift of hindsight. He says: 'Know that the least thing you hid and the lightest burden you carry is that you knew the terror of the oppressor but smoothed for him the way of deviation through your proximity to him when you approached and your responsiveness to him when you were summoned!'

So, one of the groups who were worried about the coming of a prophet were the scholars of religion–these purveyors of false faith and promoters of superstition. This group have always done everything in their power to oppose the prophets and stifle their call for liberation. We see an example of this in the story of Abraham, when the attendants of the temple found all their idols smashed. They asked: 'How did this happen?' And after much arguing and disputation, they asked Nimrod to punish Abraham by throwing him into the fire. These were not just any ordinary people–the ordinary people did not know what was happening in the temple where the idols were kept–these were priests and attendants from the temple. We see the same thing in the story of Moses in Egypt, when the priests persuaded Pharaoh to let them use their magic to overcome the miracles of Moses. We see the same thing in the story of Jesus, where the Jewish priests were his strongest opponents and the biggest obstacles to his mission. Go and read the version of the Bible that we have today–even with all of its inaccuracies and distortions, you can find all of these historical details recorded in it! So, when it comes to the preaching of Islam, it was this same group–the priesthood–that opposed our Prophet. Look at the account of the Christians from Najrān and the event of *Mubāhilah*. See how strongly people cling to their ancient traditions?

When a new idea enters a society–one which causes people to think, reflect and understand–it is only natural that people young and old will flock to hear it. People love new things and new ideas. And whatever is more acceptable to their minds is more acceptable to them. Remember: Superstitions are false. Distortions of faith are false. When someone gives a clear explanation of an idea and backs it up with reason and evidence, these superstitions are exposed as falsehoods and suppositions, and people readily accept this new idea.

On the other hand, it was always this priestly class who, throughout history and despite the clarity of the prophetic message, tried to prevent the ordinary people from following the prophets. The prophet's brought clear authority and manifest proofs. The prophets brought enlightenment to people wherever they went. They never spoke in riddles or adopted the language of philosophers to bedazzle and befuddle the masses–they spoke clearly and straightforwardly. Therefore, people should have been very quick to understand and accept what the prophets of God were saying. So why was this not always the case? Why did people react with prejudice and hostility to the prophets? Because the priestly class–whom the Qur'an refers to as 'scribes' (*aḥbār*) and 'monks' (*ruhbān*)–wanted to prevent them from doing so. So, they told people to hold on to their false ideas, maintain the traditions of their ancestors and believe in their inherited superstitions. They were terrified of the prophets because they knew that if a prophet came to them from God, and this prophet created a society in which knowledge and enlightenment were prized, a society in which new thoughts and ideas flourish, a society in which everyone is either a teacher or a student, then there will be no place left for them in such a society to lead people astray through ignorance and falsehoods. That is why these priests did everything they could to resist the prophets, their message, and their mission to resurrect society.

So, there are four classes who tend to oppose the prophets, as you will see if you refer to the Qur'an. I have not referred to the verses of the Qur'an so far. Until now, I have explained how the prophets want to change the world, I have sketched for you the kind of world that the prophets are sent to create, and the kind of society that exists within it. Next, I asked what kind of people would be afraid of such a society? Clearly the wealthy will be afraid of a society in which hoarding wealth is not allowed. Clearly the upper classes will be afraid of a society in which class divisions are abolished and not allowed to exist. After all, if someone is used to living in the upper echelons of a society and he is transplanted into a system where he is treated the same as a road sweeper or where a road sweeper is treated the same as him, he will feel that he has lost status. This is because him having status depends on other people *not* having status. After all, if everyone has status, then what value is status to him? So he will also oppose this change.

Then there are the tyrants and dictators, those whom the late Mīrzā Naʾīnī described in his *Tanbīh al-Ummah* as 'doing whatever they wish and ruling however they please'. Or in the words of the Qur'an, 'He is not questioned concerning what He does'.[20] Whatever they do, whatever they say, wherever they go–no one can ask them: 'Why?' And this is why they are opposed to the mission and message of the prophets and the government of the Prophet, because they know that if the Prophet succeeds, they will no longer be able to do whatever they want. And then there are the priestly class, whom we have just described a moment ago.

So these are the four classes which we have analysed for you. We find them named in the Qur'an. Those individuals who occupy positions of leadership and power within a nation that the Qur'an refers to as the 'elite' (*malaʾ*). For example: 'The elite of his people who were faithless said', the elite are those people who inspire awe and reverence in others (the word *malaʾ* comes from *yamlaʾūn al-ʿayn*, which literally means 'to fill the eye'). Wherever they go, people are humbled and submissive before them. And these are one of the classes that oppose the Prophet. Like whom? In Pharaoh's system

20 Q21:23.

of government, Hāmān would be one of these. 'O Hāmān! Build me a tower'.[21] See how Pharaoh turns to Hāmān to fix things for him? Pharaoh is at the top of the structure. He is the ruler. But in return for his service and devotion to Pharaoh, Hāmān is given power over everyone else. Hāmān is weak. By himself, he is just one man. But with Pharaoh's support, he becomes all powerful. That is why when he walks down the street, it is as though no mortal person can look upon him and live, because he has this power behind him.

When we look at Muᶜāwiyah's system of government, we see that these elite are men like Mughīrah ibn Shuᶜbah and Ziyād ibn Abīh. They are the ones who do Muᶜāwiyah's bidding. Who advise him and support him. They are the ones whom the Qur'an calls 'the elite'. Below them are 'the well-off' (*mutrafīn*); they have status and wealth, and they will do anything to preserve these. And when we look in the Qur'an, we are told that in every nation that a Prophet is sent to, it is the well-off who are the first to oppose the Prophet. They are the first to object to his preaching. These are another group.

As for the class of those who are the leaders of thought, whom the Qur'an refers to as scribes and monks, 'Indeed many of the scribes and monks',[22] I shall explain the meaning of the verse for you now. And I suspect that it is this group to whom the Qur'an is referring directly with the term 'rebel' (*ṭāghūt*), that we mentioned yesterday–meaning those forces which are in rebellion against God. Of course, even your own self can be a *ṭāghūt*, as we read in the tradition: 'Your most implacable foe is the self you find between your own two flanks.' By extension, it could apply to your wishes and desires, your children, your spouse, your friends–all of these could be *ṭāghūt* in opposition to God. But this term could also refer to greater things. In this sense, *ṭāghūt* has a very broad meaning. However, when we

21 Q40:36.

22 Q9:34.

look in the Qur'an, we see that *ṭāghūt* is always juxtaposed with God and performs a number of important functions. *Ṭāghūt* represents the head of an ignorant system (*niẓām-i jāhilī*). In one verse we read: 'Those who have faith fight in the way of God, and those who are faithless fight in the way of *ṭāghūt*.'[23] Elsewhere, the Qur'an says: 'God is the Guardian of the faithful: He brings them out of darkness into light. As for the faithless, their patrons are the *ṭāghūt*, who drive them out of light into darkness.'[24] We find the word '*ṭāghūt*' used in eight or so places throughout the Qur'an, and in seven of these, the way in which this word is used makes clear to the reader that what this term signifies is the head of the tyrannical forces in society.

So, these are the four classes of people who stand against the prophets, not only in the time of Moses, not only in the time of our Prophet, not only at the time of Abraham, but at all times throughout history: Wherever the truth is proclaimed, wherever the call of the prophets of God and the Heavenly Scriptures is announced, these four classes array themselves against it, whether all at once, or one after another. This is a universal principle of history. And there is a lesson on this subject we can find in these verses under discussion today.

In the first part of the first verse, God says: 'That is how for every prophet We appointed'.[25] The verse begins by saying 'like this' (*kadhālik*). What does 'like this' denote? It means as with you, or as is the case with you. It is addressed to the Prophet, O Prophet, do you see how 'for every prophet We appointed as an enemy the devils from among humans and jinn'. If you recall, we have previously discussed the meaning of 'devil' (*shayṭān*), and this verse confirms what we said before, namely that a 'devil' is any malevolent force from outside a human being. One such devil is Iblīs, who would not bow to Adam

23 Q4:76.

24 Q2:257.

25 Q6:112.

(a). He is the most infamous of all the devils, and so he is blamed for everything the devils do–the poor fellow! Whatever evil or misdeed any devil does in this world, whether the devil is a human or a jinn, people blame Iblīs for it and curse him, when some of these other devils are so evil they could teach even Iblīs a thing or two!

'As an enemy the devils from among humans and jinn, who inspire each other'–they teach each other. Sometimes the priestly class teach the elite, and sometimes the elite teach the priestly class. Sometimes the well-off teach both the priests and the elite. Usually, however, all three of these classes learn from the *ṭāghūt* whom they serve. 'Who inspire each other', these enemies teach and inspire one another 'with flashy words', with beautiful, pleasing words. Do you recall in a previous lecture, I pointed out Pharaoh's eloquence of speech? Was it not Pharaoh who said: 'Let me slay Moses'? Why does he ask to do this? 'For indeed I fear that he will change your religion'.[26] Pharaoh says that he is afraid that Moses is going to misguide people and lead them astray–is this not something that sounds good on the outside? 'With flashy words, deceptively.' Because these words spread delusion and ignorance. This is how people deceive one another.

'Had your Lord wished, they would not have done it.' They would not have been able to do it if God had not let them. If God had willed it, all four of these classes of people who opposed the Prophet could have been turned to dust in a second. God *could* have done this, but this is not how God does things: What God does is to allow these to oppose the Prophet so that the faithful and the faithless will be distinguished from one another. God makes the path a little bumpy so that those with strength and stamina will be made known, because only they will be able to traverse it. Anyone can walk on a smooth asphalt road! 'Had your Lord wished, they would not have done it.' If God had willed, if your Creator had willed, you would not have

26 Q40:26.

been able to fight against the Prophet, but God never goes against His habit (*sunnah*). 'So leave them with what they fabricate'. Leave them be with whatever lies they concoct. What does this mean? It means not to become upset or disturbed by the things they say. Not to react to them.

'So that toward it may incline the hearts of those who do not believe in the Hereafter'.[27] The result of the things they say, of these pleasing deceptive words they utter, is that the hearts of those who do not believe in the Hereafter will fall under the influence of their false propaganda–the propaganda they concoct against the Prophetic mission; the propaganda they make up to counteract the call of truth and divine unity; the lies and deceptions they fabricate to win people's hearts. Whose hearts? 'So that toward it may incline the hearts of those who do not believe in the Hereafter', those who do not believe in the afterlife. Therefore, those who do believe in the Hereafter will not be so easily led astray. 'And so that they may be pleased with it', with the pleasant-sounding things they are told 'and commit what they commit.' So, the first verse offers a general explanation that each and every prophet has enemies, that these enemies are both human and jinn, or manifest and hidden, and these enemies inspire and assist one another, they teach one another. Now, let us turn to the verses from *Sūrat al-Ghāfir* that I mentioned before, as our time is running out.

'Certainly We sent Moses with Our signs and a manifest authority',[28] as we said previously, this 'manifest authority' (*sulṭān mubīn*) could refer to a clear proof or a visible power. And what was this? His powerful logic, his true speech, his staff which transformed into a serpent, his hand which shone bright–those things which mean that everyone, whether they are an ordinary person or something more,

27 Q6:113.

28 Q40:24.

must accept what he says. God says that He 'sent' Moses. Who did he send him to? Whom did he send him to confront? And for whom was he sent? Whose side was Moses on in this society? If we ponder on these verses a little, the matter becomes very clear indeed. Social issues of this importance are discussed in the clear verses of the Qur'an–in the verses whose meanings are apparent. Who was Moses supposed to fight? To whom was he sent? 'To Pharaoh'.[29] And who else? 'And Hāmān', Pharaoh's chief minister, one of his lieutenants and a member of the elite. And who else? 'And Korah[30]'. Who was Korah? He was a man of great wealth. He was not one of Pharaoh's underlings, nor was he a leader. In fact, he survived Pharaoh, but God says that He sent Moses to him as well! In other words, for Moses, Pharaoh and Korah are one and the same and just as Moses fights against Pharaoh, he also fights against Hāmān and Korah.

Korah's wrongdoing was that he hoarded riches, that he extracted wealth from people for his own benefit, and then he squandered it on extravagance and excess. He would have a feast prepared that could easily fill the stomach of fifty people without finishing, and then sit by himself to eat from it and then leaving the food that could have fed others. So while forty-nine people might have to make do with one person's share of food between them, this Korah was taking the share of forty-nine other people for himself. That is why Moses came to fight him too.

What is amazing though is that Pharaoh was the head of the regime. He was from one class. Hāmān, his trusted advisor, was another class. Korah had nothing to do with these two, he was a man of wealth, so he was another class still. But even though these people were from three different social classes, they each responded to Moses (a) in the same way as each other. All of them adopted the same stance vis-à-vis

29 Q40:24.

30 Qārūn.

Moses. All of them spoke the same words. In fact, the Qur'an literally has them speaking as one: 'they said, "A magician, a mendacious liar."'

'So when he brought them the truth from Us'.[31] When Moses made clear the truth to these opponents of his, what did they do? Did they go silent? Did they stand aside while Moses tore down the system that they benefitted from? Of course not! As soon as they realised what changes Moses was proposing, they did everything they could to stop him. What did they say? 'They said, "Kill the sons of the faithful who are with him"'. They decided to kill the sons of anyone who believed in the new ideas propounded by Moses. They killed these sons so that they would not grow up to threaten their position in the future. Kill their sons to break their spirit and deprive them of hope.

'And spare their women.' Why do they say to spare their women? There is a reason for this. This is so that they will have to intermarry with other peoples and their descendants will no longer be fully Israelite, to promote indecency and to use them to satisfy their own desires, to humiliate them. There are many reasons why Pharaoh and his supporters did this.

Then, God says: 'But the stratagems of the faithless only go awry.' These plots and schemes of the faithless are always awry, meaning they always stray, they never achieve their goals. Like an arrow you shoot towards a target or an enemy, but then the wind blows your arrow off its course. When the divine wind blows, all these arrows are thrown in different directions–so go ahead and plot against Moses! Notice again that in this verse the three classes–Pharaoh, Hāmān and Korah–are all mentioned as though they are one and the same.

Another verse mentions the well-off (*mutrafin*)–the class to which Korah belongs. It says: 'We did not send a warner', meaning a prophet, 'to any town without its affluent ones...', the well-off, the aristocracy and the hoarders of wealth, 'saying, "We indeed disbelieve in what

---

31 Q40:25.

you have been sent with."' Why do they disbelieve in it? 'And they say, "We have greater wealth and more children"', they tell the prophet that they have more money and offspring than you; this is why they disbelieve? Do you see how low their level of thinking is? '"And we will not be punished!"'[32]

There is yet another verse on this topic in *Sūrat al-Tawbah* about the priestly class. It says: 'O you who have faith! Indeed many of the scribes and monks wrongfully eat up the people's wealth, and bar [them] from the way of God. Those who treasure up gold and silver'. Notice that the affluent are once again mentioned in this verse! 'And do not spend it in the way of God, inform them of a painful punishment'.[33]

Therefore, from these and other verses of the Qur'an, we can recognise the four different social classes who are united in their opposition to the prophets whom God sends to guide mankind.

---

32 Q34:34–35.

33 Q9:34.

The Outcome of Prophethood, Part One

Tuesday 21st Ramadan 1394
7th October 1974

قُلِ اللَّهُ خَالِقُ كُلِّ شَيْءٍ وَهُوَ الْوَاحِدُ الْقَهَّارُ (١٦) أَنْزَلَ
مِنَ السَّمَاءِ مَاءً فَسَالَتْ أَوْدِيَةٌ بِقَدَرِهَا فَاحْتَمَلَ السَّيْلُ
زَبَدًا رَابِيًا وَمِمَّا يُوقِدُونَ عَلَيْهِ فِي النَّارِ ابْتِغَاءَ حِلْيَةٍ أَوْ مَتَاعٍ
زَبَدٌ مِثْلُهُ كَذَٰلِكَ يَضْرِبُ اللَّهُ الْحَقَّ وَالْبَاطِلَ فَأَمَّا الزَّبَدُ
فَيَذْهَبُ جُفَاءً وَأَمَّا مَا يَنْفَعُ النَّاسَ فَيَمْكُثُ فِي الْأَرْضِ
كَذَٰلِكَ يَضْرِبُ اللَّهُ الْأَمْثَالَ (١٧) لِلَّذِينَ اسْتَجَابُوا لِرَبِّهِمُ
الْحُسْنَىٰ وَالَّذِينَ لَمْ يَسْتَجِيبُوا لَهُ لَوْ أَنَّ لَهُمْ مَا فِي الْأَرْضِ
جَمِيعًا وَمِثْلَهُ مَعَهُ لَافْتَدَوْا بِهِ أُولَٰئِكَ لَهُمْ سُوءُ الْحِسَابِ
وَمَأْوَاهُمْ جَهَنَّمُ وَبِئْسَ الْمِهَادُ (١٨)

'Say, "God is the creator of all things, and He is the One, the All-paramount." He sends down water from the sky whereat the valleys are flooded to [the extent of] their capacity, and the flood carries along a swelling scum. And from what they smelt in the fire for the purpose of [making] ornaments or wares, [there arises] a similar scum. That is how God compares the truth and falsehood. As for the scum, it leaves as dross, and that which profits the people remains in the earth. That is how God draws comparisons. For those who answer [the summons of] their Lord

there shall be the best [of rewards]. But those who do not answer Him, even if they possessed all that is on the earth and as much of it besides, they would surely offer it to redeem themselves with it. For such there shall be an adverse reckoning, and their refuge shall be Hell, and it is an evil resting place.'
- Sūrat al-Raʿd (13):16–18

وَلَقَدْ سَبَقَتْ كَلِمَتُنَا لِعِبَادِنَا الْمُرْسَلِينَ (١٧١) إِنَّهُمْ لَهُمُ الْمَنْصُورُونَ (١٧٢) وَإِنَّ جُنْدَنَا لَهُمُ الْغَالِبُونَ (١٧٣) فَتَوَلَّ عَنْهُمْ حَتَّىٰ حِينٍ (١٧٤) وَأَبْصِرْهُمْ فَسَوْفَ يُبْصِرُونَ (١٧٥) أَفَبِعَذَابِنَا يَسْتَعْجِلُونَ (١٧٦) فَإِذَا نَزَلَ بِسَاحَتِهِمْ فَسَاءَ صَبَاحُ الْمُنْذَرِينَ (١٧٧) وَتَوَلَّ عَنْهُمْ حَتَّىٰ حِينٍ (١٧٨) وَأَبْصِرْ فَسَوْفَ يُبْصِرُونَ (١٧٩) سُبْحَانَ رَبِّكَ رَبِّ الْعِزَّةِ عَمَّا يَصِفُونَ (١٨٠)

'Certainly Our decree has gone beforehand in favour of Our servants, the apostles, that they will indeed be the receivers of help, and indeed Our hosts will be the victors. So leave them alone for a while, and watch them; soon they will see [the truth of the matter]. Do they seek to hasten Our punishment? But when it descends in their courtyard it will be a dismal dawn for those who had been warned. So leave them alone for a while, and watch; soon they will see. Clear is your Lord, the Lord of Might, of whatever they allege.'
- Sūrat al-Ṣāffāt (37):171–180

In our previous lectures, we discussed the lofty goals which the prophets were sent by God to accomplish. Speaking today, in the 20th century, a time of learning and enlightenment, these goals seem all the more important. In practical terms, the goal of the prophets was to abolish the existence of different social classes, to make all men truly equal, and to free all men from the evils of ignorance, poverty, tyranny, inequality, and exploitation. It is for this lofty goal that the prophets of old were sent to their societies.

When we look at the lives of the prophets, we see a long series of efforts and struggles. From the moment a prophet is raised-up by God, there is no rest for them, there is no time for leisure, there is no time for frivolity or comfort. There is only the struggle. This is the destiny of all of God's prophets and messengers. As we know from our religious texts, some of these prophets met their ends in their confrontations with the tyrants and oppressors of their day, by having their heads removed from their shoulders. We are told that some of the prophets were cleft in two from heel to crown. Some died alone and in pain. None of them amassed any wealth, no matter how little. Unlike the political and religious leaders we have today, none of them, at the end of their lives, enjoyed a comfortable home in which to retire with a generous pension. This is what we know about the lives of the prophets–God's emissaries to mankind.

But this raises an important question: Based on what we read about the lives of the prophets we see that many of them became martyrs for God. Does this mean that their missions were ultimately fruitless and without benefit? Does history teach us that the prophets were defeated? Is it really as some naïve people of this world imagine (and as the anti-prophetic forces want people to imagine!) that the efforts of the prophets were all in vain? Was it really the case that throughout history, wrongdoing, injustice, inhumanity, corruption, and disbelief have always triumphed? We do not believe this is the case. We believe that these divine emissaries, beginning with Adam, Noah and Abraham, who were the best of God's creation and came in succession, one after another, not only were they not defeated, not only did they not fail, not only were all their words and deeds not in vain, but that of all human beings, of everyone who has ever pursued some goal in life, there is no one who has enjoyed the level of success achieved by these prophets! This is what we believe. We believe that the outcome of prophethood and the results of all of the prophets' missions throughout history have been exactly as intended, and they will continue to be in future too. This is what I intend to show today.

To that end, there are two main topics we must discuss. Firstly, this series of individuals who had the status of 'prophethood' (*nubuwwah*) or 'messengership' (*risālah*)–this caravan which began with Adam and ended with the Final Messenger–what did they do? *As a whole*, what did they achieve? Did they succeed or fail? This is one topic. The other topic is what God's great prophets did in their own time *as individuals*–did they triumph or were they defeated? These are the two questions we must answer, and I want to answer them both in this lecture–God-willing. These are questions that we should want to answer because their answers will be useful to us, but not only because they will increase our knowledge because there are many things that increase people's knowledge without being useful! For example, there is no harm in everyone knowing about the composition of the rocks found in volcanoes on the moon. Is it bad to know this? Of course not! But is it useful? No, it is not useful either. There is so much knowledge that we pursue as human beings: We sit, listen, speak, study, research, write and spend all of our lives pursuing such knowledge, only to realise, when we look back at it that it is of no use to us or anyone else. It has not brought us a step closer to Heaven or God's pleasure, nor has it brought us any closer to creating a genuinely Islamic society in this world. Its only use has been to make us feel pleased with ourselves and to allow us to show off to others how learned and well-read we are–no one can teach us anything we don't know already! This is the only use of such knowledge.

However, the topic I want to discuss in this lecture is 'useful' (*mufid*) in the truest sense of the word. It is not just knowledge, but knowledge that leads to action. It is like the kinds of belief we discussed in the third, fourth and fifth lectures of this series.

The first question we must answer is: This series of individuals who we call prophets, what did they do for the human race? The answer is that the prophets came to a being that was little more than an animal, who barely knew his head from a hole in the ground, a being whose instincts were not able to guide him either, and they raised this being to such a level that even the angels in Heaven would come to learn from him! They took humanity from the depths of bestiality and ignorance and raised them to the level of human beings who, if they acted on what they knew, would see manifested in their lives the highest expressions of beauty and eloquence in all creation. To put it simply, the prophets came as teachers to mankind, who were like children on the first day of their first year in school–they knew nothing, not even the alphabet–and they worked so hard to get them to the second year of school that they died in the process! Then in the second year of school, a new teacher came and raised the student to the third year, and this teacher gave their life also. So a new teacher came for the third year, and so on and so forth. And now you see this student's level of understanding, knowledge and sensitivity have increased severalfold since he began his studies, until he reaches the apex of growth and development.

Now I want you to imagine that each of these teachers, after spending a year teaching this class of students, are killed by some of their own students! Each teacher comes and delivers his lesson and dies–but has he failed? Think about this carefully. Has that teacher failed? What was that teacher's goal? Didn't he want to raise his students up to the heights of learning and enlightenment? If this is the case, then the teacher did not die in failure. True, he did not have an easy life in this world. True, he may not see the fruits of his labours. But did he fail in his mission? Certainly not! As a teacher, his goal was to ensure that his students graduated to the next year of their studies and, with struggle and perseverance, they did.

This is how the prophets were: Adam, Noah, Lot, Hūd, Ṣāliḥ, Shuʿayb (Jethrow), Abraham, Ishmael, Moses, Jesus and the thousands of other prophets who have graced this world throughout history. They came to raise humanity up: To deliver knowledge and enlightenment, to prepare them for the next life and to give them everything they need to make this journey. Even though some of these prophets gave their lives before they could arrive at their destination and before they could see the outcome of their efforts, they were still successful in their mission.

Today, more than at any other point in the last thousand years of human history, the world is ready to hear the true call of Islam. Today, more than at any other point in the last thousand years, mankind is ready for divine governance. A thousand years from now, it will be readier still. When the Imam of our age–may God hasten his reappearance–went into occultation, mankind was not ready to accept a revolutionary leader who had come with a sword in his hand to set the world right. And had he attempted to bring about this revolutionary change at that time, it is almost certain that he would not have been able to bring about the society that he envisaged on account of the unfavourable circumstances of the age.

The experience of the Imams of the Prophet's Household was that society had become so completely ruined at the hands of the tyrants and dictators from the houses of the Umayyads and Abbasids, and the ground had become so completely poisoned by their deeds, that nothing healthy could grow there. That is why the Imam had to go into hiding until the time was right. And how will it be on the day when he returns? We don't know whether this will be ten years from now or a thousand years from now. What we do know, however, is that when he returns, mankind will be ready for him. They will be ready to hear the true call of Islam and they will accept it. They will be ready to build a better society. An Islamic society. They will be ready to bear the burdens of this undertaking. They will be ready to follow the Qur'an on that day. However, when our Imam went into hiding, the time was not ripe. But what ultimately prepared the ground for his return? The teachings of the prophets and the Imams who came after them. When we get onto the topic of Imamate, I will discuss the wisdom of Imamate and why it is we need an Imam.

Therefore, as we have seen, it is not the case that the prophets failed in their missions. With each passing day, the human race takes another step on the path of enlightenment. Every day, the human race comes closer to attaining its full potential. Did the prophets ever want anything besides this? God wanted this raw material to follow its natural course of development. This is what God intended for mankind and, one day, mankind will definitely reach its utmost perfection. This is the irresistible conclusion we draw from history. This is the destiny that history lays out for mankind, and it is correct!

These are very detailed discussions, so I ask you to pay close attention to the meaning of words and terms. Destiny leads the human race on the upward path of development and refinement towards the Paradise that is promised in this world; namely, that day when true humanity will be on display and there will be no more oppression, no more evil, no more suffering–everything will be in accordance with human values. This is how the human being and the world was created; this being will ultimately follow its own path towards perfection, which is its destination. It must reach its destination. At a time when everything the human race needs to attain perfection is present, humanity will rapidly ascend on the arc of spiritual evolution towards God, towards absolute perfection. It is a truth of history that from the beginning of the human species, the human race has been journeying towards perfection, because this yearning for perfection is part of what it is to be human. This is how God created the human being, whether the human being knows this or not. However, while this is in some sense inevitable, the human being still has a choice in all of this–as will become clear in our later discussions–and, indeed, it is only possible for the human being to attain perfection through his own will and desire.

This is a fundamental doctrine of Islam and an integral part of the Islamic worldview, namely that a happy future lies in store for the human race. Why? Because God created the Heavens and the earth in accordance with truth, and the human being's very nature (*fiṭrah*) is to pursue the truth. And, since the human being has free will, he must choose the path that accords with this nature in order to arrive at his intended destination. And who is it that can show him this path? Who can show him what he must do if he is to act in accordance with this nature? The prophets! This is why the prophets were sent. They were sent to show human beings the path of humanity, of human nature. In other words, they were sent to help him on his journey towards this happy future. Therefore, human beings are advancing and, day by day, the human race is coming closer to this happy future. This is because of the efforts of the prophets. It is the prophets who sent man along this path. And if there have been delays and setbacks along the road, or at different stages of human history, this is because people have strayed from the teachings of the prophets. However, even then, the journey was continuing. This is a general point to keep in mind.

So, with regards to the first issue, we draw the conclusion that even though God's prophets may have suffered hardships and even death, their efforts to guide mankind towards perfection and growth have been successful on the grand scale of things. It was the prophets who turned the human being towards this happy future and showed him how to reach it and helped him along the way.

As for the second issue, this is exceedingly important to understand. The question at the heart of the second issue is this: When a prophet begins an awakening in the world, when a prophet starts a revolution or a social resurrection, can we say that this revolution has a good outcome or not? Can we expect it to produce a positive result? Or can we not be so optimistic? What is the general rule here?

Now, some will say that, looking at history, wherever the truth is proclaimed, wherever its notes reach people's ears, it is ultimately fruitless and without result. The truth is suppressed. They are not wrong in the experience they point to: The experience of human history shows us that the prophets have always been persecuted and oppressed, and the revolutions they initiated do not appear to have been successful–the government of truth could not be established and falsehood could not be effaced. So, what should we do with this? Does this mean we also should not raise our hands in protest, that we should stay silent and not follow the path of the prophets? After all, even in their own times, the prophets were not able to achieve anything and, ultimately, it seems that falsehood always prevails over truth, even if we say this is only a temporary state of affairs. Therefore, the truth-seekers and truth-proclaimers of this world should keep their swords sheathed, sit down, and do nothing, because taking action is pointless. And if they must do anything, they must do it in secret. This is the logic that many people follow. And it is a logic that is pleasing to the world's tyrants! This is a logic that bullies want people to believe in and to make part of their creed. They want people to believe that there is no possibility for change, that none of their actions ultimately matter, and that nothing they do will produce any positive or lasting results. This is precisely what the tyrants want.

The pages of the world's newspapers are filled with the bluffs of our national leaders for this very reason. Someone who only has a few hours, or at most days, left before his government is removed from power and he is reduced (if he is lucky) to the status of an ordinary citizen, will bluff to the very end. He will say that he is defeating his enemies, overcoming his opponents, that everything is under control and that his government will continue to rule regardless. How often have you seen with your own eyes in recent years people like this brought down from their lofty positions? Until the last, they claimed that no one could remove them from power, that they would be ruling forever. This is, in fact, why they make these bluffs. They want people to believe that no matter what they do, nothing will change, they will remain in power. They want people to believe that their power is so great that it is beyond comprehension, that they hold all the cards, that they hold all the power, and the people have nothing they can fight them with.

Do you think this is a new state of affairs? Of course not! This is something that has been happening throughout history. And that is why it is so interesting to study history. I am amazed by the cleverness of the Abbasid Caliph al-Manṣūr. He was arguably the most powerful of all the Abbasid Caliphs and the second of the dynasty to rule. It so happens that during his time there was serious opposition to his reign from sections of the religious community. He had to face an uprising led by Muḥammad ibn ʿAbd Allāh and Ibrāhīm ibn ʿAbd Allāh, two great-grandsons of Imam al-Ḥasan. For some time, these two led such a powerful movement that al-Manṣūr could not do anything about them. Even though he had all the power, in the face of the relentless struggle of these two dedicated brothers, who had nothing but their faith and a few of their believing followers, al-Manṣūr was left powerless. So, instead, rumours were spread about al-Manṣūr's power and strength, for the sole purpose of discouraging the faithful from joining their movement. For example, al-Manṣūr spread the rumour that he had an enchanted mirror that showed him all of ʿAbd Allāh's and Ibrāhīm's movements, and whose houses they were sheltering in and who was joining them. Funnily enough, this story of an enchanted mirror is virtually the same as the one told by kings like Jamshīd almost two thousand years before in order to frighten their enemies into believing that they couldn't possibly do anything without these kings knowing it.

So, what the tyrants of this world want from God–a God, incidentally, in whom they do not believe–is for people to believe that His prophets and messengers of truth were always oppressed and always defeated. What they want from God is for people to believe that no cry of truth ever prevailed against the evil nature of this material world. What they want from God is for people to be accustomed to the idea that no uprising against falsehood or oppression could ever succeed in producing a lasting positive result. The real question we must ask, however, is: Are they right? Perhaps some people who are uneducated or under the influence of these tyrants might believe that the prophets, their followers, and the Imams were always defeated, and that every uprising in this world is always defeated. But are we obliged to agree? Should we not study the Qur'an and see whether this is the case rather than taking it as fact? Because, when we look at the Qur'an, we see that it propounds exactly the opposite view. Should we ignore the Qur'an and listen to the tyrants? Of course not! We should refer to the Qur'an and learn from it because, when we do that, we see what the true outcome of prophethood was and what the real fruits of the revolutions started by the prophets and their followers can be. So, we shall first study this principle from the Qur'an, then we shall turn back to the text of history and see whether or not historical experience agrees with what the Qur'an says!

In the verses we quoted at the beginning of this lecture, the Qur'an strikes a parable for us, which tells us that in this world there is truth and there is falsehood, but ultimately, it is truth that endures while it is falsehood that vanishes! In these verses, God speaks about the water that flows down from the mountains in rivers. He says that as the water flows, a froth appears on it, but that this froth disappears while the water remains. Falsehood is this froth that will eventually vanish, while truth is the water that remains.

Here, the Qur'an is teaching us a reality that is attested to by history. Each of the prophets who appeared in this world, from the first to the last–over and above the fact that the whole series of prophets throughout history acted with a single goal in mind and took mankind forward step by step, each of them by themselves also had the possibility of succeeding. The truth is not the propaganda that al-Manṣūr poured into people's ears; that there is nothing people can do about the powers that be. This is not the case. It is not the case that, as the powerful have told people throughout history, truth can do nothing against falsehood. That truth will always be smothered out of existence by evil. On the contrary, the opposite is true. The prophets were able to succeed wherever they went, and their followers were able to succeed too, and they were indeed successful! However, there are two conditions that must be met for this result to occur–recall that I mentioned that human free will has an important role to play in shaping the future of the human race–and whenever these two conditions are met, all the uprisings that have taken place throughout history on the basis of religion, on the basis of Islamic and Qur'anic thought, have been successful and will be successful until the end of time. There is no need for any miracles, either. There is no need for miracles for the supporters of religion and truth to succeed. Without any supernatural acts, there are two practical conditions that must be met in order for Islam, the Qur'an, religion, and Qur'anic ideals to be realised. What are these two conditions?

One of these conditions is faith (*īmān*), namely belief on the basis of understanding, accompanied by a sense of moral duty and practical action. This is the first condition. The second condition is perseverance (*ṣabr*). It means to resist, not to withdraw, to be able to take action at the critical juncture.

When you look at the history of the prophets and you see that one of them was defeated by the *ṭāghūt* of his day, it is because his followers and supporters either lacked sufficient faith or sufficient perseverance. Whenever you see that truth was victorious, it is because these followers had sufficient faith and perseverance. Is there any evidence in the Qur'an for this? Of course. There are several examples of this in the Qur'an. The verses that I mentioned today are the conceptual foundation of this principle, but there are many other verses which elucidate it further. For example, there is the verse: 'Do not weaken or grieve: you shall have the upper hand, should you be faithful.'[34] This is a verse from the Qur'an–it is not a narration whose validity is open to question. It is also not an ambiguous (*mutashābih*) verse whose meaning is in doubt. No, it is clear and unequivocal in its meaning. It tells the Muslims not to slacken their efforts, or to give in to grief, because they will be superior and be victorious over their enemies. You will rule the world, on one condition. And what is that condition? 'Should you be faithful.' If you are true believers. If you have *īmān*. This is the condition for your success.

Now, you might say: But Imam al-Ṣādiq (a) struggled against the tyrant of his time and he didn't succeed in establishing his government. This is correct, but it is because many of his followers–the people claiming to be his *shīʿah*–were like me and you: They lacked faith and perseverance. Do we expect Imam al-Ṣādiq (a) to go against the divine precedent to take power at all costs, even by miraculous means? This itself shows us that the successes of the prophets and their followers did not depend on divine intervention. If the prophets were supposed to depend upon miracles, then Imam al-Ṣādiq would have performed a miracle to take power, but, instead, we see that he was assassinated by the hand of the tyrant of his own time. His son, Imam al-Kāẓim, met the same end for the same reason: Too few of his supporters and followers had the necessary perseverance and faith–the necessary belief, coupled with a sense of moral duty. Today, the situation is the same and the result is the same: Defeat. The defeat of Islam. The defeat of the Qur'an. The subjugation of the Muslims. But if today we were like those at the time of the Prophet–if we were Muslims

34 Q3:139.

with sure and unshakable conviction, with perseverance to humble the most dedicated of Heaven's angels, the kind of perseverance that means you can fight your enemies or dig a trench even while fasting in the month of Ramadan in the heat of the Arabian desert–things would be very different.

God says: 'Take recourse in perseverance and prayer'.[35] With the weapon of perseverance you will overcome your enemies. With the weapon of perseverance, you will attain your goals. This is one of the miracles of perseverance. The hand that we must raise up to do our work is the hand of perseverance. But we misunderstand the meaning of perseverance (*ṣabr*). We imagine that it means something like 'patience'–that we should sit and wait to see what the outcome will be. But I'm telling you what will happen if you do this, you don't need to wait and see! If you do not take action, if you do not make effort, if you do not get up and do something, you will suffer misfortune, humiliation and poverty, you will lose your religion and you will lose the world too. 'To become a loser in the world and the Hereafter. That is the manifest loss!'[36]

This is the outcome that the Qur'an foretells for us. Read the verses of *Sūrat al-Aʿrāf* and ponder on their meaning. What I am discussing here, I would like you to apply to your lives as a religious way of thinking. I want you to pay close attention to see whether it is really compatible with the standards of Islam, as a way of thinking. The verses we are looking at, particularly verses 126 and 127, are about what took place between Moses and Pharaoh when Moses came and invited him to God and Pharaoh not only rejected his invitation but proceeded to threaten Moses. After their debate, Pharaoh's magicians came and worked their magic against Moses' miracles but realised that they were powerless against him and announced their belief

35 Q2:153.

36 Q22:11.

in him. Pharaoh then threatened them with death: 'Why did you believe in Moses' sorcery?!' After all of these events with Moses and the magicians, Pharaoh's elite tell him: 'Will you leave Moses and his people to cause corruption in the land, and to abandon you and your gods?'[37] What are you going to do about them?

Pharaoh responds that he has a plan for dealing with Moses and his followers once and for all: 'We will kill their sons and spare their women, and indeed we are dominant over them.'[38] He says he won't leave Moses. He will not let Moses act freely in the land. On the contrary, he will adopt a new policy–killing their sons and sparing their women. After taking every possible measure to confront Moses and expecting Moses to be defeated, Pharaoh realises that even his magicians believe in Moses and that their magic is no match for his miracles. Therefore, he has to find another way of applying pressure on Moses and his followers. So, he decides he will kill the youth who have gathered around Moses. Meanwhile, he will spare the womenfolk and keep them alive. This is either with the intent of committing indecency or destroying the identity of the Israelites through intermarriage or something akin to this. Now, this is an extremely difficult situation for Moses and his followers. They are facing a new level of persecution from Pharaoh. This is a situation where even the steadiest of hearts quivers. Someone with Pharaoh's power says that he is going to torment them. He says he is not going to leave a single one of their young men alive. 'We will kill their sons'. But it is at this precise moment that Moses and his followers cannot lose heart. It is at this moment that they should not allow themselves to feel defeated!

A phrase comes to mind that was uttered by a great figure of the last century which he uttered during the era of the Constitutional

---

37 Q7:127.

38 Ibid.

Revolution. They say that he told his friends and comrades: 'You must fight. And when things seem dire, you must keep fighting. And when you think you are facing certain defeat, you must fight all the more, because then you will win!' And he was right. When people, whether as a nation, a group or an individual, want to strive for their emancipation, there are times when they are hopeful that their efforts will bear fruit. However, when things become difficult, they lose hope. Now, if they lose hope and stop struggling, their efforts will definitely not bear fruit. However, if they keep up the fight and don't give up, until it reaches the point where they think they are sure to fail, but they keep on fighting even then, it is then they are sure to succeed!

Moses used this new plan by Pharaoh to mobilise the Israelites–when the Israelites thought they were doomed because Pharaoh had decided to massacre all of their young men. Just as Pharaoh had unveiled a new plan to his advisors, Moses now unveiled a new plan to his people. What did he say to them, confronted with this new situation? 'Moses said to his people, "Turn to God for help and persevere"'. Don't leave your work half-finished. Hold onto hope and resist! And why should they do this? Because: 'The earth indeed belongs to God, and He gives its inheritance to whomever He wishes of His servants'. We are God's servants, Moses tells his people, it is Pharaoh's servants whose works will bear no fruit. 'And the outcome will be in favour of the Godwary.'[39]

This is what the Qur'an says, but history testifies to the truth of this as well! They may have thrown Abraham into the bonfire, but he founded a house of God in Makkah–a symbol of divine unity–that would endure for centuries. Moses and the Israelites suffered under Pharaoh, but then they entered the Holy Land and created a

39 Q7:128.

tawḥīd-oriented society there. 'O my people, enter the Holy Land'.[40] During his short life, Jesus's ministry did not yield any tangible results, but after just two centuries, one of the greatest empires in the world was under the sway of his followers. The Emperor of Rome–the head of this empire–fell under the influence of Christianity before himself becoming a Christian.

In Makkah, our Prophet suffered thirteen years of persecution before he came to Madinah and founded a new society. A new system which would guide people towards perfection and ultimately overcome its enemies. But what allowed him to do this? Faith and perseverance. Whenever faith and perseverance are combined, then you will be victorious. 'Yes, if you are steadfast and Godwary'[41], then you will be victorious. This is one of the divine principles at work in the cosmos and in human history. It was true yesterday, it is true today, and it will be true tomorrow. Whenever the powers of religion have managed to establish themselves and endure, it is only because of faith and perseverance. Today, those who want to see the principles of Islam, of the Qur'an, of divine unity and of prophethood manifested in the world today, those who want to see a way of life built upon the fundamental doctrines of Islam, and those who want God to govern affairs, must cultivate these two qualities within themselves: faith and perseverance. Because, when these two qualities are combined in us, we become powerful: 'The earth indeed belongs to God, and He gives its inheritance to whomever He wishes of His servants, and the outcome will be in favour of the Godwary.'

So, this is how we answer the two questions we were asked. The first question was whether the prophets as a whole were successful or not? We said that the institution of prophethood was successful. That all of the prophets taken together succeeded in their mission

40 Q5:21.

41 Q3:125.

because they wanted to lead mankind towards progress. And the analogy we drew to elucidate this was of children in a school with a series of teachers.

The prophets were, as a whole, successful in their missions. They were not defeated. However, when we look at each of the prophets as individuals, when we study each of their divine movements and uprisings for *tawḥīd*, do we draw a different conclusion or not? We said that there is a general rule at work here, and that this general rule is that wherever the prophets found followers of sufficient faith and perseverance, they were successful, but wherever they did not find followers with these qualities, they were not.

'Say, "God is the creator of all things, and He is the One, the All-paramount."'[42] God is the creator of all things, therefore only He can say what the outcome of all things will be. Because God is going to speak about the outcomes of truth and falsehood in a moment, he prepares the ground by reminding the audience that He is the creator of the world and, therefore, that He understands the principles on which the world and human history operate better than we do.

Then he strikes a parable: 'He sends down water from the sky'. There is a beauty to the way in which these verses are phrased which, unfortunately, is probably only visible to those who are familiar with Arabic. Notice that God does not begin by saying He is going to draw a parable. The audience hearing this do not know that what they are hearing now is a parable or where it is going to lead them. It is only when they reach the end of the parable that they understand what it was about. So, God begins by saying 'He sends down water from the sky whereat the valleys are flooded to [the extent of] their capacity', whether they are big or small, 'and the flood carries along a swelling scum'. The floodwaters in the valleys carry a froth on their surface. When you stand next to a flooded river, what you see first is not the

42 Q13:16.

water, but the scum and the froth that floats on top of it. The water is underneath. It is the froth that is visible first and foremost. The water is hidden.

Then the analogy changes suddenly. 'And from what they smelt in the fire for the purpose of [making] ornaments or wares', when they smelt metals such as iron or copper in order to make tools, or precious metals such as gold to make jewellery, something similar happens: There arises–'a similar scum'–similar to the froth floating on a river. When you smelt a metal such as iron or gold in the fire, scum or dross begins to float on molten metal. So, there it was the froth on the water, but what was the origin? What was the original life-giving substance: Is it water or the froth? It's the water! But what do you see? The froth which obscures the water. So, what shows itself more? The froth!

Then think, what is the desired material when a smith or a jeweller smelts metal? Is it iron or the scum? Is it the gold or the scum? It is the iron or gold, of course–they don't want the scum! But what is it you see on the surface? It is the scum rather than the pure metal beneath. Then, with this imagery in place, God immediately says: 'That is how God compares the truth and falsehood.' This is how God makes you understand the difference between truth and falsehood: In the same way as you understand the difference between water and foam, or metal and scum. What you see is not what is really there!

Now that you understand that there is a parable being struck, you want to hear the conclusion. So God says: 'As for the scum, it leaves as dross, and that which profits the people remains in the earth. That is how God draws comparisons.' The scum disappears and becomes nothing. There is not always froth on rivers. It is there for a moment, then gone. When a river is used to irrigate the fields of a farm, it is the water that is used, not the froth because the froth disappears. God says 'that which profits the people remains in the earth', meaning the water, meaning the metal, the gold–these are what remain, the scum and accretions disappear. 'That is how God draws comparisons' for you: He wants to show you how truth endures. The mission of the prophets is truth. The uprisings of the prophets are truth. The falsehoods that stand against the prophets vanish. They fade away. They collapse. They are the scum. The dross. The foam on the water. When you examine them, you see that they are really nothing.

The verse that follows this analogy turns to the social struggles of the Muslims. It says: 'For those who answer [the summons of] their Lord there shall be the best outcome.'[43] So it is those who join the uprising of the prophets whose efforts shall bear fruit. 'But those who do not answer Him', and follow the path of falsehood, 'even if they possessed all that is on the earth and as much of it besides, they would surely offer it to redeem themselves with it' and deliver themselves from their plight. Have you not seen this in history? Have you not seen how, in the clashes between truth and falsehood, the leaders of falsehood are rolled up like a school? And when this happens, they are ready to give everything they have and everything in the world besides to preserve their lives and their status? 'For such there shall be an adverse reckoning, and their refuge shall be Hell, and it is an evil resting place.'

Then, when we look at the verses of *Sūrat al-Ṣāffāt*, we read: 'Certainly Our decree has gone beforehand in favour of Our servants, the apostles'.[44] In other words, God has already made a firm decision regarding His prophets. What was this decision? 'That they will indeed be the receivers of help'.[45] Only they will receive divine assistance. 'And indeed Our hosts will be the victors.'[46] I mentioned before that the condition for the success of the prophets is that their

43 Q13:18.

44 Q37:171.

45 Q37:172.

46 Q37:173.

followers possessed sufficient faith and perseverance. In battles, God's Messenger enjoined people to persevere. In battles, the Commander of the Faithful enjoined people to persevere. They were always telling people: 'Persevere!' What does it mean to persevere on the battlefield? It means not to hold back from the fight. It means never to cease one's efforts. Not to leave anything half-done. This is the meaning of perseverance. If only the Muslims of the world would culture in themselves these two qualities, the qualities of faith and perseverance, in the cultural sphere, the economic sphere, and the political sphere, the Islamic world would have already triumphed over its enemies and adversaries!

Muslims must not allow themselves to be led to believe that the brand of ignominy, backwardness, poverty, and abasement is burnt onto the forehead of faith. No, do not believe that the enemies of religion and the enemies of Islam throughout the world should always trample the Muslims and enslave them. This is definitely not the case. If the Muslims of the world, the Muslim nations of the world, the Muslim peoples and communities–in short, the entirety of the Muslim *Ummah*–which is today six or seven hundred million strong, if they could find their faith and fortify themselves with perseverance, they could triumph against the whole world. This is the advice of the Qur'an to all Muslims at all times. This is the conclusion we draw from our discussion today. I wanted you to know that the outcome of prophethood is always good. I wanted you to know that the Qur'an has promised victory to the prophets and their uprisings. Today, we are following in the footsteps of those prophets, so why do we feel weak? Why? Why do you feel abased? Why do you think that the enemies of religion are always able to defeat the Muslim nations? Why? No. This is not the case. The truth is the exact opposite to what you have been told. However, the conditions for our success are faith and perseverance. So make sure you understand the real meaning of perseverance (*ṣabr*). If no other practical consequence comes of our sitting in today's lecture, let us at least try to fully actualise the true meanings of perseverance and faith within ourselves.

Today's lecture is at an end. I implore you to pay attention in these coming days, as we are now entering the main and most important topics of the series.

O Lord! By Muhammad and the Household of Muhammad, make us followers of the prophets!

O Lord! By Muhammad and the Household of Muhammad, enrich us with faith and perseverance!

O Lord! Grant us the fruits of faith and perseverance!

O Lord! By Muhammad and the Household of Muhammad, give victory to the Muslims and Muslim nations of the world over their enemies!

O Lord! By Muhammad and the Household of Muhammad, thwart those who want to weaken the Muslims, who want to humiliate the Muslims, who want to keep the Muslims backward, no matter where they are, or how they are doing it.

O Lord! By Muhammad and the Household of Muhammad, lend your strength to any person, wherever they are in the world, who is striving for the sake of the Muslims, for the sake of Islam, and for the sake of the higher ideals of Islam, and grant them success!

O Lord! Keep the hands of the enemies of religion off the nations and lands of Islam!

O Lord! By Muhammad and the Household of Muhammad, restrain the hands of the most implacable enemies of religion, of the Muslims, and of all humanity!

O Lord! By Muhammad and the Household of Muhammad, make us true followers of Muhammad and the Household of Muhammad!

O Lord! Make each new day of our lives wiser than the last. And increase our knowledge, determination, faith, and perseverance in it!

O Lord! By Muhammad and the Household of Muhammad, take all of the oppressed and persecuted people of the world under your protection, and throw down all the oppressors and tyrants of the world!

Accustom and habituate our souls to your remembrance,

Make our intentions and goals for our speaking, our listening, our sitting and our standing purely for you, and keep us away from idolatry, hypocrisy and eye-service.

O Lord! By Muhammad and the Household of Muhammad, hasten the freedom of all the innocents who have been imprisoned, wherever they are in the world and show special concern for them.

And please alleviate all the personal and individual troubles of the Muslims!

The Outcome of Prophethood, Part Two

Wednesday 22nd Ramadan 1394
8th October 1974

إِنَّا لَنَنْصُرُ رُسُلَنَا وَالَّذِينَ آمَنُوا فِي الْحَيَاةِ الدُّنْيَا وَيَوْمَ يَقُومُ الْأَشْهَادُ (٥١) يَوْمَ لَا يَنْفَعُ الظَّالِمِينَ مَعْذِرَتُهُمْ وَلَهُمُ اللَّعْنَةُ وَلَهُمْ سُوءُ الدَّارِ (٥٢) وَلَقَدْ آتَيْنَا مُوسَى الْهُدَى وَأَوْرَثْنَا بَنِي إِسْرَائِيلَ الْكِتَابَ (٥٣) هُدًى وَذِكْرَى لِأُولِي الْأَلْبَابِ (٥٤)

'Indeed We shall help Our apostles and those who have faith in the life of the world and on the day when the witnesses rise up-the day when the excuses of the wrongdoers will not benefit them, and the curse will lie on them, and for them will be the ills of the [ultimate] abode. Certainly We gave Moses the guidance and We made the Children of Israel heirs to the Book, as a guidance and an admonition for those who possess intellect.'
Sūrat al-Ghāfir (40):51–54

Yesterday we mentioned God's promise to His prophets and messengers to mankind-a promise filled with hope and optimism. God promised that the prophets who bore the responsibility of conveying the divine message to mankind, and all of those who summoned people towards religion and truth, would both triumph over their enemies in this world and attain a great reward in the Hereafter. We gave a brief overview of what can be said about the success of the prophets in this world from two perspectives: First, we looked at the succession of prophets as a whole from the first to the last, and we saw that these teachers of humanity were indeed successful in their overall mission. It is true that some of them suffered setbacks during their missions, or even after them, and they sometimes faced opposition from people, but when we look at the institution of prophethood, we see that the prophets as a group achieved their goals. The comparison we drew for this was with a series of teachers who, from the first to the last, want to teach a class of students, one after another, until there have been six, ten, fifteen teachers from the beginning of this class's time at school until its end, from the lowest levels of education to the highest. They wanted to take these students by the hand and lead them from the depths of ignorance to the apex of knowledge. However, their teacher in the first year only took them a little of the way and he did not see them reach their goal, as he died before this came to pass. However, how do we judge whether or not he succeeded as a teacher? Just because he did not stay with the children to the end of their studies, does this mean that he failed them? Of course not! He did his task. He discharged his duty. Then he handed them over to the next teacher to perform his share of the responsibilities.

Another analogy I usually give for this is of a heavy load that needs to be brought from one end of the mosque to the other. It is too heavy for one person to carry on their back the whole way by themselves without any help. But even altogether, people cannot carry the load all the way in one go. This leaves only one way of transporting this heavy load: The first person should come and move it a metre towards the mosque, then the second comes and moves it another metre, then the third moves it another metre, and a fourth, and so on until there are twenty, twenty-seven, thirty, more than thirty, until eventually, the distance is covered and the load reaches its destination. Each person only moved it one metre. Now, imagine that the load is so heavy that, after you've moved it a metre, you die! All these people sacrificed their lives, but in the end the distance was covered. Each of them bore the burden for just a little of the journey but, in this way, the whole distance was covered.

The prophets carry a burden such as this. Each of them is only able to move it a metre forward. Noah came and he was able to carry the burden of guiding mankind towards the pinnacle of learning and virtue for just one metre. But what hardship he endured for this one metre! He preached to people for nine hundred and fifty years, and only managed to take them a single step forward. He spent his whole life on this task but, ultimately, did he do his duty or not? Did he carry this burden a metre forward or not? You can see he did. After Noah, another prophet came and took up this burden. He carried it a metre forward. Then a third prophet came and carried it another metre forward. Then the Final Messenger (s) was raised up as a prophet, and he took up this burden and made it so that mankind would continue its march towards progress. So, the prophets–from the first to the last–were successful in their mission.

At the end of this task, the last of the divine emissaries, whom we refer to as the Master of the Age (aj) is a promise given to all the millions of theists in the world. He is the last of God's representatives on earth–he is the one whose appearance millions of believers in God are expectantly awaiting, who will bring this mission to its ultimate conclusion. Whose work does the Imam of the Age bring to completion? The work of Noah, Abraham, Moses, Jesus and the Final Messenger, the work of the Imams from the Prophet's Household. If this burden did not reach its destination, then all of Noah's efforts would have been for naught. However, it will reach its destination and when it does, this is only the last leg of a long journey–it means that Noah's efforts were not in vain, that Abraham's efforts were not in vain, that Zechariah's efforts were not in vain. None of the prophets' efforts, none of their hardships, none of their sufferings were in vain... because that burden that they carried forward through history has reached its destination. It is true that some of them were persecuted and killed. It is true that John the Baptist had his head cut off as a gift to a vicious woman. But, none of them were defeated. None of them were thwarted. Why? Because all of their suffering and hardship was in the service of a higher cause; discharging this responsibility with which they had been trusted and carrying that burden forward, even if only by a step. This is what we spoke about yesterday.

Another topic we touched on yesterday was that the ultimate outcome of prophethood means that none of the prophets should be seen as having failed in their missions. Because, in the grand scheme of things, all of them succeeded in guiding humanity towards the light. However, we also see that some of the prophets, in addition to carrying this burden forward, also enjoyed a share of success in this world in the sense that they were able to create communities and societies that were founded on the ideals of divine unity and their moral teachings. The clearest example of this is our own Prophet, who was able to create a new city, a new society, and a new system based on the ideals of Islam, the Qur'an and divine revelation. But there are many other examples of prophets who accomplished this, as we pointed out yesterday. A few centuries after Christ, the Roman Emperor himself became a Christian. After Moses's death, the Israelites founded a virtuous community. Abraham in his own lifetime was able to create a godly community, as the Qur'an explains. Solomon built a mighty empire which he ruled by God's laws. Some even say that he established his authority over the whole world and created a global *tawḥīd*-oriented society. So, we can see that some of the prophets enjoyed a special measure of success and this was manifested in the creation of a divine and *tawḥīd*-centric society and system of government.

But some of the prophets also did not have the opportunity to accomplish this. Like who? Like Zechariah, who I mentioned yesterday. Like John the Baptist. They suffered setbacks and were ultimately killed. How are we to understand this? Why were some prophets successful and others were not in changing the social order? Why weren't all of them able to create a *tawḥīd*-centric society founded on divine principles? Why were only some of them able to accomplish this? To answer in a simple formula: We saw that wherever true faith was combined with perseverance, divine leaders and righteous people were successful, but wherever this faith and perseverance was not sufficiently present, then the divine leaders, righteous people and callers to truth were defeated. This is a universal truth. Wherever the faithful who supported a prophet persevered in their confrontation with their enemies and adversaries, they succeeded. The victory of the prophets is inevitable because they speak the truth, they act in accordance with the truth, and the truth always prevails. Truth is in the very core and essence of the cosmos. The prophets speak in accordance with the truth of the cosmos. Therefore, all the elements for triumph are present in their movements. If you find a prophet in history who was defeated, this is not because they spoke the truth, no. True speech will always prevail. The truth will always prevail. Truth will always defeat falsehood and reduce it to naught. So why were these prophets defeated then? Because their followers lacked sufficient faith and perseverance. Recall, yesterday, that we read the verses of the Qur'an: 'Certainly Our decree has gone beforehand in favour of Our servants, the apostles, that they will indeed be the receivers of help, and indeed Our hosts will be the victors.'[47] These are God's eternal words. So if you ever see an instance where the word of truth appears to have been defeated, know that it was not God's host–those fighting did not meet the conditions of being God's

47 Q37:171–173.

host. Those who were defeated were defeated because they lacked the qualities of faith and perseverance, so they were not of God's hosts. When an Islamic society is God's host, it will succeed. But when it holds back from doing its duty, then it is no longer God's host.

So, to sum up what we have just said, the reason why some prophets appear to be defeated while others were successful in creating a new society is this: Wherever the followers of a prophet had true faith, and complete conviction in their cause, and relied on the truth to carry them though, they were always successful. It was not in their nature to be defeated. Yesterday I quoted someone from a great figure of recent history, who told his comrades: 'You must fight. And when things seem dire, you must keep fighting. And when you think you are facing certain defeat, you must fight all the more, because then you will win!' There is a verse of the Qur'an which appears to confirm this: 'When the apostles lost hope and they thought that they had been told lies'.[48] When it came to the point that the prophets suffered such strikes and blows from their enemies that even they had lost hope, that the prophets and those with them felt their hearts begin to waver. This not with regard to faith–they would never lose faith, their belief in God would not shake–but with regard to their belief that they would be victorious. Their certainty that they would succeed was shaken and they imagined that they had misunderstood. They were certain that God had told them they would be victorious, but things had become so dire that they wondered if they had misunderstood and God had not given them such a promise! 'And they thought that they had been told lies, Our help came to them'. Just at the moment when the pressure became unbearable and the struggle seemed insurmountable, when it seemed as though all hope was lost for the cause of faith and truth and that their enemies would surely overcome them and they saw no way of avoiding this fate–it was exactly at this

48 Q12:110.

moment, *because* they held their ground, because they didn't stop trying, that God helped them. This is what the Qur'an says!

Sometimes, we might imagine that because some of the movements that raised the banner of truth were defeated, this means that the truthful are forever destined to suffer defeat at the hands of falsehood. Zayd ibn ʿAlī died in the Mosque of Kūfah from an arrow to the forehead, Muhammad ibn ʿAbd Allah, known as the Pure Soul (Nafs-i Zakīyyah), was killed in battle with al-Manṣūr's troops, Ḥusayn ibn ʿAlī al-Ḥasanī was cut down with his followers on the outskirts of Madinah, and Ibrāhīm ibn ʿAbd Allah was killed in Kūfah or Basrah–from the deaths of all these men, it seems as though the general experience of history is this: All movements under the banner of truth and justice inevitably fall prey to falsehood and tyranny. Yes, some people who do not comprehend the logic of the Qur'an imagine this to be the case. This notion is a pleasant balm for the tyrants and oppressors of history. They want people to believe this and it is clear that they play a role in promoting this idea. However, it is completely false.

If Zayd ibn ʿAlī was martyred and his movement broken, it does not mean that truth is destined to be brought down by falsehood. On the contrary, it shows that even though the truth is the truth, upholding it requires struggle and effort. We think that because the Qur'an is God's word, God will bring it to fruition in this world–no! Of course, it is the truth and it is destined to triumph, but this still requires struggle. People must be willing to take action, to persevere, to sacrifice in order to enthrone it in its proper place! This is the lesson we must draw from the uprising of Zayd ibn ʿAlī, not that the truth is forever doomed to be swallowed by the darkness of falsehood. Why do we draw this erroneous conclusion? Zayd ibn ʿAlī proclaimed the truth–no doubt! Imam al-Ṣādiq (a) even agreed that Zayd's uprising against the regime of Hishām ibn ʿAbd al-Mālik was righteous. History attests to this fact. And Zayd went forth and fought for the cause of truth and justice but, at a critical moment, the people who were supposed to support him lost courage, made excuses–perhaps they had fallen under the influence of Umayyad propaganda–and abandoned him when he needed them most. This shows us that even if something is the truth–no less than the truth which Zayd ibn ʿAlī proclaimed!–if it is abandoned by its supporters, if no one fights for it, then it will be defeated. On the other hand, if people are willing to struggle for its sake, the cause of truth will advance! This is true for any cause in the world: How many times have we seen ideas or schools of thought brought to the fore by the efforts of their followers? Do you think falsehoods and untruths that go against the very cosmic order itself rise to prominence through the efforts of their followers, but true causes cannot? This seems absurd, but this is what some people believe to be the case!

In one of the sermons of *Nahj al-Balāghah*, the Commander of the Faithful says something which makes this very clear. I do not want to spend too much time on this in our lecture today, as I want to focus on the verses of the Qur'an we are discussing. This sermon, in which the Commander of the Faithful describes the experience of the early warriors of Islam, is one that I have mentioned on several occasions in other contexts. In it, he says: 'In the company of God's Messenger, we fought our own fathers, our own sons, our own brothers and our own uncles'.[49] In the battle against faithlessness, if we saw our uncle, our father, our son or our brother under the banner of idolatry, and we were with the Prophet, we would not say: 'He is my brother, I won't fight him', 'That is my son, I won't fight him'–we would fight them without hesitation for the sake of God. And even if we had to kill them in battle, we would not feel troubled by this. We would not say: 'O woe is us! Because of this new religion, this new idea, I killed my son!' No, our faith would not decrease because of this. It would actually increase, as the Commander of the Faithful said: 'And that

49 *Nahj al-Balāghah*, sermon no. 56.

only increased us in faith and submission, and in our determination to press on through difficulty and hardship'. Then the Commander of the Faithful describes the battlefield itself, 'and our earnestness in struggling against the foe. A man from our side and one from the enemy would launch themselves at one another like a pair of stallions vying for supremacy to see which one would quench the other from death's cup'. But I do not want to spend time explaining the imagery of warfare and bravery here, what I want to focus on is what the Commander of the Faithful says next: 'And when God saw our fidelity, he thwarted our foes and granted us His aid.' In other words, they struggled so hard that God saw that they truly believed, that they were truly Muslims. They demonstrated the depths of their faiths through their deeds. And when they did this, that was when they triumphed over their enemies with God's help and victory. There are just two or three more phrases I want to call your attention to from this sermon: 'By my life, if we then had done has you have done today, no pillar of the religion would have stood, nor would any branch of the faith have grown verdant!' Here, the Commander of the Faithful is speaking during the time of his own caliphate, at a time when many people just wanted an easy life, so that when he told them to ready themselves to fight against Muʿāwiyah, they made excuses. When he told them to arm themselves to fight Ṭalḥah and Zubayr, they brought all manner of supposedly pious reasons not to raise their swords against their brothers in faith. In short, they had become men who sought ease, who sought comfort, who preferred survival to struggle. They had strayed far from the divine teachings. These are the kind of people whom the Commander of the Faithful found himself confronted by during his reign as caliph. Weak, lax, and content with humiliation in exchange for an easy life. These were the Commander of the Faithful's forces. That is why he says: 'By my life, if we then had done as you have done today, no pillar of the religion would have stood, nor would any branch of the faith have grown verdant!' Because if this is how the first Muslims had been, there would have been no Islam of which to speak!

What do you understand from this sermon? Remember, the words of the Commander of the Faithful are no less than the words of the Prophet himself. The road taken by ʿAlī is the same road that would have been taken by his brother, the Prophet. So, why is it that in his day the Prophet was victorious, while in his own time, the Commander of the Faithful suffered setbacks? Why? This is what the Commander of the Faithful is explaining in this sermon. He is saying: In the time of the Prophet, we held fast and endured the hardships of battle. In those days, we were ready to go to the battlefield from our beds. In those days, we were ready to give up our worldly wealth and material comforts for the sake of God. Today, we are not prepared to do this. In those days, we went forth. Today, we hang back. This is a very clear and simple analysis by the Commander of the Faithful of the social situation of his day.

To sum up: The prophets of God, in addition to the fact that, as an institution and in the grand scheme of things, their mission was a success and that the outcome was in their favour, there were also prophets in this world who were successful in achieving their practical goals and establishing *tawḥīd*-oriented societies. The condition for their success was that their followers and comrades had true faith and that they were prepared to persevere and be steadfast on the battlefield. When faith and perseverance are combined amongst their followers, the prophets won victories. This is the conclusion we draw.

Now, let us return to the verses of the Qur'an. There are several excerpts from the Qur'an I would like to focus on in today's lecture. The first is from *Sūrat al-Ghāfir*, which reads: 'Indeed We shall help Our apostles and those who have faith in the life of the world and on the day when the witnesses rise up.'[50] When we look at the Arabic for

50 Q40:51.

'Indeed We shall help' (*innā la-nanṣuru*), we notice that there is both a *lām* of emphasis on the verb 'We shall help', which indicates that this is something sure to happen. It also has a particle of emphasis, *innā*, which again emphasises the certainty of this happening–there is no doubt about the fact that God will help! Notice also that God does not only say He will help His prophets but also those who have faith, as those who have faith walk the path of the prophets and so this promise encompasses them as well. Those pure-hearted individuals who follow the example of the prophets share in the promises given to them. Where will God help them? 'In the life of the world', God will help them in *this world*, and not delay His assistance until later. 'And on the day when the witnesses rise up', some commentaries on the Qur'an interpret this to be a reference to the Day of Judgement.

There is a narration about the aforementioned verse, in which the Imam (a) tells Jumayl ibn Darrāj that the meaning of this verse is that God will help His prophets during the Return (*rajʿah*). In other words, when the Imam of the Age (aj) comes and establishes a divine government over the whole world, and the banner of the Qur'an and Islam is raised in every corner of the earth, and all of the people are following the religion of God and the path of divine unity, and there is a single divine government over the whole world, and God brings back to life the prophets, the legatees, the righteous and the martyrs from amongst the faithful–in accordance with the verses of the Qur'an which allude to this and the narrations which explicitly mention it–that is when God will grant them His help. I do not want to discuss the Return (*rajʿah*) here. However, I do not think that in this tradition the Imam (a) meant to imply that 'in the life of this world' (*fī al-ḥayāt al-dunyā*) was a reference to the Return. I actually think that he meant to say that the phrase 'on the day when the witnesses rise up' (*yawma yaqūm al-ashhād*) was a reference to the Return rather than to the Day of Resurrection. After all, why should God need to give help (*naṣr*) on the Day of Resurrection? I would like to propose this as a possibility that this tradition means that God would help the prophets during the era of Return. Moreover, the apparent meaning of the phrase 'in the life of this world'–given the context in which it occurs–indicates that God is making an explicit promise to the prophets and the faithful to help them in this world in the here and now.

'The day when the excuses of the wrongdoers will not benefit them'[51] and 'the day when the witnesses rise up'.[52] When is this day? When will the witnesses rise up? On the day when the excuses of the wrongdoers will be of no use to them! There is another relevant verse of the Qur'an: 'The day when some of your Lord's signs do come, faith shall not benefit any soul that had not believed beforehand'[53] which can also be understood as a reference to the day on which the Imam of the Age (aj) rises up. Returning to the present verse, God says: 'and the curse will lie on them'[54]–the wrongdoers–'and for them will be the worst abode.'

Then, in order to demonstrate how He helps His prophets, God gives the example of Moses. *Sūrat al-Ghāfir* had focused on Moses prior to the verses under discussion and his confrontation with Pharaoh. Therefore, when God promises to help His prophets, he invokes Moses as an example of this: 'Certainly We gave Moses the guidance and We made the Children of Israel heirs to the Book.'[55] The Israelites were entrusted with a sacred scripture that contained all of God's teachings and ordinances, and this shows that they were successful in their battle with Pharaoh. After all, if the tyrants and the faithless had triumphed over the Israelites, they would not have permitted

51 Q40:52.
52 Q40:51.
53 Q6:158.
54 Q40:52.
55 Q40:53.

them to live in accordance with their sacred scripture. In fact, they would not have permitted them to keep a sacred scripture at all! God gave them this scripture 'as a guidance and an admonition for those who possess intellect.'[56]

'So persevere!'[57] What is the conclusion God draws from this example? What does God say to His Final Prophet? He tells him to persevere! He says: 'You persevere too! Stand tall! Do not allow yourself to be disheartened!' Why? Because 'God's promise is indeed true.' This promise that God gave you, that you will triumph, as we read in the verses of *Sūrat al-Ṣāffāt*: 'Certainly Our decree has gone beforehand in favour of Our servants, the apostles, that they will indeed be the receivers of help'–and as we read in many other verses of the Qur'an, is true and will come to past. You will definitely triumph, O Prophet! However, the condition for this being realised is that you persevere–'So persevere!' You must not turn back from the sacred path upon which you tread!

'So persevere! God's promise is indeed true. And plead for forgiveness for your sin'. But what sin (*dhanb*) has the Prophet committed? We should not imagine that what counts as a sin for the Prophet is anything like those sins we commit ourselves. After all, the Prophet is infallible (*maʿṣūm*), meaning he does not commit any sins. There is no doubt about this as it is a principle established by clear verses from the Qur'an and by the judgement of reason. But, if the Prophet does not commit sins, then what is this 'sin' to which God refers? The sin that God refers to in this verse belongs to the category of what we might call 'a mistake' for ourselves–however, even this is the kind of mistake that if you or I committed it, we would not even consider it a mistake! So, when God tells the Prophet to 'plead for forgiveness for your sin', he means to seek forgiveness and try to

56 Q40:54.

57 Q40:55.

redress your minor past mistakes. 'And celebrate the praise of your Lord morning and evening.' This verse shows us very clearly that the outcome of all the prophetic missions is God's assistance and success.

Now let us take a brief look at the verses from *Sūrat al-Anbiyāʾ*. This chapter of the Qur'an is in the seventeenth *juzʾ* and comes after *Sūrat Ṭa Ha*. The verses of this chapter are very inspiring, and I sincerely advise those of you who are familiar with the Qur'an, to study *Sūrat al-Anbiyāʾ* with the utmost care. At the beginning of the chapter, God very straightforwardly says that His messengers will be successful and that their enemies will be defeated in this world, to say nothing of the punishment that awaits in the next world. This is what God lays out at the beginning of the chapter. Next, after expanding on these issues a little, He turns to the discussion of history. He recounts the story of Moses, the victory of Moses, and the defeat of the forces that were against Moses; then the story of Abraham, the success of Abraham, and the defeat of the forces that were against Abraham; then the stories of Noah, Solomon, and others are dealt with in a similar fashion. All of the events recounted in this chapter of the Qur'an serve to demonstrate that the prophets always succeed, they always triumph, they always prevail, while the opponents of the prophetic revolution and of the prophetic message will always be defeated–this chapter of the Qur'an says that this is an established pattern of history.

God says: 'We did not send [any apostles] before you except as men, to whom We revealed. Ask the People of the Reminder if you do not know. We did not make them bodies that did not eat food, and they were not immortal. Then We fulfilled Our promise to them, and We delivered them and whomever We wished, and We destroyed the profligates. Certainly We have sent down to you a Book in which there is an admonition for you. Do you not exercise your reason?'[58]

58 Q21:7–10.

Then we reach the eleventh verse, where God says: 'How many a town We have smashed'[59]. This is the anthem of the victory of the prophets, it is a rousing anthem that shows how the prophets are supported by unseen divine power in this world. But this is not through unseen powers in the way that ordinary persons might wish for, such as a hidden hand smiting their enemies, no. This is through unseen forms of assistance that are hidden within the system of cause and effect that governs the cosmos, forms of assistance that are in harmony with the natural order, human nature, and human society. How much help God gave to His prophets through this unseen power! 'How many a town We have smashed that had been wrongdoing...'.

An unjust society, an unjust government, an unjust civilisation is one in which structures of oppression are employed, where class differences are created, where exploitation takes place, where one person uses another. This is the 'wrongdoing village' of which the Qur'an speaks. This wrongdoing village refers to an unjust social order, which is used by tyrants for their own ends. God exclaims: How many of these We have smashed! 'How many a town We have smashed that had been wrongdoing, and We brought forth another people after it.' Then God brought another people, another group, another class to rule.

'So when they sighted Our punishment', the misery of the wrongdoers when they saw God's wrath, 'behold, they ran away from it.'[60] When they sensed God's wrath and anger, they fled. God's punishment either means when they saw a miraculous punishment descending from the heavens, or when they saw the prophets and the faithful with them gain authority over them and raise the sword of God's justice above their heads, 'behold, they ran away from it.' No sooner had a just society and civilisation been established than they

---

59 Q21:11.

60 Q21:12.

fled elsewhere. Go back to your palaces in which you live in luxury, go back to your societies and your cities in which you lorded your status over others–where will you go? '"Do not run away! Return to the opulence you were given to enjoy and to your dwellings so that you may be questioned!"[61] They said, "Woe to us! We have indeed been wrongdoers!" That remained their cry until We turned them into a mown field, stilled [like burnt ashes]'.[62] In other words, this is what they cried out until death overtook them.

Pay close attention. There are two or three more verses we need to read, and these verses are in reality the conceptual foundations of this pattern of history the Qur'an has just expounded. Why is history the way God has described it here? Why must the oppressors fall and the oppressed rise? Why must the prophetic call always triumph over its opponents? The reason is as follows: 'We did not create the sky and the earth and whatever is between them for play. Had We desired to take up some diversion We would have surely taken it up with Ourselves, were We to do [so].'[63]

You see, God does not do things idly. He does not do things for false reasons. He does not act without a purpose. What does this mean? It means when God created the heavens, the earth, and all they contain, He did so with a purpose in mind. He created them with the intention of them reaching a particular goal. Truth (*ḥaqq*) means the path which leads the heavens, the earth, and all they contain to this particular goal. Truth is the way that takes all things towards the purpose for which God gave them existence. Any means which brings the human being closer to this goal is truth. This is not discussed in any other verse of the Qur'an but, when we ponder on this verse, this meaning is very clear. And the nature of the Qur'an is such that usually, when

61 Q21:13.

62 Q21:14–15.

63 Q21:16–17.

something is clear and obvious to the human intellect, the Qur'an does not dwell on it at length.

Following this, God says: 'Indeed, We hurl the truth against falsehood, and it crushes its head, and behold, falsehood vanishes! And woe to you for what you allege [about God].'[64] This is the way of truth, the right path, the way of human nature, the road of cosmic nature. This way will inevitably triumph over falsehood. In fact, truth's victory over falsehood will be so complete that falsehood will vanish entirely. Then the wrongdoers, the oppressors, the followers of falsehood and untruth will be woeful for the lies they have told.

Now, what follows this displays the rhetorical beauty of the Qur'an and we must strive to become more familiar with the Qur'an to appreciate this rhetorical beauty. Usually, when we read the Qur'an, these subtle points escape our notice. We are not familiar with the Qur'an. But, if a person does become familiar with the Qur'an, he becomes attuned to the tone of the Qur'an, he becomes accustomed to the way in which the Qur'an speaks–for example, on the issue I am addressing in today's lecture: That truth comes, falsehood vanishes, truth triumphs and falsehood is defeated. Then, with regard to the creation of the heavens and the earth, he knows that God is the master of the heavens and the earth and that he rules over all quarters of the cosmos. Therefore, he grasps that God must promulgate a law, He must govern, He must direct. Hence, anyone who claims authority and power against the prophets is following falsehood and is doomed to perish. And now, we pray together:

O Lord! By Muhammad and the Family of Muhammad, make us true followers of Muhammad and the Family of Muhammad!

O Lord! By Muhammad and the Family of Muhammad, do not separate us from Muhammad and the Family of Muhammad whether

---

64 Q21:18.

in the life of this world or that of the next, and grant us their kindness and their grace!

O Lord! Make us followers of the Qur'an and those who act upon the Qur'an!

The Responsibility of Belief in Prophethood

Thursday 23rd Ramadan 1394
9th October 1974

وَالَّذِينَ آمَنُوا وَهَاجَرُوا وَجَاهَدُوا فِي سَبِيلِ اللَّهِ وَالَّذِينَ آوَوْا
وَنَصَرُوا أُولَئِكَ هُمُ الْمُؤْمِنُونَ حَقًّا لَهُمْ مَغْفِرَةٌ وَرِزْقٌ كَرِيمٌ
(٧٤)

'Those who have believed, migrated, and waged jihad in the way of God, and those who gave them shelter and help, it is they who are truly the faithful. For them shall be forgiveness and a noble provision.'
Sūrat al-Anfāl (8):74

One of the issues relating to the topic of prophethood that we must discuss, and without which virtually none of the other topics of prophethood will have any practical effect, is the subject of today's lecture. This subject is a guarantee that what we have learnt in the previous lectures will be put into practice. What is it? Every day, we say: 'I bear witness that Muhammad is God's Messenger', we utter this testimony daily in the call to prayer, in the *iqāmah* before prayer, and in the course of our prayer. But what responsibility does this place on my shoulders? Does this belief and testimony of faith create any duties whatsoever for me?

For example, you might say that you believe a daffodil smells nicer than a rose. Some of us might not know which smells nicer. Others might say they believe the opposite to be the case. Equally, you are either correct in your belief that a daffodil's scent is more pleasant, or you are mistaken. In any case, once you have expressed this belief, one might ask: 'So what?' What does it matter? The answer is it doesn't! Whether you believe a daffodil smells nicer or a rose smells nicer, neither of these beliefs will have any effect on how you live your life, because neither of these beliefs create any moral responsibilities by virtue of you holding them!

Let me give you another example, in the Christian world, the head of the Catholic Church is called the Pope. However, even though people respect him, his role is largely symbolic: He does not introduce any new doctrines to Christianity, nor does he promulgate any new rules for Christians to live by that differ from previous rules. In reality, his existence or non-existence is like the existence or non-existence of a beautiful statue in a reception room–if it is there, then the room's decoration is complete, if it is not then people might feel something is missing. The existence or non-existence of the Pope today has a comparable effect on thought in the Christian world. Just imagine if, in the time in which we are living, a Christian learns that the Pope has died and someone else has taken his place, or if he refuses to believe such news–what difference will it make to him whether or not the Pope has changed? If a Christian says that they believe that the Pope today is person X, this belief does not create any moral obligations for them. In other words, his life is no different from that of a Christian who finds himself in some remote part of the world and has still not heard that the Pope has died, and another has replaced him. The state of both men is the same. In other words, the news of the Pope's death does not alter anything–the life of the Christian who learns of the Pope's death is unchanged by this fact. So this is another kind of belief that does not have any discernible practical effect on a person's life.

Now, is the same thing true when we say 'I bear witness that Muhammad is God's Messenger' in the call to prayer of our neighbourhood or town as a public slogan? As a symbol of the general belief of our society? When we say: 'I bear witness that Muhammad is God's Messenger', we are announcing our belief in prophethood. But does this belief place a responsibility on my shoulders, and a responsibility on the shoulders of the society which announces it as a public slogan? Or is it the same as the above two examples of belief? This is the key question!

The answer to this question is: Yes, of course it has an effect! What moral responsibility does it place on the shoulders of those who follow the Prophet and accept his message? Let us summarise this responsibility succinctly as follows: The responsibility or duty that a believer in prophethood undertakes refers to his or her following the path of the Prophet and accepting the responsibility to convey the Prophet's message. It is very easy to say these words–it is much less easy to live up to them, as we can see from the history of the *ummah* which bore witness to the prophetic message.

There are people who imagine that if they say: 'We accept so and so as a prophet of God', that if they give voice to the belief they have in their hearts, their work is done; they have saved themselves from hellfire and won Paradise! Think about this for a moment: Is this belief that I have just explained also in your mind or not? I'm not concerned with who believes this way and who does not. Some people imagine that there were people burning in the fires of God's wrath and displeasure when the prophethood of the Final Messenger came to pass, and some of these people who were being punished called out 'I bear witness that Muhamad is God's Messenger!' and, by the mere utterance of these words, they were brought out of the domain God's punishment and into the domain of His mercy. Now, if they had offered prayers while in this domain of mercy, they would have been a little closer to the source of divine grace. If they fasted, they would have been closer still. If they paid their *khums* and zakat, they would have been even closer than that. If they enjoined the good and forbade evil, they would have been a little closer again. The more good deeds they did, the closer they would have been to the source of divine grace but, even if they did nothing else other than uttering those words, they would still be in the domain of God's mercy. Do you see? Some people think in this manner!

The consequences of this mindset are clear: If someone wrote 'Muslim' or 'follower of the Prophet' on his national identity card–back when they actually wrote these cards by hand, today they are printed–or if someone hands them a form asking them for their religion, they answer: 'Islam'. So, merely by virtue of not writing 'Christianity', 'Judaism', 'atheism', or any other belief system–by mere virtue of ticking the box on the questionnaire that says 'Islam' or putting his finger on the option that says 'Muslim', such a person imagines that he will go to Paradise. Now, if he offered prayers, or observed fasts, or did any other good deeds, this is an added bonus, but even if he doesn't do anything else, his place in Paradise is reserved for him, it is only that while you are waiting for the Day of Resurrection in your grave, the angels will come and press you. This is a common idea and belief that people today hold onto.

But we say that this belief is not correct. Yes, it is necessary to believe in the Prophet, but believing in the Prophet also leads to the existence of certain moral duties. If these duties are fulfilled, then a person's belief is correct to the extent that he fulfils these duties. If a person believes with his tongue, or even with his heart, but does not fulfil any of the duties that this faith places on his shoulders, if he does not follow any of its precepts, if he does not act in accordance with this faith, then even if this person is outwardly a believer, he is not a genuine believer. What will God do with him on the Day of

Resurrection? In all honesty, I don't know–it isn't up to me. However, by the standards of this world, meaning judgement, meaning to the extent that we human beings are able to form a judgement about the faith or moral probity of a person, we do not consider this person to be a believer.

However, allow me to add that even though professing faith secures a person's life and property, in that we take the broad view that such a person is within the community of Islam, that is not what we are talking about here. We are not talking about whether a person's life and property are protected by law, no: We want to see whether or not this person is considered a *believer*. We are looking at the standards that the Qur'an lays down in the verses that we are currently explaining to you. We say that a person who does not fulfil the duties of faith is not a genuine believer. Someone is a believer when they actually follow the moral responsibilities that their belief in prophethood places on their shoulders.

What are these responsibilities and duties? These responsibilities are those things that we see the Prophet wanted to achieve in this world. The Prophet's mission was a tremendous undertaking. He carried a massive burden on his shoulders. He wanted to erect a great edifice. When I look at our own time today, I ask whether this goal that the Prophet wanted to reach–has it been fully achieved? That edifice that the Prophet wanted to build, has it been fully constructed? If I see that the answer to my question is 'no', meaning that the Prophet's burden has been left by the wayside, his mission has not been fulfilled, and that edifice has not been completed, then I should do my utmost to continue his work and achieve his goals. I should try to lift up this burden. And if my limbs are too weak, if I lack the strength, then I should do as much as I can and find ten other people to help me carry this load. I should find more people still to help me erect this edifice. And if I cannot finish this edifice in my lifetime, can I not at least add another row of bricks? Can I not ready its foundations? Can

I not make preparations for others to do the work? If someone says that they cannot do anything at all, this is a lie.

Someone who claims to believe in the Prophet must undertake this duty, because if someone claims to follow the Prophet but does not, they are lying. Their profession of faith in the Prophet of God is a lie. Or, if not a lie, it is merely lip service. I can bear witness that he is the Prophet, but I cannot bear witness to my believing in him as a prophet. This was the case with the hypocrites in his own time: 'When the hypocrites come to you they say, "We bear witness that you are indeed the apostle of God." God knows that you are indeed His Apostle, and God bears witness that the hypocrites are indeed liars.'[65] This is because they do not accept this fact in their hearts, only with their tongues.

The mission of prophethood is to reshape the world according to the teachings of Islam–this is what the prophets came to do. When a prophet comes, he comes to change the world to match the ideas of Islam. This is why the Prophet was sent, to change the form of human life and the structure of human society in accordance with God's instructions. So, if you see at your own time that people are not living in the way God has ordained, you see that mankind has been deprived of a godly society, you see that different schools of thought are pulling mankind this way and that, and Islam has been confined to the recesses of human hearts and minds–in such a situation, your duty and your mission is to act upon your profession of belief in the prophethood of God's Messenger and try to change the world to match the ideas of Islam. This is the prophetic mission.

Islam brought a new idea to mankind and, on the basis of this new idea, brought into being a new social movement, a new cause. We keep coming back to this simple fact when we study the verses of the

65 Q63:1.

Qur'an–religion essentially signifies the creation of a new movement and a new cause.

When people live in a society founded on ignorance and a prophet appears in this society, people are initially all meek and obedient, they are all part of the same social order. But, with the appearance of a prophet, they become divided. As we have said before, the prophets are agents of division! In the sense that the prophets split society into two camps. Pay careful attention to this if you want to repeat it to someone. Don't go and say that so and so said that the Prophet is just a causer of disunity, in the sense that prophets cause conflict and division and that's it. In what sense then? In a sense akin to the way that the carriages of a runaway train are speeding downhill, and a prophet comes and takes hold of the back of these carriages. Some of these carriages detach themselves from the grip of this prophet and continue careering downhill, while others remain in his grasp and slow down. In doing so, the Prophet has divided the wagons–but not in the conventional sense of division!

Another example: A caravan is heading towards an ambush by bandits, or it is heading towards a crumbling precipice. A prophet comes and warns the caravan to turn back; some of the caravan ignore him and press on to their doom, while others listen to him, turn back, and are saved. In this way, two groups are created–division! It is in this sense that the prophets come and cause division in their societies, because these societies were previously united in heading astray, but then a prophet came and caused some to turn back from the wrong path. It is in this way that the Prophet caused division; by coming and telling people to come back to the way of God, some return to God's path and some continued on the road [to perdition]. So, it is in this way that the prophets created a new movement, created controversy, and opened up a new front in society. The Prophet is on one side with one group, while his enemies and opponents are on the other side, in the other. Pay close attention to these two sides of the argument as I describe them. At first, it was only the Prophet by himself on his side, and everyone else was on the other side. Then the Prophet struggled and strived, and, by ones and twos, people joined him until they became a side of their own that could stand up to those who had gone astray, a side that could stand up to those who were in error. Two sides, facing each other–one is the side of the Prophet and the other is the side of his enemies.

What did the Prophet ultimately want? He wanted to take people to Paradise; a Paradise in this world and a Paradise in the world of the afterlife–a Paradise in both worlds. Because he wanted to take people to Paradise, people must go with him. If people do not go with him, they will not reach Paradise. Is that correct? The Prophet wants to bring people to the abode of felicity, but if they do not follow him, they will not reach felicity. Keep this in mind. Now, between these two sides, there is a person. He listens to the Prophet and sees that what he is saying is right. As much as he listens, he sees that what the Prophet says is good. On the other hand, he sees that if he joins the side of the Prophet, then he has no choice but to oppose the other side. He does not want to join the other side, because he sees they are heading towards Hell, but neither does he want to join the side of the Prophet because he can see following the Prophet is hard work! What does he do? He goes between the two sides and finds a safe quiet spot in which to pitch his tent. What sort of person is this? You tell me! Is someone who sits on the fence and looks for an easy life going to reach Paradise or not? It's obvious that he will not, because the Prophet is going to Paradise and anyone who is with him is going there too. This person is not with the Prophet. Anyone who is not with the Prophet is against the Prophet. Anyone who is not with ʿAlī is against ʿAlī. Anyone who is not with the truth is against the truth. This is what the Qur'an tells us. However, Imam ʿAlī makes this very clear for us when he says: 'The one who stays silent is the brother of the one who approves.' Learn this tradition: It is in *Biḥār al-Anwār*, in the volume containing the moral exhortations (*mawāʿiẓ*) of the Imams: 'The one who stays silent is the brother of the one who approves, and whoever is not with us is against us' (*al-sākit akhū l-rāḍī wa man lam yakun maʿanā kāna ʿalaynā*). Notice that he does not say anything about the one who approves, or his action, because it is self-evident what his position is–whoever is pleased with the conduct of a people is one of them! Someone who approves of the way a group or individual acts, is the same as them; he follows the same path as them and will share the same fate as them in the Hereafter. But what about the one who disapproves but stays quiet instead of voicing his disapproval? This statement from Imam ʿAlī indicates that he is the brother of the one who approves. Finally, the Imam says 'and whoever is not with us is against us'–Islam does not acknowledge any middle ground between these two positions.

For example, when the Battle of the Camel took place, the companions of ʿAbd Allāh ibn Masʿūd, such as Rabīʿ ibn Khuthaym (who is supposedly buried in Khurāsān), said: 'We are not prepared to fight alongside the Commander of the Faithful, because he is going to shed the blood of the Muslims.' So, they came and asked him to excuse them from fighting and instead send them to guard the frontiers of Islam. They thought that the battle between these two sides was like the battle between the Persian King Yazdegerd III and the Byzantine Emperor Heraclius–no matter which side won, it would make no difference for people's worldly or religious life! When someone excuses themselves from fighting, this means they do not want to get involved, they do not want to participate in the battle, so they must withdraw to a corner instead. They think that this is a war between different nations, all of whom are fighting one another for power and authority, with each nation pursuing its own interests. What they don't understand is that this is not a war between nations, but a war between truth and falsehood. This is a battle that you can't avoid. They don't understand that in the battle between truth and falsehood, if you are not with truth, then you are with falsehood. Being on the side of falsehood does not necessarily mean you are fighting the truth–if you are not helping the truth, even if you are not fighting against it, your inaction still places you on the side of falsehood. This is what they did not grasp. But the point of prophethood is to make known these two sides, and for the Prophet to say: 'Whoever is with us, then follow me!' As a poet[66] once said:

Said he: 'O people whoever does not follow our path
Should get up and leave our Karbala!'

Those people Ḥusayn ibn ʿAlī met on the road to Karbala who, when Ḥusayn called them to join him, answered: 'O son of God's Messenger! Let me give you this horse or this sword to support your cause', it is clear they were not with him. In fact, they were not only not with him, they were against him! That is why you see our scholars of *ḥadīth* say these people were 'without felicity', because they really did face a sad fate. How unhappy and ill-fated an existence they had. The prophets came to them and showed them the way. The prophets said: 'This is the path. If you are looking for the truth, if you are after God. If you bear witness to our prophethood, then make haste! This is the right way!' But then, they stay sitting where they are! They can see the way, but it looks difficult, so they don't come. It's difficult, so they don't help Ḥusayn. It's difficult, so they look away. They say: 'I couldn't see!' But, at the same time, there is a *tasbīḥ* in their hand. They bear witness to the Prophet's truthfulness without any hesitation. But this sort of bearing witness has no use! Don't just sit there and intone prayers...get up and do something! 'O you who have faith! Why do you say what you do not do? It is greatly outrageous to God that you should say what you do not do!'[67] It is a terrible sin for a person to profess belief, but not act upon it. Why do I claim to be a

66 Nayyer-i Tabrīzī

67 Q61:2–3.

follower of the Prophet when in practice I follow Abū Jahl? Why do I say I am following Islam, when in practice I follow idolatry? Why do I say I follow ʿAlī when in practice I follow Muʿāwiyah?

What was the difference between ʿAlī and Muʿāwiyah? I want you to imagine these two men and their followers facing one another. On one side is someone who, whatever he says, goes against people's ease and personal interest, he puts responsibilities on their shoulders, whatever he wants to do requires effort. He hates lying, is upset by bribery, and rejects any gift with even the hint of a bribe. He is like a lion in God's path. He does not show anyone mercy in God's laws. Even if his own brother comes to him and asks for some money from the public purse, he is ready to place a red-hot piece of iron in his hand. Such a person in the society: severe, precise, concerned with implementing God's laws and rules. On the opposite side is someone completely different: This is someone who lets people pursue a life of pleasure and ease, this is someone who will give people anything they ask for, on one condition: They do not help ʿAlī and they help him instead. He tells them: 'Don't worry, I shall not ask much of you!' Sometimes it is enough for him that they praise him before others. Now, imagine a conflict between these two sides–which would you choose if they were alive right now? Are you prepared to join the side that you know requires effort, struggle, and responsibility? Are you ready to turn your back on the side that offers you wealth, rank, prestige, comfort, influence, and power in exchange for your loyalty? If you are ready, then consider yourself fortunate: Had you been alive at the time of ʿAlī, you would have been one of his supporters. On the other hand, if you feel yourself drawn to the side offering you ease, enjoyment, wealth, rank, status and power, even if you know this side to be wrong, then you should know that, had you been alive at the time of ʿAlī, you would have been one of those people who packed up their things, saddled their horse, and stealthily rode off to Syria to join Muʿāwiyah, abandoning ʿAlī, as many respectable persons at the time did.

ʿAbd Allāh ibn ʿAbbās, the cousin of Imam ʿAlī and of the Prophet, the famous narrator of traditions and commentator on the Qur'an, whom both Shi'a and Sunni Muslims hold in high regard, did just this to ʿAlī. In *Nahj al-BalāghahBalāghah* are two letters and two speeches that the Commander of the Faithful addressed to ʿAbd Allah ibn ʿAbbās. Do you know who this is? This is someone who narrated four traditions from the Prophet, whom both Shi'a and Sunni Muslims accept. He was not actually a Companion of the Prophet, but they still accept him. If he had been a Companion of the Prophet, it would not have made a difference, as there are other companions accepted by both groups: such as Salmān, Abū Dharr, or ʿAmmār. ʿAbd Allāh ibn ʿAbbās was one of the Successors (*tābiʿīn*). He was still a child when the Prophet left this world. When we study history, we see that ʿAbd Allāh ibn ʿAbbās was one of the associates of the second caliph, ʿUmar ibn al-Khaṭṭāb–he was very close to him, in fact. So, he is a Successor rather than a Companion, and both Shi'a and Sunni Muslims accept him. What an interesting character he is! What do we call someone in Islam who when there are two groups fighting with one another, both of these groups accept him? When ʿAbd Allāh ibn ʿAbbās was the governor of Basra, in Iraq, he took all the money in the treasury to Makkah, to the holy sanctuary. Did he take all this wealth there to give it to the poor and needy? Only if you count the sellers of slave girls to be poor and needy! He bought himself several beautiful slave girls with whom to pass his days.

Now, if ʿAbd Allāh ibn ʿAbbās was alive today, what do you think he would say about the Commander of the Faithful? He narrated all of the most important traditions from the Prophet in praise of ʿAlī. He shed tears in ʿAlī's memory! Insofar as he kept company with ʿAlī, he relates many accounts about him. But do we really accept him as a devoted follower of the Commander of the Faithful? No, if he was a true follower of ʿAlī, he would have shown this when he was tested. As a tradition says: 'It is when a man is tested that he is ennobled or abased' and another reads: 'It is in the vicissitudes of life that a man's substance is known.' If you were a follower of ʿAlī, you would not have mistreated ʿAlī so badly! You would not have given him cause for grief by running away when he needed you! You, who were closer to ʿAlī than any other member of his family; you, who ʿAlī trusted above all others; you, who ʿAlī depended upon for support–you were his kith and kin and yet, when the going got tough, you ran! There is a letter in *Nahj al-Balāghah* in which ʿAlī addressed to Ibn ʿAbbās but, because the compiler of *Nahj al-Balāghah*–al-Sharīf al-Raḍī–lived under the rule of the ʿAbbāsid dynasty, instead of titling it 'a letter to ʿAbd Allāh ibn ʿAbbās', he called it 'a letter to one of his governors'–maybe because the ʿAbbāsids would have been angered by this portrayal of their forbear so al-Raḍī would have been scared to mention it this way! If you read this letter, you would clearly see the kind of person that Ibn ʿAbbās was, let alone if you look at other sources. Ultimately, he was the kind of person who abandoned his cousin and his ruler in the time when he needed him most.

So, returning to our main topic, the moral responsibility that is placed on your shoulders by believing in prophethood is this: you have a duty to follow the path of the prophet and accept the duties he gives you–whatever he bids you, you should do!

Time is short, so I will confine myself to explaining a few of the verses relating to the question of what the responsibility is that Islam places on our shoulders:

'Indeed those who have believed and migrated'[68], this is about the time of the Prophet. I do not mean that it has no relevance to other times, as it also contains a general principle, but it relates to the time of the Prophet insofar as it explicitly mentions the issue of emigration

68 Q8:72.

(*hijrah*)–emigration to an Islamic society. In those days there were Muslims who believed in the Prophet and his teachings but were not ready to leave Makkah behind. They said: 'Why should we leave our home? Our businesses are in Makkah, our friends and family are in Makkah–must we leave all this behind to follow the Prophet? Why? Isn't this about belief? I believe! A hundred times I say it in my heart, on my tongue–quietly, so people don't hear! There is only one God, and you are God's messenger! If the Prophet wants me to pray, I will pray. If the Prophet wants me to fast, I will fast for three days, or for six days! But why should I go to Madinah?' This is how some people thought at the time, but emigration was necessary. Islamic society was newly formed, so it needed them to go and strengthen it. They had to protect it from its enemies. That is why emigrating was a necessary condition for faith.

'Indeed those who have believed and migrated and struggled with their possessions and persons in the way of God, and those who gave [them] shelter and help–they are *awliyāʾ* of one another.'[69] These are the true believers, who fit together like bricks in a wall. Go and look at any building, any structure, and see how the bricks fit together, how the beams fit together, how the different parts of the structure cohere together into a single unified whole. The believers are like this in the Islamic society. They are interlinked and joined to one another with unbreakable bonds. This is what the term *awliyāʾ* means. This is what *wilāyat* means: to be bound together with firm unshakeable bonds.

'As for those who have believed'.[70] But what about those who have faith, who believe in their hearts that you are a prophet sent by God–'but did not migrate'–but did not fulfil the duties created by that faith–'you have no duty of protection in relation to them whatsoever until they migrate'–you have no bonds or link with them until they

69 Q8:72.

70 Q8:72.

migrate. As long as they remain over there and do not emigrate, they are like strangers to you. You have no connection or brotherhood in Islam to them whatsoever.

However, there is another rule that applies here. Those who are over there and have not emigrated yet, if another group comes and makes war on them, and they ask for your help, then you must still go and help them. This is because they share your beliefs and are under attack. If a group of Muslims is at war with a group of disbelievers, it is incumbent upon you to help them. Even if those Muslims are not part of your community, not part of your society, and have not yet emigrated to join you, it is still your duty to help them. The exception is if those Muslims are at war with someone with whom you have a peace treaty–in this situation, it is not incumbent upon you to help your co-religionists. So, what does this verse tell us? First of all, it tells us that it is obligatory for us to help Muslims in every part of the world, even if they have not emigrated. Second, it tells us that those Muslims who have not yet emigrated to an Islamic society–of course, no such Islamic society exists in the world today in this sense–and are living in non-Muslim lands, if they are at war with a group of non-Muslims and you have a peace treaty with those non-Muslims, then you are not allowed to go and help your Muslim brothers. Why? Because they have not yet emigrated, because they are not fully your brethren yet, they are not a part of your society. 'Yet if they ask your help for the sake of religion, it is incumbent on you to help them, excepting against a people with whom you have a treaty; and God watches what you do.'[71]

'As for the faithless, they are allies of one another.' Even if they are in two different camps, they are united in their hostility towards you. 'Unless you do the same, there will be strife in the land and great

71 Q8:72.

corruption.'[72] Perhaps what this verse means is that if you are not united, if you do not stand together, if you do not present a united front to the enemies of God, and if you do not realise that whoever is standing between the two sides might as well be on the side of the enemy, then there will be great tribulation and corruption in the land. 'Strife' (*fitnah*) here probably means to be far from religion (*dīn*), while corruption (*fasād*) means the disappearance of God's laws from society.

Pay close attention to the next verse, as it contains some interesting points: 'Those who have believed, migrated, and struggled in the way of God, and those who gave them shelter and help, it is they who are truly the faithful.'[73] Do you see? These are the true believers. As for those who believe but have not emigrated, struggled, or given shelter or help, who are they? They are not true believers: they are false believers. That is the meaning of this verse.

I would also like to briefly touch on some of the verses from *Sūrat Āl ʿImrān*, as these are essential to understanding the core topic of today's lecture: 'Behold! Allah took from His prophets a Covenant: "Certainly you are given of Scriptures and Wisdom, but in time, a Messenger will come to you to sanction what you have got, do then believe in him and give him help."'[74]

In other words, God says he took a pledge from the earlier prophets. So, for example, He said to Moses: Based on what we have given you, if another prophet comes after you and confirms what you have brought, you must believe in that prophet and help him. In other words, Moses must believe in the prophets that come after him, such as Jesus, when they come and confirm what he brought to mankind. Therefore, each prophet must believe in the prophets that come after

72 Q8:73.

73 Q8:74

74 Q3:81.

him when these prophets confirm his teachings, and–more than that–he must help them.

Now, what does it mean to help the prophet? For example, how can Moses help our Prophet? It means that he must tell his people and his companions: 'If it so happens that such and such a prophet appears with such and such a sign, do not oppose him!' This is helping him. 'Said He, "Do you pledge and accept My covenant on this condition?"' God asks these prophets: 'Do you accept this condition? Do you accept this responsibility? Will you take this pledge from your people as well until the Day of Resurrection?' In other words, the followers of Moses gave a pledge to him that they would support the prophets that came after him. What would Moses say to his followers who rejected Jesus and the Prophet of Islam? He would say: 'Shame on you! Whoever believes in Moses, didn't you pledge that until the end of time–because Moses believes in the Final Messenger–you will believe in him too and you will help him?'

Section Four

Authority (Wilāyah)

Introduction to Wilāyah

Friday 24th Ramadan 1394
11th October 1974

يَا أَيُّهَا الَّذِينَ آمَنُوا لَا تَتَّخِذُوا عَدُوِّي وَعَدُوَّكُمْ أَوْلِيَاءَ
تُلْقُونَ إِلَيْهِمْ بِالْمَوَدَّةِ وَقَدْ كَفَرُوا بِمَا جَاءَكُمْ مِنَ الْحَقِّ
يُخْرِجُونَ الرَّسُولَ وَإِيَّاكُمْ أَنْ تُؤْمِنُوا بِاللَّهِ رَبِّكُمْ إِنْ كُنْتُمْ
خَرَجْتُمْ جِهَادًا فِي سَبِيلِي وَابْتِغَاءَ مَرْضَاتِي تُسِرُّونَ إِلَيْهِمْ
بِالْمَوَدَّةِ وَأَنَا أَعْلَمُ بِمَا أَخْفَيْتُمْ وَمَا أَعْلَنْتُمْ وَمَنْ يَفْعَلْهُ مِنْكُمْ
فَقَدْ ضَلَّ سَوَاءَ السَّبِيلِ (١)

"O you who have faith! Do not take My enemy and your enemy for friends, [secretly] offering them affection (for they have certainly defied whatever has come to you of the truth, expelling the Apostle and you, because you have faith in God, your Lord) if you have set out to struggle in My way and to seek My pleasure. You secretly nourish affection for them, while I know well whatever you hide and whatever you disclose, and whoever among you does that has certainly strayed from the right way.'

-Sūrat al-Mumtaḥanah (60):1

The issue I will be discussing today is a topic called *wilāyah*. The topic of *wilāyah* as we will be approaching it, where we extract its meaning from the Qur'an, is not commonly discussed, even though the word *wilāyah* is very familiar to the ears of the Shi'a! In our invocations and supplications to God, in our narrations, in our common beliefs and ideas, the issue of *wilāyah* is treated with the utmost sanctity and reverence, and combined with a longing to preserve something called '*wilāyah*'. As Shi'as, we imagine ourselves to possess this thing called '*wilāyah*', and if we are Shi'a who are a little more precautious in our faith, then we are forever praying to God and imploring him to grant us this *wilāyah*, let us die upon this *wilāyah*, and to give us understanding of *wilāyah*. Therefore, we are very used to hearing this word *wilāyah*.

Now, I want to spend some time discussing this word and its meaning, and looking at where it comes from. We will eventually reach the *wilāyah* of ʿAlī ibn Abī Ṭālib (a), but before we get there, we must first traverse several stages of understanding. I will bring the meaning of *wilāyah* out of the verses of the Qur'an, and you will see what a sophisticated and profound concept it is, and that any society or any community that follows a certain set of ideas or beliefs but lacks this idea of *wilāyah* is ultimately rudderless and adrift. This is what we want to grasp and comprehend.

Through this discussion, you will thoroughly understand why, when someone lacks *wilāyah*, their prayers are not prayers, their fasts are not fasting, and their worship is not worship. You will understand why a society or a nation that is without *wilāyah*, even if it spends the entirety of its existence in prayer, fasting, and charity, will still never receive God's grace or forgiveness. So, to sum up, in the light of this discussion you will gain a proper understanding of the traditions we have about *wilāyah*, including the well-known saying that several scholars have narrated from the Imams (a): 'Even if a man spends his nights in prayer, his days in fasting, all of his wealth in charity, the whole of his life going on Hajj, but does not recognise the *wilāyah* of God's *walī* or take him as his *walī*, then all of his good deeds shall go to waste.'

Now, even though we discuss the topic of *wilāyah* after the topic of prophethood, it is not a separate issue to prophethood. On the contrary, *wilāyah* represents an addendum or annexe to prophethood. In fact, you will see clearly that, if there was no *wilāyah*, the very institution of prophethood would be rendered deficient! For this reason, we will have to recall some of the general points we made in previous lectures on prophethood in order to properly understand *wilāyah*. However, I will also forewarn you that this is a tricky topic to discuss, and it will be difficult to do justice to it. One of the reasons for this is that some weak, illogical, and baseless notions on the subject of *wilāyah* have taken root in ordinary people's minds. Therefore, whenever we talk about *wilāyah* in a way that corresponds to what the Qur'an and the traditions say, it is inevitable that we will encounter one of two problems: Either we will mistake what is said for the notions we have received from other sources, or we will feel that what is being said about *wilāyah* does not correspond to what we imagined it to be. That is why it is difficult. However, with God's help and your efforts, it is my hope that over the course of the next two or three days we can carefully study this matter and develop a proper understanding of *wilāyah* that is grounded in authentic Islamic teachings.

Let us begin by refreshing our memories: Why did the Prophet come? We said that the Prophet came to guide the human being towards perfection, to inculcate people with divine values, and to bring about the fulfilment of the best morals for mankind. We derived this from the *ḥadīth*: 'I was sent to complete the best of morals'–the Prophet came to make human beings; he came to nurture something called *humanity* in people.

Through what means or by what way did the Prophet set about making human beings? How did the Prophet promote *humanity*?

Did he establish a philosophical school of thought? Did he build a temple or place of worship? No! In order to produce human beings, he made a human-making factory! The Prophet was willing to wait ten or twenty years to succeed, but he did not want to produce just one or two, or even twenty human beings, he wanted to create a fully automated factory that would continuously produce perfect human beings who were accepted and liked by the Prophet [because of their worthiness]. Therefore, in order to create human beings and promote the values of humanity, the Prophet used a human-making factory.

But what exactly *is* a human-making factory? It is an Islamic society and system of government. This is the central point that I want to emphasise here. Everyone agrees that the Prophet wanted to make human beings [righteous]. Everyone agrees that the Prophet came to educate and enlighten people. Everyone understands this. But what we need to understand–the detail that is sometimes missed–is that the Prophet did not come to change people one by one through speaking to individuals, nor did the Prophet create a moral or philosophical school of thought in order to produce a crop of students whom he could send to guide people in different parts of the world. The Prophet's mission was much deeper and more fundamental than this. What was his mission? To create a factory that would produce only human beings, and that factory was the Islamic society.

Now, what is an Islamic society? What defines it and makes it what it is? This is another conversation. I will provide a short explanation here but, know that this is just a glimpse at a much fuller discussion. An Islamic society is a society which is ruled by God, and whose laws are the laws of God, where God's ordinances are applied, and where God appoints and removes those in authority, so that, in the pyramid of society–if we imagine society diagrammatically, as some sociologists do–God sits at the top of the pyramid, and beneath God is all of humanity and the humans. The religion of God brings into being the institutions of society, and God's decrees determine foreign policy, social relations, economic policy, government, laws... all aspects of society are determined by God's religion; God's religion is implemented, and God's religion stands behind this system of laws. This is what we mean by an Islamic society.

Where can we see an example of this? In Madinah. The Prophet came and formed a new kind of society in Madinah. Of course, the Muslims had been in Makkah before this, and wherever they were in the world before Madinah, they could worship God as individuals–but this was not enough. They came to Madinah and created a society, and at the head of society it was God who ruled. God's representative ruled over that society–who was this, in practice? It was the Prophet. Who was it that issued the decrees? Who was it that promulgated the laws? Who was it that directed policy? It was the Prophet. Who implemented the laws? Who ensured people followed the laws? It was the Prophet.

In a society where everything is from God, the congregational prayers and the sermon that follows the prayer are no different than the military march played in the war. In the same mosque as the Prophet stood to lead prayers, delivered sermons from the pulpit, and educated and guided people, they would bring the battle standard, and the Prophet would give it to one of his commanders–such as Usāmah ibn Zayd–and tell them to go forth in the name of God to fight such and such a foe, or undertake such and such a mission. It was in the same mosque that the Prophet of God implemented criminal punishments. It was in the same mosque that the Prophet heard legal cases. It was from the same mosque that the Prophet governed society and the economy. It was in the same mosque that taxes were collected and distributed. It was a place of worship, a place of learning, a place for the mustering of troops, a place of government–it was a place which brought together all of the affairs of this world and the Hereafter under the leadership of the Prophet in the House of God. This is what we mean by an Islamic society. All of the prophets came to create precisely such a society. It is through the existence of such a society that human beings are made [righteous]. And even if members of such a society are not perfect human beings, they are still forced to observe basic standards of human decency. Whoever wants to be good can be good in the society of the Prophet, while this is not the case in societies that are not governed by God's guidance.

In non-Islamic and non-religious societies, even the people who want to be good cannot be good. You want to avoid paying or charging interest–you can't. A woman wishes to remain modest because of Islam's values, the social environment pressures her to do the opposite. All of the elements and forces of this society keep people away from God's remembrance. In a non-Islamic society, the images, spectacles, details, comings-and-goings, dealings, and conversations take a person far away from thoughts of God and removes all trace of God from a person's heart. In an Islamic society, the opposite is true. In an Islamic society, markets, mosques, government buildings, friends, family, old and young alike, all foster a mindfulness of God in people, draw people towards God, make them familiar with God, and strengthen their relations with God. An Islamic society produces people who are God's servants and who serve nothing except God. If the Islamic society founded by the Prophet had lasted another fifty years under his leadership or under the leadership of his designated successor, ʿAlī ibn Abī Ṭālib (a), then you can be sure that after fifty years all of the hypocrites (*munāfiqīn*) in this society would have been transformed into true believers. If the rule of the Prophet had been immediately followed by the rule of ʿAlī, that human-making society would have naturally reformed people's characters, changed their hearts, inspired their spirits with faith, and made them know God and faith properly. This is the natural function of an Islamic society. Prophets come in order to make something. When they have made it, it is like a human factory; it does not make Muslims by ones, by tens, or even by hundreds, it makes them in generations. It makes both outward Muslims, who outwardly observe the rules of Islam, and inward Muslims, who are true believers in their hearts. This is the ultimate goal of the prophets.

Previously, I said we want to study *wilāyah* from its foundations. When the Prophet first brought Islamic ideas, when he first began preaching his message, was he able to immediately form a society for himself to govern? Did he not want to create a society? Did he not want to establish social institutions? Did he not want to raise an army to protect this society from its enemies and keep its people safe? Is it not necessary for the Prophet to gather people to help him and spread his message? The answer to all of these questions is 'of course!' but all of this had to be achieved through normal means. In most of their activities, the prophets used the usual means at their disposal. When a prophet comes, in order to be able to create the desired society that will act as a human factory, he must first create a unified group around himself who believe in his mission, who believe in the very depths of their hearts, and who will stand firm and go forth to achieve this goal. Therefore, the first thing a Prophet must do is assemble a group like this. He does so by reciting verses of the Qur'an and through beautiful preaching. 'Invite to the way of your Lord with wisdom and good advice...'.[1] In this way he brings Muslim hearts into being around his person. These constitute a group. In short, the Prophet's first task when he begins his mission, is to bring into existence a group of people, a movement, or a side to oppose the side of disbelief. Who will constitute this movement? The true believers, those whom 'do not pay any heed to reproach when it comes to following the path of God.' These are Muslims of the highest degree.

When a prophet brings such a group or a movement into being, in what kind of society are they living? In a society founded on

1 Q16:125.

ignorance. For example, our Prophet and his first followers were living in the ignorant society of Makkah. Now, if they want this fragile movement called 'Islam' which they brought into being to survive, to endure in that society full of contradictions and hassle–if they want this movement of theirs not to vanish or disappear–then the Prophet must forge his followers together like steel. These Muslims must be so closely connected to one another that nothing can drive them apart. To use a modern term, there must be a strong sense of partisanship amongst these Muslims. To do this, they must be bound together as strongly as possible and they must be kept apart from other movements and other ideas, because they are a minority. When you are a minority, your ideas could be influenced by those of the majority. There is a risk that their behaviour, identity, and character, if brought into contact with that of the rest of society, which might differ from theirs, could disappear as a distinct group. It is because of this pressure that they face that means they must remain united as a group so that, in future, they can bring an Islamic society into being, govern that society, and come to the aid of the Prophet. So, the more closely they are bound to one another, the further they are from other movements.

For example, if there are some climbers taking a difficult route over the mountain, ten people amongst the snow, sticks in their hands, following a narrow and dangerous trail–they must follow this steep and winding path in order to reach the summit of the mountain. In order for them to safely traverse this trail, they must tie themselves to one another with ropes around their waists and move not as individuals but as a group, because if they remain by themselves, there is a risk of falling. That is why they tie themselves firmly together. As well as tying themselves together, they do not take heavy loads with them, nor do they look here and there–they focus on the path in front of them and where they are putting their feet. They tie themselves together with rope around their waists so that if one or two members of their party slip, the others can pull them to safety. The way in which these mountain climbers are tightly bound to one another is a perfect representation of how the early Muslims had to be bound to one another in their mission. Is there a name for this kind of close bond or not? This bond that existed between the members of the Muslim movement at the advent of Islam, who were so closely bound to one another that they could not be separated, who completely isolated themselves from other movements, who held fast to one another as tightly as they could–is there a name for this in the Qur'an and traditions? Indeed there is! That name is *wilāyah*.

Now, there is a long way to go from here to the *wilāyah* of ʿAlī ibn Abī Ṭālib (a) or 'the *wilāyah* of ʿAlī ibn Abī Ṭālib is my protection'. There is another hour or two of discussion before we reach that–we are not there yet, so pay close attention.

So what is the original meaning of *wilāyah* that we find in the Qur'an? The original sense in which the Qur'an uses this word *wilāyah* means for a group of people to be bound to one another, to be part of the same movement, to be on the same side, because they share a common idea, are pursuing a common goal, and following a single path. They are striving for a single purpose, on the basis of a single idea and a single worldview. The more closely bound together the members of this movement are, the further they must keep themselves from other movements and other poles in society. Why? So that their movement survives. This is what the Qur'an calls *wilāyah*.

At the outset of his mission, the Prophet created a group of followers who were bound together in exactly this manner. They were joined to one another, they were brothers to one another, they moved as a single caravan. It was through them that the Muslim *Ummah* came into being, that an Islamic society came into being. They avoided becoming joined to the enemies of the Prophet, his opponents, his rejectors, and with other groups, as we will see in the verses we discuss in the next lecture. They kept themselves apart from other movements in society, whether Jews, Christians, or idolaters, and they did everything they could to strengthen their ranks. Why? Because if they were not like this, if they did not have *wilāyah*, if they were not one-hundred-percent committed to one another, then disagreements would have emerged between them and they would not have been able to carry out the important mission with which they had been charged. They would not have been able to reach their destination.

However, later, when the Islamic society had grown into a great nation, *wilāyah* was still necessary. Now, as for what *wilāyah* means on such a grand scale and why it is necessary, I will explain this when we come to discuss the concept of *wilāyah* in the sense it is used by the Shi'a today. We said that a small group of believers came into being in a world of darkness and ignorance, and that they must be tightly bound to one another if they are to have any hope of surviving. If they are not united, if they do not walk hand in hand, then the movement they have created will not last. We gave an example of the state of the Muslims at the advent of Islam in Makkah, or in the very earliest days of the existence of an Islamic society in Madinah.

Is there another situation where this also applies? Yes! When is that? When there is a small group of Shi'a during the era of the anti-Shi'a and anti-Islamic caliphates in the early period of Islamic history. Do you think the Shi'a could easily survive under such regimes? Do you think that the propaganda war on the one hand, the suppression and repression on the other, and the imprisonment, torture, and execution on the other, left much room for the Shi'a to survive in society? A movement like the Shi'a, who were so implacably opposed to the powers that be and a constant thorn in their side, how could they survive this? Because of *wilāyah*. It was *wilāyah* that enabled them to survive. It was because of their remarkable unity and bonds of faith that they were able to endure under the oppressive yoke of the so-called caliphates. This *wilāyah* was fostered by the Imams (as) in order to preserve the Shi'a movement in a hostile environment in which there were many other such movements.

Imagine a great river into which numerous tributaries flow. The waters move quickly. Their surface is choppy and uneven. There are whirlpools, rapids, and all manner of currents pulling this way and that, competing with one another as the waters churn. Amongst all of these different currents with their muddied, turbid, dirty waters, is a current whose water is clear, clean, and sparkling that follows its own path in the vast and heaving river. You can sometimes see currents like this in some rivers and seas; the waters are of two different colours, two different kinds, right next to one another without mixing. This is, of course, due to natural causes, which we will not explain here. So, amidst the vast and fast-flowing waters of this river, there is a current which takes its own path and, strangely, never mixes with the others, its colour never changes, its flavour never changes, becoming bitter, but always remains sweet, its waters are always clear and pure, without turbidity. And it goes on.

Now, the Islamic world under the rule of the Umayyads and 'Abbasids was exactly like this river, in that it was filled with all manner of intellectual and political movements that were competing with one another and mixing together. However, from the beginning until the end, you see that the Shi'a movement, exactly like the pure current in the river, moved between the heaving waters. It may have seemed small or insignificant, but it was there, never mixing with the others, never changing its colour, never changing its taste, never losing its purity, never becoming like the other waters. What was it that kept it this way? What element ensured the survival of Shi'ism during these times? The existence of that *walī* who enjoined people and his followers to have *wilāyah* amongst themselves, who enjoined them to be united, who enjoined them to be kind to one another, who spread *wilāyah* amongst them. This is the same kind of *wilāyah* that existed at the time of the Prophet. This is the Shi'i *wilāyah*, the *wilāyah* whose importance everyone emphasises. This is one dimension of it. There are other dimensions too, which we will come to. Here, we are only discussing one aspect of *wilāyah*–there are still more to come. This is *wilāyah* in the sense of being joined to one another.

The Qur'an describes the faithful as guardians (*awliyā'*) of one another. Those people who are of true faith, who share the same orientation, who are bound to one another, and who are called 'Shi'a'. The word 'Shi'a' is used in the narrations to signify a true believer. If you look at the words of the early scholars and in many narrations, there are conditions mentioned for attaining certain spiritual ranks in Islam. For example, they say that there is Islam, and after Islam comes faith (*īmān*). You might be wondering: 'What is faith?' The meaning of faith means having the particular Shi'a mindset. It means to understand Islam from a Shi'a point of view, and to follow the logic of Shi'ism. This is the meaning of faith. We can see that at the time of the Imams (a), the Shi'a were united and joined together as brethren in faith. It is by this means that they were able to preserve the Shi'a movement throughout history. Were this not the case, Shi'ism would have disappeared a thousand times before today, its ideas would have vanished a thousand times before today. It would have been no different to any other sect which has long since faded from the pages of history.

In any case, this is one of the aspects of *wilāyah*. Tomorrow, God willing, we will deal with another that is perhaps even more important than what we discussed today–and that is the *wilāyah* of God's *walī*. The *wilāyah* of the Shi'a between themselves is now known, but what does the *wilāyah* of God's *walī* mean? What does the *wilāyah* of 'Alī ibn Abī Ṭālib mean? What does the *wilāyah* of Imam al-Ṣādiq mean? If you and I are supposed to have *wilāyah* for the Imams today, what does that mean? Some imagine that the *wilāyah* of the Imams simply means that we should love the Imams–what a big mistake this is! How far off the mark! *Wilāyah* is more than just loving the Imams, otherwise do you think you can find anyone in the Muslim world who didn't love the Imams of the Prophet's family? So, does everyone have *wilāyah* then? Is there anyone who is their enemy? Do you think everyone who fought them at the advent of Islam hated them? Many of those fighting against them loved them, but they their love for this world made them ready to fight them. There were many who knew how important the Imams were and recognised their great spiritual status. When the Abbasid caliph al-Manṣūr learned of Imam al-Sadiq's death, al-Manṣūr began to weep! Was this just an act? Who was he acting for? Do you think he was making a show of weeping for the sake of his servants? Do you think he was making a show of weeping for his chamberlain, Rabīʿ? This was not an act, al-Manṣūr was truly grieved by the death of Imam al-Ṣādiq–he was genuinely distressed! But who was it that killed him? None other than al-Manṣūr! It was al-Manṣūr who gave the order to poison Imam al-Ṣādiq. But when he learnt that Imam al-Ṣādiq had died as a result, his heart broke. Does this mean that even al-Manṣūr had *wilāyah*?

The same sort of mistake is made by those who claim that the caliph al-Maʾmūn was Shiʿa. What does it mean to be a Shiʿa? Does being a Shiʿa simply mean knowing that Imam al-Riḍā was right? Is that all? If that's all it takes to be a Shiʿa then al-Maʾmūn was a Shiʿa, and so was his father Hārūn al-Rashīd, and al-Manṣūr, and even Muʿāwiyah and Yazīd. In fact, they would be more Shiʿa than anyone else if that were the case! Were ʿAlī's rivals at the meeting of Saqīfah not aware that he was right? They all knew he was right! So were they Shiʿa too? Didn't those who fought the Commander of the Faithful also love him? Of course, they did! So were they Shiʿa? Did they have *wilāyah*? Definitely not–*wilāyah* is something else entirely. *Wilāyah* is more than this. It is only once we know what the *wilāyah* of ʿAlī ibn Abi Ṭālib and the Imams means that we have the right to look at ourselves and ask whether or not we meet the criteria of *wilāyah*!

Then, if we see that we do not, we should ask God to help us obtain the *wilāyah* of the Imams and do our utmost to gain it!

Now, there are some people who are very pleased with themselves. They imagine that they truly have the *wilāyah* of the Imams purely by loving them. Purely by believing in them. They think this is all it takes to have *wilāyah*. But this is not *wilāyah*. *Wilāyah* is something more than this, as we shall see tomorrow. Tomorrow we will see what it really means to have the *wilāyah* of the Imams: How can we recognise the Imams as our *walī* and hold fast to their *wilāyah*? That is when we will see how different the reality of *wilāyah* is from what some people claim!

Whenever ʿĪd al-Ghadīr comes around, it is customary for people to say: 'Praise be to God, who made us of those who hold fast to the *wilāyah* of ʿAlī ibn Abī Ṭālib (a)' (*al-ḥamdu lillāhi-l-ladhī jaʿalanā min al-mutamassikīn-a bi wilāyat-i ʿAlī ibn Abī Ṭālib*). However, it would be better to avoid saying 'Praise be to God, who made us', as we might be untruthful! Better to say: 'O God, make us of those who hold fast to the *wilāyah* of ʿAlī ibn Abī Ṭālib (a)!' (*allāhumma-jʿalnā min al-mutamassikīn-a bi wilāyat-i ʿAlī ibn Abī Ṭālib*). Let us see whether or not we qualify. This is another topic we will discuss, and it is yet another dimension of *wilāyah*. What I have said today can be summed up as follows: The *wilāyah* of the Muslim *ummah* and the *wilāyah* of that group that is striving in the path of God and for the sake of God means that there should be strong bonds of brotherhood between the members of this movement. The closer the hearts of these people can be to one another, and the further they are from other poles of attraction, and from those who believe differently to them and struggle against them. This is the meaning of *wilāyah* in this context.

The verses of *Sūrat al-Mumtaḥanah* clearly illustrate this point, as I shall now explain:

'In the Name of God, the All-beneficent, the All-merciful. O you who have faith! Do not take My enemy and your enemy for allies (*awliyāʾ*)'.[2] Some explain the verse as follows: 'You should not take the disbelievers, who are My enemy and yours, as helpers.' This is very close to the meaning I have in mind for this verse. Others say it means: 'You should not take My enemy and your enemy as friends'. However, this meaning is not complete. This verse is not only about friendship and affection, it is more than that: Do not take them as your *walī*, in other words do not think of them as being on the same side as you. Do not place yourself in the same line as them; in other words, in your heart, do not suppose you and they are on the same path. They are your enemy and God's enemy. Do not think they are with you–see them as opposed to you and the opposite of you.

'[Secretly] offering them affection (for they have certainly defied whatever has come to you of the truth)'. You know that they reject the truth that has come to you from your Lord, '(expelling the Apostle and you, because you have faith in God, your Lord) if you have set out for jihad in My way and to seek My pleasure.' If you are truthfully striving for my sake, you have no right to take my enemies as allies.

This chapter of the Qur'an is incredibly important and interesting. As we read the next few lines, it will become clear what God means. God does not mean that you should not be friends with any of the disbelievers. God does not say you should cut off all of your relations with the disbelievers. No, He makes clear which groups of the disbelievers this applies to. God divides the disbelievers into different groups–if we have time in the next lecture, I will explain these to you.

God says next in this chapter: 'You secretly nourish affection for them, while I know well whatever you hide and whatever you disclose, and whoever among you does that has certainly strayed from the right way.' Whoever knowingly takes the enemies of God as friends and protectors has surely gone astray and left behind the middle path!

---

2 Q60:1.

Then, in order that the Muslims will be rationally convinced as to why they should cut their ties with these disbelievers. God describes them. It is worth noting that the original context of this verse's revelation was concerning Ḥāṭib ibn Abī Baltaʿah. Ḥāṭib was a Muslim of somewhat weak faith. When the Prophet wanted to go to war against the idolaters of the Quraysh, Ḥāṭib was worried that the Prophet might be defeated, and that some harm might come to his relatives in Makkah if this were the case. So, he decides to be clever. He goes with the Prophet to fight by his side and earn God's pleasure, but at the same time he writes a letter to the Quraysh showing his friendship towards them. What's the matter with this? It's not like he's going to help them if he meets them in battle, so what's wrong with writing a letter to the Quraysh to hedge against the Prophet's defeat in battle? He can have the best of both situations in this way!

So Ḥāṭib wrote a letter to the leaders of the Quraysh, in which he made himself known to them and reached out to them in friendship. He gave this letter to a woman, and the woman concealed the letter in her clothes, and set out for the Quraysh.

However, the Prophet became aware of this through God's revelation. So he sent the Commander of the Faithful and one or two trusted persons after the woman. They intercepted her, pressed her into surrendering the letter, and returned to the Prophet. Now the Prophet asked Ḥāṭib: 'Why did you do this? Why did you divulge our movements and strategy to our enemies?' He replied: 'O Prophet of God! I have friends and family there, and I was worried they might come to harm. So, I wrote a letter to the Quraysh in the hope of softening their attitude towards me!' This verse gives a clear response: 'Don't make a mistake! Their hearts will not be softened towards you! Those who believe the opposite to you, those for whom your beliefs and your faith are detrimental to their interests, those who want to destroy your religion and your faith, they will never be your friend!'

The next verse explains this further: 'If they were to confront you they would be your enemies'.[3]

O Ḥāṭib, you fool! Do not imagine that just because you help them now, tomorrow they will help you–no, by God! The more you help them, the more power they gain over you. The more you help them, the better they can oppress you and do you wrong. 'They would be your enemies, and would stretch out against you their hands and [unleash] their tongues with evil [intentions]'. They will stretch out their hands to put you under more pressure. They will turn their tongues towards you with evil. They will abase and humiliate you. They will not see you as a person, let alone an equal! So if you're helping them now, do not think that this will be of any benefit to you 'and they are eager that you [too] should be faithless.' When they gain power over you, they won't allow you even a grain of faith in your heart, they will want to bring you back to disbelief. Do not think that they will leave you free to practice your faith or to follow its teachings.

The next verse contains a definitive statement about Ḥāṭib's people and family, and the peoples and families of all the Ḥāṭibs of human history. For the sake of your children, for the sake of your people and kin, for the sake of your noble-born, for the sake of giving your relatives an easy life, you are ready to befriend the enemies of God? In order to win the friendship of God's weak servants and gain some short-term benefit for yourself and your family, you are ready to abandon God's commands? How much do these family ties actually benefit a person? You do this for the sake of this young man, for the sake of his job, for the sake of his salary, for the sake of his earning a living amongst the disbelievers of the Quraysh. How much benefit will this be to you? How much of God's punishment will this save you from? You fool!

---

3 Q60:2.

Ḥātib is willing to collaborate with the enemies of the Prophet to keep his family and relatives in Makkah safe from harm! How much use will these kin be for him against God's wrath and punishment? 'Your relatives and your children will not avail you on the Day of Resurrection: He will separate you [from one another].'[4] As God says elsewhere: 'the day when a man will evade his brother, his mother and his father, his spouse and his sons'.[5] In other words, the same child you are so worried for today, you will flee from on the Day of Judgement, and both of you will flee from everyone else, you will not have the time for one another, you will not have any concern for one another–'that day each of them will have a task to keep him preoccupied.' On the Day of Judgement, each person will be so worried about his own predicament that he will not give any thought to the predicament of others, not even of his own children. Today, if a thorn pricked your child's hand, you would give anything in the world to make them feel better, wouldn't you? And yet on the Day of Resurrection you will flee from them! If we can grasp the logic of the Qur'an in this regard, we would understand that those people who are ready to give up this world and the next for the sake of their children, who are willing to suffer for all eternity for the sake of their children, if they understood the logic of the Qur'an here, they might be shaken. This child, this daughter, this son, this little darling that is leading you towards Hell, while you are not willing to let the slightest harm come to them and are willing to suffer anything for their sake, to what extent will this child help you in the next life? Will this child carry any of your burdens on the Day of Resurrection? No! God says: 'Your relatives and your children will not avail you on the Day of Resurrection: He will separate you [from one another], and God watches what you do.'

---

4 Q60:3.

5 80:34–37.

'There is certainly a good exemplar for you in Abraham and those who were with him'.[6] This verse is the climax of what we have read so far. God tells the faithful: Look at what Abraham and his companions did, and you do the same! What did they do? They took a clear stand against the people who had gone astray in their own time, disassociated themselves from the servants of false gods and idols of their own time: 'when they said to their own people, "Indeed we repudiate you and whatever you worship besides God. We disavow you, and between you and us there has appeared enmity and hate for ever, unless you come to have faith in God alone"'. Until you come over to our way of thinking. Here, God tells the faithful to adopt the same approach as Abraham:

'There is certainly a good exemplar for you in Abraham and those who were with him, when they said to their own people, "Indeed we repudiate you and whatever you worship besides God. We disavow you, and between you and us there has appeared enmity and hate for ever, unless you come to have faith in God alone"'.

Then the Qur'an says: 'There is certainly a good exemplar for you in them–for those who look forward to God and the Last Day–and anyone who refuses to comply [should know that] indeed God is the All-sufficient, the All-laudable.'[7] So if you collaborate with the enemy and forsake your humanity and give up dignity, you should know that God does not suffer any loss from this. We should remember these words that Abraham and his followers said to the disbelievers of their own time: 'Indeed we repudiate you'.

Imam Sajjād and his followers dealt with the misguided people of their own time in the same way. There is a tradition in *Biḥār al-Anwār* which says that Yaḥyā ibn Umm Ṭawīl, a disciple of the Fourth Imam, would go to the Mosque of Madinah and stand up in

6 Q60:4.

7 Q60:6.

front of the people. The people amongst whom Imam Ḥusayn and Imam Ḥasan had lived amongst for twenty years. People who were neither Umayyads nor pro-Umayyad in their views. So what were they? They were cowards who, even though they believed in the Prophet's Household, abandoned them during the events of ʿĀshūrāʾ and Karbalāʾ out of fear of Umayyad persecution.

Yaḥyā ibn Umm Ṭawīl stood up in front of the people and uttered the following verse of the Qur'an: 'We disavow you, and between you and us there has appeared enmity and hate for ever'! In other words, the same words that Abraham spoke to the disbelievers, idolaters, and misguided people of his time, Yaḥyā spoke to the people of his own time. See how this is the same *wilāyah* in both cases? Abraham and his followers had *wilāyah*, and the followers of Imam Sajjād at their own time had *wilāyah*. If one of Imam Sajjād's followers, whether out of fear or greed, went over to the other side, he would have gone out from the *wilāyah* of Imam Sajjād and would not be counted as being on the side of the Imam! That is why Imam Sajjād's disciple, Yaḥyā, one of his closest and most-excellent disciples, would utter these following words to them: 'We disavow you, and between you and us there has appeared enmity and hate for ever'!

The fate of this righteous believer was that the Umayyad governor, Ḥajjāj ibn Yūsuf, took him and chopped off his right hand, then his left hand, then his right foot, then his left foot. However, Yaḥyā would not stop preaching, so Ḥajjāj cut out his tongue and he died. And this was at a time when he had organised the Shiʿa and had established the main cornerstones of the edifice of Shi'ism after the time of Imam Sajjād.

Relations of the Ummah

Saturday 25th Ramadan 1394
12th October 1974

يَا أَيُّهَا الَّذِينَ آمَنُوا لَا تَتَّخِذُوا الْيَهُودَ وَالنَّصَارَى أَوْلِيَاءَ بَعْضُهُمْ أَوْلِيَاءُ بَعْضٍ وَمَنْ يَتَوَلَّهُمْ مِنْكُمْ فَإِنَّهُ مِنْهُمْ إِنَّ اللَّهَ لَا يَهْدِي الْقَوْمَ الظَّالِمِينَ (٥١) فَتَرَى الَّذِينَ فِي قُلُوبِهِمْ مَرَضٌ يُسَارِعُونَ فِيهِمْ يَقُولُونَ نَخْشَى أَنْ تُصِيبَنَا دَائِرَةٌ فَعَسَى اللَّهُ أَنْ يَأْتِيَ بِالْفَتْحِ أَوْ أَمْرٍ مِنْ عِنْدِهِ فَيُصْبِحُوا عَلَى مَا أَسَرُّوا فِي أَنْفُسِهِمْ نَادِمِينَ (٥٢)

'O you who have faith! Do not take the Jews and the Christians for allies: they are allies of each other. Any of you who allies with them is indeed one of them. Indeed, God does not guide the wrongdoing lot. Yet you see those in whose hearts is a sickness rushing to them, saying, "We fear lest a turn of fortune should visit us." Maybe God will bring about a victory or a command from Him, and then they will be regretful for what they kept secret in their hearts.'
Sūrat al-Mā'idah (5):51–52

Allow me to speak succinctly, even though there is much that requires further discussion–of course, I will go into detail as much as I think is necessary–so that we can explain this topic properly in the next day or two. In short, we are looking at what is necessary about *wilāyah* for our day and age, namely if we want to create an Islamic society or a community called 'the Islamic *Ummah*'–meaning that we want to govern this society in accordance with the divine decrees, divine thought processes and divine legislation, and implement these laws and decrees through God's power. This society, which we call the Islamic *Ummah* must have *wilāyah*, in the sense that we extracted from the Qur'an yesterday and that we will continue to explore the proper meaning of this term gradually through these lectures. We are not interested in the idea that most ordinary people have about *wilāyah*. We are interested in *wilāyah* as understood by the scholars and sages who are familiar with the teachings of Islam and Shi'ism. That is what we are going to discuss shortly. However, right now, we are talking about the Qur'anic concept of *wilāyah*. If we want to grasp the Qur'anic notion of *wilāyah*, and secure for the Islamic *Ummah* this notion of *wilāyah* as it is laid out in the verses of the Qur'an, then we must pay attention to two aspects in particular. One aspect is that of internal relations within the Islamic society. The other aspect is that of external relations, or the relation of the Islamic world, the Islamic society, and the Islamic *Ummah* with other societies.

With regard to internal relations, when the Islamic *Ummah* has *wilāyah* in the sense laid out by the Qur'an, this means that they are joined to one another and united together to the greatest extent possible, encompassing all individuals and wings of the community. In other words, there should be no division or disagreement anywhere within the great Islamic *Ummah*. There should be a single, cohesive whole.

In the event that war breaks out between two parts of the Islamic *Ummah*, for example let us imagine that a war breaks out between a group in the eastern Islamic lands with a group in the north-east, then the general principle is as follows: The remainder of the Muslims must do everything in their power in order to bring about peace between the two groups. If they see that of these two groups, one is willing to make peace and the other is not, or that the position of one side is unjust while the position of the other side is right, and those on the side of wrong are not willing to listen to the side of right, then in this situation the entirety of the Muslim world must be united in taking action against the side which is unjust and putting them in their place.

The Qur'an says: 'If two groups of the faithful fight one another, make peace between them. But if one party of them aggresses against the other, fight the one which aggresses until it returns to God's ordinance.'[8] This is what God has decreed with regards to maintaining unity amongst the Muslims.

As for external relations, the Islamic world must try to organise its relations with the non-Islamic world and the world that is not part of this *Ummah* so that it does not even fractionally fall under the latter's control, or even fractionally fall under the influence of its ideas. In short, it must pursue a policy of independence, and it cannot achieve independence under the influence of the latter's policies. Muslim nations should not be allowed to pursue unity or cooperation with those nations if this leads the Muslim *Ummah* to fall under their influence and control.

There is a famous story on this topic. I will not go into the full details here, but there is a narration mentioned in the reliable books of Shiʿa traditions. This story dates to the time of Imam al-Bāqir (a) or Imam al-Ṣādiq (a), when the Muslim world typically used Roman coinage. The Romans threatened to cut-off this supply of coins, and the Muslims were left helpless. At this point, the Imam advised the Caliph to do something. This is a very strange event, an exceptional situation that only occurs once or twice in history, where we see the Imams (a) helping the Caliphate! This is one such event. The Imam advised the Caliph to strike his own coins. Now, the Muslims did not

8 Q49:9.

know how to mint their own coins, what dimensions or weight they had to be, where or how to obtain the precious metals to make them, for example whether to mint one dirham, half a dirham, and so on. The Imam instructed them in all of this.

Therefore, from the perspective of external relations, it is forbidden to even come fractionally under the influence of non-Islamic–and especially anti-Islamic–powers. The Islamic society and the Muslim *Ummah* do not have the right to form relations with the non-Islamic world except from a position of strength and superiority. In other words, the connection between the Muslim *Ummah* and a non-Muslim nation should never be based on exploitation, as for example we saw with the Tobacco Monopoly in Qajarid Iran. The Islamic world has no right to form such agreements. Or, for example, as the Mughals did in India, where they allowed foreign powers to come and create companies, which then were able to act against the *wilāyah* of the Muslim world. They should not have allowed such companies to come–whether they knew what would happen or not, and they should have known–like the British East India Company who, when they came to India, what devastation they wrought on the region and its peoples. Their heinous activities ultimately culminated in the establishment of British colonial power in the Indian Subcontinent. The Mughals should have known better, but they did not. The Muslim world must never again allow such relations to form.

Pay close attention here. When I say that these sorts of relations with non-Muslim and non-Islamic nations need to be severed, I do not mean that the Muslim world needs to withdraw from the rest of mankind. No, this is not a question of political isolation, such that you might imagine the Muslim world has no trading, political, or diplomatic relations with other nations–no, this is not what I mean. There should be normal relations. What this means is that there should not be *wilāyah* with them, there should not be unity with them. There should not be an essential connection with them.

It should not be such that they are able, should they wish, to spread their influence through the Muslim world.

Hence, *wilāyah* has two aspects from the Qur'anic perspective: The interior aspect, which pertains to relations within Islamic society, whereby every element of that society must be directed towards a single goal, follow a single path, and move with one step. Then, the exterior aspect, which pertains to relations with other societies, whereby the Muslim world does not allow itself to fall under the influence of any non-Islamic block or movement.

Here, there is a subtle point to be made, namely that *wilāyah*, in the sense it is used in the Qur'an, is the same sense as we Shi'a use it. Pay close attention to my explanation of this so that you grasp how the Shi'a concept of *wilāyah* relates to the Qur'anic concept of *wilāyah*. It is possible that a few people, or a previous generation, were ready to blindly accept some of the things they heard about *wilāyah*. However, a young person who wants to understand the meaning of this term and how it derives from the Qur'an must pay close attention to understand from whence *wilāyah* in the Shi'a sense originated.

When we say that our relationship with the Imam is so important, when we say that the Imam has the right to direct all aspects of our social life, why is this? Where does this come from? This is what the Qur'an says to us: If we want to create a society or a nation, in which the Qur'anic notion of *wilāyah* exists, in the sense that we want all of the internal capabilities of that society to be directed towards a single purpose and a single goal, and we want that society to follow a single path, and for all of its strength to be mobilised against the external anti-Islamic powers, then there must be a point in the fabric of that society in which those powers are concentrated, a point to which all of these powers are connected, from which all of these powers take inspiration and direction, a point which is aware of the best interests of the society, and which, like a powerful and farsighted commander, can issue orders to each individual on the battlefront. There must be a leader, a commander, a central power in Islamic society who knows how its strength must be directed, who knows what each person must do, and can issue instructions to them accordingly.

For example, look at carpet weavers. A group of them sit down to produce a carpet. Everyone who is there working on this carpet, whether young or old, weaves the carpet all day long for a couple of *tūmān*s. Each of them works hard as an individual, but if their work was not coordinated by someone in charge–if there wasn't someone supervising and planning how they should weave, guiding their work in line with the plan for the carpet, so that each of them knows which thread must go where–then how will this carpet turn out? It won't be remotely symmetrical; the right side will look one way and the left side will look another! One side will be Turkoman and the other will be Kurdish! When there is no plan and no guidance, the result will be something worthy of mockery.

When you look at a well-made carpet, you see that all of the threads have been laid out according to a precise pattern, without any excess or deficiency. What ensures that this is the result? First, having a plan, second having a foreman in charge of the work and telling them how to do their job. And this can't be just anybody; I don't know how to direct the work, even a carpet seller doesn't necessarily know how the carpet is made–someone who understands carpet weaving must be in charge.

Now, if we want all of society's resources and energies to be directed towards a particular task or goal, so that none of them go to waste and all of the forces of society come together like a single fist to safeguard the best interests of mankind, then there must be a central power. There must be a heart for the body of the Muslim *Ummah*. However, there are conditions for this heart. This heart must be very aware, it must be very knowledgeable, it must be very resolute, it must look at the world in a particular way, it must not be afraid of anything in the way of God, it must be willing to sacrifice itself if necessary. Now, what name do we give to this heart? We call it the Imam.

An Imam is the ruler and leader appointed by God to govern human society. What do I mean when I say this person is appointed by God? It means that God has appointed him either by name or by the qualifications that they should possess. Appointing by name such as appointing Imam ʿAlī (a), the Commander of the Faithful, such as appointing Imam Ḥasan (a), Imam Ḥusayn (a) and the rest of the Imams. The Prophet was himself an Imam, as God says in the Qur'an to Abraham: 'I am making you the Imam of mankind.'[9] The Imam is the ruler and leader of a society.

So, sometimes God appoints this leader for society by name. For example, He says that after the Prophet, the leader of the Muslims should be ʿAlī ibn Abī Ṭālib (a). Sometimes, however, God does not specify the Imam by name. Instead, he describes the qualifications he must possess. This is like the words of Imam al-ʿAskarī (a), who said: 'As for those of the learned who protect themselves from sin, preserve their religion, turn away from their desires, and obey the command of their Lord, the ordinary folk may follow them.' Here, the Imam says that people with these qualities are also Imams. That jurist, who is the successor of the divinely appointed Imam, is also an Imam in his own right. He is an Imam, but he was not appointed by name. He was appointed by his qualifications. Therefore, anyone who meets these requirements is also an Imam. Now, let me explain what the word 'Imam' means. 'Imam' literally means a leader, it means a ruler, it means someone who is in control, it means a person that wherever he goes, people follow. An Imam is a leader who must be appointed by God, who must be just, who must be fair, who must be pious, who must be resolute, and so on, in accordance with the

9 Q2:124.

criteria laid down in discussions of the Imamate, which are not our concern at present.

So what is it that the Qur'anic principle of *wilāyah* necessitates? The existence of an Imam. However, this is not the end of the story–pay close attention! If this great body, which is the Muslim *Ummah*, is going to live, if it is going to be successful, if it is going to be strong, what must it do? It must make its connection to this centre, to this heart, to this motor, to this lifeforce strong and lasting. Therefore, what does *wilāyah* mean? Think about this! *Wilāyah* means a strong connection between the individual members of the *Ummah*, in whatever circumstances they find themselves, with this heart. What kind of connection is this? A theoretical and a practical connection. In other words, it means following his example, it means following his ideas and his viewpoints, it means following his actions and behaviour.

If this is the case, then what does the *wilāyah* of ʿAlī ibn Abī Ṭālib mean? It means to follow ʿAlī in your thoughts. It means to follow ʿAlī in your actions. It means to have a firm and unshakeable bond with ʿAlī, so that you will never be apart from ʿAlī. This is the meaning of *wilāyah*. So, now do you see why *wilāyah* is so important? On this basis, we can properly understand the saying of God: 'The *wilāyah* of ʿAlī ibn Abī Ṭalib is my fortress, so whoever enters my fortress is protected from my punishment.' This is a very profound statement! What does it mean? It means that the Muslims, the followers of the Qur'an, if both in terms of their thoughts and ideas, and in terms of the actions and behaviour, are connected to ʿAlī ibn Abī Ṭalib, then they are safe from God's punishment! Is it anything other than this? Is there any other way of understanding this? If ʿAlī ibn Abī Ṭalib was known today and, once he was known, I model my behaviour on his, then I have found his *wilāyah*. This is the meaning of *wilāyah*.

Now if someone says that we cannot understand the Qur'an by ourselves–God forbid!–then how can he claim that he has the *wilāyah* of ʿAlī ibn Abī Ṭālib, or that his ideas are connected to those of ʿAlī, when it was ʿAlī who said in *Nahj al-Balāghah*: 'And know that this Qur'an is the advisor who never deceives, the guide who never leads astray, and the speaker who never lies. And know that no one sits down with this Qur'an save that he rises with an increase or a decrease; an increase in guidance or a decrease in blindness.'[10] This is how the Commander of the Faithful introduces the Qur'an to people, and this is how he encourages people to read the Qur'an. So, does someone who says we cannot understand the Qur'an really have the *wilāyah* of ʿAlī ibn Abī Ṭālib? Never! For it is this same ʿAlī ibn Abī Ṭālib who was willing to give all of his being for the sake of God–this is the behaviour of ʿAlī ibn Abī Ṭālib. Meanwhile, this person is not ready to give an atom of his wealth, of his life, of his reputation, of his ease, or of his pride for the sake of God. Does such a person have the *wilāyah* of ʿAlī ibn Abī Ṭālib? The *wilāyah* of ʿAlī ibn Abī Ṭālib means having an unbreakable bond with ʿAlī, both in terms of one's thoughts and beliefs, and its terms of one's actions.

If you grasp *wilāyah* as I have just explained, then you have access to the deepest and most profound sense of *wilāyah* as expressed by the Qur'an. Now let us turn to the verses of the Qur'an itself. The verses I am about to discuss are from *Sūrat al-Māʾidah* and they touch on both the affirmative aspect of *wilāyah*, namely the internal relationship it entails, but also on the negative aspect of *wilāyah*, which is the severing of external relations. We will also see how these relate to the other aspect of *wilāyah*, namely the connection with the *walī*–in the sense of that pole, that heart, that ruler and that Imam.

God says: 'O you who have faith! Do not take the Jews and the Christians for allies (*awliyāʾ*)'. *Awliyāʾ* is the plural of *walī*, and *walī* is from *wilāyah*, which is that connection, so a *walī* is someone with whom you are connected; so, this is saying do not take the Jews and Christians as your affiliates–'they are *awliyāʾ* of each other'–meaning

10 *Nahj al-Balāghah*, sermon no. 176.

some of them are allies and supporters of the other; do not look at how their blocs are opposed to one another, because insofar as they are against you, they are the same. 'Any of you who allies with them is indeed one of them. Indeed God does not guide the wrongdoing lot.'[11]

'Yet you see those in whose hearts is a sickness rushing to them'.[12] They rush to join the side of the enemies of the faith; they don't just go over to the other side, they rush over to them; they are not content being beside them, they want to be amongst them! And if you ask them: "Why are you working so closely with the enemies of the religion? Those who you know are the enemies of your faith? Never mind not opposing them, why are you their friend?" If you ask them this question, they respond, 'saying, "We fear lest a turn of fortune should visit us"'. They say, if we do not become their friends, we are worried that some harm will come to us (and how often do we hear these things!); they say they are worried that their faith will put them in danger, they are worried they will get into trouble for their faith (see how familiar these words are even today?).

What is God's response to these people? 'Maybe God will bring about a victory' for the faithful 'or a command from Him'–or something will happen by His will that is to their benefit–'and then they will be regretful for what they kept secret in their hearts'. Then they will say: 'What a terrible mistake we made! If we had known that the faithful would triumph and become strong like this, we would never have cooperated with the enemies of faith and humiliated ourselves like this!'

After these people have humiliated themselves by helping the enemies of the religion, what will the faithful say? 'And the faithful will say: "Are these the ones who swore by God with solemn oaths

11 Q5:51.

12 Q5:52.

that they were with you?!'"[13] The faithful will be perplexed by this! They will be surprised that it was these outwardly friendly faces, who swore solemn oaths that they were with the faithful, who did such a thing. The faithful will say: 'Whatever we said to them, whenever we told them anything, they said: "Yes, we agree with you. We believe as you do. We do not differ from you. We say the same as you do!"' This is what they gave as their seemingly sincere position, but it later became clear that they had a sickness in their hearts, and, in spite of their pleasant exteriors, their insides were filled with hypocrisy. The faithful will be shocked by this and ask: 'Are these the ones who swore by God with solemn oaths that they were with you?!' In other words: 'Are these really the same people who made these promises?' 'Are these the same people who said they were with you?' God says: 'Their works have failed, and they have become losers.'

So, this is with regard to external relations. Now let us turn to internal relations: 'O you who have faith! Should any of you desert his religion, God will soon bring a people'.[14] This 'people' (*qawm*) refers to the ideal followers of Islam. The ideal society of the followers of Islam, with regard to their internal and external relations and connections is what this verse describes: 'whom He loves'. God will bring forth a people whom He loves 'and who love Him'. Do we love God? No! This does not mean the little bit of love you sometimes feel which makes you say: 'O God! I give my life for you!' Even though God doesn't need you to tell Him this, and He doesn't need you to give Him your life–because when we say this, we are not speaking truthfully, as we are in no way ready to follow-through on our words! Therefore, this is not love. So what is the love of God then? 'Say, "If you love God, then follow me; God will love you"'[15] This is what the Qur'an says: If

13 Q5:53.

14 Q5:54.

15 Q3:31.

you love God, follow the Prophet and God will love you. Therefore, when the Qur'an says, 'He loves them and they love him', this means they submit fully to the commands of God. This is the love of God.

So, this is one quality which they possess; there exists a relationship of love between them and God. What else distinguishes these ideal Muslims? 'Humble towards the faithful'–this shows the intimate relationship that exists between the faithful. In other words, when they are dealing with the faithful, with their fellow Muslims who are the fabric of the Islamic society, they are not arrogant, they are not demanding, they do not make baseless claims. When they deal with people, they see themselves as of the people, with the people, in the way of the people, and for the people. They do not see themselves as being separate from the people in an ivory tower, seeing people from a distance and sometimes feeling sorry for them. They are humble with the faithful, but by contrast they are 'stern towards the faithless'–they are stern towards the enemies of the faith and the opponents of the Qur'an, meaning they are not influenced by them, they are proud, they protect their Islamic beliefs so that the faithless cannot influence them.

'Struggling in the way of God', the other quality they possess is that they struggle in the way of God, without any condition or reservation, just as the verse says. 'Not fearing the blame of any blamer.' They do not worry about what other people think, what kind of blamers are these do you suppose? 'That is God's grace which He grants to whomever he wishes, and God is all-bounteous, all-knowing.'

Then, the relationship between the different parts of the Islamic society and its heart, its centre, and its leader, which is none other than the Imam is addressed in the next verse. Do you see how beautifully this is put together? Do you see how pondering on the Qur'an makes clear these topics which one might not have even realised were there in the Qur'an? Do you see how clearly the Qur'an speaks? It discussed external relations, then internal relations, and now it turns to what sits at the heart of those internal relations, namely the leader of the society. It says: 'Your guardian (*walī*) is only God'.[16] Recall that the *walī* is the one who undertakes the affairs of governance, the one who directs all the energies and activities of the Islamic society and the Islamic nation, the one from whom all other parts of Islamic society draw inspiration. The Qur'an says this centre is God. However, God cannot take on a physical form to come and rule people in person, so who does this on his behalf? 'And His Messenger'. Clearly there is no contradiction or competition between God and His Prophet. After all, the Prophet is His messenger. So the *walī* is God and His Messenger. But the Prophet will not always be here: 'You will surely die, and they will die too.'[17] So what about after the Prophet? We read in the verse: 'and the faithful...' But which of 'the faithful'? Will anyone who has faith do? No. The verse goes on: 'who maintain the prayer and give the zakat while bowing down.' Now, who does this refer to? Commentators on the Qur'an agree that this refers to the Commander of the Faithful, ʿAlī ibn Abī Ṭālib.

Now someone might doubt this. They might say: No, this refers to all of the faithful, as they all pray and give charity. But I would say: But who epitomises these qualities most out of all the members of the Islamic society? There is no one but ʿAlī ibn Abī Ṭālib. Out of all the members of the Islamic society, the only one who exemplifies such firm and unshakeable faith is ʿAlī ibn Abī Ṭālib. So, even if this verse was not revealed about ʿAlī, it still refers to him because of the historical facts which have come down to us about him!

However, gentlemen, I would just like to remind of something about our discussion today and yesterday. When we speak about Imamate and *wilāyah*, we do so from a Shiʿa perspective, and we are looking only at affirming this perspective–we are not trying to negate

16 Q5:55

17 Q39:30.

anything else. As I have said before, I think it is important for the Shi'a to know their own beliefs and strengthen their own faith. In our discussions, we want to establish the teachings of Shi'a Islam, but we are not interested in negating anyone else's beliefs. We don't want to open up pointless academic debates. However, you need to know how to understand Shi'ism. Don't think to yourself: We should establish Islam first and then later talk about Shi'ism, no, because the Shi'ism we are discussing is nothing other than Islam itself, and Islam is nothing other than this Shi'ism. Shi'ism is the true Islam, even if there are ten other ways to see Islam. The Shi'i understanding of Islam and the Qur'an is the correct, logical, objective, and rational understanding of Islam and the Qur'an. Do you see? Therefore, we are discussing the fundamental principles of Islam itself. In our mind and from our viewpoint, we are explaining the ideological principles of Islam. I do not think you disagree with me on this point. However, I just wanted to remind you that we are merely affirming our own position, rather than negating the position of others.

In these lectures we are explaining Islam according to the Shi'a school of thought. We are not interested in other branches of Islam which might understand the teachings of the Qur'an in a different light. We have no argument with them, but neither do we pretend that there are no differences. They are our brothers and we extend the hand of friendship to them, why? Because we have a common enemy, and that enemy is standing outside our house. Whatever our differences, we two brothers do not have the right to argue with one another right now. This is our approach, as you well know, which I wanted to remind you of. Our discussion is about Shi'ism because we believe Shi'ism represents the original teachings of Islam. Therefore, we discuss Shi'ism and we understand Islam from a Shi'a perspective. This is not because we want to stir up discord between Shi'a and Sunni Muslims, as we believe all such discord is forbidden.

So, we were discussing the verse: 'Your guardian (*walī*) is only God, His Apostle, and the faithful who maintain the prayer and give the zakat while bowing down.'

Now, if we observe all the different aspects of *wilāyah*, what will happen? Will it have an effect? We said that *wilāyah* has three aspects: First, maintaining internal relations; second, cutting off exterior relationships with opposing currents; third, maintaining a continuous and deep connection with the heart of the Islamic body, and the heart of the Islamic *Ummah*, which is the Imam or leader. We explained these three aspects of *wilāyah*. Now, if we act on these three aspects of *wilāyah*, what will happen? The Qur'an answers this question: 'Whoever takes for his guardians (*awliyā'*) God, His Apostle and the faithful [should know that] the confederates of God are indeed victorious.' They are the most successful of people and they will overcome all other factions of humanity!

The Paradise of Wilāyah

Sunday 26th Ramadan 1394
13th October 1974

الَّذِينَ إِنْ مَكَّنَّاهُمْ فِي الْأَرْضِ أَقَامُوا الصَّلَاةَ وَآتَوُا الزَّكَاةَ
وَأَمَرُوا بِالْمَعْرُوفِ وَنَهَوْا عَنِ الْمُنْكَرِ وَلِلَّهِ عَاقِبَةُ الْأُمُورِ
(٤١)

'Those who, if We granted them power in the land, will maintain the prayer, give the zakat, bid what is right and forbid what is wrong, and with God rests the outcome of all matters.'
Sūrat al-Ḥajj (22):41

There are a number of points worthy of mentioning following on from the subject of our previous lectures on the topic of wilāyah: First, a general description of the society that has wilāyah and the individual that has wilāyah; second, an overview of a society which has wilāyah. In the lectures of the last two days in which we discussed this topic, we pondered on the meaning of the Qur'an's verses and extracted meanings from them in the light of the teachings of the Prophet's Household on the subject of wilāyah. In short, on the basis of the Qur'an and the ḥadīth, we saw that wilāyah has several aspects.

One of these is that in a Muslim society, there should not be connections with elements outside of itself, there should not be a reliance on non-Muslims. However, we explained that this lack of connection does not mean there should be no relationship whatsoever. We would never say that the Islamic world should withdraw from the world political and economic stage and have no relationship whatsoever with any non-Muslim nation, country, or power, no. This is not what we mean. The issue is one of dependency–Muslims should not be dependent upon or follow non-Muslim powers. They must stand on their own two feet.

Another aspect of *wilāyah* is the strong and harmonious connection of Muslims to one another. In other words, when we speak or think about an Islamic society, what we call *wilāyah* is the unity and commonality of the Islamic society. Just as we read in sayings from the Prophet and others: 'The similitude of the faithful in their mutual affection and concern for one another is like unto a single body.' The Islamic nation is like a single body or structure, whose components are joined to one another as a single edifice. Muslims must be united; they must be bound to one another with firm ties. They must be as one, united against the attacks of their enemies. This is what we discussed yesterday. Just as we read in *Sūrat al-Māʾidah*, the faithful are 'humble towards the faithful, stern towards the faithless.' There is yet another verse which makes this even clearer: 'Muhammad, the Apostle of God, and those who are with him are hard against the faithless and merciful amongst themselves.'[18] When they confront an external threat, you will find nothing more impenetrable or firm than they are, you will find nothing more powerful or committed than they are. They are independent. However, when it comes to dealing with one another, and the different branches of the Islamic society, there is no harshness, there is no sternness. On the contrary, the faithful influence one another and call each other towards goodness and righteousness, they advise one another to follow whatever is true and good, they encourage one another to stand up to whatever is evil

18 Q48:29.

and corrupt, and they look after one another. This is exactly like the example we gave the other day about the mountain climbers; how they tie themselves to one another as they ascend the mountain so that if one of them loses his footing and slips, rather than plunging a hundred or more metres to his death, the others are able to hold on to him and pull him to safety. So the faithful hold on to one another as tightly as possible; they make sure no one slips, no one gets lost, no one gets left behind, that no one goes hungry. They see if there are any amongst them who is weaker in his thinking, in his material wellbeing, or in his knowledge of the truth, and if there is someone like this, then everyone strives to help him and guide him to the right path. In short, the faithful are like members of the same family. This is another manifestation of *wilāyah* in the Islamic society.

Another aspect of *wilāyah* that we mentioned in our previous lectures and said that it is very important to understand–in fact, it is arguably the most important of all the aspects and the one that guarantees the existence of the others–is that the Islamic society needs a central leadership with very specific qualifications. This is because the Islamic society must be like a single body whose constituent parts are joined to one another internally, and which externally is like a single fist, like a single mass, facing other opposing forces. This unity is essential in Islamic society. But unity cannot come about without there being a focal point for all of this society's energies. If there is a different power in control of each corner of the Islamic society, then these different parts will eventually come apart, separate from one another, and take different paths, just as would happen if the central nervous system of the human being was altered so that instead of a single controlling organ–the brain–there were two, one for the right side and one for the left. Now, when both sides of my body are controlled by one brain, it is easy for me to get them to work in harmony. This is because both sides are receiving instructions from a single source. If someone wants to carry a heavy load from one side of this hall to another, they can manage this because both sides of their body are working together in harmony with one another; one hand grips one side of the load and the other hand grips the other, and both move the load in the same direction, and both sides set it down together. On the other hand, imagine if there were two different centres of control for our central nervous system–one for the right side and one for the left–how can the right and left side work together? The right hand goes to pick up this heavy load while the left hand sits immobile, because each of them are receiving orders from a different centre of control! The right hand tells the left to come and help, but the left pays no attention and does not answer. The more the right hand insists that the left hand helps, the more adamant the left hand becomes that it will not. Now imagine if the two sides of the body are facing a common foe, and the left hand calls on the right to come and help it fight, but the right hand remembers when the left didn't help it lift that load, so it does nothing. Do you see how if the human body has two centres of control, what this body is reduced to? It cannot even carry a load from one place to another, let alone protect itself from a foe!

Now, if the Islamic society wants to defend itself from an enemy, but one part of that society wants to launch an attack tomorrow while another wants to attack the day after tomorrow, this will also not be of any use! If this society wants to be like a single body to fight its enemy, then there must be a single point of leadership that directs all the faculties of that society against its enemy. If each part of the society wants to attack on a different day–one today, one tomorrow, and one the day after tomorrow–then the enemy will be able to rest easy. This is like the story, as told by Rumi, of the three people who went into a grape orchard together and, in order to get rid of them, the owner of the orchard used trickery to separate them from one another, then he could easily chase them off one by one. And how many times has this happened in the history of Islam!

So, if the Islamic community wants to secure its wellbeing and protect itself from harm, its constituent members must be joined to one another internally so that, externally, it forms a single body against its enemies, and if the whole of the Islamic society is to work together as one, then it requires a single controlling organ to direct it and marshal all of its constituent parts towards a single goal, whether these are intellectual or practical, and whether this is for the sake of its own life-giving activities or to face the threat of an external enemy–all of its members must be connected to a single central leadership.

That centre of control that sits within the fabric of Islamic society, directs all the wings of that society, employs each individual as befits his status and ability, and prevents disagreements. It directs all the energies of that society towards a single goal. This leader must be appointed by God, he must be a scholar, he must be aware, he must be trustworthy and protected from sinning, he must be someone who fully embodies all of the different elements of Islam, he must be a physical manifestation of the Qur'an. By what name do we call this leader? We call him a *walī*. Therefore, *wilāyah* in Islamic society, in the two senses that we have described, necessitates the existence of a *walī* in that society. This is yet another dimension of the issue of *wilāyah*. And this summarises what we covered in previous lectures until now.

The question that logically follows on from this discussion is: Do we have *wilāyah* or not? Now, you or I as individuals might have *wilāyah*, but does our society as a whole have *wilāyah* or not? You might be wondering whether there is a difference: There is. It is possible for one organ to be healthy, but just because one organ is healthy, it does not mean that the whole body is. This is the first point. Second, even if the organ itself is healthy, if the body is sick then the organ cannot fully benefit from its own health. These are the two points we need to consider. So, first of all, we must ask what an individual who has *wilāyah* looks like, what kind of person is he? This way we can know whether or not we have *wilāyah* as individuals. Once we have discussed this, it will be clear–God willing–that you and I have *wilāyah*. Then, we must ask how society must be in order to have *wilāyah*?

Now, there is no reason to suppose that a person who lives in a society without *wilāyah* cannot attain *wilāyah*. I am not saying there are no problems with this, only that there is nothing to rule out this possibility. But has this person fulfilled their moral duty? This is the question! Can he have *wilāyah* while living in a society that is deprived of it? Is this the right way for him to live? If someone lives in a society that has *wilāyah*, but lives in a society that is without *wilāyah* and feels no sense of responsibility to those without *wilāyah*, does this lack of a sense of responsibility not clash with the very principle of *wilāyah* itself? These are the questions that you Muslim men and women, and especially you, the Muslim youth, must reflect upon. Perhaps I will not have time to discuss each of these topics in detail. In fact, if I wanted to do justice to each of these topics in such a way as to make sure that everyone here understood them, then each of these topics would require a lecture in of itself, and we do not have enough time for that.

So, the topics we must consider are as follows: First, when a person has *wilāyah*, what kind of person are they? How should I be when I have *wilāyah*? How would I be when I do not have *wilāyah*? This is first. Second, we must ask how we must be if our society–in the sense of a group of people who have gathered together in a single place–is to have *wilāyah*, and what is it like when our society does not have *wilāyah*? What form does a society take when there is a *walī* and the people follow the *walī* in accordance with the teachings of Islam? And in what form and what conditions is a society without *wilāyah* as prescribed by the teachings of Islam?

These are two topics. Third, when an individual person has *wilāyah*, is his moral duty discharged merely by him having *wilāyah* as an individual? Does he not have a duty to create a society that is founded on *wilāyah*?

Fourth, if there is an individual person with *wilāyah* who lives in a society that is deprived of *wilāyah* but does not feel any sense of responsibility to instil *wilāyah* in that society, does this absence of sense of responsibility invalidate his *wilāyah*? It doesn't matter whether other individuals with *wilāyah* are doing this or not, the question is whether or not this lack of sense of responsibility weakens or impairs his own *wilāyah* in any way.

These are the topics we must discuss. I am going to focus on one or two of them. However, as I am discussing them, I want you to compare the way in which *wilāyah* is presented in the Qur'an and *ḥadīth* with the way in which it is imagined by those lazy people who just want to enjoy an easy life.

Some imagine that having *wilāyah* means just crying in the *majālis* we hold for the Prophet's Family. They think that *wilāyah* means when the name of the Prophet's Family is mentioned, they say 'peace be upon them'. They think this is all it is. They think that having *wilāyah* means that a person loves the Prophet's Family in their heart. That is all it takes. Of course, it is a duty to love the Prophet's Family. It is a duty to mention their names with respect. It is important to hold gatherings in their name, to mourn their deaths, and celebrate their births, to learn from their lives, to commemorate and remember their deeds, to weep over their tragedies, their martyrdoms, and their suffering...all of this is necessary, but all of these by themselves do not constitute *wilāyah*. *Wilāyah* is something more than these. When you sit in the *majlis* of Imam Ḥusayn (a) and shed tears, you are doing something good–it is good and proper to cry for him! However, you are doing something bad indeed if you believe that shedding these tears is enough to qualify for *wilāyah*.

I want to make sure you understand what I am saying. Those whose minds are under the influence of the slogans of some ignorant or corrupt preachers should pay close attention here. Let it not be said that anyone is opposing shedding tears for Ḥusayn! No. And if anyone is opposed to this, we are not opposed to it. We say that shedding tears for Ḥusayn is enough sometimes to save a whole nation of people! The Penitents (Tawwābīn) gathered at the grave of Ḥusayn ibn ʿAlī and spent one, two, or three days weeping for him. But what was the outcome of their weeping? The outcome was they made a pact of blood and self-sacrifice. They said: We are going to the battlefield and we are never going to turn back. We pledge not to return alive! This is crying for Ḥusayn–and no one opposes this!

No reasonable person opposes mentioning the names of Ḥusayn (a) and ʿAlī (a) with reverence–not only does no Shiʿa oppose this, no Sunni opposes this either. Nor does any disbeliever oppose this! Anyone who knows these people acknowledges that their names are worthy of being mentioned with respect! Those of you who were here on the twenty-third night will recall that I said that a family whose legacy is martyrdom, a family whose dearest memories are of abnegation and sacrifice for the sake of God, a family all of whose energies and being are directed purely for the sake of God–is this not a family any human being would hold in esteem? They must!

I make all of you a promise: Go to Europe, to America, to any country outside the Muslim world, any place where there is no Islam, any place where the people have not heard of Islam, and tell them that there was someone called ʿAlī ibn Abī Ṭālib and tell them about his life. Tell them his life story, and you will see how they will respect and praise such a person, to the extent that his name will remain lodged in their minds. This is not something only for the Shiʿa! Do you think you've done something outstanding by saying 'upon him be peace' (*ʿalayhis-salām*) after the name of ʿAlī ibn Abī Ṭālib? Is this something momentous you've accomplished? Do you think that *wilāyah* is nothing more than this? What a mistake! The *wilāyah* that takes the human being to Paradise is not this. Yes, this can be considered an important component of the totality of *wilāyah*, as can weeping for Ḥusayn. But some people, without realising it–God-willing without realising it, not intentionally–distort these issues. The matter of weeping for Ḥusayn (a) is something people who oppose the Prophet's Household with their words–rather than their ideas–distort in this way. They make Shi'ism and *wilāyah* seem very shallow and restrict *wilāyah* to these issues. They restrict it to the point where it is so small and narrow that it hardly seems worthy of being considered one of the fundamental teachings of Islam.

Wilāyah in an individual person refers to that person's connection in thought and practice with the *walī*. Find the *walī*, recognise God's *walī*, that person who is the rightful *walī* of the Islamic society, and identify him. Once you have identified him, then your thought, your practice, and your spirituality must be guided by him; connect yourself to him, follow him. If his struggle is your struggle, if his fight is your fight, if his friend is your friend, if his enemy is your enemy, if his side is your side, then you have *wilāyah*. Do you see? This is what it means for someone to have *wilāyah*. Know the *walī*, know what the *walī* thinks, align your thoughts with his, know what the *walī* wants to do, act with the *walī*, follow the *walī*, connect yourself to the *walī* in practice and in thought. This is what it means to have *wilāyah*.

Who here will raise his hand and claim that he has this *wilāyah*? Who here will raise his hand and admit that his *wilāyah* is incomplete? We have reduced *wilāyah* to feeling affection for ʿAlī ibn Abī Ṭālib and shedding a tear for him, even if our actions are the opposite of his, even if our thoughts and ideas are the opposite of his. Do we call this *wilāyah*? We have made this myth and superstition for our own benefit, to keep us happy, so we can say we are followers of ʿAlī ibn Abī Ṭālib (a) and claim that we have his *wilāyah*. That way, we can please ourselves with the idea that everything that has been promised to the followers of ʿAlī ibn Abī Ṭālib is also promised to us for sure! This is foolish, and it does not do justice to ʿAlī ibn Abī

Ṭālib! In fact, it is an injustice to Islam because it is an injustice to the fundamental teaching of Islam that is *wilāyah*. We are not ready to understand *wilāyah*.

Imam al-Ṣādiq (a) told his own followers–those who had *wilāyah*, whose value he recognised, and whom he esteemed–that *wilāyah* required action. He said that he who acted righteously was the ally (*walī*) of the Prophet's Household, while he who did not act righteously was the enemy of the Prophet's Household. This is what we are saying here. Imam al-Ṣādiq explained *wilāyah* in such a way that the difference between *wilāyah* in his vocabulary and *wilāyah* in the vocabulary of that ignorant person who thinks he is living his life in the name of Imam al-Ṣādiq could not be clearer. Why do we not understand the true meaning of *wilāyah*? Why do we not grasp the profundity of this Islamic principle? Why are we content to ossify and regress, to stray from Islam, and to lose this world and the next? Sometimes I worry that we spend our lives in Hell in this world out of hope for Paradise in the next, only to find, when we are brought back to life on the Day of Judgement, and we see deeds for what they are, our hopes come to naught–and there is no Paradise for us. How regretful we would be then! So, the *wilāyah* of an individual person is his connection and relation with the *walī*. He must be connected to the *walī*. This is first of all.

But what does *wilāyah* mean at a societal level? What is *wilāyah* in society? *Wilāyah* in a society means that the *walī* in that society is, first of all, known–in the sense that people know that this person is the *walī*–and second, that this *walī* guides and directs all the energies and activities of that society, and serves as the axis around which all the elements of that society arrange themselves. The *walī* should be the centre who issues all directives and implements all the laws in the society. He should be a point at which all the veins and sinews of a society converge. All should look towards him. All should follow him. He should be the one who ignites the engine of life in that society. He should be the driver and leader of the caravan of life in that society. This society is one which has *wilāyah*.

After the Prophet, the Commander of the Faithful (a) was deprived of his rightful place for 25 years as the leader of the society the Prophet had founded. After the Prophet, the Islamic society spent twenty-five years without *wilāyah*. It vanished. In that society, Salmān was an individual who had *wilāyah*. Abū Dharr was an individual who had *wilāyah*. But what about the Islamic society? The Islamic society after the Prophet did not have *wilāyah* for twenty-five years. Only when the Commander of the Faithful returned to rule did the Islamic Society have *wilāyah* again. To what extent? To the extent that Imam ʿAlī (a) was a source of guidance and direction for the society. The *wilāyah* of a society is nothing other than this. When the Imam rules over a society, when the Imam is the source of the commands and prohibitions of a society, when all the different branches of that society go back to the Imam, when the Imam is actually organising the affairs of the society, when it is the Imam who ties the battle standard, when it is the Imam who gives the order to attack, when it is the Imam who writes the peace treaty, it is then that this society can be said to have *wilāyah*. In any other set of circumstances, this society does not have *wilāyah*.

Now, if we have *wilāyah* in our society, then we must thank God! But if we do not have *wilāyah* in our society, then we must take steps to bring it about. If you have been blessed with this divine gift, be grateful to God. There is no blessing greater than *wilāyah*. Let me explain why *wilāyah* is such a great blessing so that, if you do not have it, you will do whatever it takes to obtain it for yourself and human society. We must try to live like ʿAlī. We must try to follow ʿAlī's example. We must try to create a strong bond between ourselves and ʿAlī, who is God's *walī* for us. This requires effort, struggle, and sacrifice. I tell you that the Imams (a) themselves, after the martyrdom of the Commander of the Faithful, all struggled in the path of *wilāyah* without exception. All of their efforts were for the sake of keeping this *wilāyah* alive, to revive the Islamic society, to nurture this sapling we call a human being in the garden of this world with the life-giving water of *wilāyah* so that it would grow tall and thrive. This was the goal the Imams struggled for their entire lives.

When we speak about making an effort to bring *wilāyah* into society, this does not mean that we should sit here stoically and tell Zayd and ʿAmr what to do. This is not how *wilāyah* comes about. In fact, by doing this, we only make *wilāyah* harder to obtain. The way to bring about *wilāyah* is by striving to give power to God's *walī*, to the *walī* God has appointed. In the previous lecture, I explained how God appoints the *walī*. I said that sometimes God names the *walī* specifically, while at other times He designates the *walī* by signs. Sometimes, God designates the *walī* like he designated ʿAlī ibn Abī Ṭālib (a), Ḥasan ibn ʿAlī (a), Ḥusayn ibn ʿAlī (a), ʿAlī ibn Ḥusayn (a), and so on until the last Imam, by name and a specific description of him. Other times, God does not name his *walī* specifically, instead he says: 'As for those of the learned who protect themselves from sin, preserve their religion, turn away from their desires, and obey the command of their Lord'. He designates the *walī* in this way. This also means they are appointed by God. So, the *walī* can be appointed by name, or by qualifications, so that you can determine for yourself, for example, that the *walī* is someone like Ayatollah Burūjerdī, for example. Do you see? When a person wants to revive the divine teachings and the laws of Islam in society in accordance with the principle of *wilāyah*, he finds a way to do so. He learns the different ways and methods that the world presents to the human being to do so. At the moment, we are not talking about ways and methods however–we are interested in the principle itself.

So, when a society has *wilāyah*, what happens then? To put it in a single sentence: This society becomes like a dead person who has been brought back to life. This single sentence sums it up perfectly. Imagine a dead person, someone who has lost their life, who does nothing. He has eyes, but he does not see. He has a mouth, but he does not eat. He has a digestive system, but it cannot extract nutrition from the food. He has veins, but his blood does not flow through them. Why? Because he is not alive. He has hands, but he cannot protect himself from the smallest insect. He has feet, but he cannot move out of the sun and into the shade. He is dead. Now imagine you bring him back to life: His brain works. His nerves work. His hand grasps things. His mouth eats things. His stomach digests things. His blood flows. The energy reaches all parts of his body. His body becomes warm again. He can strive. He can walk. He can lash out at his foes and look after his friends. He can improve himself and make himself better.

This analogy will help you understand the importance of *wilāyah* for a society. The human body is the society, and *wilāyah* is the soul. A society without *wilāyah* has potential, but it is unrealised, wasted, fading away, or–worse still–being used to suppress human flourishing: It has a brain, and the brain is thinking, but its thoughts are of corruption, of murder, of destruction, of misery, of exploitation and tyranny. There is an eye, but it does not see what it should and instead sees only what it should not. There is an ear, but it does not hear the words of truth, and the nerves do not convey the words of truth to the brain, and the brain does not send instructions in accordance with the truth to the limbs and organs, so the limbs and the organs do not act in accordance with the truth in objective reality. The conditions of the world do not allow a person to act in accordance with truth. This is a society without *wilāyah*.

In a society without *wilāyah*, not only are the lamps not lit, but there is no oil with which to light them. The oil which the Prophet poured into the lamps of guidance has been used up and the wicks are drying out. Do you see how in the days after the death of the Prophet, they lit the lamps and illuminated the world? It was the Prophet who poured this oil into the lamps, but because the hand of *wilāyah* was not above these lamps to refill them, the oil was gradually exhausted and their flames died down, and the lights dimmed. It came to the time of ʿUthmān and power was transferred to Muʿāwiyah. Do you see what happened? The very things that Fāṭimah (s) foretold to the women of the Emigrants and the Helpers came to pass, but they had not paid attention to her. The things she had warned the Muslim community about were happening, but they had not understood her warning. They all happened. The sharp and bloody sword, the spear that had killed virtue and goodness, the hand that had smothered humans and humanity. These were the things that Fāṭimah had warned people about, and before her, the Prophet. The two of them had foreseen these things, they had warned of these things, but the Muslim society had not given any heed. They closed their ears to the predictions of doom. But today the warnings of Fāṭimah are still reaching our ears–O heedful ears! Can you hear her warning?

A society that has *wilāyah* is a society in which all human potential is realised, a society in which all the things which God gave the human being for his growth and perfection are safeguarded. The human sapling grows tall. Human beings flourish. Humanity is strengthened. In this society, the *walī* is the ruler; he is the one who is in charge of all of its different faculties and departments; and the society as a whole is walking the path of God and living in the remembrance of God. In terms of wealth, the *walī* divides wealth fairly amongst the people. He tries to promote good and erase evil.

The Qur'an says: 'Those who, if We granted them power in the land, will maintain the prayer'.[19] Prayer here symbolises God's remembrance and turning towards God on a societal level; maintaining the prayer means they go towards God, and they organise their life in accordance with God's directives. 'Give the zakat', this refers to the fair distribution of wealth; the word zakat in the Qur'an has a very

19 Q22:41.

broad meaning, and I suspect, although I am not yet certain, using some evidence I have, that the word zakat in the Qur'an refers to all forms of monetary expenditure and charities.

So giving the zakat, generally speaking, means a fair distribution of wealth in society, based on the narrations on the topic which say that zakat has this overall effect. 'Bid what is right and forbid what is wrong'–they try to uproot all wrongfulness. We sometimes imagine that 'bidding the right and forbidding the wrong' (*al-amr bi al-maʿrūf wa al-nahī ʿan al-munkar*) means that we go and tell someone not to do something bad and tell them to do something good instead. However, this is only one aspect of bidding the right and forbidding the wrong. People asked the Commander of the Faithful: 'Why are you fighting Muʿāwiyah?' He gave a very comprehensive answer. I will not repeat the whole *ḥadīth*, but in it, one of the reasons he gives is that bidding the right and forbidding the wrong is an obligation. Pay close attention and reflect! They asked him: What business do you have with Muʿāwiyah at Ṣiffīn? You should go to Kufah and he should go to Damascus. What does ʿAlī say? He tells them that God has made bidding the right and forbidding the wrong a duty. Imam Ḥusayn (a) rises up and they ask him: Where are you going? He says: 'I want to bid the right and forbid the wrong.' Do you see how broad the scope of this is compared to the narrow way in which we imagine it? When *wilāyah* exists in a society, this is what happens: Prayer is maintained, zakat is given, the good is enjoined and evil is forbidden. In short, a lifeless corpse is brought back to life!

The Walī: The Central Authority

Monday 27th Ramadan 1394
14th October 1974

إِنَّ اللَّهَ يَأْمُرُكُمْ أَنْ تُؤَدُّوا الْأَمَانَاتِ إِلَى أَهْلِهَا وَإِذَا حَكَمْتُمْ
بَيْنَ النَّاسِ أَنْ تَحْكُمُوا بِالْعَدْلِ إِنَّ اللَّهَ نِعِمَّا يَعِظُكُمْ بِهِ إِنَّ
اللَّهَ كَانَ سَمِيعًا بَصِيرًا (٥٨) يَا أَيُّهَا الَّذِينَ آمَنُوا أَطِيعُوا اللَّهَ
وَأَطِيعُوا الرَّسُولَ وَأُولِي الْأَمْرِ مِنْكُمْ فَإِنْ تَنَازَعْتُمْ فِي شَيْءٍ
فَرُدُّوهُ إِلَى اللَّهِ وَالرَّسُولِ إِنْ كُنْتُمْ تُؤْمِنُونَ بِاللَّهِ وَالْيَوْمِ الْآخِرِ
ذَٰلِكَ خَيْرٌ وَأَحْسَنُ تَأْوِيلًا (٥٩)

'Indeed God commands you to deliver the trusts to their [rightful] owners, and, when you judge between people, to judge with fairness. Excellent indeed is what God advises you. God is indeed all-hearing, all-seeing. O you who have faith! Obey God and obey the Apostle and those vested with authority among you. And if you dispute concerning anything, refer it to God and the Apostle, if you have faith in God and the Last Day. That is better and more favourable in outcome.'
Sūrat al-Nisāʾ (4):58–59

Following on from the previous lectures, I would like now to discuss some of the issues that surround the matter of *wilāyah*. These are not questions about the fundamental aspects of *wilāyah* such as: what is *wilāyah*, where is it found in the Qur'an, what are the different dimensions of it–these are the topics we have covered already. However, there are a series of issues that arise from *wilāyah* and are subsidiary to it, but which are nevertheless each essential in their own right for the proper direction of the Islamic society. Today we will, God-willing, touch on two of these and tomorrow, God-willing, we will deal with two more.

One such issue arises from the fact that we established from the Qur'an that maintaining the internal cohesion of a Muslim society and cutting-off entanglements with external powers depends on there being a central authority and power in Islamic society to direct all of its energies and activities towards a single goal, and to govern all of the different tendencies and axes of society, and that this central power is called the *walī*. This *walī* is the leader, from whom all the different elements of society must draw inspiration, and to whom all activities must ultimately devolve. In short, it is the *walī* who manages Islamic society, whether from the theoretical or practical aspect. We established all of this from the Qur'an. Now, one might ask: So who is the *walī* of Islamic society? Do we have a simple answer to this question, if someone turns around and says: Ok, we want to know who this *walī* is! Who can be this *walī*? Who is this power around whom all the energies of Islamic society must converge, and from whom they must take orders? If someone asks this question from us, do we have an answer or not? Yes, we have an answer. We have already made references to the answer to this question in previous lectures–this is not something completely unknown. So, now, we want to address this in a logical and scientific fashion.

The Qur'an gives a straightforward answer to this question. It says that the one who is the true *walī* of the Islamic society is none other than God. It is God who rules Islamic society and no one else. This is what *tawḥīd* itself teaches us. There is none aside from God. Prophethood also affirms this point. Now let us see whether *wilāyah* does the same. Here, I would just like to make a brief point, that the fundamental doctrines of a school of thought or movement must be such that each of these doctrines is in perfect harmony and conformity with all the others. It should not be the case that one of these doctrines, taken to its logical conclusion, will produce a result that is opposed to all of the others. And yet, unfortunately, this is exactly how it is in the hearts and minds of many simple Muslim folk. They derive things from some of their fundamental beliefs that are completely at odds with others.

Therefore, the person in Islamic society who has the right to command and prohibit, and to implement these dictates and direct the orientation of the society, and who has the right to govern all aspects of human existence, is God. 'God is the *walī* of the faithful.'[20] Having looked at all of the verses in the Qur'an that use the terms *walī* and *awliyāʾ*, I can safely say that doctrines such as God being the *walī* of the Muslim community, that the faithful have no *walī* or helper except God, that God governs all aspects of human life, are taken for granted in the Qur'an. However, to avoid anyone misunderstanding this point, I want to make clear that this is not about God's authority over creation. That is a separate discussion, namely that God has complete control over the heavens and the earth and that He directs all their affairs. However, what we are talking about here is the fact that even the laws that govern human life, and individual and social human relations, must also come from God. In other words, in a godly and Islamic society that is founded on Islamic principles and governed by the Islamic system, or the Qur'anic system–or better to say, the system of ʿAlī, or the government of ʿAlī–is one in which God rules over human affairs.

Now, someone might ask: What do you mean that God rules over human affairs? God does not come and appear directly to people in order to command or prohibit things. There must be a person ruling

20 Q3:68.

over people! There must be a person who directs all the organs of society. Now, by this I do not mean there must be just one person–I am not saying there cannot be a group of people–but, ultimately, the ruler of human society must themselves be human. Otherwise, there will only be laws and ordinances and, even if that law comes from God, there is no ruler such as the Commander of the Faithful (a) or a group of persons to lead that society and *implement* those laws and ordinances. In which case, how will human society be organised? Therefore, there must be a person. Now, who is that person?

This person or people whose role it is to govern human society is, in practice, the *walī* of that society, and they have *wilāyah* of that society. So who is this? Different schools of thought have given different answers to this question, and historical realities have also answered it in a variety of ways. There have been those who have said that power belongs to whoever can take it–the law of the jungle. Others have said that whoever is better able to govern should rule, while others still have said that whoever the people accept should rule over them. Frequently, the dynastic principle has been invoked, saying that leadership belongs to people of a particular family or lineage. And there have been other theories about this also.

Religion and religious thought answer this question with the Qur'anic verse 'Your *walī* is only God, His Apostle'.[21] The one who is given command over society by God himself is God's messenger. Therefore, when a prophet comes to a society, it is meaningless for people to choose a ruler other than this prophet to govern them. The prophet is the person who must take hold of the reins of power in society. The prophet must rule. When the Prophet left this world, what was people's duty then? When the Prophet of God, like all other people, dies and leaves this world to return to his maker, then what are we supposed to do? The same verse of the Qur'an also answers this

21 Q5:55.

question 'and the faithful'–the faithful are your *walī*. To which of the faithful does this refer? Does it mean that anyone who believes in the religion's teachings can be the *walī* and ruler of Islamic society? If this is the case, then there are as many rulers as there are believers! What should we do in this case? No, the verse does not just say 'faithful' and leave it at that, it singles out those faithful with a particular quality. Clearly, this verse of the Qur'an wants to designate a particular individual for this role. It wants to point at one specific person and identify them as the rightful ruler of society, while at the same time explaining the criteria by which this appointment has been made. Pay close attention to this! The Qur'an wants to say that this person who has been selected by the Lawgiver should rule over people, but at the same time, it wants to explain the criteria for this decision. In other words: The reason we have selected this person to rule over you is this criterion. This is why God chose him and appointed him to lead. So, the Qur'an begins by saying 'and the faithful' (*wa alladhīna āmanū*), which is a categorical statement. Faith here refers to genuine faith and not just the outward profession thereof. So it is already pointing to someone who has spent the entirety of his life being faithful, and who has confirmed his faith through his actions. Therefore, 'and the faithful' is the first condition; this person must be a true believer. However, there are other conditions too: 'who maintain the prayer'–so the faithful who maintain the prayer. They do not just offer their prayers–offering prayers is something else–they *maintain* or *establish* prayer. If God had wanted to say they offered prayers, he would have said 'and the faithful *who pray*', not 'and the faithful *who maintain the prayer*', as the former is more succinct and direct.

Maintaining prayer in society means keeping the spirit of prayer alive in society, so that the society is the kind of society that offers prayers. You know that a society which prays–meaning a society in which all of its elements are mindful of God and remember God–creates a wave...and you know that a society in which the mindfulness and remembrance of God creates a wave–this is a society in which the values of humanity are upheld and never betrayed. The society in which the remembrance of God creates a wave is one in which the majority of people are mindful of God, in which they orient themselves in accordance with God, and in which everything people do is for the sake of God.

The cause of theft, the cause of crimes, the cause of wrongdoing, and the cause of allowing wrongdoing–from both sides–the reason for the transgressions that take place, and the reason why transgressions are allowed to take place, is entirely down to people's distance from the remembrance of God. A society in which God is remembered will have a leader like ʿAlī ibn Abī Ṭālib (a), who neither wrongs others nor allows others to do wrong. It will have citizens like Abū Dharr al-Ghifārī who, even though he was beaten, even though he was exiled, even though he was threatened with death, even though he was isolated from friends and family, he never wronged anyone, and never turned away from the path of God. This is a society in which God is remembered. This is a society in which prayer is maintained.

When a person of faith maintains the prayer, this means he turns the society towards God, and promotes the remembrance of God in society–'who maintain the prayer'. However, the Qur'an has not finished: 'and give the zakat'–they divide wealth fairly, they give the zakat, they spend in God's way. Then God says: 'while bowing down.' In other words, they give the zakat while in a state of bowing down. This, of course, refers to a particular series of events with which we are familiar. There are those commentators on the Qur'an who say that this phrase 'while bowing down' simply means that these faithful are always in a state of prayer, and that it does not refer to any particular occurrence. However, the Arabic language does not allow for this interpretation, because 'while bowing down' here means that they give zakat while in a state of bowing down then and there. This corresponds with the point I made yesterday, when I said that this refers to all forms of spending in God's way, as the ring that the Commander of the Faithful gave to the supplicant was not technically zakat, but rather a simple act of spending in God's way, and yet this was called zakat in the Qur'an: 'and give the zakat while bowing down.' This means that there was someone who was so concerned with fairness, and so committed to spending in God's way, to the extent that seeing poverty was so painful for him that he could not even wait to finish his prayer out of fear that this beggar might leave. Rather than signal for the beggar to wait so that he could give him something, he gave his own ring while still praying. This person is so attracted to giving to others, this person is so determined to fulfil his duties that he does not allow himself to wait. He sees a poor person, he sees his poverty, he sees something which God does not like and which, by extension, he does not like. He has nothing but his ring, and he is in the middle of prayer, so he gives that ring to the beggar.

This is a reference to a particular historical event in the life of ʿAlī ibn Abī Ṭālib (a): While ʿAlī was praying, a poor person came and ʿAlī gave alms to him. As a result, this verse was revealed. So, as you can see, this verse is somehow designating ʿAlī ibn Abī Ṭālib was the *walī* after the Prophet. This is not the same as what wrongdoers have done throughout history; for example, when Muʿāwiyah wanted to appoint a successor, he appointed his son to succeed him as Caliph. This is not how God appointed ʿAlī as the successor of the Prophet. God said that ʿAlī must succeed the Prophet as ruler of the Muslim community because he possesses the qualifications necessary to lead. What are these? Complete faith in God, maintaining the prayer in society, and a commitment to giving zakat to the extent that he neglects his own needs. So, at the same time as appointing the Prophet's successor, and designating ʿAlī ibn Abī Ṭālib (a) for this role, God also explains the criteria and the philosophy behind this choice. This is what this verse of the Qur'an is saying. Therefore, in Islam, the *walī* must be the one whom God has sent and the one whom He has appointed to the role because, seeing as all people are equal in their nature and creation, no person has the right to rule over others.

The only person who has the right to rule over human beings is God, and because God has this right, He can give this right to others based on what He knows to be in the best interests of humankind. We know that nothing God does is without benefit for us. He is not a dictator! God does not act like a bully or a tyrant! God acts in the interests of human beings. So, when God appoints someone to lead us because it is to our benefit, we should submit to God's choice. He sends the Prophet. He appoints the Imam. After the Imam, He says that those individuals who meet these criteria and possess these qualifications should lead; He says that anyone who has these qualities, after the infallible Imams, should rule over Muslim society. So it is God who appoints the *walī*. He is Himself the *walī*. The Prophet is the *walī*. The Imams are *awliyāʾ*. The Twelve Imams from the Prophet's Household, one after another, were appointed as successors to the Prophet. Following them, those people who have these qualities and qualifications are appointed as rulers and leaders. The issue of designating the *walī* is this. And this is just one verse of the Qur'an that I have presented to you. There are other verses in the Qur'an as well, some of which you will be familiar with, and others you will need to go and find. There are many verses on this topic.

What the matter ultimately devolves to from the perspective of Islam is that power should not fall into the hands of those who will lead humanity towards hellfire. Is this not also the lesson that history teaches us? Have we not seen what happened shortly after the bright dawn of Islam? Have we not seen what became of the Prophet's society? A society in which people did not give power to good men, a society in which people changed the standards of goodness, a society in which people could not recognise who was sincerely trying to look after their best interests? How much work it must have needed to reduce the society of the Prophet to this state! Poisonous propaganda from the tyrannical and unjust regime spread through the Muslim society, to the extent that it completely changed the horizons of people's thought and perception, to the extent that these people saw black as white and white as black. This is why we study the history of the second and third centuries, we see the terrible crimes carried out by the government and the Caliphate, and we see how indifferent and confused people were. Are these the same people? Are these the same people who would not put up with ʿUthmān? Are these the same people who came and besieged him in his home and, in the end, removed him from power? Are these the same people? Are these the same people who saw no problem with the ʿAbbāsid caliph spending exorbitant amounts of wealth on his wedding? When they saw what debauchery he created by spending out of the public purse? I'm not even talking about morality; the ʿAbbāsid caliph spent enough money for a thousand people on himself. Even if he was not spending this money on debauchery, but on prayers and fasting, would it be allowed? These events were happening right in front of people's eyes, and yet they were utterly heedless. They did not care!

Another example of this opulence is what happened at the wedding of Jaʿfar Barmakī, the favourite vizier of Hārūn al-Rashīd. He was a young man of between twenty-eight and thirty years when he got married. Of course, he was only thirty-four or thirty-five years of age when the ʿAbbāsids put him to death. However, when he was at the peak of his influence and favour, he got married. Hārūn al-Rashīd himself had a close relationship with this vizier. So, to celebrate his marriage, instead of throwing sweets over the heads of the bride and groom as was customary at a wedding, Harūn al-Rashīd threw something else over their heads. When the guests came close picked up these things from the floor, they saw that they weren't sweets, or even coins. They were little cases, no bigger than a finger, made from gold. Inside they found a folded piece of very fine paper and, when they unfolded it, they saw it was actually very large! They read the piece of paper and, to their amazement, it was a deed of ownership for a piece of land. It was a land grant (*iqṭāʿ*).

So, in a single night, God only knows how many of these were given out–five hundred, eight hundred, a thousand!–on very fine pieces of paper, wrapped in golden cases, and thrown over the heads of the bridge and groom, without the caliph knowing who would receive them! Imagine ownership of a big piece of land being given to a child, or a drunkard, or a common thief–a person who has no idea what to do with such a piece of land. The caliph had no idea, these grants were literally thrown away and whoever picked them up, got one. As for this region which was now in the hands of such a person, how the people there would now suffer; their wealth and livelihoods would be ruined, their rights would be usurped, they would lose everything! The caliph didn't think about this, of course. At the same time, class differences in society were so severe that, while the caliph was quite literally giving away land grants and living a life of opulence and excess, a descendant of Imam Ḥasan by the name of Yaḥyā ibn ʿAbd Allāh ʿAlawī was fighting against tyranny and oppression in the mountains of Ṭabaristān, and he and his family only had a single cloak between them so that when they wanted to pray, they would have to use the same cloak one after another to cover themselves. The family of the Prophet were fighting against tyranny while living such difficult lives, while the caliph and his entourage could not care less.

But I am not interested in Hārūn al-Rashīd personally. If Hārūn al-Rashīd had not done these things, he would not be Hārūn al-Rashīd. It was the ruling class, to which Hārūn belonged, that had decided that so long as they existed, they would live like this. So this isn't about Hārūn al-Rashīd–this is about the people who had lost the sensitivity that had existed at the advent of Islam and forgotten what the Prophet had stood for. Faced with such clear wrongdoing, they felt no sense of responsibility, they felt no sense of duty, they were of no use! What for? From all the harmful and corrupting propaganda that people had been exposed to. This kind of propaganda and the ones responsible for spreading it were dispersed throughout the Muslim world and found in every Muslim land, and they had spent years corrupting people's souls and people's minds, until it had reached this point. So, do you see how important it is for the right person to rule Islamic society? The person whom God has appointed as the head of this society.

The Qur'an says: 'O you who have faith! Obey God and obey the Apostle and those vested with authority among you.'[22] Who are 'those vested with authority' (*ulu al-amr*)? Do those ignoramuses who call themselves Muslims imagine that anyone can hold authority? That anyone who can take power has the right to it and can be called one 'vested with authority'? We say that this is not the case. These people are not the ones God has vested with authority. If we think that anyone who issues orders is the holder of authority who is recognised by the Qur'an, then in some mountains somewhere there is a bandit leader who issues commands, is he one vested with authority? Is it a religious obligation to obey him?

What about the person who told everyone that only women could come out of the home for three nights and men were banned from leaving the home–this is one of the Safavid notables who, according to some accounts, made this ban a norm in Isfahan. An eyewitness wrote this report, but we do not know whether it is accurate or not, that only women were allowed outside in public places, like markets and shops, so that in every place women and girls were working and men were not allowed outside. So, were there no men in the city? So that women could be at ease without any strangers around? Not at all! This leader allowed his own associates outside during this time. Men whose mother or sister were in the market had no right to come

22 Q4:59.

outside, but this man and his friends were allowed outside. Are these people 'vested with authority'? Should these people's commands be obeyed? Is their command God's command?

According to the Shi'a, who are 'those vested with authority' whom God expects us to obey? It is those people who, while they are 'among you', they are people like you, they have been granted *wilāyah* by God–they have received authority from God.

Now, is Hārūn al-Rashīd 'vested with authority'? This man who mistreated people, who lived an opulent and excessive life, who butchered so many people, including the vizier Ja'far Barmakī and many of his family members in a single day? Including many of the true believers and the Muslims? Who committed so many crimes that only God knows their number? So, Abū Ḥanīfah says this man is vested with authority. Abū Ḥanīfah was always at odds with Imam al-Ṣādiq (a). He was always arguing with him. He asked him: 'Why do you oppose the one vested with authority in your time?' He meant Hārūn al-Rashīd! Do you see?

So the Shi'a observe a very subtle and meticulous logic in this issue. As well as deriving the fact that God must appoint the *walī* from the Qur'an, they also provide criteria and conditions for people to protect them from being led astray, so that the people would not say we accept ʿAlī ibn Abī Ṭālib as our leader, but we also accept Hārūn al-Rashīd as his successor! This was exactly the argument that the ʿAbbāsids themselves had made: that they were the true successors of ʿAlī or the Prophet! The ʿAbbāsid caliph Manṣūr would say that he accepted the caliphate of Imam Ḥasan, but claimed that Ḥasan had sold the caliphate. Well, this is the logic of Manṣūr: Ḥasan sold the caliphate, so he has no right to it! On the other hand, we took the caliphate by force from those to whom he sold it, so it belongs to us now. This is what they say. So they accepted ʿAlī ibn Abī Ṭalib and respected him, at least outwardly, but they saw no contradiction between this and the rule of someone like Hārūn al-Rashīd.

On the other hand, the Shiʿa say that this is not correct. The Shiʿa say that if you accept the rule of ʿAlī ibn Abī Ṭālib, then you must also accept the criteria for the caliphate and *wilāyah*. You must accept that the reason why ʿAlī ibn Abī Ṭālib was appointed by God as the *walī* is because he possessed the necessary qualifications for this office. Therefore, if someone lacks these qualifications or, in fact, has the opposite qualities in him, he has no right to call himself ʿAlī's successor. He has no right to claim to hold *wilāyah* or to be one of those 'vested with authority', and no one has the right to accept such claims made by him. This is the first issue that arises concerning the issue of *wilāyah*.

However, there is a second issue we must also address, namely: What is God's *wilāyah* for? If someone asks you why you say God must choose the holder of *wilāyah*, how do you answer? The answer stems from a philosophy of the natural order that is laid down by the Islamic worldview. According to the Islamic worldview, everything in the world is the result of God's power: 'To Him belongs whatever abides in the night and the day'[23] so, when everything that exists only does so because of Him, and He directs all the affairs of the cosmos, then the government of the human realm should also be His to direct, there is no avoiding this conclusion. This is the second issue. Consider the following verses:

'Indeed, God commands you to deliver the trusts to their [rightful] owners, and, when you judge between people, to judge with fairness. Excellent indeed is what God advises you. God is indeed all-hearing, all-seeing.'[24] This shows that whatever God commands you to do is good, and that His commands emanate from his perfect knowledge, awareness, and wisdom. He hears even your innermost needs, he sees your fate, and, therefore, whatever it is you need, he gives you.

23 Q6:13.

24 Q4:58.

This verse also speaks about trusts (*amānah*) and says that you should deliver them to their owners. In reality, this prepares the ground for the second verse, because fulfilling a trust does not just mean giving you a *tūmān* that is due to you or collecting one from you that is due to me. In fact, the most important manifestation of fulfilling a trust is that whatever God has entrusted mankind, man should put it in its proper place and deliver it to its rightful owners. Obedience to God is part of the covenant God has made with mankind; fulfilling it means obeying God and obeying the one to whom God has made obedience obligatory. This is the most important form of trust there is.

Next, the Qur'an says: 'O you who have faith! Obey God and obey the Apostle and those vested with authority among you.'[25] This verse shows how Islam's thesis of government differs from that of other schools of thought. Islam's thesis does not say that government will one day be unnecessary. Islam does not predict a day in the future when there will be no need for a state or government in society–this is unlike some other schools of thought which foretell the advent of an ideal society, one of whose features will be the absence of any form of government or state apparatus. Islam does not accept such a view.

The Khawārij used the pretext of supporting divine rule in order to say that ʿAlī ibn Abī Ṭālib should not lead the Muslims. They relied on the slogan 'there is no rule except that of God!' (*lā ḥukma illā lillāh*). In response to this, the Commander of the Faithful said: 'A true word with a false meaning' (*kalimatu ḥaqqin yurādu bi-hā al-bāṭil*). Yes, it is correct that the true ruler is only God, as it is He who promulgates laws and determines life's outcomes. However, when they said: 'There is no rule except that of God!' or 'There is no command except that of God!' The question they must answer then is who applies God's laws? No doubt, their response would be: 'People must have a leader'

25 Q4:59.

because, ultimately, there must always be someone ruling over society. It is human nature to want to live in a society that is governed by laws; it is not enough just to have laws, there must be someone to ensure these laws are properly implemented. This is why the Qur'an says: 'And those vested with authority among you'. But is this anyone who has authority? Does this mean anyone who issues commands should be obeyed? Sometimes a person gains authority but human reason and wisdom judges him unfit to rule, is he still one of 'those vested with authority'? Here is a fundamental difference between Shi'a and Sunni thought. We say that 'those vested with authority' are those who meet the God-given criteria for leadership. On the other hand, they do not consider this a necessary condition. I cannot say I have thoroughly researched the contents of their works of jurisprudence. However, what they frequently say in their public statements is that anyone who occupies a position of power and authority should be respected and recognised as legitimate.

'And if you dispute concerning anything, refer it to God and the Apostle, if you have faith in God and the Last Day. That is better and more favourable in outcome.' This verse makes clear that good leadership produces good outcomes and bad leadership produces bad outcomes.

The third verse then criticises those who reject this general command: 'Have you not regarded those who claim that they believe in what has been sent down to you, and what was sent down before you?'[26] These people think they believe in your religion and the religion which was revealed to those prophets who came before you; they fancy themselves faithful, but they do things that are contrary to their faith in God. What are those things? 'They desire to seek the judgment of the satanic entities'–in other words, to solve their problems they turn to illegitimate authorities (*ṭāghūt*), receive

26 Q4:60.

judgements from them, and organise their life according to what they tell them. This is contrary to the tenets of their own faith! 'Though they were commanded to reject them, and Satan desires to lead them astray into far error.' They follow the satanic entities, heedless of the fact that this Rebel–this devil, whom the Qur'an calls Rebel–wants to lead them off the right path so they become lost. The Rebel, Satan, wants to take them so far from the path that it is not easy for them to find their way back to it with ease. This is what the Qur'an says.

To sum up, the faithful accept God's *wilāyah* on the basis of a philosophy which has been laid down under the Islamic worldview and is therefore a natural matter. When we say that we must obey God and that God is the *walī-yi amr*, this is based on a clear natural philosophy because everything belongs to God. As the verse says: 'To Him belongs whatever abides in the night and the day'.[27]

In our next lecture, we will continue our discussion of this topic, God-willing.

27 Q6:13.

Wilāyah to the Ṭāghūt

Tuesday 28th Ramadan 1394
15th October 1974

فَإِذَا قَرَأْتَ الْقُرْآنَ فَاسْتَعِذْ بِاللَّهِ مِنَ الشَّيْطَانِ الرَّجِيمِ (٩٨)
إِنَّهُ لَيْسَ لَهُ سُلْطَانٌ عَلَى الَّذِينَ آمَنُوا وَعَلَى رَبِّهِمْ يَتَوَكَّلُونَ
(٩٩) إِنَّمَا سُلْطَانُهُ عَلَى الَّذِينَ يَتَوَلَّوْنَهُ وَالَّذِينَ هُمْ بِهِ
مُشْرِكُونَ (١٠٠)

'When you recite the Qur'an, seek the protection of God against the outcast Satan. Indeed, he does not have any authority over those who have faith and put their trust in their Lord. His authority is only over those who befriend him and those who make him a partner [of God].'
Sūrat al-Naḥl (16):98–100

The topic we wish to address with the above verses today is as follows: We previously understood that every Muslim and everyone who claims to be a servant of God, must recognise the *walī* appointed by God to direct all the activities of his life, he must deliver his obedience to that *walī* that God has appointed. In short, he must make God the sole arbiter and director of the affairs of his life, and anyone whom God has appointed as His deputy on earth. We also discussed the identities of those whom God chooses as His representatives. We said that these are first the prophets, and then the *awliyā'*–those whom you already know as *awliyā'*, meaning the divine leaders and rulers. In short, we said that the divine *walī* and ruler must be appointed by God, whether specifically by name, or generally by qualifications. This is what we spoke about yesterday. Today, we will discuss what it means when someone rejects God's *wilāyah* and delivers his obedience to someone other than God. First of all, how do we judge such a person? Second, what is this action called? Third, what is the outcome of such an act? This is what we will discuss regarding *wilāyah* today. Once we have grasped this, we will discuss some of the fundamental practical principles of Islam; our main discussion is on *wilāyah*, but these issues that derive from it will be secondary and pertaining to practice, while *wilāyah* itself is a fundamental doctrine.

The Qur'an calls every form of *wilāyah* other than that of God '*wilāyat al-ṭāghūt*' or '*wilāyah* of the Rebel.' Anyone who is not under the umbrella of God's *wilāyah* is under the *wilāyah* of *ṭāghūt*. But what does *ṭāghūt* mean? The Arabic word *ṭāghūt* is derived from the root *ṭughyān*, which means rebellion and overstepping the proper bounds of human nature. For example, if we say that humanity came into being in order to attain perfection, someone who stops humanity from attaining perfection is *ṭāghūt*. If we say that human beings must live in accordance with God's religion, this is something natural and innate to the human being. If someone causes humans to reject this and brings about changes in them so that they live in a way that does not accord with God's religion, this person is *ṭāghūt*. The human being must always be striving to bring his own existence to fruition, so anything that leads the human being not to strive, not to make an effort, to become lazy, to seek a life of comfort and ease, that too is *ṭāghūt*.

Human beings must obey God, anything that that causes human beings to disregard God's command, anything that causes them to abandon God's command, anything that causes them to act in disobedience to God–this is *ṭāghūt*. Therefore, the word *ṭāghūt* does not refer to any one thing, as some might imagine–for example, that *ṭāghūt* is the name of an idol. Yes, it is the name of an idol, but not any specific idol. Sometimes, that idol is your own self. Sometimes, that idol is your wealth. Sometimes, that idol is you seeking an ordinary and comfortable life. Sometimes, that idol is your ambition. Sometimes, that idol is the person who takes you by the hand, closes your eyes, and takes you wherever he pleases. Sometimes, this idol is gold and silver, unliving metal. Sometimes, this idol is a human being, your nearest and dearest. Sometimes, it is the social order. Sometimes, it is the law. Therefore, *ṭāghūt* is not the name of any one thing–although on the topic of social classes that we discussed in the lectures on prophethood, we did see that the verses of the Qur'an placed *ṭāghūt* above the elite, the wealthy, and the priesthood. However, this is another topic and is beyond the scope of our present discussion. Therefore, anyone who is not under the *wilāyah* of God is inevitably under the *wilāyah* of *ṭāghūt* and Satan.

What is the relationship between *ṭāghūt* and Satan? Is there any relation between the two? Yes! Satan is the *ṭāghūt*, and the *ṭāghūt* is Satan. Look at the language of this verse from the Qur'an: 'Those who have faith fight in the way of God, and those who are faithless fight in the way of the satanic entities. So fight the allies of Satan; indeed the stratagems of Satan are always flimsy.'[28] Do you see in this verse, how God uses the terms Satan and *ṭāghūt* interchangeably? Any element that is external to the human being's own existence and that prompts him to do evil or immoral things, to oppress, to wrong, or to tyrannise, we call that element 'Satan' or 'a devil.'

There are human devils, there are *jinn* devils, they are devils who are our nearest and dearest, there are devils who are our leaders, there are devils who are strangers, there are devils who are our feelings. We call all of these 'Satan.' One of the exemplars of these devils is

28 Q4:76.

Iblīs, who refused to bow down before Adam when God commanded him to do so. But this Satan, whose story we know and who we curse almost every day of our lives–poor guy!–is just the first of the devils. He is not the only devil. In fact, he may not have even been the first, and he certainly was not the last! We have God only knows how many devils. We can even reach out and touch some of them. We can hold some of them. We see some of them. Sometimes, we can even live with them. Each of these devils is fully a devil. Anything that leads the human being away from the path of God and towards corruption, moral decline, and evil, is a devil.

Every *wilāyah* besides that of God is a *wilāyah* of Satan and *ṭāghūt*. Anyone who does not live under the rule of the true *walī*, should know that he lives under the rule of *ṭāghūt* and Satan. Now you might ask: 'What's the problem if he lives under the rule of Satan and *ṭāghūt* and follows their commands?' This is one of the points addressed in today's verses. The Qur'an gives several answers on this topic.

The first answer is that if you submit to the *wilāyah* of Satan, this means that Satan gains control over all the useful, creative and fruitful energies that are contained within your existence. This is the first thing, that if you bow down to Satan and *ṭāghūt* and they gain authority over your being, there is no escaping them: Everything that is in your existence, all of your energy, your creativity, your agency, your brilliance, will fall into their grasp. And when all of your existence is in their grasp, it is easy for them to drive you down the same path that they chose, and take you to the same destination as they reached–just by wanting it, they will take you with them. It is clear that Satan and *ṭāghūt* will never guide man to spiritual enlightenment, wisdom, or ease. This is not the goal of Satan and *ṭāghūt*; their primary goal is securing their own individual interests; so they will use you for their own ends.

If you consider each of the series of things I have just enumerated, these words and phrases, you will see that they each have their own specific meaning, and you will see how they apply to historical realities, from the earliest recorded events until the present day. If you submit to the *wilāyah* of *ṭāghūt*, then all of your energy, your creativity, and your potential will fall into the grasp of *ṭāghūt* and, when this happens, this will not be to your benefit, because Satan and *ṭāghūt* do not even consider what is beneficial to you. On the other hand, if they have to sacrifice you for their own ends, they will sacrifice you without hesitation. If they have to lead you astray, they will lead you astray. If they deem it necessary that you should suffer for their sake, then you must suffer for their sake. This is Satan we are talking about, after all! With the power that he has–and that you have given him–he can take you wherever he pleases.

The verse of the Qur'an that we will discuss today is a verse that is very worthy of reflection upon. Sometimes, even if you ponder on the meaning of the Qur'an's verses, with a little extra effort, you sometimes find something new. I am always deeply regretful of how little time we spend pondering on the Qur'an.

God says in the Qur'an: 'Whoever defies the Apostle', whoever argues with the Prophet and opposes him, 'after the guidance has become clear to him', by turning aside from the path the Prophet has made clear to him, 'and follows a way other than that of the faithful', a way other than that of the Islamic society and a way that does not lead to the objectives of his faith, and separates himself from the Muslims. 'We shall abandon him to his devices'[29], literally, we shall leave him to that which he takes as a *walī*, that to which he bows down, the *wilāyah* which he accepts, we shall permanently colour his unfortunate existence with this. He himself chose to go and live under that *wilāyah*, so we will abandon him there. 'Indeed, God does not change a people's lot, unless they change what is in their souls.'[30]

29 Q4:115.

30 Q13:11.

It was you yourself who handed over the reins of your life to Satan, so leave those reins in the hands of Satan. This is what We do. This is the law of creation. This is for this worldly life of yours–and what about your afterlife in the next world? 'And We will make him enter Hell', when you close your eyes on this world, you will enter Hell and suffer eternal divine punishment. And when any person looks at human history, they see this is exactly how it was.

These are very important social issues. Very little work has been done to understand these issues from the viewpoint of the Qur'an, and we have done very little work on applying these issues to the history of Islam. How good it would be for those people who are interested in the Qur'an and have reflective minds to ponder on its social and especially, historical issues. Then, from studying the Qur'an and the trends in history, it would be clear which explanations of the Qur'an's verses correspond to reality. I would like to take a moment to discuss an episode in history in light of the verses we have just covered. I know that this is not my usual approach in these sorts of gatherings–to discuss history–but today I would like to do just this!

The city of Kufah is a very interesting city in the history of Islam. You will already know some facts about Kufah–you are not only hearing about it just now. For example, you will recall that it was Kufah, out of all the cities of the Islamic empire, that the Commander of the Faithful (a) chose to make his capital. This is one positive point, as they say. You will also recall that the inhabitants of Kufah fought for the Commander of the Faithful at the Battle of the Camel, and at the Battle of Nahrawān, and at the Battle of Ṣiffīn also, along with tribes from the vicinity of Kufah and elsewhere, but that it was also in this battle that the Commander of the Faithful (a) reprimanded them: 'Why is it that, when I call you for battle, you do not respond?' It was the same people of Kufah whose leaders wrote a letter pledging their allegiance to Imam Ḥasan (a) and promising the support of their city. It was the same people of Kufah who wrote to Imam Ḥusayn (a), saying: 'We have no leader', we have no ruler, we have no commander, God has given this tyrant authority over us, so come and lead us. Some were faithful in their pledge–men like Sulaymān ibn Ṣurad, Ḥabīb ibn Maẓāhir, Muslim ibn ʿAwsajah and others–but most participated in the massacre of Ḥusayn (a) and his outnumbered band of supporters. Of course, it was also the people of Kufah who brought something into being the likes of which has been rarely seen in the history of Islam: The Tawwābīn or 'Penitents'. They were determined to sacrifice their own lives fighting the Umayyads in order to repent for their part in the killing of Ḥusayn at Karbala. This spirit of resistance and rebellion persisted throughout the reigns of the Umayyad and ʿAbbāsid caliphates, as time and again the people of the city rose up against tyranny; how many gave their lives, how many were slain, how many brave struggles they gave! But at the same time, it was also the people of Kufah who became weak, lazy, and impotent in spirit and in thought, as demonstrated on a number of issues.

So how to explain this? Did they have two spirits, two natures, or two faces? The same people to whom Zaynab bint ʿAlī said: 'O people of Kufah! O people of betrayal and perfidiousness!' The issue of Kufah is something worth reflecting on. I believe it would be worthwhile and very interesting to study the psychology of the city of Kufah through the ages. If someone is qualified to do this; a sociologist or a psychologist perhaps. It would be fascinating to hear their thoughts on this strange city. At one moment, the people of Kufah seem to embody the best qualities of humanity, at another, they exhibit weakness, laziness, and ineptitude. What can explain this? Were there two types of people in Kufah? Were there two factions in Kufan society? Kufah was a region that was under the direct rule of the Commander of the Faithful, and it was he who nurtured its society. Kufah was an environment that produced real human beings. Therefore, in the history of Shi'ism, nowhere produced as many valiant fighters as Kufah. Why is this? Because of the teaching and guidance of the Commander of the Faithful (a) for those four years! It is no joke for someone like ʿAlī ibn Abī Ṭālib to rule a place for four years! Yes, it is true that his rule, when looked at with regard to the entirety of the Islamic world, was ultimately unsuccessful. However, it was successful at the level of Kufah itself. In Kufan society, the Commander of the Faithful had a profound effect. For this reason, Kufah became the cradle of Shi'ism, and the birthplace of Shi'i values and virtue. Is that right?

However, just because somewhere is the birthplace of some values, that does not mean that everyone there shares these values or the virtues that accompany them, or that even those that do are ideal followers of these values. In every society, there are always the good and the bad. Out of a million people, there are perhaps tens of thousands or even just thousands who do something heroic and inspiring, so that all one million people become known for their valour. There was a class of people in Kufah who were very interesting. They were not a class in the strict and technical sociological sense of the term, rather they were a group of people who exhibited these qualities. As for the vast majority of the Kufans, the masses, they were like ordinary people anywhere in the world. No better and no worse. Just like the people of Mashhad, Tehran, Isfahan, Madinah, or other places. However, that small group of people in that corner of the Islamic world were a major source of anxiety for the governments of their time. The Umayyads always made sure to appoint the vilest, cruellest, and most obedient of their servants to govern the city in order to deal with these elements, which by outright persecuting them, by spreading negative propaganda, or by presiding over the pauperisation of the city's people, in order to corrupt them and lead them astray.

Why did they do these things? Because that resistance group were only found in this city and not in others. Because they wanted to smash the basis of this resistance and make use of this city for their own ends. Because they could not bend these people to their will, they destroyed the land which made them instead. They spread propaganda to poison people's minds, they put people under pressure, they weakened people economically, and, in short, they placed the city under siege and created harsh conditions found in no other city in the empire. And it was as a result of these activities that the ordinary people fell under the influence of the regime and began to oppose this group. However, this was not because the people of the city were innately bad. It would be very good for someone interested in this topic to study it.

Let me give you some further explanation. The Umayyad caliph, ʿAbd al-Malik, sent Ḥajjāj ibn Yūsuf to Kufah because he knew that no one other than Ḥajjāj could possibly break the spirit of resistance that was there. Ḥajjāj was possibly the most brutal, ruthless, and loyal of ʿAbd al-Malik's governors. So, Ḥajjāj entered the city in the middle of the night, so that people would not know that he had arrived. It seems the people of the city had expelled his predecessor or somehow forced him to leave. Ḥajjāj had thirty, forty, or one hundred armed men with him. He and his men came to the central mosque of Kufah, which was filled by the murmuring of night worshippers. He withdrew into a corner of the mosque and issued orders to his men.

When the time came for morning prayers, and the call to prayer went out, people gathered at the mosque to pray. They came for worship. However, it became clear that they were not as aware as they should have been in their prayers. The reason for this is what I just said, namely that Ḥajjāj ibn Yūsuf had come, but no one knew why he was there or even that he was in the mosque. He came and sat near a crowd, without drawing anyone's attention. Then, all of a sudden, he ascended the pulpit. At first, people did not realise what was going on. He sat atop the pulpit without saying a word. Someone looked up at saw Ḥajjāj sitting atop the pulpit but did not recognise him. He turned to the person next to him and said: 'Who is that on the pulpit?' That person made a face. Ḥajjāj was wearing a turban made from red fur, with a strip of cloth hanging beneath his chin. Then he loosened his turban and drew the cloth around his face so that only his eyes were showing. Now the people saw the strange countenance of this armed man in a red turban and cloak sitting on the pulpit of the mosque of Kufah, they fell silent and people gathered around to see how this was.

Keep in mind the verse of the Qur'an we quoted: 'We shall abandon him to his devices'–it says that someone who leaves the path of faith and the faithful, a servant who turns aside from the right path, we will put a noose around his neck. You are a Muslim. Some unknown person is sitting on the pulpit. Why are you gathering around him passively? You should be going up there and challenging him, saying: 'Who are you? Explain yourself!' Imagine one person, two people, three people asking this question. This would change the situation entirely. But they were lax. Their passivity and weakness meant that they sat there waiting for him to speak.

Once he had everyone's attention, he said: 'It seems that the people of Kufah do not know me. People saw me but they clearly did not recognise me. So, allow me to introduce myself!' He removed the turban and the face covering, looked at the people gathered there, and recited the poetry:

'I am the son of clearness and the climber of defiles [full of vigour],
If I take off my turban, you will know me.'

And as he removed his turban before the onlookers, the people began telling one another: 'It's Ḥajjāj!' They were overcome by shock and awe, that Ḥajjāj had suddenly come and sat himself on the pulpit. People sat there, terrified. No one said to himself: 'Ḥajjāj is but one man, and I am one man too; he is just sitting up there, and I am sitting down here. Everything he has, I have.' Do you see how spineless these people were not to see this?

Ḥajjāj spoke: 'O people of Kufah! I see heads that have ripened hanging from their necks ready to harvest!' People became even more terrified. The hollowness of their slogans was revealed. It's not like Ḥajjāj had taken an atom bomb to Kufah. If he had set off an atom bomb, there would have been no one left to rule. He could not kill everyone–some had to survive. If he killed everyone, who would he rule over? Over a door and four walls? Where was the fun in that? He may as well go and rule the empty desert if that was the case! But people did not think of this.

He told them that their heads were ripe low-hanging fruit and the time for the harvest had come. Then he said: 'Now I will tell you whose heads are to be cut,' and told his servant to read the Caliph's letter. The servant stood before the pulpit and read out the letter of the caliph ʿAbd al-Malik ibn Marwān. It began: 'In the name of God, the Compassionate, the Merciful. From the Commander of the Faithful, ʿAbd al-Malik ibn Marwān, to the people of Kufah. O people of Kufah! Peace be with you'. At this point, Ḥajjāj stood up and silenced his servant. Then he turned to the people there and said: 'How poor your manners have become! The Commander of the Faithful sends you greetings of peace, and you do not respond to his greeting in kind!' Then he told his servant to start again. This time, when the servant read the words 'Peace be with you', the whole mosque repeated loudly 'And peace be upon the Commander of the Faithful!' Ḥajjāj must have given himself a self-satisfied smile and said in his heart: 'Mission accomplished.' Because he knew then that his work was as good as finished.

God says in the Qur'an: 'Whoever defies the Apostle, after the guidance has become clear to him, and follows a way other than that of the faithful, We shall abandon him to his devices'. You have accepted Ḥajjāj as your governor? You send peace on his so-called 'Commander of the Faithful' (better to call him the 'Commander of the Faithless' or 'Commander of the Sinful'!), OK–God will leave you with your Ḥajjāj then. God will not perform some miracle to make Ḥajjāj go away. And Imam Zayn al-ʿĀbidīn will remain where he is. This Ḥajjāj will be with you until you make him go away. So long as you accept Ḥajjāj, your life, your thoughts, and your souls will be in his hands. This is the cosmic order of things. This is the rule that governs human history.

These are the lessons that history teaches us. As Iqbāl says:

It is more fitting that the sweethearts
Be described in the words of others.

History is a kind of exegesis of the Qur'an. You can find the Qur'an in history. In the words of Saʿdī:

The wise experienced man
Must live twice in these days,
The first to gain experience,
And the second to put it into practice.

We must pay attention to history. We must familiarise ourselves with history. But you must always try to draw a lesson from history! Do not content yourself with stories and tales from the past. See instead what message history has for us today. What, for example, is the message that the events surrounding Ḥajjāj send us now?

Go and see what lessons history has to teach us and what messages it conveys to us! Plunge into the depths of history.

Now let us see how the history I have just recounted relates to the verses of the Qur'an we will discuss today: 'When you recite the Qur'an, seek the protection of God against the outcast Satan.'[31] Now that you have read the Qur'an, now that you have learnt something of the Islamic sciences, and understood some of God's word, seek protection lest Satan afflict you and make you forget the Qur'an or unable to comprehend it. How should you seek protection? Try to take the knowledge of the Qur'an that has entered your heart and keep

31 Q16:98.

it with you, so that you are not deprived of a deeper understanding. 'Seek the protection of God against the outcast Satan.' Can we seek God's protection? Can he ward off Satan's evil? Of course! 'Indeed he does not have any authority over those who have faith and put their trust in their Lord.'[32] Satan's evil and corruption cannot overcome those who have faith in God and rely on God in their affairs. Those who try to place themselves under God's *wilāyah* are protected from Satan.

'His authority is only over those who take him as a *walī*'.[33] So Satan only has power over those who accept his *wilāyah*, just like the authority of Ḥajjāj was only over those who sat and listened to his harsh speech. So Satan's authority is only over those who accept his *wilāyah* 'and those who make him a partner [of God]'.

'Whoever defies the Apostle, after the guidance has become clear to him'[34], whoever leaves the path of the Prophet and does not act on the responsibilities that his profession of faith has placed upon his shoulders, 'and follows a way other than that of the faithful, We shall abandon him to his devices'. We shall make that thing whose *wilāyah* he accepted his *walī*, 'and We will make him enter Hell, and it is an evil destination.'

'Indeed God does not forgive that any partner should be ascribed to Him'.[35] Refer back to our discussions of *tawḥīd* and idolatry and see how we explained these two terms; what kind of sin is it that God does not forgive? 'Indeed God does not forgive that any partner should be ascribed to Him'. If we want to be even more precise, we can. God's forgiveness does not encompass the state of a person who accepts idolatry. A person who is an idolater is under the *wilāyah* of someone other than God, so he has gone from the domain of God's

---

32 Q16:99.

33 16:100.

34 Q4:115.

35 Q4:116.

influence to the domain of another's influence. The sin of associating partners with God inflicts a wound on the soul of the one who does so that it cannot be healed, meaning it cannot be forgiven. This is what the word forgiveness (*maghfirah*) means, as we explained previously. Forgiving a sin means healing the wound it inflicted and undoing the harm and error it caused. When this wound is healed, it is then that forgiveness encompasses a person. When you are forgiven it means that the pain and suffering caused by your bad act, by your straying from the path of God, is effaced–'but He forgives anything besides that to whomever He wishes'. Of course, God's will is not arbitrary; He wishes to forgive those who repent to Him and return to His way. 'And whoever ascribes partners to God has certainly strayed into far error.'

Sometimes in the desert you lose your way, but only by a kilometre. Other times, you lose your way by tens of kilometres and it is not easy to find your way back to the road. It needs more effort to get back–a person who is so thoroughly lost needs stronger guidance. Equally, those who associate partners with God have truly strayed far from the right path 'and whoever ascribes partners to God, he has certainly strayed into far error.'

'They invoke none but females besides Him, and invoke none but a obstinate Satan'[36], a devil who is utterly disobedient, and without goodness or virtue, 'whom God has cursed,'–'and who said,'–this means that the nature or essence of all devils is this–'"I will surely take of Your servants a settled share"'[37]–meaning that he will separate some of God's servants from the right path and take away their reasoning, and deprive them of their insight and their wisdom, so that they will not be under God's *wilāyah* but his own instead–'and I will lead them astray and give them [false] hopes' with no basis in reality.

36 Q4:117.

37 Q4:118.

Pay attention to this phrase 'give them [false] hopes.' Far-fetched or unrealistic hopes mean anything that lead a person away from the path of God. Far-fetched hopes for ten years of living in comfort and ease, far-fetched hopes for finding a match for your son or daughter, far-fetched hopes to extend your small house, or to expand your shop front, or far-fetched hopes to be the head or manager of a company or organisation, to make money, for my son to be an engineer or for me to be one–these are far-fetched hopes. Hopes which are like a millstone hung round a person's neck, weighing them down and holding them back; hopes which, no matter how much you strive for them, are forever out of reach. All at once you find the freedom you found in the path of God gone. 'And give them [false] hopes'.

'And prompt them to slit the ears of cattle', this is an example of a wrongheaded pre-Islamic practice. However, this phrase may also symbolise something greater. I haven't given it much thought–there are a couple of issues on which I have not had the time to study everything that has been said–but it is possible that there is another meaning latent in this verse. I will say what I think this is, but you should also ponder on this. So, this verse mentions a pre-Islamic practice whereby people would cut the ears of animals, perhaps in order to obtain some blessing or secure some worldly benefit. It is a pre-Islamic practice. However, this could be a symbol for many ungodly practices and ideas. What's more, even if the followers of these practices do not find them worthless, they are certainly worthless in the eyes of any rational person.

The next phrase is very interesting: 'and I will prompt them to alter God's creation."' Satan says that those human beings who are under his command, who live under his authority and *wilāyah*, he will make them bring about alterations in the natural order that God created, and go far astray from the path that you had originally laid out for them. He says: I will make a law for them that goes against human nature; I will give them commands that go against the natural order;

I will lead them down a path that will take them to a destination far from the destination for which they were intended. I will certainly give them a command so that they will surely change your creation and disrupt the God-given order of things. This is Satan's promise to God.

This is the nature of Satan's covenant with God, it is a covenant of disobedience, of insolence, of opposition to God. And isn't this how we are? All the devils are like a plague upon creation. All of the devils of this world are after this end. Be certain that if there is someone who wants to live his life in the way that God and nature intended, Satan will not allow him to. No matter how he achieves this, those who are under his *wilāyah* are under his authority and power, and they are far from their God-given nature. This is so because, otherwise Satan would be failing in his mission. This is why, immediately after this, God says: 'Whoever takes Satan as a friend instead of God has certainly incurred a manifest loss.'

'He makes them promises and gives them [false] hopes, yet Satan does not promise them anything but delusion.'[38] Satan makes promises to them about their future lives, but it is all lies; he inflicts far-fetched hopes upon them and, in the end, all he offers them is deceit and delusion.

38 Q4:120.

Migrating to the Wilāyah of God

Monday 29th Ramadan 1394
16th October 1974

وَمَنْ يُهَاجِرْ فِي سَبِيلِ اللَّهِ يَجِدْ فِي الْأَرْضِ مُرَاغَمًا كَثِيرًا
وَسَعَةً وَمَنْ يَخْرُجْ مِنْ بَيْتِهِ مُهَاجِرًا إِلَى اللَّهِ وَرَسُولِهِ ثُمَّ يُدْرِكْهُ
الْمَوْتُ فَقَدْ وَقَعَ أَجْرُهُ عَلَى اللَّهِ وَكَانَ اللَّهُ غَفُورًا رَحِيمًا
(١٠٠)

'Whoever migrates in the way of God will find many havens and plenitude in the earth. And whoever leaves his home migrating toward God and His Apostle, and is then overtaken by death, his reward shall certainly fall on God, and God is all-forgiving, all-merciful.'
Sūrat al-Nisāʾ (4):100

The issue of emigration for the sake of God (*hijrah*) is connected to the issue of *wilāyah* in the broad sense that we have discussed the latter concept in these lectures. We said that *wilāyah* refers to the creation of a firm bond between the faithful and one another, and the cutting of ties between the faithful and those who are not faithful. At the next level, we said that it signifies the creation of a powerful link between all the individuals on the side of the faithful with the central power and focal point that is responsible for governing Islamic society, namely the Imam, *walī*, or Islamic leader. Aside from this, we also discussed who this leader of Islamic society must be. We found our answer in the Qur'an: 'Your guardian is only God, His Apostle, and the faithful who maintain the prayer and give the zakat while bowing down,'[39] which contains a reference to the Commander of the Faithful. If we are able to comprehend *wilāyah* in this broad sense without relegating this issue to a secondary or subsidiary matter in relation to *wilāyah*, as some do without realising it, then emigration becomes one of the *consequences* of *wilāyah*. Why is this so? Because if it is necessary for every person to live under the *wilāyah* of God and His *walī*–as indicated by the doctrine of *wilāyah* itself–and if we accept that all of the human being's energies and potential, in body, soul, and mind, must be directed in accordance with the will of God's *walī* and, in short, that all the elements of his being must be serve God and not serve *ṭāghūt*, then the inescapable conclusion we must draw is that if there is somewhere where all of our being and all of our energies are not under the *wilāyah* of the Imam but are, in fact, under the *wilāyah* of *ṭāghūt* and Satan, then it is our God-given duty to escape the prison of *ṭāghūt*, to save ourselves, to free ourselves, and flee to the *wilāyah* of God. In short, we must escape the authority of the unjust and flee to the authority of the just. This is known as emigration (*hijrah*). So, do you see how the matter of emigration is a natural corollary of *wilāyah*? Therefore, we have already mentioned three issues pertaining to *wilāyah*. This is the fourth.

Why must the human being escape the *wilāyah* of *ṭāghūt* and Satan? This is a question that is worthy of serious consideration. What I would really like, when I pose this question, is for you dear audience to immediately take it in to your minds and analyse it for yourselves, and for you to try and formulate an answer for it on the basis of the teachings and principles of Islam. If your answer and my mine–the answer I am about to present–are at odds, then there is still more to discuss. So the question is this: Can we not be

39 Q5:55.

both Muslims and under the *wilāyah* of *ṭāghūt*? Can we not imagine a Muslim living under Satan's authority, while still serving the All-merciful? Is this something that can happen or not? Is it possible somewhere in which all the horizons of human existence have been occupied by an ungodly force? For the human body to be under the dominion of an ungodly force, for the human mind to be under the dominion of an ungodly force, for the spirit, emotions, and feelings of members of society to be dragged this way and that by such an ungodly force? Can there be a person under the dominion of such ungodly and rebellious powers who is, at the same time, a servant of God and a true Muslim? Is this something possible or not? Ponder this for a moment and formulate an answer in your mind. See whether or not you think this can happen. To properly answer this question, we must do some analysis and reflect on the Qur'an so that the answer becomes clear: Can someone live under the authority of Satan while being a Muslim, or can they not?

This question is made up of two parts. The first part is what does it mean for a person to live under the *wilāyah* of Satan? What does *wilāyah* mean in this context? If we give it the same meaning as we derived from several verses of the Qur'an, then it becomes clear what the *wilāyah* of Satan means: The *wilāyah* of Satan is when Satan–in the general meaning we mentioned previously, rather than referring to any specific being–holds sway over all the power and potentiality that exist within the human being. Whatever a human being does, he follows the path which Satan has laid out for him. Whatever he thinks, he follows the path that Satan inclines towards. It is exactly like someone who has fallen into a river and is being pulled along by a fast-moving current. This poor soul does not want to be swept against the big rocks where he might dash his head or be dragged beneath the surface and drowned. However, even though he does not want it, the current is so fast and strong that it carries him along no matter how hard he struggles, no matter where he turns or what he tries to grab a hold of, the current is too strong for him.

The *wilāyah* of *ṭāghūt* and the *wilāyah* of Satan are no different to this. That is why the Qur'an says: 'We made them leaders who invite to the Fire'[40]–there are leaders who lead their followers into the fires of Hell, who lead them towards misery. Another verse says: 'Have you not regarded those who have changed God's blessing with ingratitude and landed their people in the house of ruin?–Hell, which they shall enter, and it is an evil abode!'[41] God asks whether we have considered those people who were ungrateful for God's blessings? To which blessings does he refer? This could actually be anything: The blessing of power, which is a manifestation of God's power, the blessing of worldly power, the blessing of being charged with looking after the affairs of thousands, the blessing of having the abilities, thoughts, potential, energy of people at your command–these are all forms of blessings; these are all resources which can be a source of good for humankind.

The people who are under the authority of the kind of person this verse is discussing can become great human beings, they can become God's foremost servants, they can attain the highest levels of perfection, but they have shown ingratitude for these blessings by using them in a way that they should not. In doing so, they have 'landed their people in the house of ruin'. They have brought their own people to the threshold of nothingness and destruction. They have brought them to 'Hell, which they shall enter, and it is an evil abode!'

Mūsā ibn Jaʿfar (a) recited this verse to the ʿAbbāsid caliph Harūn al-Rashīd, to show him that it was he who was leading his own people towards ruin and destruction instead of towards goodness. When

40 Q28:41.

41 Q14:28–29.

Imam Kāẓim recited this verse, Hārūn was taken aback. He said: 'Are we disbelievers, then?' The Imam had recited this verse to him so that he would see that the word *kāfir* did not just mean those who do not believe in God or deny the truthfulness of the Qur'an or the Prophet of God–this is just one kind of *kāfir*. In fact, this is the better kind of *kāfir*, because they explicitly say what they believe and people can see what their stance is in order to respond.

A worse kind of *kāfir* is someone who is ungrateful for the great blessings that God has bestowed upon him (*kufrān al-niʿmah*) by using them in an incorrect way. It is not only that this person takes himself to Hell, though, he takes everyone under his authority with him as well. This is the real meaning of the *wilāyah* of *ṭāghūt*.

So, when someone lives under the *wilāyah* of *ṭāghūt*, it really seems as though he does not have control over his own life. By this, I do not mean that such a person has no free will whatsoever–the verse of the Qur'an we just examined makes everything clear–but the current of the river carries him along. He wants to grab hold of something, but he can't. He wants to pull himself away from the path to Hell, because he sees that everything is sliding towards Hell and taking him with it. But there are many people there, so even if you want to turn back, you are carried along by the crowd. You want to be good, you want to live a good life, you want to live like a human being, you want to remain a Muslim and die a Muslim, but you cannot. In other words, the currents of society have caught you and are taking you with them–there is nothing you can do to resist. Even if you try to resist, you are just wasting your own energy–it won't work. Not only can you not resist, worse still is the fact that sometimes you don't even realise what is happening.

I don't know whether you have seen how fish swim in the ocean when they are being caught by fishermen. Sometimes hundreds of fish are caught in a single net and dragged to shore. They are caught out in the middle of the ocean, many kilometres away, but this net carries all of them to the shore across this distance. They don't even realise what is happening. If you ask a fish caught in a net: Where are you going? The fish might think it is going by choice, but the reality is the fish has no choice; it will go wherever the fishermen carry it to.

The pre-Islamic way of life was like an invisible net cast over human society, carrying people to wherever those who controlled the net wanted to take them. People did not know where they were going. Sometimes they even believed that they were actually being led to happiness and felicity, unaware of the fact that, no, they were actually going to Hell–'Hell, which they shall enter, and it is an evil abode!'

So, this is what the *wilāyah* of *ṭāghūt* looks like. This is the *wilāyah* of Satan. This is the first part of our question. The second part is the core of the question. Remember, we asked whether it was possible for someone to live as a Muslim while simultaneously living under the *wilāyah* of *ṭāghūt*? Is it? Now that we have understood in general what it means to live under the *wilāyah* of *ṭāghūt*, in order to grasp the particulars of this we must refer to examples from history.

When we study the time of the Umayyads and the ʿAbbāsids, we see that the Islamic world was full of energy, we see the amount of knowledge and learning that was taking place in Islamic society; what great physicians there were, what great translators! At a time when there was a drought of language and learning in the rest of the world, the Islamic world was busily translating the amassed learning of the ancients into Arabic and making this available to people. In all fields, whether history, science, medicine, astronomy, and even art, Muslims took great strides forward. Today, when someone like the French thinker, Gustave Le Bon, or another European scholar of the east, studies these phenomena, he refers to the second, third, and fourth Islamic centuries as a 'golden age'. Adam Metz wrote a book on Islamic civilisation of the fourth century hijri which reads almost like a lament for the loss of this great civilisation. He describes a resplendent culture of learning and scientific advancement in the fourth century. Why do these European scholars behold the second, third, and fourth centuries of Islam with such wonderment? Because of the amazing dynamism and vitality on display from the Islamic society. Let me ask you a question: Do you think all of this energy and activity from that time was to the benefit of Islamic society and humanity as a whole?

Almost ten centuries have passed since that time. Without showing any partiality to those days, it is safe to say that compared to the non-Muslim world, it was the Islamic world that was the beacon of knowledge and learning. It was the Islamic world that was building universities, debating philosophy, and making advances in science and medicine. But amongst ourselves, if we want to be honest, did all of that activity ultimately end up benefiting humanity and Islamic society? What does Islamic society have of this heritage ten centuries later? And what has it lost? Why do we no longer possess this intellectual and scientific wealth? Why is it that in today's world we no longer shine as we did in the golden age? Is it for any other reason than the fact that all of these efforts, even if they were valuable for the benefit of all humanity, ultimately took place under the auspices of *ṭāghūt*? As the poet Ḥāfiẓ says:

I shall never grasp the jewel of Solomon
Lest one day it falls into the hands of Ahriman.

It was these *Ahrimans* or devils who played with Islamic society. Even if they encouraged and sponsored these translations, it was only so that they could take credit for it as one of the achievements of their reign. Even if they did the same for all the scientific, mathematical, astronomical, literary, legal and other activities that took place under their authority. If, instead of all of these mathematical, scientific, astronomical, literary, and legal advancements, they had simply allowed the Imams (a) to rule, if they had allowed Imam Ṣādiq (a) to take control of affairs, and placed all of the power and energy of society at his disposal, even from the perspective of learning, literature, and the issues in which the world takes pride today, even if this had delayed work by a hundred years, it would have been of more benefit to the human race. This is because humanity would have grown, Islam would have flourished, and human energy and potential would be channelled into the correct path. On the other hand, under the ʿAbbāsids, even though great strides were being made in science, what about individual morals and societal ethics? Is it ok to leave this so weak so that class divisions remain an entrenched component of society?

It is exactly like the disgraceful and corrupt civilisation of the world today. The world powers boast of their scientific discoveries, they boast of their wonderous inventions, they boast about every medicine, every formula, every undertaking. This is from the perspective of science. However, from the perspective of humanity and ethics, nothing has changed from a thousand years ago. Today, we still see fabulous wealth side by side with terrible hunger and poverty. We still see a very small percentage of the world's population enjoying the benefits of the modern world, while millions live hungry in impoverished nations. They boast of their achievements, but this is exactly the state of the great Islamic civilisation that prevailed in the second, third, and fourth centuries of Islam. It is the same issue now as it was then. Great scientific advancements are taking place, but there is no concern for the values of humanity or virtue; huge class differences remain, and at the same time as one part of the world is starving, the other part eats itself to death. It is the same now as it was then. What is the cause of this misfortune? Why was it the case that Islamic society at that time, with all of the intellectual energy and dynamism it had, why was it not a rose in the garden of virtue and humanity? Why not?

Now, when we look at the history of the second and third centuries of Islam, we can mention those people whose names truly belong on the list of great figures in world history, those who fought against the injustice of the societies in which they lived. There is Muʿallā ibn Khunays, whom they hung in the marketplace, Yaḥyā ibn Umm Ṭawīl, whose hand and foot they cut off and whose tongue they tore out, Muḥammad ibn Abī ʿUmayr, whom they scourged a hundred times, Yaḥya ibn Zayd, a young man of eighteen years who they killed in the mountains of Khurāsān, Zayd ibn ʿAlī, whose corpse they left on display for four years. These are the people whose names we can mention proudly as great figures in world history, these are the ones who had nothing to do with this glorious society that Gustave Le Bon described as a 'golden age'. In fact, they fought against that society. So, you can see how when the *wilāyah* of *ṭāghūt* or Satan governs a society, rules over its people, and holds the reins of power, it makes use of the energies of its people, and of their potential, but how? In the same way as we see in the world today, in the same way as we saw in the Islamic society ten or eleven centuries previously. It is in such a way that has no value in the estimation of the values of humanity or on the scales of virtue! This is the *wilāyah* of *ṭāghūt*.

Can one live as a Muslim under the *wilāyah* of *ṭāghūt*? What does it mean to live as a Muslim then? To live as a Muslim means to place all of your potential, your energy, your ability, and your power at God's disposal. It means to offer God everything you have: your wealth, your life, your daily activities, your sleep at night, your thoughts and ideas. 'Can you give any examples of this?' I hear you ask. Of course! Whether for communities that exist as a whole society, as a city, or as a group, especially in rebellious groups who rose up against *ṭāghūt* and emigrated to God.

The first example I will give is of the society of Madinah during the lifetime of the Prophet. When the Prophet was alive, the society of Madinah was a society that served God. It was a truly Muslim society. Every step that society took was a step taken in the path of God. There, Jews and Christians lived under the rule of Islam, and their life was an Islamic one. In an Islamic society, Jews are protected (*taḥt al-dhimmah*) and so are Christians, and all members of society move together in the path of Islam. Yes, as individuals, this person is a Jew or that person is a Christian but, as members of society, they are Muslims. In fact, they live a more authentically Islamic life than Muslims living in pre-Islamic society. During the lifetime of the Prophet, one's wealth was used for the sake of God, one's sword was used for the sake of God, one's tongue was used for the sake of God, one's thoughts and ideas were used for the sake of God. In fact, whatever a person did, they did for the sake of God. Even their emotions and their feelings were for the sake of God. This is at the level of society. During the time of the Commander of the Faithful too, it was more or less the same. Insofar as the Commander of the Faithful (a) was himself a divine ruler and God's *walī*, there was no distinction between him and the Prophet. However, he inherited a bad society. He inherited many problems from his predecessors. In fact, had the Prophet himself come back after twenty-five years and ruled in the Commander of the Faithful's place, he would have confronted exactly the same problems as the Commander of the Faithful did. This is at the level of society.

As for groups, there are many examples of the groups of Shi'a who surrounded the Imams (a) throughout history. The month of Ramadan is coming to an end and we have not even gotten onto the discussion of Imamate. If we had more time, we would discuss Imamate after *wilāyah*. If we had more time, I would have told you how the Shi'a were as a unit at the time of the Imams: I would have shown you how the Imam's connections and relations with the Shi'a were, and how the connections and relations of the Shi'a with the society that surrounded them were. However, for the time being, we will provide a summary of this. The Shi'a outwardly appeared to be living in a social order dominated by *ṭāghūt*, while inwardly they were working against this system. Like the small band of followers that were with Ḥusayn ibn ʿAlī at Karbala. These Shi'a stood firm against the deluge and were ready to go against the direction of the current. Therefore, in history, we have examples at the level of society and at the level of groups. But what about at the level of individuals? In general, an individual can be a Muslim in such a society. Can he place all of his being, all of his potential, and all of his abilities at God's disposal, even while living in the sort of society we have described? This is not possible, because when a person lives in an environment dominated by a system of *ṭāghūt*, a fraction of his being a Muslim ultimately is drawn into the way of *ṭāghūt*, a part of his life is spent serving *ṭāghūt*, he cannot be one hundred percent devoted to God.

There is a tradition in *al-Kāfī* that has been narrated in a number of versions. The book, *Uṣūl al-Kāfī*, is one of the oldest and most reliable works of Shi'a traditions. It contains a few versions of the tradition I am about to quote. You can find it in *al-Kāfī*, in the *Kitāb al-Ḥujjah*, under the heading *Man dāna Allāh-u ʿazz-a wa jall bi ghayr-i imām min Allāh* ('Whoever follows God's religion under an ungodly ruler'). In this tradition, the Imam relates what God has said: 'I will surely punish every flock in Islam that accepts the *wilāyah* of any unjust leader (*imām*) who is not from God, even if that flock is pious and righteous in their deeds, and I will surely forgive every flock in Islam that accepts the *wilāyah* of any just leader appointed by God, even if that flock is wrongdoing and sinful in themselves.' This is an astounding tradition. It says that those people who are under the *wilāyah* of God's *walī* are the people of salvation, even if in their personal conduct they sin or fall short of the mark, while those people who live under the *wilāyah* of Satan and *ṭāghūt* are the people of punishment and ill-fortune, even if they are good and righteous in their personal conduct. This is most astounding. There are several versions of the tradition and all of them give the same meaning, it is found in *Uṣūl al-Kāfī*, and as far as I remember (although I am not fully certain), the chain of its narration is also good.

I always draw an analogy for this tradition. I say it is like a car which you are riding in to go somewhere, let's say to Nishapur! Now, if the car is going to Nishapur, then you will reach your destination. However, if the car, instead of Nishapur, is going to Sarakhs or Qūchān, then you definitely will not reach your destination! So, if the car is travelling to Nishapur and taking you where you want to go, if your fellow passengers in the car are polite, considerate people who treat each other kindly, then so much the better. On the other hand, if they are not particularly polite or friendly, you will still reach your destination. Now, if, on the way, you or they do something wrong, that will be punished, it will have effects, it will have consequences. And they will have to bear those consequences, but they will still reach their destination. On the other hand, if the car is taking you in the opposite direction to Nishapur, even if all the passengers in this car are polite, considerate, and respectful in how they treat one another, even if they behave well together, it is still not going to get you to Nishapur–it's going to take you to Qūchān! And no matter how the people in the car behave, this will not have any effect on this outcome. They might be very good people. They might be very kind people. But will they reach their destination? Obviously not!

In the first instance, the driver was someone reliable, who knew where he was going–a 'leader appointed by God' as the tradition says–and, so, the passengers will reach their destination–'even if that flock is wrongdoing and sinful.' In the second example, the driver does not know the way, he is not reliable, he is greedy, he was drunk, he lost his way, he has something to do in Sarakhs or Qūchān and his needs come before the needs of others, he was going there anyway–the passengers in his car will definitely not reach their destination. It doesn't matter that inside the car, everyone is treating one another well, everyone is friendly, everyone has good manners–'even if that flock is pious and righteous in their deeds', ultimately, 'I will surely punish'–they will suffer God's punishment. They will not reach their destination. Therefore, when there is a society organised under the *wilāyah* of *ṭāghūt*, human beings will not reach their destination. They cannot be Muslims.

What should they do, then? What should they do? Here the Qur'an answers us in the following verse: 'Indeed, those whom the angels take away while they are wronging themselves'[42]–when the angels come to take their souls, while they were wronging themselves, those people who were wronging their futures and are now dying, the angels have been charged by God with taking their souls. 'They ask', the angels ask these people: 'What state were you in?' Where were you? This question makes you wonder what kind of awful state these people were in for the angels to ask this! It's just like when a doctor comes to treat a patient and sees what a bad condition the patient is in, and the doctor asks: 'Where have you been living? How have you been living?' This is a good analogy to explain the significance of the angels' question; it shows they are surprised by how bad a state these people are in, how ruined their souls are, and the punishments and misfortunes that await them in the afterlife. They ask: Where were you living to become like this? How did you wrong yourself so much? Why are you leaving this world while wronging yourselves? Where were you? How were you living?

How do these people respond? 'They reply, "We were oppressed in the land."' We were oppressed by the people around us, we did not have any choice. The 'oppressed' (*mustaḍʿafīn*) are those members of society that have no control over the direction of that society. They cannot influence what it does, what stances it takes, or how it behaves. Just as we said previously, they are pulled along by the current, they have no choice over where they end up.

Imagine a child in the first year of primary school, not even seven years of age (because seven-year-olds today are very clever!). A child

42 Q4:97.

of four or five years of age, going to primary school, learning to read and write like they used to in the old *maktabkhānahs*[43]. When we used to come out of school to go home, we'd come out in a big group, not knowing where we were going. Small children don't pay attention to where things are. Instead, there has to be someone older there keeping an eye on them: 'Go this way! Go that way! Watch out for the car! Cross the road!' (*laughter of audience*) They don't know where they are going–one time they might end up at their own home, another they might end up at a friend's home.

Those who are oppressed in the land are those who have no information about what's going on in society. They do not know what is going where. They do not know where they are going. They don't know where they will end up when they leave where they are, who is taking them there, or how they are going. They just keep their eyes down, like the windmill's blinkered horse[44] whose eyes are covered and simply keeps moving forward. It just goes and goes and goes, turns and turns and turns; if this horse was of a reflective temperament, it might wonder whether or not it has reached Paris with all the distance it has travelled! (*laughter of the audience*) But then, at the end of the day, when the blinkers come off, it sees that it is back where it started this morning. So, you see, it has no idea where it went. It doesn't know where it is going when it moves. The oppressed in the land are these people in society; the majority of uninformed people. However, in those societies which are being properly governed, in which humanity is valued; in those societies which hold the human being and the human will in esteem; meaning those societies which are being led by the Prophet–the Qur'an says 'and consult them in the

43 [Before the emergence of modern education in Iran, children would attend *maktabkhānahs* where they would learn to read and write.]

44 [A horse used in olden times in a mill that would move the mill by moving around it in circles.]

affairs'[45], even though the Prophet has no need to consult anyone, but the Qur'an commands him to in order to show that it respects people and to encourage their growth–these sorts of societies do not have these [oppressed] masses. It is only in societies which are dictatorial or oppressive, or governed by a non-Islamic system in which the majority of people are those abased in the land.

They say: 'We were oppressed in the land.' We didn't know what our leaders were doing. How they were oppressing others. How they were embezzling wealth. And now we are dying! This is the excuse of the abased. But see how the angels respond to this excuse, in a moment. They say they were abased in the land, that they were weak and oppressed, that they had no choice. The angels answer them. Look at the flawless logic of the angels, because what they say is what any reasonable person would say. As Saʿdī said seven or eight hundred years ago:

Let no companion detain you, nor abode
For the land and sea are spacious and there are many people.

Saʿdī clearly agreed with the opinion of the angels: 'They say, "Was not God's earth vast enough so that you might migrate in it?"' Ok, you were abased there, but was there nowhere else you could go on God's earth? No matter where you lived, no matter which society you went to, were you also abased? Was God's earth not broad enough for you to escape this prison and go somewhere that was free? Couldn't you find somewhere that you could worship God, somewhere that you could use your potential as God intended, somewhere that has no abased people? Was there nowhere in the world like this? 'Was not God's earth vast enough so that you might migrate in it?' The abased in the land have no answer for this. These poor souls know that the angels are right. And that is why, in the end, the Qur'an says about them–the abased in the land, whose potential and freedom were in

45 Q3:159.

the hands of the *ṭāghūt*–: 'The refuge of such shall be Hell, and it is an evil destination.' Where will they end up? In the worst of places.

There is one exception to this: Those who cannot emigrate (*hijrah*), who were unable to free themselves from the bondage of a tyrannical regime. Some cannot do this. Some are too old. Some are too young. Some are women who cannot leave. These are all exempt: 'Except those oppressed among men, women and children, who have neither access to any means nor are guided to any way.'[46] They find no way towards the light, towards Islam, towards serving God. There is nothing they can do. 'Maybe God will excuse them'[47], see how the Qur'an speaks? It is hoped that God will excuse them. This is how moral responsibility works–'for God is all-excusing, all-forgiving.'

Then, lest those who have been told to emigrate imagine that emigrating might be a source of loss or misfortune for them, or lest they worry that they might not be able to make a life for themselves there, the Qur'an says: 'Whoever migrates in the way of God will find many havens and plenitude in the earth.'[48] Those who emigrate will be amazed by how high they can soar in this world, they will be amazed by the fulfilment of their heart's desire in the Islamic society, whereas beforehand there was a ceiling that limited how high they could fly. What a boundless horizon they shall find! In Makkah, these people offered their prayers under pressure. If they were very quick, they could offer two *rakʿat*s of prayer in the Holy Mosque, but then they would receive a terrible beating! This was the limit of the Muslims in Makkah, they could do no more. However, after they emigrated to Madinah, they came to a free land, with a free atmosphere. They came to an Islamic society that was under the *wilāyah* of God and His Messenger. They were amazed by the place they had come to; this

46 Q4:98.

47 Q4:99.

48 Q4:100.

was the place where people 'vied with one another in good deeds.' Here, with the verses of the Qur'an, with piety and worship, the level of individuals was clear and known. Whoever did more for the sake of God, worshipped more, strived harder, fought harder, spent more, they were more highly respected and esteemed in the society.

Before, they knew that if they spent one dirham for the sake of God in Makkah, they would have heated up the same coin and tortured him with it. Now that they had emigrated to the city of the Prophet for the sake of God, when they saw that this was a place where they could roam free and take flight, this was a place where their hearts' desire could give them wings. 'Whoever migrates in the way of God will find many havens and plenitude in the earth.' Meaning in the divine and Islamic society they will find freedom, openness and the space to roam.

Now, if you leave Makkah–the abode of faithlessness–for the sake of God to go to the abode of emigration, but you died before you could reach your destination, what happens then? They say that when this happens, your reward lies with God, because you did what you had to do. You set off as you were supposed to. As Saʿdī says:

Heading off to the desert is better than sitting with falsehood
For even if I do not reach my destination, I have tried my utmost.

This is all Islam wants. Islam wants everyone to walk God's path to the extent of their ability, to the extent of their capacity, to the extent that they have the strength to do so.

'And whoever leaves his home migrating toward God and His Apostle, and is then overtaken by death, his reward shall certainly fall on God, and God is all-forgiving, all-merciful.'

Since this is our last lecture, I want you to pay close attention to this point. Our work is only half-finished. There is so much more to say. So I just want to make one point. Emigrating from the abode of faithlessness (*dār al-kufr*), from the *wilāyah* of other than God, from the *wilāyah* of Satan and *ṭāghūt* means to set off the abode of emigration (*dār al-hijrah*), to the abode of faith (*dār al-īmān*), to live under the *wilāyah* of God and the *wilāyah* of the Imam. To live under the *wilāyah* of the Prophet and the divine *walī*, you must emigrate. This is the meaning of *hijrah*. Now, if such a place does not exist in the world, what must we do? Must we remain in the abode of faithlessness? Should we give up all thoughts of a place to emigrate to? Remember that even the Prophet was an emigrant, was he not? The Prophet also emigrated. However, before the Prophet emigrated, there was virtually nowhere to emigrate to. It was through his own act of emigration that the Prophet created a place to which Muslims could emigrate.

Sometimes it is necessary for a group of people, through their own emigration, to create a starting point for the emigration of others. To create a divine and Islamic society, to bring an abode of emigration for other people, so that the faithful can emigrate. This is the conclusion we must draw from our discussion of emigration.

All praise be to God for the completion of this discourse.

www.ingramcontent.com/pod-product-compliance
Lightning Source LLC
Chambersburg PA
CBHW011617020526
44118CB00039BB/2523
* 9 7 8 0 9 9 5 7 5 8 9 1 9 *